THE **Black** Press, U.S.A.

SECOND EDITION

THE Black
Press, U.S.A.

SECOND EDITION

ROLAND E. WOLSELEY

WITH A FOREWORD BY **ROBERT E. JOHNSON,** EXECUTIVE EDITOR, **JET**

IOWA STATE UNIVERSITY PRESS / AMES

Roland E. Wolseley is professor emeritus of journalism, Newhouse School of Public Communications, Syracuse University.

First edition © 1971 by Iowa State University Press

Second edition © 1990 by Roland E. Wolseley
All rights reserved

Manufactured in the United States of America

♾ This book is printed on acid-free paper.

First edition, 1971
Second edition, 1990

Library of Congress Cataloging-in-Publication Data

Wolseley, Roland Edgar, 1904–
    The Black press, U.S.A./Roland E. Wolseley: with a foreword by Robert E. Johnson.—2nd ed.
      p.   cm.
    Bibliography: p.
    Includes index.
    ISBN 0–8138–0494–9
    ISBN 0–8138–0496–5 (pbk.)
    1. Afro-American press—History—19th century. 2. Afro-Americans—Race relations—History. 3. Afro-American newspapers—History—19th century. 4. Afro-American journalists—United States—Biography. I. Title. II. Title: Black press, USA.
PN4882.5.W64 1990
071′.3′08996073—dc20
                                        89–31302
                                           CIP

Dedicated to Robert W. Root, 1915–1970

friend and colleague, educator, author, and
journalist whose books on the church and race
are a contribution to better interracial relations

CONTENTS

This mass of Negro newspapers may be the most interesting footnote to contemporary national history; the journalism of a caste, the journalism of involuntary expatriates, the protest and 'community newspapers' of a people exiled on their own soil.

EARL CONRAD IN **TOMORROW**
1946

FOREWORD

A JOURNEY OF JOURNALISTIC REFLECTIONS
BY **ROBERT E. JOHNSON,** EXECUTIVE EDITOR,
JET NEWSMAGAZINE

When Professor Roland E. Wolseley asked
me to write an introduction to his book, *The Black Press, U.S.A.*, he
said, "Your introduction can say what you wish, good and bad alike.
Any observations about your own experience or views on the black
press will be welcomed by readers and reviewers alike."

As a member of the black press establishment and an alumnus of
Syracuse University's School of Journalism, I accepted this honor
with misgivings because it casts me in the role of a student doing a
critique of his teacher's writing.

After reading press proofs of *The Black Press, U.S.A.*, profound
in its scholarship and significant in the scope of objectives, I was
propelled on a journey of reflections.

This book had to be written. It asked me to write it in 1948 when
I was a Morehouse College senior and editor of the *Maroon Tiger*,
student newspaper whose 1938 editors V. Trenton Tubbs, Moss H.
Kendricks, and Bernard Milton Jones founded Delta Phi Delta journalistic society which originated the celebration of "Negro Newspaper
Week" in March each year. Nobody, I reasoned, would take seriously
anything written by a student.

This book urged me to write it in 1950 when I was a "veteran" of

---

Foreword from first edition replicated for second edition, as is, at request of
Robert E. Johnson.

two years of reporting for the Atlanta (Georgia) *Daily World*. At that time, my resources not only included the libraries of Atlanta's accredited black colleges—Morehouse, Spelman, Clark, Morris Brown, and Atlanta University—but included such World and Scott Newspaper Syndicate journalists as Emory O. Jackson, William Fowlkes, Marion E. Jackson, V. W. Hodges, Joel Smith, and William Gordon. Moreover, there were such *World* alumni veterans as Robert Ratcliffe, Lucius (Lou Jo) Jones, Ric Roberts, and the late Cliff W. MacKay. I didn't write the book then because I was convinced that no one would believe a good book on the black press could be written by a black reporter whose fingers were not yet saturated with printer's ink.

This book begged me to write it in 1952 when I was enrolled at Syracuse, studying for a master's degree in journalism. I declined, this time with distaste and disdain. This was a result of the fables of the 1950s. Integration was the "in" thing. It was the decade of the negro backlash when it was considered a put-down for a white professor to advise a negro student to select a black subject for his master's thesis or Ph.D. dissertation. It wasn't hip to be that black and proud. It was a time to be ashamed if your white classmates caught you reading a black newspaper. This was the decade when a negro student thought it to be more relevant to write a thesis on, say, "An Interpretative Analysis of John Milton's Areopagitica and Its Literary Impact Upon the Liberty to Print Tracts without License" rather than, say, "The History of Black Journalistic Thought from John Russwurm to John H. Johnson."

At the end of the decade of the 1960s, I was executive editor of *Jet* with sixteen years of newsmagazine experience. Finally, in 1970, this book demanded that I write it. Immersed in administrative rather than writing responsibilities, I deferred again.

Blacks should plead their own cause since we know our condition better than anyone, the founders of the black press, Samuel E. Cornish and John B. Russwurm, tell us. But if we fail to do so, it behooves anyone to come forth, reminds Dr. Howard Thurman, former Howard and Boston universities theologian who was voted by *Ebony* magazine as one of the "Ten Best Preachers in America."

Professor Wolseley came forth to do this book because black journalists like myself could sleep at night rather than yield to the pressure of the unwritten manuscript of the 144-year journey of the black press in America.

The Black Press, U.S.A. is a redeeming document of black men and black media struggling to overcome chaos and establish community in a racist society against incredible odds. To whites who read this book, it may be described as a case for chauvinism. My reaction to this is contained in the conversation a group of black journalists and myself had in Tel-Aviv, Israel, November 21, 1969, with Foreign Minister Abba Eban. He observed, "You, as members of the black press, may be accused of being a selfish press. Everybody who looks after himself is said to be selfish by those who have already looked after themselves." Drawing a parallel of blacks and Jews, he allowed: "There is a beloved quality that men call patriotism if they possess it themselves, and chauvinism if they see it in others. It's obvious that those who have to fight for survival—whether as groups within the nation or nations within the 126 sovereign states of the world—they are obviously going to be more preoccupied than those whose survival is assured."

Similarly, Professor Wolseley offers this kind of empathy and insight in his book.

The only quarrel—and it's really not a quarrel—is that I prefer to speculate on the future of the black press. Nearly always, whites ask about the future of *Jet* or *Ebony* or the black press in an integrated society, but they don't ask about the future of *Life* or *Look* or the white press. I'm reminded of the response of Dr. Benjamin E. Mays, president-emeritus of 104-year-old Morehouse College, when a similar question was raised about the future of the black college. To paraphrase him, if we really get rid of white racism we will concede the fact that the black press has just as much right to exist as the white press. Nobody ever raises the question of what is the future of the white press, and they have been discriminating more than the black press all through the years. But when you ask about the black press, you want to know what's going to happen to it. This is a kind of discrimination which is abominable.

Professor Wolseley's book is an invaluable ally in helping the black press convince white America that blacks can mobilize their own talents, their own genius, and take fate into their own hands. That is the secret to black emancipation—black liberation!

Chicago, Illinois
April 30, 1971

PREFACE

A body of publications like the black press is called black mainly on the basis of color: the color of the readers, staff members, owners, and the fact that the content deals largely with the black society.

That terminology is insufficient, however, because being black is something more than having a certain skin tint. As was pointed out by a sociologist colleague, blackness can stem from no more than point of view. Under this concept the holder of that view need not be of the black race.

That, according to the social scientist friend, means that a white person who knows the history of the black race, is familiar with the psychology and physical characteristics of that race, and is cognizant of its lifestyles and problems could be far more nearly black than a man or woman of jet skin color devoid of the knowledge and viewpoint of that white person.

As anyone who is acquainted with visitors to the United States from African nations knows, some black Africans have no identification with black Americans and act much like foreigners from Western nations. Africans who come to the United States, especially in the recent years of relative calm in the American black society, pay little or no attention to black publications or broadcasts.

So if blackness is largely a point of view there need be no concern for skin color. The practical difficulty with applying this view in professional circles is that there are so few nonblacks with a black point of view. In the days of abolitionism the whites sympathetic to the slaves actually were the major readers and financial supporters of the earliest black publications. Not so today, however. As their cause was won few if any abolitionist whites produced newspapers for black U.S. citizens. Such journalism had to be provided by persons of black skin. Even the abolitionists had no interest in becoming part of the black social order, just as blacks had no interest in becoming an integral part of the white order until many years later. This separation of labor has continued ever since.

So I acknowledge that there may be ideological shortcomings in this book. These result from the fact that, despite my more than four decades of awareness of the black society, its problems, and its press, and despite my empathy for black people, I am white and grew up and lived in a white environment filled with the usual racist attitudes. That environment was not—most of those years—always one of understanding of the black people by any means, but the taint of racism did not cling.

White on Black

Ever since the first edition of this book was published in 1971, I have been asked many times: "Why are you so interested in the black press?" Or: "Why are you, a white man, writing a book on that press?" Or: "Why didn't a black write the book?" It is not only Caucasians who raise such questions. They also come, largely in a critical tone, from blacks. Some of the blacks making such observations do so as if I had no business probing the subject, others say they should have done so first and it is their own fault for letting it go to a white author. And still others are resentful; one prominent black journalist wrote me four abusive letters in succession. To all such reactions I point out that I needed a text for my course in the subject at my university. Since none existed I produced my own after two years of research and teaching and the use of information gathered over a score of years.

These objectors to a white author dealing with a black subject are guilty of racism, although they would be the last to admit it. A prime example is a reviewer (though not of this book) for the *Black Scholar*. In reviewing books on neo-African literature, some of them written by whites, S. E. Anderson warned against "the danger of depending upon a white analysis of our existence that is plaguing not only the cultural component of our liberation struggle . . . [but] is infecting all facets of the struggle." At the review's end he wrote: "When white authors publish detailed 'scholarly' works about blacks we should not relax and sigh, relieved that someone is doing the necessary work. Instead, we should be intensely committed to developing more accurate understanding of the meaning of blackness and black revolution.[1]

Divisive or Unifying?

A reader of the manuscript of this book opined that it could be considered divisive. "You object," the critic said, "when I mention that someone is black and you say that it is irrelevant. So why single out the black press from the press as a whole? Isn't that discrimination?"

The perpetuation of the black press is desirable for these reasons: to help preserve the culture and heritage of the black race, and to assist in fighting for justice for a still often unjustly treated human group, even in the free society we know as the United States of America.

The history and nature of the black press should be put on record, since that press has had a part in our national development. It is not a matter of separating one press entity from another to prove that one or the other is superior. It is a matter of preserving identity, accepting the plurality that exists culturally and racially, and bringing about more harmony between the two.

Books on black art, literature, and communications can be divisive if their authors claim that black is best and should be the standard for all. That attitude is resented by blacks and Asians when made by writers on white art, literature, and communications.

The Black Press, U.S.A. is descriptive and diagnostic, not a race champion. It points out what the author sees as faults and virtues. For years such books have appeared about various foreign groups residing in the United States; a few books deal with the press of such enclaves and have helped gain understanding of their culture, lifestyles, and customs. These presses also have encouraged the unity and loyalty of these groups to their new country. In the late 1980s we are seeing the development of a strong Hispanic press, serving a rapidly increasing segment of the U.S. population.

This book, then, is part of the needed literature in this egalitarian nation. It seeks to promote understanding, not divisiveness.

Other Purposes

Other purposes exist for this book. The Report of the National Advisory Commission on Civil Disorders in 1968 published these words: "The Negro Press . . . could be a particularly useful source of information and guidance about activities of the Black community." This function is encouraged by constructive books on that press.

This book seeks to answer certain questions for the enlightenment of black and white readers alike. Among them are: What is the black press? What are the leading publications? Who are the leaders? What are the press' organizations? What is the historical background? How influential is this special press?

Most Americans, including many of the black race, do not know the answers to such questions. Nor can they be expected to know them. Little is taught in schools, colleges, and universities about journalism other than the techniques of producing publications or airing programs. The larger schools of journalism and communications have courses on the ethics and social significance of the media, but out of the total of the university population in this country few persons take such classes.

For scores of years, supported by the publishing business for its own good as well as for that of the public, efforts have been made to teach people how to read newspapers and magazines and how to use the electronic miracles of radio and television. But the level of public taste remains low. So another purpose of this book is to suggest higher standards for the black press.

During the years since the first edition of this book was published numerous changes have occurred not only in black American society but also in the black print journalism. The economic condition of many black persons has changed, some for the good and some for the bad. Middle-class blacks with greater disposable income have increased in number. There still is enormous poverty in the black community, easily visible in the substandard neighborhoods of dozens of cities. The steps taken to fight poverty, hunger, joblessness, and illness have been reversed or hampered by federal government regulations and budgeting.

Nevertheless, there has been progress. Education for blacks and other minorities has become more accessible. The first rush to take advantage of opportunities and financial aid at colleges and universities had subsided somewhat by the late 1980s, but black enrollments had improved.

Although financial aid is more readily available in the educational world, the high cost of living still handicaps some young blacks who wish to be better educated. Also, they are needed by their families to be wage earners in a period of high unemployment. Even when they are well educated there is no guarantee of employment in their chosen specialty.

The outlook for the future can be disheartening to young people of any race or color in the United States. They live in a country spending billions on weapons and the military system while hunger and misery persist in the cities, race prejudice continues, and the Ku Klux Klan and other race extremists carry on their terrorism. The general situation of the early 1970s has survived to the brink of the 1990s.

The changes in the black publication world have been marked as well. Numerous publications have failed for a variety of reasons, as detailed in this book. More black journalists are employed in the nonblack media. Black publishers still are complaining about their best writers and editors being lured away to nonblack newspapers, agencies, and periodicals. The costs of production have increased greatly. Wages have gone up, but not competitively with the nonblack offices. Circulations have dropped dangerously and dramatically in numbers of publishing firms. Advertising space still is difficult to sell.

The black identity is being lost somewhat in the term *minority*. It is joined with the Native American, Asian, and Hispanic populations in the granting of awards and the provision of education and training. That policy generates competition, imbalance, and even friction.

So numerous and lengthy is my treatment of certain of these changes that some details have been left in the first edition that are chiefly of historic interest. Otherwise this book would have reached encyclopedic proportions.

Changes in the Book

Numerous changes from the first edition have been made without destroying the fundamental structure of the book. An outdated chapter has been dropped to make room for more recent material. All chapters have been revised and updated. Many more biographical and historical sketches have been included. The Bibliography has been expanded and classified; many of the photographs are new and were taken expressly for this book.

Scope of the Book

It should be understood that the word *press* in the title stands for print journalism, and covers chiefly newspapers, magazines, and news agencies. Radio and television are dealt with as competitors for the press; but they are deserving of their own books. *Press* and *journalism* as used here do not embrace advertising, circulation, and production—they are considered auxiliaries that also need to be dealt with in depth in other volumes. The word *media* is used to mean all of the mediums of mass communications: newspapers, magazines, newsletters, radio, television, cassettes, and videocassette recorders. The focus, however, is on print journalism.

Syracuse, New York　　　　　　　　　ROLAND E. WOLSELEY
October 1988

Acknowledgments

An author's wife often is helpful, usually as a cheerer-on or as a provider of quiet.

Isabel Wolseley went far beyond the usual helpfulness.

She took and processed dozens of photographs. She served as preliminary copy editor of each chapter, with all that implies. She passed the entire manuscript through her electronic typewriter, the home computer bug not having bitten us hard enough yet. Being herself a professional photojournalist she provided a backstop of precious value.

So the greatest weight of my thanks goes to her.

Scores of professional colleagues, friends (including many former students), editors, publishers, librarians, secretaries, administrative assistants, public relations people, and personnel of advertising agencies also have my thanks.

Singled out for special appreciation are Raymond H. Boone, James W. Carty, Jr., Ruth K. Kent, Sheila Maroney, and the late J. William Snorgrass. All five sent information, new publications, and other important materials unasked and contributed data from libraries in their areas or other sources. The death of Professor Snorgrass in September 1987 not only deprived this book of further material but also ended a new friendship.

Many thanks for their painstaking editing go to Gretchen Van Houten, sponsoring editor of this book, and her assistant, Sarah Brown. They have saved the author from faults missed by all other critics.

Dozens of other persons helped and deserve mention. They cooperated on one or both editions of this book. They are: O. Rudolph Aggrey, Daryl Alexander, Harry Alexander,

E. Lance Barclay, Lionel C. Barrow, Jr., Marilyn Batchelor, Fred Beauford, Lillian Bell, Sherilyn Cox Bennion, Thomas L. Berkley, Elwood Berry, Carolyne S. Blount, Robert H. Bontrager, Bernice L. Borgeson, Eric J. Brewer, Sherman Briscoe, Robert U. Brown, Les Brownlee, Ronald K. Burke, Philip Ward Burton, Rhea E. Calloway, Diane Camper, Caroline Dillon Carpenter, Claudia Caruana, Wesley C. Clark, Jamye Coleman, David Collington, George M. Daniels, Lawrence Davis, Steve G. Davis, Kent W. de Felice, Micheline Del Gatto, James A. Doyle, K. E. Eapen, Rosemary Eng, W. Leonard Evans, Alson Fitts III, Carlton J. Frazier, Elizabeth Gardiner, Bernard E. Garnett, W. Rick Garr, Gene Gilmore, Ulysses Glen, Carlton B. Goodlett, Thelma Thurston Gorham, Earl G. Graves, Meg Hale, Pat Jones Hillman, Sue Holaday, Betsy Homer, Everett Hullum, Barbara L. Jackson-Hall, Bert Johnson, Gerald O. Johnson, John H. Johnson, Robert E. Johnson, Kuumba Kazi-Ferrouillet, Geraldine Keating, Frank Kent, Marilyn Kern-Foxworth, Lettie S. Knight, Henry La Brie III, Alfonso Lankster, Timothy A. Lester, James E. Lewis, Charles-Gene McDaniel, Louis E. Martin, Henry Lee Moon, Elizabeth Murphy Moss, Earle E. Newman, Karen A. Newton, Herbert Nipson, John J. Oliver, Jr., Thomas Picou, Ida Phillips, Theodore Pratt, Armistead S. Pride, George C. Pryce, Gary A. Puckrein, Robert H. Reid, Lawrence Ragan, Carolyn Watson Redenius, Garth C. Reeves, Jay Reidel, Lillian Reiner, Frank Render II, Thomas A. Richards, Jr., Dan Ritey, Susan Rittenhouse, Patricia Roesch, Sue Shields Rosenberg, Linda Chiavaroli Rosenbloom, C. A. Scott, John H. Sengstacke, Mary Luins Small, Kenneth Sparks, W. David Stephenson II, Chuck Stone, Nora Swindler, William Howard Taft, Susan L. Taylor, Eunice Trotter, Margaret Troutt, Debra Washington, Thomas H. Watkins, Jr., S. Jack Weissberger, Brian White, Eva M. Willard, Charles V. Willie, Valena Minor Williams, James L. Winston, Samuel F. Yette, and Sherri York.

    Librarians at Northwestern University, Syracuse University, and various public library systems have been patiently helpful. I especially appreciate the courtesy of the Department of Afro-American Studies at Syracuse University in opening its Martin Luther King, Jr., Memorial Library to me whenever I needed it, even in vacation periods.

    Extremely valuable were the membership or client lists provided by the National Newspaper Publishers Association and the Amalgamated Publishers, Inc.

    Numerous newspaper and magazine editorial offices provided information and materials. Among the newspaper offices that sent information for use in this edition were: *Afro-American* Newspapers, Atlanta *Daily World*, Baton Rouge *Community Leader*, Birmingham *News*, Charlotte *Post*, Chicago *Defender*, *Christian Recorder*, Cleveland *Call and Post*, Cleveland *East Side News*, Cleveland *Independent*, Indianapolis *Recorder*, Los Angeles *Sentinel*, Miami *Times*, *National Catholic Mentor*, New York *Amsterdam News*, New York *Daily Challenge*, Norfolk *Journal and Guide*, *Post* Papers, St. Louis *American*, *Star of Zion*, and Washington *New Observer*.

Among the magazine offices were: *A.M.E. Church Review*, *about . . . time*, *American Visions*, *Black Collegian*, *Black Enterprise*, *Black Family*, *Crisis*, *Ebony*, *Essence*, *Excel*, *Jet*, *Josephite Harvest*, and *Message*.

Scores of other publications were drawn upon, but their materials were not obtained directly.

For the first edition materials were received from the following publications, now discontinued but referred to in the new edition: *Encore*, *New Lady*, *Sepia*, *Soul*, *Soul Illustrated*, *Tuesday*, and *Tuesday at Home*.

Picture Credits

Associated Publishers, Inc. — Fig. 3.5.
Florida A. & M. University — Fig. 11.1.
Ulysses Glen — Fig. 6.2.
Johnson Publishing Company — Figs. 10.3, 10.4.
Moorland-Spingarn Research Center, Howard University —
    Figs. 2.2, 2.3, 3.2, 3.3, 3.4.
Negro History Bulletin — Figs. 2.5, 2.6, 2.7.
Ethel L. Payne — Fig. 10.5.
Armistead S. Pride — Fig. 11.2.
Publishers-Hall Syndicate — Fig. 10.1.
Thomas A. Richards, Jr. — Figs. 3.1, 5.2, 5.3, 5.4, 6.4, 8.2b,
    8.2d, 8.3.
George S. Schuyler — Fig. 10.2.
John H. Sengstacke — Fig. 4.1.
Charles E. Simmons — Fig. 3.6.
Isabel C. Wolseley — Figs. 2.1, 5.1, 5.5, 6.1, 6.3, 7.1a, 7.1b,
    7.1c, 7.1d, 7.2a, 7.2b, 7.2c, 7.3, 7.4, 8.1, 8.2a, 8.2c, 8.4,
    8.5, 11.3, 12.1.

PREFACE

"The Negro press has become the most influential Negro business in the Twentieth Century. . . . Unfortunately, [it] has not received the scholarly research attention it deserves."

Erwin K. Welsch, author of *The Negro in the United States*, makes this observation at the outset of his discussion of the black press and the literature on it. He then notes that the only general book was published in 1922. *The Black Press, U.S.A.* was written to provide information about this ethnic press at a time when the black citizens and all their problems, interests, and enterprises have taken on a new importance. It is not a textbook about the techniques and methods of black journalism, which are similar to those of any other in this country, although some distinctions are drawn.

After an opening chapter discussing the validity of the entire concept of a black press and setting the stage in general come three chapters that briefly relate the history. Not all background is confined to these chapters, however; additional historical information appears in various other sections where it contributes to understanding of a particular facet. The history is followed by four chapters that examine the newspapers and magazines of today; another chapter describes types of material offered, although that is evident in many other sections as well. Next come chapters on reporters and editors of the present and past, followed by a chapter about the training and educational problems and possibilities for the journalist. From there the book considers the problems facing owners and publishers, the ideologies of the times and their impact upon the press, and a number of practical areas: advertising, circulation, and production. In another chapter syndicates, public relations, and black radio are treated. The attacks upon and defenses of the press then are reviewed, after which comes the evaluation of black journalism. Finally, the traditional and essential discussion of what may be ahead is provided.

The book attempts, therefore, to explore the nature of a heretofore neglected and subordinated press, depicting it today against its background. It seeks, also, to relate the press to the social movements now attracting many black or Afro-American people. Its objective is neither to put the black press in a necessarily positive light nor, on the other hand, to emphasize shortcomings, but simply to report on that press with a grasp of how it came to be and why it is what it is.

As is customary at this point in a preface, the author invites readers to inform him of significant omissions. He is aware that many persons and publications have gone unmentioned, but this book does not pretend to be an encyclopedic record.

Syracuse, New York   R. E. W.
1971

THE **Black** Press, U.S.A.

SECOND EDITION

The Black Press Defined

When a course on the black press in the United States was launched at Syracuse University in fall 1968, several professors in other areas of knowledge raised doubts about the existence of such a press.

"How do you tell?" a political scientist asked.

"What determines it?" came from a historian, who went on to inquire: "Is it that the readers are black-skinned?"

Indeed, how does one tell? And is it important that there be a distinction?

This problem was one of the first presented to the students, as in every offering of the course. For in such a class, as in this book, it is a central point. If there is no black press, then there is no point in publishing books about it or scheduling courses concerned with it. The skepticism is not one that springs from ignorance only of this ethnic press; some black publishers also question such a distinction.

The conclusion by the class, at term's end, was that there is such a press and that it definitely is important that a distinction be made between it and other press groups. One graduate student, Kent W. de Felice, selected the problem for deeper investigation and obtained reactions from several leading black journalists.[1] His report concluded that there are certain qualifications that a publication must meet to be considered a unit of the black press. They are:

1. Blacks must own and manage the publication; they must be the dominant racial group connected with it. (In support of that requirement it can be said that if the publication is not black-owned and

3

black-operated, its aims, policies, and programs can be altered by persons unsympathetic to the goals of black editors and publishers. An instance occurred in 1968 when an apparently black-owned newspaper supported George Wallace during the presidential campaigns. Investigation brought out the fact that the paper had been black-owned until shortly before the campaigns began, when whites bought it and altered its policy.[2] The black press otherwise backed Hubert H. Humphrey strongly but included supporters of Richard M. Nixon as well.)

It is not enough, as is suggested by some writers on black communications, for a publication to be called black because the newspaper or magazine appeals to a majority of black readership.

Such a simple yardstick would mean that the major papers of cities with high black population figures, such as Washington, Detroit, and Oakland, California, could be categorized as belonging to the black press. In Oakland, the situation is different in one way but the same in result. The Oakland *Tribune* is owned and edited by a noted black journalist, Robert C. Maynard, but its appeal is not mainly to the interests of a black readership. It could as readily be owned and produced by nonblack owners. Oakland, in fact, has a genuine black paper, the *Post*, one of a chain in California. The *Tribune* had a paid circulation in 1987 of 151,669. The *Post* had a controlled circulation of 62,496.

2. The publication must be intended for black consumers. (A science magazine presumably is aimed at scientists or persons interested in scientific matters. A paper about music is directed to persons responsive to its contents. Advertising sales depend upon such identification of reader with subject. Similarly, a magazine or newspaper for black citizens deals with their interests and concerns and is not primarily for whites. So long as there is a cultural and ethnic distinction in society between black and white citizens there will be a place for black journalism. These differences still are acute.)

3. The paper or magazine must, the report concluded, "serve, speak and fight for the black minority." It also must have the major objective of fighting for "equality for the Negro in the present white society. Equality means the equality of citizenship rights," de Felice said.

Moses Newson, then executive editor of the Baltimore *Afro-American*, one of the major black newspapers, noted that the black press of the United States was "founded for the purpose of serving, publicizing, speaking, and fighting for the colored minority." The late E. Washington Rhodes, publisher of the Philadelphia *Tribune*, a leading semiweekly, although denying the validity of the use of the word *black* or the existence of a black press and accepting *Negro press* as a term, went on to write that the units of this press are intended "to secure for their readers absolute equality of citizenship rights." And from the late William O. Walker, editor of the Cleveland *Call and Post*, came the clear view that "Black is a color — Negro is a race; so there is a Negro press. It serves the interests and needs of the Negro people."

A parallel can be drawn with another area of communications: theater. Peter Bailey, writing in *Ebony*, insisted that black theater is one that is written, directed, produced, financed by blacks, located in a black community, and uses the community "as its reference point."

Similarly, some black journalists believe that the black press is that owned, produced, and intended for black readers in a black environment. This third proviso, then, makes the black press a special pleading institution, one with a cause, goal, or purpose going beyond the basic one necessary for survival in the American economy — the making of a profit.

As the twenty-first century approaches, the purposes of some of the present black media vary from those of the past.

The primary purpose, 160 years ago and for many years thereafter, was to campaign for freedom of the slaves. After the Civil War it was for more fair treatment of black citizens in many areas of their lives, such as access to public eating places, attendance at white colleges, and use of public beaches.

Although these goals have not yet been fully achieved, a measure of success has attended those fighting for such objectives.

After a time, the black media as a whole did not need to depend upon subsidy for survival, as the slave era papers were forced to do. As subsidy became more and more difficult to obtain, because of the low earning power of black citizens the press seeking these persons as readers had to turn to advertisers for support.

The black newspaper and magazine thus became more and more a business operation, less a crusader. Editorializing for social causes was not always acceptable to white business enterprises that might be chief advertisers.

For the sake of survival, and to give owners and their employees a viable business or professional product, attempts to be professional became more important. In time the aims of the black press were more complex, varying by the type of medium of communication.

Black newspapers now exist primarily to report the news of the black population and the particular local community, to give space to their own and others' opinions on many racially oriented matters, to promote the activities of the society in which they exist, to present advertisers with a billboard or a spoken message, and to be the advocate for the black population. All these purposes, of necessity, are superseded by that of earning a profit from advertising and circulation or reaching the listeners and viewers essential to independent survival.

The Differences Discerned

Applying the de Felice specifications to white newspapers and magazines brings out the differences between the black and white presses. Although usually owned by whites, the white press need not be. It could be owned by blacks but aimed at whites, as in the case of the Seaside *Post News-Sentinel* in Seaside, California, for the white press generally hopes to have readers of all hues. The main difference exists in the goals of white publications. Usually they are concerned with the problems of whites, the majority group readers, and only incidentally with those of blacks, Orientals, or other minorities, racial or political. This policy accounts for the complaints against the dominant press which have been made for a century and a half by the black society. During most of the white press' history, in fact, there has been indifference to the black minority's problems, if not downright opposition to that race, giving rise to the black press as a corrective force as well as a weapon with which blacks have been fighting for their rights.

It should be noted, however, that by no means are all black publications dedicated to social causes dear to the country's black citizens. Just as with any other business, there are publications whose goal chiefly is financial profit, sometimes to be used in the interest of the race, other times, as with white entrepreneurs, for the personal benefit of the managers and owners.

Black, Negro, or Colored?

The black press has existed for more than 160 years, but should it be called a *black* press? This point has become sensitive. A *Playboy* cartoon once showed a white man talking to a black one in an integrated cocktail party scene. Says the white to the black: "I don't want to make any social blunders. What are you people calling yourselves these days?"

Although certain labels have hung on for generations, in the 1960s change came rapidly: *negro* replaced *colored*, *Negro* came in for *negro*, *Negro* went to *black*, *black* then became *Black*. Now the last two are being used interchangeably, with lower case *b* the more common. All were surrounded by other less widely used terms, although in the black press some at one time were popular: *Afro-American, Aframerican, colored, non-white, race*, and similar variations. In 1988 *African American* was debated.

Certain writers and publishers preferred *Negro-oriented* press. *Ebony*, for example, called itself a Negro magazine during its early years, but in its promotion in the later 1960s called itself Negro-oriented, and by the 1980s was using Black. D. Parke Gibson, throughout an entire book, *The $30 Billion Negro*, refers to the "Negro-oriented press," a reflection perhaps of the greater readership of these publications by whites and the desire to direct advertisers' attention to coverage in depth. The term also accommodates the dozens of white-owned radio stations which carry programs for black listeners.

When *Negro Digest*, once a companion magazine to *Ebony* and *Jet*, underwent a change of name to *Black World* in 1970, the editors explained that "Negro" was in harmony with the times in 1942, when it was founded, but not in 1970. Not only had the magazine's formula changed after its death in 1951 and rebirth in 1961 but its policies also were altered. The editors said that the new name reflected the actual character of the publication.

Although the debate may seem as it did as long ago as 1950 to Roi Ottley, the historian of the Chicago *Daily Defender*, only "a tempest in a teapot," it is worthy of serious discussion because of the semantics of the situation. These terms reflect attitudes. They can indicate the evaluation of a whole race as well as of individual members of the group. For example, a reader sensitive to the various views of this minority would comprehend that someone calling himself editor of a Negro-oriented paper perhaps is conservative socially, certainly at this time nonmilitant, for the militant abhors *Negro*, considering it a term applied by whites who feel superior to him. The debate has added importance because it is related to what people of black-colored skin call themselves. One needs to know what is acceptable, as the *Playboy* cartoon implies, so as not to offend any group needlessly. Ethnic minorities are particularly tender on this point, as can be seen in the Jewish protests about Fagin and Shylock in theatrical productions and the objections of Chinese, Poles, Italians, Japanese, and the clergy to the various stereotypes of themselves still encountered on cinema and television screens.

By the late 1980s, the press itself and various organizations in this group of Americans have settled down mainly to use of *black, Black*, and *Negro*, with the first two seen more and more in print. The Black Academy of Arts and Letters was founded in Boston in 1969, one of dozens of organizations and publications using *Black. Colored* has virtually disappeared except in distinctive and long-used names like that of the National Association for the Advancement of Colored People (NAACP). *Race* for a time also was widely used by the press, but now is uncommon. *Afro-American* survives more strongly than *colored*, since it is in the name of a widely read group of newspapers, and appears as well in some organization titles.

Negro, although for so long acceptable to both white and black groups (some of the best black magazines have used it for years, *Journal of Negro Education*, for instance), was opposed as long ago as 1896, when Dr. J. C. Embry, a Philadelphia pastor, argued that *Negro* was objectionable because it was derived from color only. He held out for *Afro-American*, since Africa is the land of origin of black Americans. More recent objectors say that *Negro* is a word coming from whites and suggests Uncle Tomism. The Congress of Racial Equality barred a Columbus (Ohio) *Dispatch* newsman and a photographer from its 1968 convention because the paper had used *Negro* in reporting its sessions. Dick Gregory, the entertainer, objected to *Negro* because it is related, he once said, to the opprobrious term *nigger*, which in turn is derived from the Latin *niger*, for black. His view had been voiced many years before by a noted black journalist, T. Thomas Fortune, thought to have originated *Afro-American*.

Among the black people there is no uniformity of attitude or practice. But concern over what nonblacks call them is rising as part of the developing consciousness of status and pride in accomplishment.

The term *black* is used in this book because in the author's view it is the choice of many persons actively concerned with the welfare of this ethnic group.

The use of *black* has been defended eloquently by the writer of a letter to *Editor & Publisher*. She discussed a point made by Roy H. Copperud, the magazine's lexicographer-columnist, who expressed surprise that *black*, which might well strike many people as derogatory because of its frequent association in literature and elsewhere with servitude of one kind or another, had been accepted so quickly. That was early 1968.

"It's part of the quest for self-identity, that precious, subtle pride that was so painstakingly crushed in slavery, and has been suppressed all these decades," wrote Elinor Diane Harvin, then of the public relations staff of the Michigan Bell Telephone Company. "It goes along with the rejection of whitey's insistence that straight hair is better than kinky hair, thin lips are better than thick lips, white skin is better than dark skin.

"It's a way of saying 'Hold on, baby. White is not better than black. We see who we are. Black is on the same level as white. We will define who we are and how much we're worth. You're not going to tell us who we are or who we have to be anymore.' And one doesn't have to be a radical to feel this. . . .

"Whether America's newspapers displace the ever-popular name 'Negro' for black or Afro-American is up to each paper of course. (The black press has already swung overwhelmingly in favor of the 'new' language, still using 'Negro' when they need a nice 'neutral' word)."[3]

The Need for a Black Press

Whatever they may be called, the black newspapers and magazines and their auxiliaries exist. How they developed is related in subsequent chapters. Why they came into being is part of that history.

The aims of the early publications, from *Freedom's Journal* of 1827 to those issued in Reconstruction days, are clear. The exploitation of slaves, their mistreatment, and the limitations placed upon them are examined in the historical perspective. But the black citizen of the United States is a free man or woman, education is available (if not always the best), employment can be had at least by some (even if still mainly in the lower echelons), and civil rights slowly are being won. What, then, is the need for a black press still?

It is needed mainly because all the old battles have not yet been won and because there are so many new ones. "Without the black press, the black man would not know who he is nor what is happening to his struggle for the freedom of citizenship," in the words of Valarie Myers, former editor of Syracuse (New York) *Challenger*, one of the many new community papers of recent years that had short lives. And perhaps less important now than in the past but still vital is the need for facts about themselves, i.e., coverage of the black society, still largely not covered by the general press and not likely ever to be. The number of ethnic minority citizens is mounting daily and a single viewpoint press cannot be expected to cover this huge population. The standard press will continue to deal mainly in racial conflict, crime, and news of blacks known to whites from the sports and entertainment worlds, for such news fare is a staple of U. S. journalism regardless of race, including the white.

Also, for many years the black people have mistrusted the white press. As Roi Ottley has explained, the white press and news services earned the suspicion of black citizens in the first half of this century because they could not be trusted to tell the truth about blacks. These white agencies were accused of favoring whites against blacks, i.e., tailoring the news to fit the publications' prejudices or at least those of their owners. Both northern and southern papers followed the practice of race identification of blacks only and of ignoring entirely anything but unfavorable black news.

Complaints about the white press treatment of blacks' news today, however, are no less numerous, perhaps more selective because they single out regions, and merely different in nature from those of the early years of black journalism. Representatives of various types of black organizations, for example, met in Washington in 1969 with editors and reporters from the city's three white dailies to discuss "The Minorities and the Press." The session was typical, in the matter of criticisms of the white press, of others held in various parts of the United States by newsmen's organizations, schools of journalism, and newspaper unions.

The black critics in Washington objected to the papers' practice of displaying civil rights stories next to crime stories involving blacks. They objected also to all news concerning black citizens being handled as civil rights news instead of being put in appropriate departments, such as financial or women's sections. News about blacks, it also was charged, is always negative and the newspapers tend to deal only with conflict stories about what goes on in the ghetto.[4]

Twenty years later the critics would have to admit that the white press carries many more positive stories about blacks than at any time in journalistic history.

Using its *Afro* Survey feature plan, in 1987 the Richmond (Virginia) *Afro-American* asked eight persons at random to answer the question, "Is the black press still needed today?"

The inquiring reporter spoke with an electrician, a businessperson, a minister, an aide associate, an administrator, and two computer clerks. The eighth was unemployed. Three in the group were women. All were black citizens. They appeared to be between twenty and forty years of age.

All eight said the black press is needed. Their reasons:

". . . it better relates to the problems that blacks face."

". . . because of the tide of racism that has emerged. This is the only media that is positive toward the gains that blacks have made."

". . . because blacks are doing more and going further and these things need to be mentioned."

". . . to have a two-way communication for fairness of the media."

"Only the black press can give an adequate account of what is happening to the black community."

". . . because the white media does not give us the full picture."

". . . to give us information about blacks that we don't get from the white press."

"The black press can give us a black view of things."

All eight either directly or by implication were critical of the general press, saying it failed to cover black news or that it cannot give the black view of black events. This common complaint has existed for years. There are answers. So long as black news is handled by white reporters and writers it cannot give the black view with full understanding. To cover more black news than already is handled in the most tolerant liberal newspapers and newsmagazines provides a service to a small group in whose lives and activities the majority of readers have little interest, a defense that has been used against more coverage of all ethnic groups or other minorities.

The result is that there must be a black press for the reading matter not found elsewhere and for the advertising that is too costly to run in the standard press, whose rates are much higher because of larger circulations.

There is an additional concern. It would be of interest to learn what black publications these eight persons read and how faithfully. Probably in Richmond the *Afro-American* is one, but not necessarily. Regardless of what is read, do these readers wholly support the black press by subscribing to it or buying it regularly and reading it? Do they support it by patronizing the advertisers in the black publications?

Over the years the author has questioned black friends and total strangers encountered in traveling, on the streets and in shops, and on college campuses. It is an unscientific canvass, just as is the *Afro* Survey, but it may still be a small indicator. These inquiries show that most respondents read *Ebony, Essence*, and/or *Jet*. A considerable number read *Black Enterprise*. A few mentioned such specialized publications as *Black Scholar, Black Collegian*, and *Black Family*.

Newspapers were named according to region. In the northeastern United States it was weeklies from Boston, New York, and Philadelphia, most often the New York *Amsterdam News* and the Philadelphia *Tribune*. Farther south it was one of the five *Afro-Americans*. In the Midwest blacks named the Kansas City *Call* and the Chicago *Defender*. On the West Coast, where there are several chains of newspapers, one or another of them were mentioned. (See Table 1.1.)

But when asked where they see these papers and magazines the respondents revealed that few put down money for them—there is much pass-along circulation in the black press market. There are reasons: Their cost has gone up, with papers selling at from twenty-five to fifty cents a copy and magazines from one to two dollars a copy. They are not always accessible, even in cities with considerable black population. Buyers are spread too thin. Libraries usually stock the more popular papers and magazines, especially in black neighbor-

TABLE 1.1. Circulations of top black newspaper groups in 1986

Newspaper	Number of Papers	Frequency[a]	Circulation	Audit[b]
Wave Group (Calif.)	7	W	160,230	PR
Hartford *Inquirer* Group (Conn.)	5	W	125,000	NI
Post Group (Calif.)	5	W	124,000	TMC
San Francisco *Reporter* Metro Group	7	W	104,700	PR
Sacramento *Observer* Group	3	W	99,466	SWP/F
Chicago *Citizen* Group	4	W	77,215	CPVS
Afro-American Newspapers[c]	5	S-W (2), W (2), NI (1)	34,030	ABC (2), PR (2), NI (1)

Sources: *Editor & Publisher International Year Book,* 1987; *Gale Directory of Publications,* 1987; Publishers' statements.

[a]W = Weekly; S-W = Semiweekly; NI = Not indicated.

[b]PR = Publisher's report; NI = Not indicated; TMC = Controlled circulation; SWP/F = Publisher's statement paid and free; CPVS = Community Papers Verification Service; ABC = Audit Bureau of Circulations.

[c]Figures for the New Jersey edition are not available. The Baltimore and Washington papers are semiweeklies; the two figures for each week have been combined.

hoods. Some bars, barbershops, beauty parlors, and smoke shops are outlets for publishers and sources of free reading for consumers.

Some unusual answers were received in the author's inquiries. One young bank teller said instantly that she reads only one periodical of any kind. "Guess which," she said. The usual leading black ones were named. She disavowed them all. It was *Cosmopolitan.* She could not identify with the magazines aimed at her. Her friends were mostly young white women, and that was their favorite as well. The Cosmo Girl was all she needed. (See Table 1.2.)

Several others confidently named magazines that had, in some cases, long disappeared, such as *Encore, Sepia, Ebony Jr!,* and *Black Sports,* leading one to distrust their replies. It was the aura reaction: they wanted to be well thought of, to appear loyal to their own press, and wanted to say what they thought was expected.

As in the early years, blacks turn to their press to fight their battles. A look at almost any black paper and most magazines dramatizes this point. To the middle-class white or other nonblack reader, the black world is a separate realm. The use of *world* in black publication titles, such as *Our World, Bronze World, Black World* magazines or Garvey's paper, the *Negro World,* all indicate that this separation was realized in the past. The fault is not all that of white publishers. The general white press does not cover the details of life in most industries or professions or other specialized groups of humans, for that would be impossible; that explains the existence of thousands of

TABLE 1.2. Black magazines with circulations of 100,000 or more in 1986

Publication	Frequency[a]	Circulation	Audit[b]
Ebony	M	1,724,249	ABC
Essence	M	800,241	ABC
Jet	W	790,373	ABC
Crisis	M	300,000	PR
Black Enterprise	M	234,760	ABC
Players	M	206,474	PR
Excel	M	130,000	VAC
American Visions	B-M	100,000	NI
Right On!	M	350,000	NI
Black Family	B-M	200,000	PR
Black Collegian	Q	133,955	TMC
Message	B-M	120,000	PR

Sources: *Gale Directory of Publications,* 1987; Publishers' reports.
[a]M = Monthly; W = Weekly; B-M = Bimonthly; Q = Quarterly.
[b]ABC = Audit Bureau of Circulations; PR = Publisher's report; VAC = Verified Audit of Circulation Corporation; NI = Not indicated; TMC = Controlled circulation.

special publications to compensate for the lack of their news in the consumer or general press.

An example of what has been described as the continued discrimination against black citizens occurred in 1987. The National Newspaper Publishers Association (NNPA) had arranged to hold its annual convention in Arizona. It was set for January 21–22. But when Governor Evan Mecham refused to observe the birthday of Martin Luther King, Jr., which his predecessor had promised to do by giving the employees the day off with pay, the NNPA reconsidered its plans. Members were polled and the convention was canceled, the food paid for and donated to a Phoenix Catholic charity.

Arizona's black people were upset by the governor's action, which was based on the view that it was illegal to grant the day off because only the state legislature could make such a decision. About fifteen thousand citizens marched on Phoenix in protest.

Clyde Reid, a Howard University public television public information officer, summarized the need for a black press in such circumstances as the Arizona incident:

"1. We live in a segregated society with glaring disparities in socio-economic conditions which must be made public.

"2. Only the black press can help preserve the culture and heritage of America's black people.

"3. The black press is a 'special press,' comparable to the Jewish press or the Spanish press, with a special mission; it is not dependent upon the deficiencies of the white press for its existence."[5]

Extent of the Black Press

A visitor to the United States from India, whose citizens, being people of color other than white, often have an interest in and sympathy for the nonwhites anywhere, once remarked to the author that he saw no publications for blacks in his travels here although he saw many black people. When he was told that at the time the country's black population amounted to 18,870,000, he was astonished.

The experience is a common one for whites as well, although not to be taken too literally. The Indian friend was shown a variety of black periodicals and then recalled having seen several of them on newsstands but of being unaware of their origin. Unless one knows the titles it is not always easy to identify black publications, especially with the greater use by white papers and magazines of black models on covers or the photographs of black celebrities on front as well as inside pages. In general, however, it is true that the black press has little newsstand exposure, for the obvious reasons that only those newsstands where there is substantial black traffic, such as in largely black neighborhoods, would benefit from selling such publications, and that the earning power of almost all blacks has kept down the purchase of publications by single copies. Furthermore, it is too expensive to place publications on newsstands through distribution companies unless wide sale is likely. Perhaps one stand on a main street may stock a magazine or two. (See Table 1.3.)

Library holdings also have been sparse. Exceptions are private and public institutions patronized by blacks, such as college libraries especially interested in black history and culture, only a recent interest in most instances. It is the unusual public library that receives more than one or two magazines and that number of newspapers aimed at black readers.

Most whites and not a few blacks are unaware of the extent of the black press. College people, except those deeply involved in social movements embracing racial problems, rarely can remember seeing a black publication, a situation the author has become aware of through classroom work during thirty-five years of teaching journal-

TABLE 1.3. Ten highest circulations of individual (nongroup) black newspapers in 1986

Newspaper	Frequency[a]	Circulation	Audit[b]
Black American (N.Y.)	W	77,000	SWP
Chicago *Metro News*	W	76,793	CPVS
Philadelphia *Metro*	W	73,000	CAC
Big Red News (Ill.)	W	53,766	PR
Atlanta *Voice*	W	50,000	SWP/F
Dallas *Weekly*	W	50,000	CVPS
Daily Challenge (N.Y.)	D	46,308	SWP/F
Cleveland *Call and Post*	W	43,285	ABC
Benton Harbor *Citizen* (Mich.)	W	42,000	SWP/F
Dallas *Examiner*	W	40,000	TMC

Sources: *Editor & Publisher International Year Book,* 1987; *Gale Directory of Publications,* 1987; Publishers' statements.

[a]W = Weekly; D = Daily.

[b]SWP = Publisher's statement paid; CPVS = Community Papers Verification Service; CAC = Certified Audit of Circulation; PR = Publisher's report; SWP/F = Publisher's statement paid and free; ABC = Audit Bureau of Circulations; TMC = Controlled circulation.

ism courses in which total or only some attention has been given to the black press.

As their circulations attest, most black magazines, aside from a few popular ones, seem to exist in secrecy. White scholars have vague impressions of such capably written and well-edited periodicals as *Phylon* and the *Journal of Negro Education*. Several dozen other meritorious publications have functioned for years in quiet, surrounded by white indifference. In their effort to understand the black society, some whites look into these publications.

An accurate or nearly complete list of newspapers and magazines aimed at black readers is not available. Far more complete are the lists of black radio and television broadcasting operators.

In preparing this book, the author attempted to compile for his own purposes as nearly complete a list as possible on the printed journalism. Lists from several sources, including the NNPA membership, the clients of the Amalgamated Newspapers, Inc. (ANI), the *Gale* (formerly *Ayer*) *Directory of Publications*, the *Editor & Publisher International Year Book, Standard Rate and Data Service, Directory of Advertising Agencies*, and *Ulrich's International Periodicals Directory* were consulted.

Several other reference books were also examined, but all were too old to offer a reliable list because they were incomplete in their coverage and did not go past 1986. There are several reasons for these incomplete statistics. Black publications not only appear and disappear quickly but many ongoing enterprises do not join their own or general media organizations such as the NNPA, the American Society of Newspaper Editors (ASNE), the American Newspaper Publishers Association (ANPA), or the American Society of Magazine Editors (ASME), each of which has only a smattering of black members. Nor do they usually join their state organizations. The expense of dues (costly for the national organizations), the costs of participating in distant conventions and workshops, and the belief that they have too little to gain explain this reluctance to work in such organizations.

Black radio and television station owners are organized, as are the newspapers, but the magazines have no national organization of their own.

Further complicating a count is that numbers of papers are given away (sometimes called shoppers or throwaways). They are on record nowhere except for those that use the U.S. Postal Service for distribution.

Similarly obscure in some instances are some others, also of free circulation or partly free, that consider themselves community newspapers or magazines.

No publication or organization of any kind attempts to keep an absolute record of the movements in the black media world. Certain scholars, usually on university faculties, keep systematic records of the aspects of the black press of deepest interest to them. One such was Dr. Armistead S. Pride of Lincoln University in Missouri, who specialized in the newspaper.

Such a reference work as *Who's What and Where*, first published in 1985, is concerned largely with a listing of black journalists. That information is for media administrators so they can obtain staff members from the directory's alphabetically arranged brief biographies. Although the appendix contains a list of black newspapers, it is a combination of the NNPA and the *Editor & Publisher International Year Book* compilations. The magazine tally of thirty-six periodicals is incomplete, since it omits several times that number.

The broadcasting industry provides better information of this sort about itself than does the publishing industry. The National Association of Black-Owned Broadcasters is the principal such organization.

The Scope Today

What do these publications tell their readers? What appears in them? The newspapers give their audiences news of the black community as well as of national and international events directly affecting black citizens. The emphasis is on local or regional news. They also provide entertainment and editorial guidance, although largely the former, as with newspapers anywhere in the United States. The magazines also seek to entertain, but more and more are informing their readers and promoting ideas and organizations. None of this is done with uniform thoroughness or quality. But, along with black radio and television, the black press is still the main source of the black citizen's information and comment about his or her life. Through advertising these publications fulfill the commercial function. (See Table 1.4.) The segment of the press known as specialized magazines serves as a literary outlet, an opinion forum, or a guidebook for business and professional people. As the late Henry

TABLE 1.4. Black-and-white display advertising line rates (in dollars) of fifteen
            black newspapers

Newspaper	Open Rate
Atlanta *Daily World*	8.40
Baltimore *Afro-American* Group (6 papers)	85.28
Baton Rouge *Community Leader*	9.56
Charlotte *Post*	5.60
Chicago *Defender*	15.02
Cleveland *Call and Post*	35.00
Indianapolis *Recorder*	8.51
Los Angeles *Sentinel*	17.50
Miami *Times*	12.60
Michigan *Chronicle*	16.30
New Pittsburgh Courier Group	15.04
New York *Amsterdam News*	33.00
Philadelphia *Tribune* (4 editions)	36.12
Portland (Oreg.) *Observer*	6.58
St. Louis *American*	15.24

Source: *Standard Rate and Data Service,* 1987.

Lee Moon, director of information for the NAACP and editor of its magazine the *Crisis* put it: "Colored citizens still look to the Negro press for their side of the story and for an interpretation of the news that affects their vital interests."[6] Or as a perceptive white student expressed it: "A black publication actually is one which helps establish the black identity and serves the black community."[7]

These functions and different kinds of content, are, of course, not unique to the black press. The newspapers and magazines of any nation or any minority group have more or less the same purposes if not the same content. The black press differs from the white not so much in kind as in message and in quality. It often reports news not covered by other journalism. It interprets that news differently, from an uncommon standpoint. It ventures opinions about matters not dealt with by other presses and its opinions frequently vary from those of other publications treating the same topics. The reporting and writing, for understandable reasons to be explored in this book, often are superficial; the editing frequently is careless; the printing, especially of the newspapers, is slovenly in many instances.

By and large, the physical patterns of these papers and magazines are like those of others in the United States. The newspapers, at a glance, look like any to be found on the ordinary display. The main news—or news that will sell papers or hold readers—is on the first page; other news stories are scattered throughout the rest of the paper. An editorial page has all the usual characteristics of such pages: two or three essays on local or national affairs down the left; to their right a cartoon on some national topic or event involving black citizens; and columns and letters to the editor in other areas of the page. The columnists frequently are one or two of the nationally syndicated or otherwise regularly available black leaders. Local columnists abound.

One or two pages each may be devoted to sports, church, society, and entertainment news. A good deal of this often is obvious publicity material. Occasionally columnists appear on sports and society pages. Syndicated copy, obtained from one of the few black feature companies or, more likely, a regular white-oriented one, and news from United Press International (the latter a white agency), or in some instances special services, appear sparingly, and chiefly in the larger papers. Some of the little weeklies are hardly more than composites of lifted material with datelines and the symbol showing the source chopped out before the item is pasted for photo-offset reproduction. The rest is advertising, both classified and display. Space is being bought by large corporations as well as by local enterprises seeking to employ blacks, but the bulk of the space is filled by the ads of small firms or service-oriented businesses.

Tabloid-size is becoming more common among black newspapers, particularly because many of the new community weeklies were using that dimension in 1987. Magazines were mainly of two sizes, eight-by-twelve-inches (or newsmagazine-size) and the six-by-nine-inches used by scholarly journals. Both letterpress and offset remain in use as printing methods but photo-offset reproduction, especially with new publications, is taking hold rapidly.

The magazines are too varied for a single description, the *Journal of Negro Education* having little in common with *Right On!* Just as the newspapers resemble their white counterparts, the magazines, type by type, are much like periodicals for whites serving the same function. *Ebony* is a small *Life*, superficially. *Phylon* resembles the serious literary and public affairs quarterlies of the *Southern Review* type.

Points of View

The opinions of these publications, since they descended from a press known for its strong protest function, have in common certain positions. But beyond these particular uniform beliefs there is great variety. It goes without saying that pleas and demands for greater recognition of civil rights can be heard from all except a few dissidents and the highly specialized, technical publications (and even they have their say on the subject now and then).

On racial matters the black press is by and large vigorously outspoken. Although the publications have the same goals, they differ considerably in how they propose to achieve them.

For the most part, on national issues aside from race, the bigger publications are socially and politically conservative or moderate but not reactionary. Liberal viewpoints are to be found in the small community weeklies, the publications of militants, and some of the purely opinion publications more often than in the big-circulation newspapers and periodicals. Although traditionally loyal to the Republican party, more and more of the black press members in the 1970s turned their support to the Democratic party, led to that viewpoint by President John F. Kennedy, Vice-President and then President Lyndon B. Johnson, Vice-President Hubert H. Humphrey, and Senator Robert F. Kennedy. In the 1980s the opposition to President Ronald Reagan has been strong. The magazines, issued in a different frequency than the newspapers, with some exceptions avoid commitment on current issues or find it impractical to have a timely position on any subject outside the publication's realm.

The Old and New Readers

Sharp differences exist between what the older generation black people read in the way of black journalism and what is preferred by the younger generation. Judging by detailed descriptions of their reading choices from representatives of both groups a generalization or two may be offered. People aged fifty or more are likely to stay with the standard consumer publications (large circulation black magazines and major black newspapers) and listen to some black radio. People in the twenty to thirty-five range read no black publications whatsoever or listen to no black radio stations. Or if they read black journalism their preference leans to some of the newer periodicals or at least the older ones that have taken a position on today's problems facing members of the black race.

Here are some typical responses from the older generation, this from a retired U.S. diplomat:

In a number of ways I have been close to the black press all of my life. Growing up in North Carolina—fatherless from the age of one— as a child I waited anxiously for each week's edition of the Baltimore *Afro-American* and Norfolk *Journal and Guide*. My mother bought these two papers faithfully. My aunt, who lived with us during the summer and the school holidays, contributed the Pittsburgh *Courier*. At Livingstone College across the street from our home, where both my parents had taught earlier, the librarian encouraged me to read the Chicago *Defender*, the New York *Amsterdam News*, and the New York *Age*, as well as the *Carolina Times*. S. W. Garlington, a sociology professor at Livingstone, founded the short-lived *Salisbury Citizen*, a local black weekly and we talked often of the Black press. We were to renew our acquaintance in New York during 1949–50 when Garlington was managing editor of the *Amsterdam News*.[8]

The next testimonial comes from the editor of a prominent white-published religious international magazine:

I read or browse through as many [Black publications] as I can get my hands on, or as many as time permits. Among them: *Ebony, MBM, Jet*, the *Crisis, Black Enterprise, Essence*, the *Amsterdam News*, the *City Sun* (which I prefer over the *Amsterdam News*), the Chicago *Daily Defender* (to keep up on things in Chicago, where I lived for nine years), the St. Louis *Sentinel* (my hometown paper), and the Jackson *Advocate* (the best newspaper in the state of Mississippi and one of the most courageous Black papers in the country).

I read the above magazines and newspapers regularly because I want to know what is going on in my own immediate community and among Black Americans everywhere in the U.S. When I include these with "other" publications (*Time, Newsweek, Business Week, Atlantic, Harper's, Money, Sports Illustrated, Reader's Digest*, New York *Times, Wall Street Journal*, Washington *Post*, etc.), then I consider myself fairly-well up on things. [9]

A different group of publications is read by an Ivy League university professor:

Years ago, when growing up as a young boy in Dallas, I sold the local black weekly in Dallas, then called the Dallas *Express*. It and a host of black weeklies in other Texas cities, including Houston, were published by an enterprising black businessman whose name was Carter Westley. As I recall, he was not much of a journalist. The editing of the paper was sloppy. But it was well-read in the black community for details about black tragedies—deaths, including murders and lynchings, property destruction, news of what was happening in the churches and sports in the segregated high schools. There were no reporters. Institutions like churches and the "Negro Branch" of the YMCA sent news releases which were published as sent. The local paper, as I recall, published more about the bad times in the black community and less about the good times. I also sold by way of home delivery, the Pittsburgh *Courier*, Chicago *Defender* and *Afro-American*. There was something mystical about these "national" papers to me. They seemed to open up foreign territories. My family subscribed to the Dallas *Morning News*. But it did not carry any news about blacks in Dallas in those days.

After moving to Syracuse, I felt cut off from happenings in the black community. I particularly wanted to keep up with new names — new presidents of colleges and universities, new politicians and public administrators. Thus, I subscribed to *Jet, Ebony*, and the *Afro-American*. Even though I was in New York State, I preferred the *Afro-American* over the *Amsterdam News* because I wanted to keep up with names of people in the South, particularly in Georgia where I was a college student and in Texas and Alabama and Tennessee where I had family. *Jet* has served as the one magazine that gives me the names I want to remember and read about nationally. Although it has gone overboard on featuring athletes and entertainers, *Jet* still does a good job in reporting on political leaders. I therefore keep up with what is happening by reading *Jet* weekly and *Ebony* monthly. I also subscribe to the *Afro-American* now.[10]

These choices are unlike those of several young blacks, under forty and active in journalism, all of them on white papers, which is significant in itself.

The first is a young reporter on the West Coast, working for a daily:

She reads *Black Enterprise, Ebony*, and *Essence* regularly. "Many of my friends," she writes, "read the same magazines. My family reads *Ebony Man, Essence* and the *Michigan Chronicle*, periodically."

Another, working as an editor for a major East Coast daily, says she reads many periodicals but "only the *Amsterdam News* and *Black Enterprise*" (both, along with *Vanity Fair, W*, and *Spy*, are read for their curiosity value). Her parents read a Twin Cities black weekly, the *Spokesman*. "My friends don't follow the black press (monthlies included) to any extent. The only exception is a friend on the *Amsterdam News*."

This particular young reader had important experience as a staff member on a leading black magazine for women.

Another major newspaper staffer, an editorial writer, believes that she represents her race in her job. Although all of her professional career has been on white publications she is perhaps more aware of the black press as an influence upon her thinking as an editorialist. She is a free-lance writer for black magazines.

She reported that she reads the *Amsterdam News, Jet,* and *Black Enterprise* regularly, and *Ebony* and *Essence* less regularly. She sees a new weekly called *City Sun* at her office.

"Family members," she reports, "read *Ebony* and *Jet.* My friends read *Essence, Black Enterprise,* and *Jet* with some frequency."

No mention was made of black radio by any respondent.

The author has made many inquiries over the past two decades about the use of black media. In recent years more and more blacks have disavowed any interest in the black publications or stations. They read entirely in white publications. When asked why, the reply always is the same: "There is nothing in them to interest me." The older people sometimes continue to read newspapers from their former places of residence because they want to keep up on the news in those towns and cities and may still have friends or own property there. But people twenty and thirty years of age who grew up in the North would have few ties to the South. And Northerners who grew up on the West Coast have little stake in the area of their birth.

Typical of what observant whites have said or written about the reading and listening practices of their black friends is this quotation from a letter to the author describing the situation in 1987:

". . . Many blacks I know wouldn't read a black-oriented newspaper. They want to be 'homogenized'—they want to be in the main stream, and don't view themselves as part of an ethnic group . . . Because of labor troubles at the *Amsterdam News* many blacks call management exploiters . . . None of my black students ever consider working for the black press although some of my Caribbean students do work, either for pay or on a volunteer basis, for these special-interest publications."

All these testimonials coming from black people are by writers who hold one or more college degrees and work in one of the professions, primarily teaching or journalism.

The Beginnings

The black press in the United States is approximately half the age of the white press, having begun in 1827, when the white press already had existed 137 years.

Particularly during the early period – 1827 to the Civil War – the black press was a leader of protest against injustices to the race; not only that, it was also a journalism almost totally committed to a cause. After 1865, however, it began to resemble the white press in its division: some publications continuing to crusade for more freedom, others supporting reaction, and still others interesting themselves more in profits than in social progress.

Earl Conrad, a white journalist who worked for the black press in the 1940s, saw that press of the 1830–60 period not merely as a crusader against slavery but also as "the spiritual ancestor of the essentially agitational press of this day [1946] but possibly of the modern labor and radical press," he wrote. It was not a community press in the sense that it did not exist exclusively for the Negro group, he added.[1]

These first publications, despite the African descent of their originators, were modeled after European publications, especially the British, as were all American papers and magazines. No evidence of African influence is apparent; in fact, the first newspaper in West Africa, homeland of many slaves, was founded by Charles L. Force, who went to Monrovia, Liberia, from the United States. He brought with him a hand-run press given him by the Massachusetts Colonization Society of Boston and on it, in 1826, printed a four-page monthly paper, the *Liberia Herald*.[2] He died a few months later and the paper was suspended. But it was revived in 1830 by John B. Russwurm, who was one of the two founders of the first American black paper.

Russwurm had joined with Samuel E. Cornish in bringing out

America's first black publication; their weekly *Freedom's Journal* originally was issued in New York City as a means of answering attacks on blacks by another newspaper of that city, the white New York *Enquirer*. I. Garland Penn, one of the few historians of black journalism, wrote that the attacking paper was edited by "an Afro-American-hating Jew" who "encouraged slavery and deplored the thought of freedom for the slave" and "made the vilest attacks upon the Afro-Americans."[3] Editor of the *Enquirer* at the time was Mordecai M. Noah.

Although it had newspaper format, *Freedom's Journal*, whose first issue was dated March 16, 1827, was in content more of a magazine than a newspaper. On the first page of one issue, for example, appear three articles: "Memoirs of Capt. Paul Cuffee," "People of Colour," and "Cure for Drunkenness," none of which can be said to be news. The masthead carried the sentence, "Righteousness Exalteth a Nation." Its columns, as Conrad describes them so well, "were packed with a religious wrath."

The little paper must have been aimed mainly at white readers, since the literacy rate of blacks in the early part of the nineteenth century was low. It is likely that the editors wished to influence the whites, for they were in a position to help free the black man. Doubtless, also, the publishers needed white support, since blacks were not able to help financially.

The two founders and their associates were not experienced journalists. Russwurm, whose name now is borne by both a Harlem public school and a national award given each year by black publishers, was one of the early black college graduates. He received a degree from Bowdoin the year before he helped begin *Freedom's Journal*. After he left the paper he went to Liberia; there are hints that he was dragooned. There he earned his living as a teacher and school administrator but also embarked again on journalism with the *Liberia Herald*. At his death in 1851 he was governor of the Colony of Maryland at Cape Palmas, Liberia.[4]

Enoch R. Waters, in his "personal history of the black press," insists that it was Cornish, not Russwurm, who was the father of the black press; he raised the money and hired Russwurm to be editor. It was Russwurm who resigned and closed the paper and left the United States.

The two men disagreed over the question of colonizing blacks, Cornish opposing it and Russwurm favoring. As a result, six months after they had launched *Freedom's Journal* Cornish resigned, and Russwurm ran it alone. Within a year, however, Russwurm had left

2.1. The first black newspaper published in the United States.

for Liberia, and Cornish returned, changing the paper's name to *Rights of All* in May 1829. It continued to plead for Afro-American freedom and citizenship. Penn records that it suspended publication in 1830;[5] Pride, a more careful and more recent historian, reports that the last issue extant is dated October 9, 1829.[6]

Other Early Publications

Cornish, a free black man and Presbyterian clergyman, edited or published other black papers. After he left *Freedom's Journal* to stay, he edited the *Weekly Advocate,* sometimes considered the second black publication because of its tenure. Like its predecessor, it was a New York City paper, and had to rely on the abolitionist movement for support. It, too, went through a change of name. It had many editors in a short time. It first appeared in January 1837, but in two months became the *Colored American*. As the *Advocate* it was managed by Phillip A. Bell, who was to have something of a career in black journalism, and published by a Canadian, Robert Sears. Financial support, Penn records, came from the antislavery movement, including such leaders as Lewis Tappan of the silk merchant family, an organizer of a large abolitionist society. When Cornish left, the editorship went successively to James McCune Smith, an Edinburgh University graduate, and Charles Bennett Ray, a clergyman. There is evidence that it had a Philadelphia edition; if so, it was the first black paper to serve more than one community with separate editions.[7]

Penn was himself a man of journalistic experience for his day. Ernest Kaiser, while on the staff of the Schomburg Library, a Harlem branch of the New York Public Library, wrote a brief biographical sketch of Penn for a facsimile edition of *The Afro-American Press and Its Editors*. Penn was busy all his life in organization work. At one time or another Penn was a school principal, editor of a black newspaper, and a correspondent for other publications.

He edited the Lynchburg *Virginia Laborer*. Among the papers using his dispatches from the South was a leading black weekly, the

2.2. Samuel E. Cornish, cofounder of *Freedom's Journal*.

2.3. John B. Russwurm, the other founder of *Freedom's Journal*.

New York *Age*. His history book was written when he was only
twenty-four years old. Kaiser called it a landmark for its period.

After he moved to Cincinnati he returned to school teaching and
other educational work and to write other books. He coedited several
volumes and programs, and coauthored two educational books.

The number of publications issued by blacks before the Civil War
has been verified as "forty or more."[8] These, the scholar who verified
them observes, were journalistic vehicles for views and feelings that,
until then, had expression in chants, spoken poems, folk songs,
hymns, orations, and sermons, all unprinted forms. Even many of the
journalistic publications issued after 1827 were hardly more than
pamphlets and were short-lived; thus the career of the *Weekly Advo-
cate-Colored American,* 1837–42, was unusual.

The names of many publications that followed reveal the antislavery aims: *Aliened American, Mirror of Liberty,* the *Elevator,
Freeman's Advocate, Palladium of Liberty,* the *Genius of Freedom,*
and *Herald of Freedom*. Most were from New York State. The rest
were organized in other northern or western areas. They contained so
much opinion rather than news (with their concentration on propaganda for the antislavery movement), that they were of far more
consequence as persuaders than as news organs.

Samuel Ringgold Ward

The Reverend Mr. Ward is better remem-
bered today as a public speaker than as publisher of three black newspapers, part editor of another, and a contributor to two more, both
among the more famous antislavery journals of their day.

The U.S. papers he ran himself were the *True American* and the
Impartial Citizen. The third was a Canadian publication. He acquired
his first paper in 1846, and published the *True American* until 1848 in
Cortlandville, New York. He suspended it to begin issuing the *Impartial Citizen* in nearby Syracuse, New York, in 1849. Both papers gave
him problems; survival was difficult in those days for all antislavery
publications. Ward had difficulty collecting money from subscribers.
The *Impartial Citizen* was moved to Boston in June 1850, and continued there for another year.

Ward persisted on the lecture circuit, speaking out against slavery
and the lack of rights for his fellow blacks. He supported the views of
the white abolitionist Gerrit Smith.

2.4. Samuel Ringgold Ward, pioneer editor and publisher.

Ward was born into a Maryland slave family in 1817, but his parents soon left the mid-South to live in New York City, where their son grew up. He was an agent against slavery and also engaged in his first journalism by selling the *Colored American* for three years. He became a Congregationalist minister in 1839 and served churches in central New York. For a time he carried on his antislavery campaigns in Canada. He established the *Provincial Freeman* there.

As a corresponding editor of one of the leading papers of the day, the *Aliened American*, Ward shared editing responsibilities with another minister, the Reverend J. W. C. Remington, and with William H. Day. He was connected with this Cleveland paper from 1852 to 1856.

Although not on the staff, he wrote letters from Canada frequently for another and even more famous black publication, Frederick Douglass's *North Star*.

A man of religious convictions, a press was only one more tool for the advancement of his views. He died poor in Jamaica in 1866; he had visited England and Jamaica on speaking tours in his later years.[9]

The name of his paper lives on; it was adopted by a Syracuse, New York, bimonthly that seeks to be a social critic of Ward's type. (See Chapter 6.)

The *Ram's Horn*

Although it lasted only a year, the *Ram's Horn* symbolizes the conditions which gave rise to many black publications over the years. Penn relates that in 1846 the New York *Sun* published editorials proposing the curbing of Negro suffrage in that state. A black man, Willis A. Hodges, wrote a reply which was published only when he agreed to pay fifteen dollars and run it as an advertisement. At that, its sentiments were modified. Hodges was told by a staff member, when he protested the changes in his reply, that "the *Sun* shines for all white men, and not for colored men." If he wanted the Afro-American cause advocated, he was told, he would have to publish his own paper.[10] In 1847 Hodges established the *Ram's Horn*.

His partner in the venture was Thomas Van Rensselaer; neither had capital with which to work, so Hodges agreed to raise money and write for the paper. He spent two months earning what was needed by doing whitewashing. He paid for the first issue and wrote its first article. January 1, 1847, saw publication of 3,000 copies, with the motto, "We are men, and therefore interested in whatever concerns men." A weekly, it had as contributors a distinguished black journalist, Frederick Douglass, and a noted white fighter for blacks, John Brown, although Penn wrote that Douglass did little writing but mainly lent his prestige to the paper as editor in name if not in fact.

Penn reports that it reached 2,500 subscribers and survived until 1848, Hodges having withdrawn in a dispute and Rensselaer remaining as editor and owner for its last few issues. Penn called it a strong antislavery paper that "had done good work for the race, in whose special interest it was run."

Douglass and the *North Star*

In its forty-third issue the *Ram's Horn* carried a prospectus for a new antislavery paper, to be called the *North Star*. A weekly to come from Rochester, New York, it was to sell for two dollars a year (if paid in advance, fifty cents more if not within six months) and to be published by Frederick Douglass.

The *North Star* was the first of a series of newspapers and maga-

zines edited or published by Douglass, the great journalistic and oratorical hero of American blacks and one of the outstanding leaders in
their struggle for freedom. He set forth the platform for his new
paper thus:

"The object of the *North Star* will be to attack slavery in all its
forms and aspects, advocate Universal Emancipation; exact the standard of public morality; promote the moral and intellectual improvement of the colored people; and to hasten the day of freedom to our
three million enslaved fellow countrymen."[11]

November 1, 1847, saw the paper born. It was the *North Star*
until 1851 when it was merged with the *Liberty Party Paper* and
renamed *Frederick Douglass' Paper*. Doubtless that is what everyone
actually called it, for he was by then a widely known and admired
lecturer. Douglass said he did it to distinguish it from the many other
papers with *Star* in their names.

The $2,175 with which the paper was established came from Eng-
lish friends. It cost two dollars an issue to produce and had an average
circulation of 3,000. Assisting at first as an editor was Martin R.
Delaney, who had edited and published the Pittsburgh *Mystery* and
was the first black graduate of Harvard. Delaney, sometimes considered the original black nationalist, began the *Mystery* when he was
thirty-one and edited it from 1843 to 1847. He met Douglass when the

2.5. Martin R. Delaney,
editor and Douglass's aide.

orator visited Pittsburgh in 1847. After six months he parted with Douglass, leaving journalism to study medicine, and went on to a career of importance in that field. He wrote books also, including at least one novel.[12]

Douglass not only met local opposition in Rochester from anti-black elements but also after a time the plague that besets black journalism even today set in upon him: lack of both money and staff help. With the aid of his sons and many friends, however, he kept the paper alive until 1860, pouring into it what money he could make in public speaking, at which he excelled, and writing.

Several inches larger overall than the regular eight-column standard newspaper of today, *Frederick Douglass' Paper* would not be considered particularly readable. Each of its four pages contained six wide columns packed solid with type; its front page usually carrying no breaks except spaces between its small headlines. It consisted largely of abolitionist material, looking and sounding much like the *Liberator*. But that was the journalistic vogue. The vigor of Douglass's writing and the excitement of the times compensated to some extent for the lack of typographic attractiveness.

Frederick Douglass

The words and works of Frederick Douglass appeared for many decades chiefly in biographies written by blacks and anthologies of black writing edited by black scholars and literary people. White authors and scholars usually relegated him to the footnotes. But in recent years children's books about him have been issued, his autobiography has been republished, estimates of his importance and contribution have appeared, as have new biographies and collections of his writings. The U.S. government has issued a postage stamp carrying his portrait. The emphasis today has not been upon his journalism as much as upon his leadership of his race, which is as it should be, for he was only secondarily a journalist, although an extremely active one. Whatever the emphasis, his story is extraordinary.

Originally his name was not Douglass but Lloyd. He was born in Maryland in 1817 or 1818 (he was unsure of the year, as slaves' children often were) of a slave owned by a wealthy planter, one Colonel Edward Lloyd. His mother was Harriet Bailey. As was the custom, he bore his master's name. The boy knew nothing about his father, as slave children often did not. But Colonel Lloyd was gossiped as the father; in his autobiography Douglass allows the reader to think that the colonel might indeed have been his parent.[13]

Until he was seven he was reared by his grandmother, and then taken to the plantation home. There for three years he saw the cruelty with which slaves were treated, sights that never left his memory. When he turned ten he was sent to Baltimore to live with a relative of the Lloyd family. There he learned to read and write a little, taught secretly by the mistress of the house. But when the white master found out he prohibited his wife from continuing the lessons to the slave boy.

Douglass soon was allowed to hire himself out. He earned three dollars a week as a shipbuilder's employee. While doing such work he tried many times to escape slavery, succeeding finally in 1838 and fleeing to Philadelphia. From there he went to New York and New England, taking laboring jobs. He used the name Lloyd, but after several years took the name Bailey, was married, and continued work as a laborer. he shortly assumed the name he retained for life:

2.6. Frederick Douglass.

Douglass. At about the same time he came to know a man who was to influence his life sharply: William Lloyd Garrison, the abolitionist-journalist. Garrison helped educate him and encouraged him to become a writer and author, Douglass having improved his reading and writing ability while working.

Douglass's first public writing was letters to newspapers, in which he attacked slavery. As Quarles and some of his earlier biographers point out, his experiences on the plantation provided him with graphic examples of the effect of the system. He also attended anti-slavery meetings; at these he had opportunities to demonstrate his oratorical ability, beginning a public speaking career which was to bring him to international fame. In 1845 he went to Europe to lecture there, stirring opposition to the evil he was fighting. Still a slave, he was in constant danger of recapture by Colonel Lloyd. Realizing this, English Quaker friends collected $750 and in 1846 bought his freedom.

Upon his return to the United States the next year, Douglass went to Rochester, beginning the venture which most entitled him to a place in American journalistic history but which until recently was scarcely mentioned in the volumes on that history. His editorship of *Frederick Douglass' Paper* was interrupted in 1859 when he was rumored to have been involved in the John Brown raid and threatened with arrest. Friends spirited him to Canada; from there he went to England. After the threat died down he returned and resurrected the paper. In it he urged Lincoln to use black troops and to issue a proclamation of emancipation. By now he had come to oppose the Garrisonites, many of whom had failed to support his publications because of disagreement over policies in combating slavery. He refused to believe, as did most abolitionists, that the Constitution was proslavery per se. He also had no confidence in the view that politics was unavailing in fighting slavery. He wanted to use the Constitution and the democratic right to vote as weapons against evil.[14]

Douglass again gave his name to a publication when in mid-1860 he issued *Douglass' Monthly*, a magazine aimed mainly at British readers and devoted largely to abolitionist material. It came to an end three years later. As the magazine began the newspaper ceased, deeply in debt and almost devoid of support. Little sustenance was coming from whites and virtually none from blacks — who were in no economic condition to provide it in any case.

For the next decade Douglass devoted his time largely to lecturing and working with labor and political groups, at which he was impressively successful. A big man with a powerful voice, he was an eloquent speaker invited everywhere in the fight of the black man for justice. In his prime he resembled Mark Twain or Walt Whitman, for he had a striking head and beard of white hair.

Douglass returned to journalism in 1870. A new weekly, the *New Era*, appeared in Washington, with Douglass as corresponding editor. It was devoted to righting the wrongs against black people. But it soon, despite Douglass's warnings, went into debt deeply. Douglass rescued it by buying a half interest, changing its name to *New National Era* and assuming its editorship.

Its policies, he wrote, were: "Free men, free soil, free speech, a free press, everywhere in the land. The ballot for all, education for all, fair wages for all." He published many of his own articles on issues confronting the black citizens in the 1870s. But by late 1874 it failed again; it had absorbed another paper, *New Citizen*, but the financial panic of 1873 was too much and Douglass's two sons, who had bought it, could not save it, even by making it antiunion and a Republican party voice. It ceased in 1875,[15] Douglass saying later "This misadventure"—it had cost him ten thousand dollars—had been a useful investment, for from the experience he had learned to stay out of newspaper work, which he did thereafter. His main interest became his activities in government appointments.

Douglass died in Anacostia Heights, D.C., in 1895, aged seventy-eight. His Washington home has become a shrine; in 1969 the House of Representatives passed a bill appropriating $338,000 to rehabilitate it.

What was his contribution to journalism? He had a clear idea of what it might be, as he explained it in one of his several autobiographies in a passage written just before he launched his major publication:

> The grand thing to be done, therefore, was to change the estimation in which the colored people of the U.St. were held; to remove the prejudice which depreciated and expressed them; to prove them worthy of a higher consideration; to disprove their alleged inferiority, and demonstrate their capacity for a more exalted civilization than salary and prejudice had assigned to them. I further stated that, in my judgment, a tolerably well conducted press, by calling out the mental energies of the race itself; by making them acquainted with their own latent powers; by enkindling among them the hope that for them there is a future; by developing their moral power, by combining and reflecting their talents would prove a most powerful means of removing prejudice, and of awakening an interest in them. I further informed them—and at that time the statement was true—that there was not, in the United States, a

single newspaper regularly published by the colored people; that many attempts had been made to establish such papers; but that, up to that time, they had all failed. These views I laid before my friends. The result was, nearly 2,500 dollars were speedily raised toward starting my paper.

In spite of his difficulties, he was to persist, and in the long run be successful. For it was not a small accomplishment, in those pre–Civil War years, to keep a black paper which we now would call an example of advocacy (or militant) journalism alive for more than a dozen years. It was an encouragement to other black publishers; it went on to be a source of inspiration for dozens of others to follow, even today.

Clearly the positions Douglass took in his papers provided leadership against the slavery system. And, although he differed later with other abolitionist leaders, his editorials and articles helped clarify the direction in which the movement was going.

Thus Frederick Douglass fulfilled several of the traditional functions of the newspaper publisher: he provided information as well as guidance and encouraged others to continue with their efforts.

The Early Magazines

Although little news appeared in these early papers and much of the material that did appear was of the kind now usually bound into magazines of opinion, they are classified generally as newspapers rather than periodicals because of their appearance, frequency of issue, and their habit of calling themselves news organs. Charles S. Johnson, a black scholar and editor, has observed that the first black publications were like magazines. But there were orthodox periodicals of a type other than *Douglass' Monthly*. Conflicting claims exist about which was first, largely revolving around whether it was one of broad or specialized appeal. Johnson notes that the first with a black editor was the *National Reformer*, the monthly issued by the American Moral Reform Society of Philadelphia.[16] Because it had more white readers than black and was intended for abolitionist readers and had integrated ownership and management, it is not by definition a black magazine. Penn records 1833 as its year of first issue; Johnson gives 1838.

A general magazine edited and owned by blacks and aimed at black readers was the *Mirror of Liberty*, a quarterly issued in New York City, edited by David Ruggles. It lasted from 1847 to 1849. It was not the first magazine, however, for from the black church denominations came several, including the *African Methodist Episcopal Church Magazine*, a short-lived quarterly started in September, 1841, but halted in the following December, and published from Brooklyn.

Another early one was the *Christian Herald*, later called the *Christian Recorder*. It grew, as did so many church periodicals and newspapers, out of the common goals of the black church and the black press. Like white church publications of the time, some of this religious journalism for blacks ventured into social problems. The *Herald*, a Pittsburgh publication sponsored by the African Methodist Episcopal Church, had grown out of *Mystery*, the Pittsburgh paper edited by Douglass's aide, Delaney. Founded in 1848 as a quarterly, after four years it was moved to Philadelphia, where the name change occurred and it was issued each week.[17] As the *Recorder* it was to continue into the twentieth century and rank among the longest-lived of black publications. Penn called it a bishop-maker among church periodicals, for Jabez Campbell, its first editor according to Penn, later rose to the episcopacy, as did his successor, John M. Brown.[18] It was being published in newspaper format in Nashville, Tennessee, in 1970, and claiming seniority among black church weeklies.

Subsidy, as with many religious publications still, was the only practical means of financing magazines like the *Recorder*. That circumstance accounts for the existence, over the years, of numerous church, lodge, club, educational, and college publications. Detweiler records that in some states even this relatively innocuous kind of journalism suffered from the fact that blacks were not allowed to go to school or read papers, magazines, and books.[19] It was one reason for the scarcity of publications before Emancipation.

During the Civil War establishment of new publications naturally fell off. Penn and other early writers were able to discover only one black paper founded between 1860 and 1865, the *Colored Citizen* of Cincinnati; it died once the conflict ended. But there were others. An important one, significant because it was the first to be established in the South, was *L'Union* of New Orleans, a French-English weekly started in 1862. The next year it became a triweekly, but could not survive past 1864.[20]

After the Civil War

When the Civil War ended there was a rush to establish new black publications. Pride's study shows that a dozen were begun just from April 1865 to January 1866; half were in the South, the first real breakthrough for that area.[21]

During the decade after 1865, black newspapers sprang up in eight states that had had none and in four others that already had papers. From 1875 to 1895, more were founded, for this was a period of migration to the North. In 1887 alone 68 papers were begun. And by 1890, according to Pride, 575 had been established. Many of these were intended to be regular newspapers, but various other types of black publications were born as well, some as political organs, others to serve churches or other special groups. One of the religious papers survives. The *Star of Zion* of the African Methodist Episcopal Zion Church, begun in 1867, today is a tabloid newspaper published for the denomination in Charlotte, North Carolina.

Another paper that reached into the next century, although unlike the *Star of Zion* it lacked subsidy and so did not live, was the Washington *Bee* which was published from 1882 to 1926. Founded by William Calvin Chase, who had edited the Washington *Plaindealer* from 1879 to 1881, and the *Argus* from 1880 to 1883, the *Bee* left "a record for endurance, forthrightness, and racial appeal," Pride observes.[22] And Penn wrote that "Nothing stings Washington City, and in fact, the Bourbons of the South, as the *Bee*." A weekly, during its forty-four years Chase made it an exciting if bitter paper. He was fond of exposés. He took sides on many subjects; his position always was clear if not consistent.

The war's end meant not only more publications but also a change in their content. The dominating subject of slavery was replaced with material of great variety. Immediately at the end of the war, for example, a Friday publication, using the name of an earlier, Albany, New York, paper, the *Elevator*, was launched in San Francisco by Phillip A. Bell, who had managed the *Colored American* some years before. It contained material on science, art, literature, and drama.

Another new element was illustrated by a paper issued later in 1865 by Republican party members in Augusta, Georgia. The *Colored American* again was to serve as the flag of a newspaper "designed," as its prospectus put it, "to be a vehicle for the diffusion of Religious, Political, and General Intelligence." The new element in this publication's formula was the plan to devote it "to the promotion of harmony and good-will between the white and colored people of the South. . . ." It was to cost four dollars a year, a reflection of the rise in expenses. Its publisher, however, had bad luck with his shareholders and the paper was sold in 1886 and its name changed to the *Loyal Georgian*. After two years it was merged with the *Georgia Republican*.

In certain other states postwar papers came into being quickly and were serving black readers of different sections. Among the earlier ones noted by Penn were the *Colored Tennessean* and the *True Communicator*, the latter of Baltimore. Neither survived for long nor, for that matter, did many of those in the rush to the presses. Among the more important new black papers were the New Orleans *Louisianian*, the first to be issued twice a week; *Our National Progress*, of Wilmington, Delaware; the *Progressive American*, of Syracuse, New York; the *Argus* of Washington; and the *Western Sentinel* of Kansas City, Missouri.

Penn included in his account a table showing the growth in the number of papers by states from 1880 to 1890. Texas began with one and a decade later had fifteen, according to the tabulation. Georgia went from none to ten; Pennsylvania, Virginia, and Alabama each added nine to their original one publication. In 1880, Penn calculated, there were 31 publications; at the end of the following decade 123 had been added, for a total of 154.[23] Years later Pride was to prove that many more were founded but that most did not survive to 1890.

Six reasons for the upsurge of black papers after the Civil War have been given by Pride.[24] The black populace was becoming better educated; freedmen were able to earn a little more; social service and other groups gave financial support to the press; religious organizations entered journalism to advance their views; the blacks able to vote provided an audience for politically sponsored publications; the last, suggested to Pride by Rashey B. Moten, Jr.'s, thesis at the University of Kentucky, was that it was realized that the editor of a paper is a person of wider influence than some other professionals.

To these reasons can be added the fact that social changes other than the end of slavery and war were affecting the black citizens at this time as well. During the Reconstruction years blacks were pushed into ghettos in the larger cities of both North and South. Segregation became the enforced way of life for them. Conrad, commenting on this change, observes that it led to a community-conscious press devoted to protest against discrimination as well as to reporting the minutiae of black life.[25]

Such protest kept the papers alive when other content failed, as in the instance of the Chicago *Defender* (see Chapters 3 and 4), which lived on scandal and crime stories for a time but did not thrive until it became the champion of the black people.

Female Journalists of the Period

The female journalists of the black race in America who have achieved distinction through their accomplishments on newspapers are largely those of the present century. Perhaps "attention" is a more nearly fair word than "distinction," for the female editors and writers of the nineteenth century have been ignored as journalists by almost all who have written on black journalism before 1970. An exception is I. Garland Penn. His writing is so gushy, however, that it is impossible for one reading his history today to depend upon his judgments. At least he exhibited a sensitivity about the minority within a minority. A sixty-page chapter in his *Afro-American Press and Its Editors* tells the stories, in his usual somewhat florid style, of nineteen women engaged in black journalism in this period. An example of his style in this portion on Professor Mary V. Cook, chiefly a teacher who in the 1880s and 1890s wrote columns for the *American Baptist* and the *South Carolina Tribune* and edited a magazine, *Our Women and Children*: "There is a divine poetry in a life garlanded by the fragrant roses of triumph."[26]

Victoria Earle Mathews

A black journalist no longer much heard about but one of the most able of those in the post–Civil War years is Victoria Earle Mathews.

Victoria was born a slave in 1861 in Georgia, one of nine children. She was left in the care of a nurse by her mother, Caroline Smith, because the master mistreated her mother, who escaped after numerous efforts to get away. Her mother returned after the Civil War. In the meantime five of the children had died. Victoria and her siblings were taken to New York, where her mother, after much deprivation, had a job and now was able to take care of her children.

While going to school in the big city, Victoria became interested in writing, eventually working as a reporter on several of the major papers of the metropolis, including the New York *Age* and the New York *Globe*. She managed, as well, to sell short stories or articles to numerous magazines for women and various religious and other specialized journals.

Toward the end of the century her interest in social work moved her to start the White Rose Mission on New York's East Side. It gave migrants to the city, as her mother once was, a social center.

Because she wrote for his paper, the *Age*, Victoria had come to know T. Thomas Fortune, the noted editor. While she was working to open the mission he was asked to help her financially, but he was unable to do so. He did, however, appeal to Booker T. Washington for aid for the project, and obtained it. Fortune took Washington to see the sewing and other training classes at the mission. Washington was impressed with the efforts Victoria Mathews was making but depressed by the condition of the people she was helping.

Later she worked for Fortune in Atlanta on the staff of the *Southern Age*, a short-lived paper. Along with this work she edited, in 1898, a book of Washington's speeches. By now Victoria had become a close friend of Mrs. Washington. Fortune wrote the introduction to the book, which was titled *Black-Belt Diamonds*.

In the reports on her life now available there is no record of when she married and became Mrs. W. E. Mathews nor of when she died.

Ida B. Wells-Barnett

Possibly the one female journalist of the 1800s remembered in this century is Ida B. Wells-Barnett. Penn compares her to the once internationally known Mrs. Frank Leslie, widow of the English editor whose name was on various versions of a once highly popular illustrated magazine during and after the Civil War. Bontemps and Conroy, writing many years after both Penn and Barnett had died, have provided a little sketch of her career. A Mississippian born about 1869, she was left by her parents' death to support four (Penn says five) younger brothers and sisters when she was fourteen. She worked but also studied. After a time, at Fisk University, her interest in journalism cropped up when she wrote for the student paper. She then became a Memphis teacher but continued her journalism by writing for a local black paper, the *Living Way*. She was Ida B. Wells but used only Iola in her byline. In the ensuing years she wrote for many other black publications and also entered publishing by becoming half-owner as well as editor of the Memphis *Free Speech*, a black paper that campaigned against racial injustice.

2.7. Ida B. Wells-Barnett, editor and champion of black women's rights.

In 1892, however, her paper's plant was sacked because it had carried accusations that white competitors had inspired the murder of three black businesspeople. The hoodlums, Bontemps and Conroy relate, demolished the press and the paper's offices. Wells had to move from the city to save her life. Because she had been free-lancing to the New York *Age* she went to that paper, then published by T. T. Fortune. She worked also with Douglass and William Monroe Trotter in their civil rights enterprises. Like Douglass she made a strong impression when she lectured against lynching in the British Isles. In the mid-1890s she settled in Chicago, organizing various women's clubs and kindergartens. Antilynching leagues were formed after her lectures in both Britain and the United States. She continued to write for both the black and white press, particularly the Chicago *Inter-Ocean*. In 1895 she married Ferdinand L. Barnett, a lawyer and part-owner of the first black newspaper in Illinois, the *Conservator*. After their wedding they continued to fight racial injustice and Barnett began planning an ambitious political and teaching career, but in 1931, aged 62, she died suddenly. Nine years later a large low-rent housing project in Chicago was named for her; certain women's groups carry her name today.[27]

Black Journalism Enters the Twentieth Century

Some of the most important papers extant were launched just before or after the turn of the century, as the American black press became better established. More newspapers were founded as commercial ventures and to serve as news rather than propaganda organs, but cause papers continued to appear as well. Some weeklies were to become leading papers in later years. The magazines, however, were for the most part still organs of opinion or of organizations rather than vehicles of entertainment.

The turn of the century saw the rise of several important black leaders in American history—men able and skillful enough to use journalism as a tool to support their causes and views.

The Philadelphia *Tribune*

The Philadelphia *Tribune*, which considers itself the oldest continuously published black newspaper in the country, was organized in 1884 by Chris J. Perry, Sr. One of the most substantial of the black papers, it owns its own plant and engages in various public enterprises, such as charities and scholarship programs (see Chapter 14). After Perry died in 1921, the paper was published by

43

his widow and two of his daughters. The husband of one, E. Washington Rhodes, a lawyer, was publisher and editor until his death in 1970. Rhodes had taken a decided position about the black race, singling out what he called "affluent middle-class Negroes" because they did not in his opinion do enough to help the poor.

The *Afro-American*

The *Afro-American* is the name for a Baltimore paper with five editions, four regional and one national, which have made it one of the oldest and most powerful black journalistic institutions in the United States.[1] Like so many other black papers, the *Afro*, as it is called by most readers, had its origin in religious circles. Three Baltimore church people figured in its first few years. The first was the Reverend William M. Alexander, who had started a provisions store in the city. Wanting to advertise Sharon Baptist Church and community enterprises, he published on August 13, 1892, a four-page paper to which he gave the name *Afro-American*.

Another churchman, a layman who was superintendent of the Sunday School in St. John African Methodist Episcopal Church in the same city, wanted all such black church schools to organize statewide, as did the white groups called the Epworth League and the Christian Endeavor Society. This man was John H. Murphy, Sr., a whitewasher by trade. He, too, thought a publication would be a force for achieving his aim. He bought type fonts and a press; from the cellar of his home in Baltimore he printed *Sunday School Helper*, a small paper.

A third man printed a paper with the same purposes as the Reverend Mr. Alexander's, calling it the *Ledger*. This editor was the Reverend George F. Bragg, pastor of St. James Episcopal Church.

Murphy acquired the *Afro* by borrowing two hundred dollars from his wife and buying it at auction; it had a circulation of 250. When in 1907 the *Afro* was merged with the *Ledger* it was called the *Afro-American Ledger*. Murphy was publisher and Bragg wrote the editorials. For the publisher it became a lifetime occupation, for he owned the paper until his death in 1922; his family continues it still.[2] It went first into the hands of a son, Carl Murphy; by then it had gained recognition as a national publication. D. Arnett Murphy, still another of John Murphy's sons, served as vice-president and advertis-

3.1. The *Afro-American* group of newspapers.

ing manager. A grandson, Howard E. Murphy, was business manager. Elizabeth Murphy Moss, a granddaughter, was at one time assistant managing editor and a war correspondent. John J. Oliver, Jr., is now chairman of the board and publisher; Frances M. Draper is president, and Robert W. Matthews III, executive editor.

The *Afro* has during its history followed a policy of moderation in direct editorial opinions and an emphasis on news coverage as a tool with which to inform and mold public opinion. A credo formulated in 1920 by John H. Murphy, Sr., and published regularly since on its editorial pages sets its tone (see Chapter 8).

In New York and California

Booker T. Washington frequently is linked with the New York *Age*, a prominent weekly that stemmed from a downtown New York tabloid, the *Rumor*, begun in 1890. In 1903, Washington said he believed that a strong national Negro paper was needed. Remaining behind the scenes, he began to subsidize the *Age* and by 1907 had completed purchase of the weekly. "His influence over the Negro press was achieved by loans, advertising, printing orders and political subsidies," wrote one of Washington's critics. "He saw to it that critical papers received editorial material favorable to his cause and at times was even able to disrupt the distribution of such publications."[3]

Because of Washington's connection with the paper it was severely criticized by W. E. B. Du Bois and other black leaders who disagreed with a philosophy that they believed condemned the black man to segregation and subservience to whites.

. In its earlier, less controversial days the paper, as *Rumor*, called itself "A Representative Colored American Newspaper" and was published by George Parker, who changed it from a twelve-page tabloid to standard size and renamed it the New York *Globe*. As *Rumor* it carried news, verse, short stories, and articles; its first page usually was a woodcut of some black leader; on one occasion it was Douglass. Parker took on two partners, W. Walter Sampson and T. Thomas Fortune, who was to become a leading figure in black journalism.[4] In a few years Parker sold his interest to Bishop William B. Derrick. But the bishop could not pay his share so the paper went into the hands of the marshal. Fortune took over as sole owner in 1884 and changed the name once more, to the *Freeman*. After also withdrawing for a time he returned in 1888; by now it had become the New York *Age*. On rejoining it, Fortune became co-owner with Fred R. Moore, as well as editor. Moore bought Fortune's share in 1907, continuing to publish it until 1943, and it remained in the Moore family after his death that year. During Moore's regime the paper exposed the Ku Klux Klan before white papers brought that organization's actions into the open. Moore, however, was better known for his business and political activities than his journalism. He worked in New York banks, in 1893 organized the Afro-American Building and Loan Company, and in 1903 was elected national organizer of the National Negro Business League, four years before joining the *Age* staff. He once was U.S. minister to Liberia.[5] A later editor who became even more widely known was James Weldon Johnson, the poet.

A white couple, Mr. and Mrs. V. P. Bourne-Vanneck, of England, bought the *Age* in 1949. The Chicago *Defender* took it over from them in 1952 and merged with it; for a time the *Defender*'s New York edition was called the *Age-Defender*, but within a few years the *Age* name no longer appeared in the flag.

Another paper which made some, if less, impression, and which did not survive was the *California Eagle,* founded in 1879 in Los Angeles. Of standard-size, it became the property in recent years of a leader of the NAACP, Loren Miller, but he sold it in 1964 when he was appointed a municipal judge. It ceased in 1967.[6]

T. Thomas Fortune

In any occupation there always is someone who, during the latter part of his life is called "the dean" of whatever it may be. T. Thomas Fortune was so dubbed. Ottley, the biographer of Robert S. Abbott and author of several essays on the black press, wrote that Fortune was in his time considered the dean of black journalism in America. Fortune, along with Frederick Douglass and William Monroe Trotter, is recalled almost a century later, unlike most black journalists of the past. He deserved Ottley's title because he had a far greater background of professional experience than most of his contemporaries and was treated as a spokesman for the black press. He came of slave parents, and was an errand boy in a southern white newspaper office. After working as a mail agent and then a

3.2. T. Thomas Fortune, editor of New York *Age.*

special inspector of customs in Delaware, he went to work in a composing room, and then joined *Rumor*. Meanwhile, he was an assistant to Amos Cummings on the New York *Evening Sun* and later wrote for the companion daily, the New York *Sun*, when the noted Charles Anderson Dana was its editor.[7]

Many years later, in a magazine article, Fortune recalled his early journalism.

> When I entered upon the active work of journalism, in New York City in 1879, my partner and I were the first to set the type of the *Globe*. At night we prepared the forms for the press, and in the day we worked as compositors. Mr. William Walter Sampson and I had worked together as compositors on a daily newspaper, now the *Daily Times-Union*, at Jacksonville, Florida. Through him I secured a position on the *Daily Witness* in New York. Here I found my previous experience of great value, for it had been my good fortune to have met and collaborated with such men as John W. Cromwell, Charles N. Otey, and Robert Peel Brooks, among the most brilliant men that the race has ever produced. My acquaintance also included the great Frederick Douglass, the lion of them all. . . .[8]

While editor of the *Age*, Fortune attracted notice in the white press with his editorials. Ottley quotes Theodore Roosevelt as saying: "Tom Fortune, for God's sake, keep that pen of yours off me." Fortune helped Booker T. Washington with the writing of his autobiography. Late in his life he came to believe in the back-to-Africa movement of Marcus Garvey, discussed later in this chapter.

Trotter and the *Guardian*

The first important paper born after the turn of the century was the weekly Boston *Guardian*, founded in 1901 by William Monroe Trotter and George Forbes. Both were 1895 college graduates, Trotter from Harvard and Forbes from Amherst. A provocative paper, it would now be considered militant. W. E. B. Du Bois, himself a perceptive journalist, described the *Guardian* as "bitter, satirical, and personal . . . well edited . . . earnest, and it publishes facts." He reported also that "it attracted wide attention among colored people; it circulated among them all over the country; it was quoted and discussed." Few blacks agreed with it wholly, he believed.[9]

3.3. William Monroe Trotter, publisher, Boston *Guardian*.

Of greatest significance was the fact that it was the start of organized opposition to Booker T. Washington. When he came to Boston in 1903 to speak, Trotter and Forbes raised questions with him about his views on black education and voting. The result was "a disturbance," as Du Bois described it, and "a riot" in the view of Boston's white dailies. Trotter was arrested and served a jail term. The whole incident led to a major event in black history in America. Du Bois's resentment of the treatment of Trotter led to forming of what in 1905 became incorporated as the Niagara Movement, so named because its founders originally met near Buffalo, New York. Among its principles were promotion of freedom of speech and criticism and "an unfettered and unsubsidized press." More will be heard of this movement when Du Bois's own career as a journalist is examined.

Trotter also worked for improvement of the lot of the black people through the New England Suffrage League and the National Equal Rights League. Because he had experienced race prejudice he dedicated himself to its defeat through journalism. On one occasion he led a delegation to a personal interview with President Woodrow

Wilson to protest prejudice against blacks. This editor's place in black journalism can be gauged from a statement by Lerone Bennett, Jr., a specialist in black history, who credits Trotter with having "laid the first stone of the modern protest movements" and "mobilized the forces that checked the triumphant advance of Booker T. Washington's program of accommodation and submission." Washington replied to the assault on his views by subsidizing another paper to compete with the *Guardian*, Bennett reported.[10]

Unlike many other black journalists who came to positions of power, Trotter was reared in a comparatively luxurious home in a predominantly white Boston suburb, Hyde Park. He was born in 1872, in Chillicothe, Ohio, a son of a white merchant and a former slave. His family moved to Boston when he was a baby. At Harvard he was a cum laude graduate and elected to Phi Beta Kappa, the first black to be accepted by that elite group of scholars. He then completed a two-year master's program in one year. From his father he learned to fight for equality. James Monroe Trotter, while a Union Army lieutenant, led a successful campaign to equalize the pay scales for black and white soldiers. After graduation William Trotter began a real estate business; in 1901 he started his paper. Judging by a 1902 issue, it was one of six columns, with cartoons and halftones and the familiar unbroken columns of type so common in all U.S. newspapers in those days.

When the offices were moved into a Boston building where Garrison's *Liberator* once was published, Trotter, an admirer of the abolitionist leader, found this fitting. He spoke out against segregation in federal employment and protested *The Birth of a Nation* film as racist; it then was banned. Bennett calls him the "Boston Cato."

But all was not well with his paper. For a time Trotter had been well off, but in the second decade of the century he and his wife lost their home and lived in poverty; the paper was too great a drain on their resources. He held on through the depression years of the early 1930s but died in 1934, in what was either an accidental fall or suicide. The paper was continued by his sister, Maude, until her death in 1957. An indication of new appreciation of his fight for his people was the naming of a high school for him in 1969 in Roxbury, Massachusetts.[11]

Abbott and the *Defender*

Trotter may have laid the first stones for the modern protest movements but Robert S. Abbott, after a somewhat slow start, built the foundation, using his Chicago *Defender*, now the anchor newspaper in a small group or chain of black publications and itself one of the only three dailies in black journalism.

Roi Ottley, his biographer, ranks Abbott with "the giants of his time: Booker T. Washington and W. E. B. Du Bois." Abbott's activities and personality were far different from those of the other two men, who were more personally conservative and more politically distinctive. Ottley notes that Abbott was "almost inarticulate" and humble, whereas Du Bois was clearly an intellectual and a considerable egotist. The greatest praise of Abbott came from an influential white scholar, a keen analyst of American life, the Swedish economist Gunnar Myrdal, who considered him, as Ottley summarized it, "the greatest single force in Negro journalism, and indeed the founder of the modern Negro press."[12]

Abbott's background was complex. A Georgian, he was born in 1868 on St. Simons Island. His father, Thomas Abbott, had been head butler in an aristocratic household. His mother was a hairdresser in a Savannah theater. Various relatives worked as servants in Thomas Abbott's employer's household. His family, apparently of Ibo stock, was literate. After the Civil War his parents ran a small grocery store on the island. Thomas, despite his record of service, is reported by Ottley to have neglected his wife, and was not even on the island when Robert was born.

Robert's mother, Flora Butler Abbott, was snubbed by the other Abbotts. She had learned to speak German, going for a time to a secret slave school; learning that language was to change her and her son's lives. When Thomas Abbott died the family brought legal proceedings against Flora because she refused to surrender her son. John H. H. Sengstacke helped her fight the case and won it for her. Sengstacke was the son of a well-to-do German merchant, Herman Sengstacke, who had married a slave girl in 1847. John was their first child. He was taken to Germany by his father, who did not want his children reared as slaves. When the elder Sengstacke returned to Savannah, he was defrauded of his inheritance and John came to the United States to find out why. It was then that he met Flora Abbott and became Robert's stepfather.

As a youth Robert and his seven brothers and sisters (Flora and

John's children) lived in a black settlement in Savannah. Robert's first exposure to journalistic work may have come when his stepfather became a translator for the city paper, the *Morning News*. His own first newspaper job was in the print shop of the Savannah *Echo*, but he botched it by damaging an imposing stone. After periods at several colleges he went to Hampton Institute, but left in 1888 to resume work at the *Echo*. About this time his stepfather decided to enter the publishing business by founding a paper, the Woodville *Times*. Alexander, a brother of Robert, was editor when the elder Sengstacke died.

At Hampton the future founder of the Chicago *Defender* had studied printing as well as an academic program, which he completed in 1896. During this period he was influenced by Frederick Douglass and Ida B. Wells, two noted black journalists whom he had heard speak. After graduation he became a printer in Woodville and helped get out the *Times*. Printing jobs being hard to get and ill-paid at that, and lack of money having thwarted him in a romance, Robert decided to study law. He took his own father's name, changing from Sengstacke to Abbott. The only black in a class of seventy getting law degrees, he was not admitted to the bar. His search for work in several midwestern cities was no better as lawyer than as printer until 1904, when a political friend pried him into a printing house job despite his color. After his stepfather died Robert resolved to be a teacher, and began in a Woodville school. Journalism continued to beckon, however, so after a time he decided to start his own newspaper.

Founding of the *Defender*

Abbott selected Chicago because it had a large black population, about forty thousand then. Before the paper was launched in 1905 he had attempted a daily; apparently the two or three numbers issued were scrapped and none has been found. He ignored the fact that the black press field was crowded; Chicago had three already: the *Broad Ax, Illinois Idea*, and the *Conservator*. The black citizens also had access to two important out-of-town papers, the *Indiana Freeman* and the New York *Age*. The goal Abbott had for his paper was to fight for the black race, so he called it the *Defender*. In rented space on State Street he put a card table and a borrowed chair; he arranged for the paper to be printed on credit, since his total capital was twenty-five cents — needed for paper and pencils. His staff was himself, helped by his landlady's teenage daughter. One early issue of the weekly, displayed at the Chicago *Defender* building, is impressive for so feeble a foundation. The first was dated May 5, 1905, but all copies now are lost. It was, in contrast to its rivals, an offering of news, much of it in the form of personals. Politics and black problems at first were avoided. Paid advertising was there, but not enough. In fact, the paper would have died if Mrs. Lee, Abbott's landlady, had not let him use her dining room as an office, provided his meals, given him money for small expenses, mended his clothes, and let him use her telephone. It remained the paper's address until 1920. These good deeds not only saved the paper but also saw it to prosperity. In time Abbott showed Mrs. Lee his gratitude by giving her the deed to an eight-room house.

With the paper beginning to catch on, Abbott began a policy of muckraking, running campaigns against prostitution in the black community and for black causes. Accompanying the muckraking was a policy of sensationalism, but the use of so many crime and scandal stories brought the paper heavy criticism. During World War I he combined support of the war with the battle for black rights.

The campaign for which Abbott and the *Defender* are best remembered came during and after World War I. When the black soldiers returned it was still obvious that blacks would not be granted first class citizenship, even though many had lost their lives or been wounded. By 1916 the Ku Klux Klan had gained new strength, boasting of its five million members. They and their sympathizers were tarring and feathering, branding, hanging, and burning the black people; in one period in 1919 as many as seventy were lynched.

Abbott had suggested through the paper in 1917 that the blacks come north, pointing out that conditions were better. The paper led in formation of clubs that could get group railroad rates. And north they came. Ottley reported that 110,000 moved to Chicago alone, almost tripling the black population.

One result Abbott had not counted on, however, was the race riots in Chicago after the great migration. He tried to calm the rioters but was not heeded. The *Defender* did not come off well in a report of a commission on race relations, being accused of irresponsible journalism, although complimented for running balanced editorials.

The *Defender* nevertheless went on to prosperity, its own presses, and another, larger building. Abbott's personal characteristics now became more evident in his paper's tone: Ottley notes a tendency toward penuriousness, but self-indulgence about automobiles. His policy about black progress, at first militant, gradually changed to one of moderation, in his biographer's opinion. He saw to it that the paper emphasized black accomplishments and abandoned an earlier abrasive tone. It continued, however, to sensationalize crime for the sake of sales. When he was fifty Abbott married and began to travel. He went to Brazil, where he learned of the low status of blacks, which prompted demands for more reforms in the United States, including integration, a stand that lost him supporters. A European trip, in which he met discrimination, moved him to write a series of articles for his paper. Ottley writes that Abbott came to fear personal attack and was cautious when traveling, sometimes disguising himself or using another name.

The *Defender* Goes On

The *Defender*'s history illustrates the use of sensational treatment of news in order to sell papers. After it no longer was necessary for Pullman porters to bring newspapers from other cities so that Abbott could rely on them for news of the black people, the paper stayed in a leading position primarily because of what then was called race-angling the news. Ottley notes such headlines as "White Gentleman Rapes Colored Girl" and "100 Negroes Murdered Weekly in United States by White Americans," those lines being in red ink. The stories, he discovered, at times were from the imagination of a staff member.

By 1915 the paper was enlarged; branch offices were opened, including one in London. Several thousand agent-correspondents worked to increase sales and gather local news. By that year circulation reached the astonishing figure of at least 230,000, a total found by Ottley's own investigation. Along with this prosperity came evidence of influence, for whites began attacking it as divisive of the races and subversive because it challenged racial traditions. Ottley reported that several cities tried to prevent distribution by confiscation. Ku Klux Klan members threatened owners of copies. Two distributors were killed. A riot broke out in Texas that resulted in whites burning blacks' homes and the public flogging of a black school principal because a black teacher covered a lynching for the paper.

But after World War I circulation dropped gradually to 180,000. By now readers were getting much for their dimes: thirty-two pages, although a few years before it had been four to eight. The circulation decline was to be expected; no war or riot news was there to whip up sales. Also, competition had appeared in the Chicago *Whip*, which sold for a nickel.

The *Defender* was the first unionized black paper as well as the first integrated one. Technically trained black men were scarce, so a white foreman and printers were hired, as were advertising salesmen, but not without bringing criticism and a fall of support. After the early 1930s the paper settled down to a modified news policy on racial events, a social philosophy asking patience, and moderation in matters of racial change and conflict. The *Defender* had suffered during the depression, like all other businesses, and by 1935 was down to 73,000 circulation. It also was showing the effects of absentee ownership, for Abbott was away much of the time. Slashes in personnel and salaries were ordered; Abbott cut his own earnings to two hundred dollars a week and subsidized the paper to the tune of more than a quarter of a million dollars, Ottley discovered. Misdealings with the paper's funds also occurred at this time.

The paper continued the fight for fairer treatment of black citizens at the same time that it added features such as cartoons and personal columns. Much space was devoted to society, cultural, and fashion copy, a practice that later moved E. Franklin Frazier, the sociologist, to write: "Since the Negro newspaper makes its appeal to the awakened imagination of Negroes in urban communities, it provides a romantic escape for Negro city-dwellers."[13]

Advertising was still slim; circulation revenue remained, as with the black press in general, the main income source. Ads often were the kind long ridiculed by critics—hair straighteners, magic symbols, sex books, and skin color potions.

Politically the paper up to the 1920s had been independent but leaned toward the Republicans, the traditional stand of the black press. In 1928, however, Abbott opposed Herbert Hoover and supported Alfred E. Smith. When much of the responsibility for the *Defender* was turned over to John H. Sengstacke, the weekly not only regained its secure foundation financially but also took different political stances than in the early days.

Although the *Defender* no longer has the extraordinarily high circulation it possessed in its heyday, it retains its place of respect in the black journalism world, for it is issued four times a week as a daily and adds a weekend national edition. The familiar tabloid is still led by John H. Sengstacke, who heads a chain including three large weeklies. The editorial tone is moderate. News coverage is better than that of some papers with larger circulations.

Abbott's Decline

When the depression struck the nation, Abbott tried to discourage a new migration of blacks from south to north, but this time was as ignored as he had been heeded earlier. This failure, plus the loss of his mother in 1932, affected his health, and

Ottley says he often was away from the office. Meantime, he also had begun a magazine, *Abbott's Monthly*, the attention to which did not help his health, for by now both the magazine and the paper were in financial trouble. The magazine died in the depression and bank failures affected his personal fortune. The next calamity was a suit for divorce, which was costly.

The year Abbott was seventy-one he decided that his nephew, John H. Sengstacke, son of his brother Alexander, should carry on the paper. In 1939 he willed two-thirds of the estate to the young man and a third to his second wife, whom he had married in 1934. Most of his time was spent in bed, for he was becoming weaker daily. He began to dictate an autobiography; it never was completed. Death came in February 1940.

Enoch R. Waters, a twenty-five year *Defender* staff member, portrays Robert S. Abbott as a strong individualist. He knew Abbott well, but had divided emotions about the publisher's methods and views, yet an overall admiration for his courage. In his autobiography, Waters describes the goings-on in the plant, and tells of some of the unusual reporters and editors who were on the staff and of the difficulties the paper had in its early days in getting the news.[14]

Lochard and Harper

A characteristic of newspaper and magazine publishing is that certain publications attract talented writers and editors. They are not always large publications; the *New Yorker* is an example. The black press has had a similar experience. *Ebony* magazine, the Atlanta *Daily World*, the Chicago *Defender*, and the Pittsburgh *Courier* among them have had as staffers most of the more capable craftsmen (see Chapter 10). Few of these stars are known as stars in the world of journalism in general; only a few, in fact, have received recognition within the black press itself. Glances at two will be found here; a dozen more could be listed, some tragic, some amusing. Metz Lochard and Lucius Harper have been selected because they represent different types.

Metz P. T. Lochard appears to have been one of the best educated of the *Defender*'s staffers. Although Ottley, historian of the *Defender* and its publisher, thought Lochard was "the first foreign editor in the Negro press," this distinction, if correct (as it probably was), was not Lochard's major contribution. A Frenchman educated at Oxford University as well as at the University of Paris, he had been an interpreter for Marshal Foch and then a language teacher at two noted black universities, Fisk and Howard. His French background and linguistic ability attracted Abbott. After the publisher's death Lochard became editor in chief of the paper.

Lucius C. Harper is remembered around the *Defender* office, at least among those who recall any of the old-timers, as the staff member who once headed two of Robert Abbott's major enterprises, for he served as editor both of the paper and of *Abbott's Monthly*, the short-lived venture into periodical publishing. Outside the office, however, he was known because of his "Dustin' Off the News" column, a lively and popular feature that appeared in the 1940s and 1950s.

Harper's first connection with the Abbott enterprises came through a fluke. Somehow his letter of application in 1916 to *Overton's*, a black magazine, was delivered to the *Defender* offices in error. Harper had a typewriter and could use it—few black people were interested in journalism in those days, and the few scarcely ever were thus equipped. He was hired. Harper had learned barbering, but had come to the paper with more than that skill and a typewriter. A graduate of Oberlin College, like Abbott he began as a printer's devil, working for the *Georgia Baptist*. He wrote articles for the Indianapolis *Freeman*, the Cleveland *Gazette*, and the New York *Age*. His interest in being a journalist arose, Ottley writes, from knowing newsmen at the Chicago Press Club, where he once worked as a bellboy. When Abbott hired Harper in 1916 he began a term of service that lasted thirty-six years.

W. E. B. Du Bois the Journalist

So controversial was William Edward Burghardt Du Bois's life—he was the center of disagreements as a teacher, as an NAACP executive, and as a political partisan—that his close association with black journalism is submerged. He founded five magazines, two of which still are published; he was a correspondent for four newspapers, columnist for numerous both black and white papers, and contributor of articles to many general as well as scholarly periodicals, black and white.

Journalism to Du Bois, it is true, was only a tool to advance his sociological studies of the black race or to aid him in his plans to help the race. But he used it effectively and far more than some others who

considered themselves journalists but engaged in that profession as
entrée to another: politics.

A New Englander, he was born in the same year, 1868, as Abbott.
He was of partly slave and white ancestry, for his parents both were of
partially white descent. He barely knew his father, who had left to
make a home for his wife elsewhere in the country. Du Bois's mother
was too timid to follow. She and the boy lived in near poverty, aided
by family and friends. He attended public school in Great Barrington,
Massachusetts, and also was active in church there. He was a book
lover.[15]

Yet in none of his town life did he personally encounter racial
discrimination or segregation. He learned of it by being told by
others.

Du Bois's first journalism was the editorship, with a white class-
mate, of a short-lived hand-produced high school paper called
Howler. A local bookshop operator got him his first professional
news job — as correspondent for the Springfield *Republican*, a famous
white daily. He also wrote for the notable black weeklies, the New
York *Age*, the *Freeman*, and the New York *Globe*. When he went to
Fisk University in 1886, his first venture into the South, he edited the
Fisk Herald. Many years later, in 1924, he helped bring out what
might be called an off-campus version of it in New York in support of
a student rebellion at his alma mater.

From Fisk he went to Harvard, but did no journalistic work
there, nor again until his return late in the century from graduate
study in Germany. He began contributing sociological articles to the
Atlantic Monthly and *World's Work*, two of the most important white
periodicals then being published. A clue to his developing concept of
journalistic responsibility appeared when a committee made up of
several dignitaries, including Walter Hines Page, editor of the *Atlantic*, approached him about editing a magazine to be published at
Hampton Institute. When he said, in submitting his plans, that he
would expect all editorial decisions to be his own only, the project was
dropped. This position was to disturb his journalistic life ever after
but also may account for the effectiveness of several of the publications he edited.

By 1905 Du Bois had become fully aware of the power of the
press. He wrote to a wealthy man he had met two years before, he
relates in his autobiography, about the need for "a high class journal
to circulate among the Intelligent Negroes. . . ." In his letter he
characterized the black press of the time thus: "Now we have many
small weekly papers and one or two monthlies, and none of them fill

the great need I have outlined." He thus described that need: "The Negro race in America today is in a critical condition. Only united, concentrated effort will keep us from being crushed. This union must come as a matter of education and long continued effort."

The publication he had in mind would tell black readers of their own and their neighbors' needs, "interpret the news of the world to them, and inspire them toward definite ideas." And it would be a monthly. But the wealthy men he approached expressed sympathy and nothing more. There it ended until a few years later.

Du Bois's proposal of a magazine reflected his social views. They put him into conflict with Booker T. Washington. Du Bois himself "believed in the higher education of a talented tenth who through their knowledge of modern culture could guide the American Negro into a higher civilization." Washington believed that blacks would gain their best place by being skilled workers and businesspeople and finally capitalists.

Du Bois saw his plans for a publication born at last in 1906. With the help of two Atlanta University graduates, he had started in Mem-

3.4. W. E. B. Du Bois, founder of five magazines, sociologist, and educator.

phis a small printing establishment. It now produced the *Moon Illustrated Weekly*, and may have given the editor the formula for the magazine he edited later, the *Crisis*. The *Moon* soon ranged itself against Washington. It contained miscellany, much of it reprinted from other black publications but also original editorials and biographical articles. After a year it was discontinued and in 1907 replaced by *Horizon*, which its founder dismissed by merely calling it "a miniature monthly." Rudwick, one of Du Bois's biographers, reported that *Horizon* was begun as a voice for the Niagara Movement. It failed, he believed, because the black people of the period were not ready for the Niagara philosophy. But producing this periodical laid more of the foundation for Du Bois's later editorial work. *Horizon*, in turn, gave way in his affections to the *Crisis*.

That magazine came from Du Bois's decision to resign his faculty post at Atlanta University and become director of publications and research for the NAACP, of which he had been an incorporator. His work brought him into association with Oswald Garrison Villard, publisher of the *Nation* and editor of the New York *Evening Post* as well as a grandson of William Lloyd Garrison. Ever the egotist, Du Bois was critical of Villard because the far more experienced white journalist gave him advice on editorial matters.

He began the *Crisis* on his own and despite, as he put it, "the protests of many of my associates." He saw in the magazine a chance to interpret to the world "the hindrances and aspirations of American Negroes." His work with it was a deep interest for nearly a quarter of a century: 1910 to 1934. During those years he made the magazine a vigorous critic of any national policy or event which resulted in harm to the black people—whether it was discrimination in the military services or the wartime lynchings of the 1914–19 conflict.

"As *Crisis* editor," Bennett has written. "Du Bois set the tone for the organization and educated a whole generation of black people in the art of protest."[16] But he was so possessive of the magazine and so prone to use it to comment on the NAACP itself (of which, it should be remembered, it was the official organ) that there was dissension within the organization. Through the magazine he advocated a program which certain other NAACP leaders could not accept.

Another Du Bois journalistic idea was founding a magazine for all children but written from a black standpoint. Launched in 1920, it was called the *Brownies' Book* and was intended to "help foster a proper self-respect," as its editor put it years later. It lasted two years, becoming one of the few black juvenile publications.

When he turned sixty-five, Du Bois resigned from the NAACP

and the editorship of the *Crisis*, returning to Atlanta University in 1934 as sociology department head. One of his purposes, he said, was "to establish . . . a scholarly journal of comment and research on world race problems." It took six years for this goal to be reached. The result was *Phylon*, being published still at the university as a scholarly and literary quarterly. He was editor for four years. It was to be his last major journalistic editorial work. Thereafter he wrote articles for black as well as white publications: *New York Times Magazine, New Masses, Nation, Journal of Negro Education, Negro Digest, Freedomways, Masses,* and *Mainstream,* among others. He was the author, from 1896 to 1963, of a score of books, editor of a dozen more, author of countless articles, and regularly contributed newspaper columns.

Because he placed his confidence in college-educated blacks to "save the race," as Rudwick puts it, Du Bois naturally believed in the use of books, magazines, and newspapers as vehicles of communication.

In the 1960s, as attempts were made to catch up with black history, it was popular to name schools for noted black people. Du Bois was not overlooked. The Chicago Board of Education in 1969 renamed a South Side elementary school for him; not without a debate, however. For toward the end of his life he joined the Communist party, moved to Ghana, and became a citizen of that African nation. He died there in 1963, aged ninety-five. His new publishing project he was not to live to see realized—the *Encyclopaedia Africana* he had been commissioned to direct. His views were recalled in 1970 when his widow, Shirley Graham, also a writer and a New Yorker living as a Ghanian citizen in the United Arab Republic, for a time was denied a visa to enter the United States. The reason given by the Department of Justice was based on a section of the McCarran-Walter Act that forbids entry into the country of persons associated with subversive activities, as a New York *Times* dispatch put it.

A memorial park was dedicated to Du Bois on October 18, 1969, at Great Barrington, on the site of the farmhouse where he spent his childhood. It was opposed by the John Birch Society and a white weekly, the Berkshire *Courier*, but supported by many other cities and the white daily, the Berkshire *Eagle*.

Other Magazines of the Period

Du Bois's magazines were not the only important ones of the first few decades of the century. One group now remembered because of the social climate then and today was what might be called mildly leftist in sympathies. These included *Opportunity, Crusader, Promoter, Triangle, Messenger, Black Man*, and *Negro World*, most issued from New York City. Like so much of the black press, several of these were organs of protest, some asking for a black state, others espousing a vague radicalism that avoided both socialism and communism of the brands then current, a radicalism centered on battling for the rights of blacks or for blacks to be in all government departments. But others supported some brand of socialism as a social order, with stronger labor and farmers' unions and cooperatively owned businesses.[17]

Black Man was among the more than half-dozen publications of Marcus Garvey, whose journalism will be noted in more detail. Intended as a monthly and published from Jamaica, the periodical, according to Cronon, a Garvey biographer, was irregularly published. It first appeared in 1933, carrying organization news and much of Garvey's own writing, such as poetry, editorials, and other communications from the messianic editor. It had many financial problems but managed to maintain an international circulation and continue for five or six years to help unite members of Garvey's Universal Negro Improvement Association. In one of its final issues was an appeal for support of a bill asking repatriation of U.S. blacks to Africa. It had been introduced by a notorious racist, U.S. Senator Theodore G. Bilbo. But it tied in with the magazine's and Garvey's program for American blacks.

An earlier Garvey magazine was *Negro Churchman*, launched as an organ of the denomination which the Black Moses, as Cronon calls him, had stimulated, the African Orthodox Church. A monthly, it supported Garvey's belief in an all-black religion, to which much of the rest of the black press gave no encouragement. The bulk of the other religious groups rejected it, evidently thinking the new denomination and its organ were merely political tools for Garvey.

Probably as much condemned and feared in its day—toward the end of World War I—as the *Black Panther* was at the other end of the century, the *Messenger* today seems placid. At first it was edited jointly by Chandler Owen and A. Philip Randolph, the latter a revered black leader long identified with the labor movement. Openly

Marxist, a dangerous position for those days of government interference with the press, it opposed Du Bois as much as Washington,
although they were in sharp disagreement. Representative James
Byrnes, of South Carolina, attacked the *Messenger* (as well as the
Crisis) in the House and blamed black journalists for the postwar race
riots. Consequently it was investigated by the Department of Justice.
Its report named the *Messenger* as "the most dangerous."[18]

Detweiler illustrated the tone of the *Messenger* when he noted
that a poem by Archibald H. Grimke, "Her Thirteen Black Soldiers,"
had been rejected by the white *Atlantic Monthly* and the black *Crisis*
but accepted and published by the *Messenger*. He describes the verse
as "a sombre invective against the nation, which is held guilty for the
fate of the Negro soldiers who rioted at Houston in the summer of
1917."[19] Another issue of the *Messenger* carried a cartoon showing a
black riding in an armored car and shooting down his white opponents in race riots. Claude McKay, one of the best of the black poets,
published in this magazine one of the poems for which he is best
remembered, beginning: "If we must die, let it not be like hogs." And
the magazine devoted itself to urging blacks to form and join labor
organizations of their own. George S. Schuyler notes in an autobiography that the magazine began as the *Hotel Messenger*.

Like Henry R. Luce, founder of the Time Inc. empire, Robert S.
Abbott started a magazine during an economic depression, one
sharply in contrast to the radical *Messenger*. Luce's *Fortune* went on
to thrive, but *Abbott's Monthly*, as already noted, did not last. Roi
Ottley assigned it the distinction of being "the first popular-style periodical published for Negroes," perhaps a challengable assertion in
1919, when it first was issued. Ottley also called it a forerunner of
Ebony, although that picture magazine owes as much to *Life* and
Look as to any other, and *Abbott's* little resembled either.[20] It was a
melange of articles on many different topics, international and national, of special interest to black readers. Much of it was race-
angled. Poetry and photographs were included. It was going well until
the depression caught up with it. Unlike *Fortune*'s readers, its clientele
were persons to whom the cost of a magazine was a personal sacrifice
from an always low income. Its diffuse content and absence of any
discernible formula may have undone it also. In any case, it was no
more after 1933.

Perhaps far more to be lamented was the death of a periodical
begun in 1923 which outlasted Abbott's magazine. This one was *Opportunity*, often confused with a later salesman's journal but actually
the voice until 1949 of the National Urban League. Charles S. John-

son, one of the few scholars interested in black periodicals, not only wrote about them but also began and edited *Opportunity*, making it one of the best in its day. He saw the need to give the magazine an auxiliary activity by sponsoring the Harlem Writers' Guild and set up literary competitions. As Frank W. Miles, a writer on black periodical journalism, noted of it, "thus living up to the Urban League's motto—not alms but Opportunity."[21] Bearing the subtitle *Journal of Negro Life*, it was a quarterly of about fifty pages an issue, carried serious articles on black problems, reviewed books, and reported on business and professional opportunities. Personality sketches and literary work were staples, as was League news. When it ceased it had a circulation of 10,000. The League explained that it was discontinued because "many other outlets are now available for the creative work of Negro writers and for serious articles on Negro life" and because increased costs of production made the deficit too great. In those words rests the explanation for many subsequent publication failures.

During the 1920s new magazines of a more specialized type than *Opportunity* appeared quickly: *American Musician, Master Musician, Music and Poetry*, and *Negro Musician* were those particularly devoted to music. In another decade, a dozen and a half more were begun, including *Brown American* and *Challenge*, but did not live to see the last of the 1930s. But in the 1940s, as to be seen later, came the surge that produced several highly successful consumer magazines and the rise of various more specialized periodicals, these dealing with the trades, education, travel, and other topics. *Pulse, Negro, Spotlighter*, and *Headlines*, among the general ones, did not survive; *Negro Digest* did, although it was buried for a decade and in 1970 became *Black World*.

Washington and Garvey

The newspapers during this period had just as unsteady a history. Prominent in the first quarter of the century were two figures, one an educator, the other a politician-editor-churchman, both interested in newspapers rather than periodicals as tools for their purposes. These men were Booker T. Washington and Marcus Garvey.

Washington's vague connections with black newspapers already have been noted. He was thought, according to Rudwick, to have provided some with financial assistance; it may or may not be significant that his articles appeared in those particular papers. Du Bois accused him, as early as 1905, of having provided several with three thousand dollars in hush money the year before. In time Du Bois even named them: the New York *Age,* Chicago *Conservator*, Boston *Citizen*, Washington *Colored American*, Indianapolis *Freeman*, and *Colored American* magazine, all now defunct. Rudwick asserts that Washington secretly invested that sum in the magazine and assumed its operations.

Rudwick also goes on to say that advertisements were bought in papers which supported him, such support including publication of editorials sent to the editors. Among the papers so favored, he declares, were the Charleston *Advocate* and the Atlanta *Independent*. These editorials appeared in several papers simultaneously, a situation to be expected in chain or group papers but not in those independently owned and separate. To these assertions Ottley adds the view that Washington gained press support by persuading supporters to buy financially weak papers; at one time as many as thirty-five were available to publicize his work or that of supporters. Among them were the Chicago *Broad Ax* and Chicago *Conservator*.[22]

Washington did more than operate behind the scenes, however. After publication of his classic of black literature, *Up From Slavery*, he was asked to write magazine articles. Ever his opponent, Du Bois declared in one of his autobiographies that these were prepared by black and white ghost writers, with their headquarters at Tuskegee, of which Washington was president.[23] Perhaps, like many a presidential and gubernatorial speech and article, his were composed with the help of others. Nevertheless, they were important in advancing Washington's views, especially that the black man was best able to improve his lot by using the worlds of labor and business as the paths to power.

If Washington was largely on the fringe of black journalism, Marcus Garvey, at least in the early part of his life, was steeped in it. Unlike other prominent editors and publishers such as Du Bois, White, Abbott, and Trotter, Garvey was racially pure, for he was entirely of black ancestry. Born in 1887 in Jamaica, his story differs from most of theirs also in that he was prone to demagoguery and had a most unhappy end to his career.

One of his first jobs was as a printer, at which he worked from his fourteenth to his twentieth year in Kingston. In 1907 he became a master printer and a foreman. When he took part in a printers' strike that year he lost his job, an experience that led him to begin what was to be a lifelong career as an organizer for members of his race to improve their social, political, and economic condition. His plans were not limited to the West Indian or U.S. black, but were international. The organization for which he is most remembered, the Universal Negro Improvement Association, he formed and headed in 1914. It was his platform. Garvey had a sense of the dramatic that made his own and his followers' activities newsworthy. In appearance they were attention-getting. The men were part of what he called the African legion; they wore blue uniforms and red trousers. The women belonged to a Black Cross Nurse Society.[24]

His following was large among the working class blacks but not among the middle class or its leaders, many of whom were disaffected by such bombast as calling himself the Provisional Ruler of Africa in Exile. His plans were far too big, involving establishment of a Black Star Line, a steamship company with small vessels in poor condition. American blacks invested $750,000 in the firm, which could not carry out his glowing plans. Garvey was indicted on fraud charges, accused of making rosy promises which were not kept. He received a five-year sentence and later was deported to Jamaica. The account in his paper, the *Negro World*, on August 11, 1926, carried the headline: "150,000 Honor Garvey" and the story began: "Harlem, the largest Negro community in the world, paid a tribute today to the greatest Negro in the world."

Garvey, who would have been one hundred years old, remained in the news in 1987. The debate over the merits of his policies and actions continued. Representative Charles E. Rangel, backed by the Congressional Black Caucus, of which he was a member, introduced two measures in Congress in 1987 because of new evidence that Garvey's conviction may have sprung from pressure brought by J. Edgar Hoover, who investigated Garvey. Dr. Robert A. Hill, editor of the Marcus Garvey Papers project at the University of California, found new papers in the National Archives that show Garvey was the victim of Hoover's practice of seeing both blacks and communists as conspirators against the United States.[25]

Black journalism played an important part in Garvey's life. His first venture into publishing began while he was on a government printing office job in 1910 in Jamaica. He started a magazine, *Garvey's Watchman*, the first of a series of short-lived publications he was to sponsor. Next came a fortnightly, *Our Own*, a political organ.

By now he had concluded that organization was needed if he was to help improve the conditions of his people. He quit his job, went to Costa Rica and while there started *Nacionale*, but it too failed through lack of response. Then came another Spanish-language paper, *La Prensa*, likewise short of life. He traveled through South America, where he saw more exploitation of black workers. Eventually he reached England, where he spotted *Up From Slavery*. It inspired him to more efforts to lead his race; it was then that he returned to Jamaica to form the Improvement Association. In two years he went to the United States, and in another two he started the New York paper which was his most important journalistic contribution: the *Negro World*, the Association organ.

A weekly, the *World* rapidly became popular and went to a circulation of about 200,000 at its best, perhaps 50,000 in an average week, with a wide distribution. Garvey was responsible for the paper, writing editorials and at times longer articles, but the bulk of the writing was done by others.[26] It was more an opinion organ than a newspaper, hitting hard for the nationalistic aims of Garvey's group, harking frequently back to Africa. Among the several capable journalists who wrote for it were T. Thomas Fortune and John E. Bruce. The *Negro World*, in fact, for a time was a rival for the Chicago *Defender* as a leading black paper. Garvey's strong personality and the actions of some followers put the *Defender* in the opposite camp. The *Negro World* naturally espoused Garvey's major campaigns for his shipping company, a Black House to match the White House, black generals, black congressmen, and even a Black God.

When Garvey was not relating his accomplishments, he wrote forcefully and convincingly. An example of his writing is this portion of an article in the *Negro World* in 1921:

> Some people ask, "Why hasn't the Universal Negro Improvement Association protested against so-and-so, and why hasn't it sent a telegram to the President denouncing lynching? Why hasn't it asked for interviews from Congressmen and Senators over the question of injustice to the Negro?" Why should you want to do this when other organizations have been doing this for the last twenty years without any result?[27]

The *Negro World* was suspended in 1933, a depression year, outliving several other short-lived Garvey ventures, such as *Negro Times*, a daily; *Black Man*, a monthly magazine; *African World*, a paper distributed in South Africa; the monthly *Negro Churchman*; and the *Negro Peace Echo*. When Garvey died in 1940 a follower revived the *World* in Cleveland as the *New Negro World*, in magazine form, but it soon ceased. Garvey himself has not been forgotten, however. On the contrary. His nationalism appealed to the new separatist movement of the 1960s and 1970s. The black press reported various Garvey Day ceremonies in August during recent years, with proclamations, parades, and entertainment in his memory. A Garvey housing project was launched and a New York park was given his name.

The Rise of the *Courier*

Today it calls itself the *New Pittsburgh Courier*, but it is one of the oldest black newspapers of general distribution. Founded in 1910, the *Courier* at one time had the largest circulation of any black paper in the country, close to 300,000. Credited with developing the paper was Robert L. Vann, whose manner of directing it was continued after his death by his widow, who became publisher in 1940. Until recently the *Courier* has been one of the top papers in circulation, and still is influential because of its traditions.

Vann was brought in by the four Pittsburgh Methodist church people who founded the paper but who could not make a go of it financially. He was a lawyer with journalistic experience on two other black papers in the same city. His formula was to launch the paper on numerous crusades in behalf of the black community and black citizens generally. These campaigns were against Jim Crowism and discrimination against blacks in major league baseball, two of the classic targets of papers out to fight for black rights. He put the *Courier* behind nationally known black figures, such as Jackie Robinson and Joe Louis, early in their careers. Vann did something even more difficult: he saw to it that the paper was taken into the South, for in some localities black citizens were prohibited from reading black publications.

The story of the *Courier* follows what now is a familiar pattern: printing sensational news for the sake of sales, running campaigns in the news columns, printing editorials in behalf of readers, and struggling for advertising. But it went a step further: it attracted to its staff some of the major black journalists of the first half of this century, such as George S. Schuyler, P. L. Prattis, William G. Nunn, and a good many young writers who later became important on other papers.

In recent years there has been new appreciation of P. L. Prattis. When he died in 1980 he was eighty-five. More than his associates, such as George Schuyler and Robert Vann, he brought considerable valuable professional experience to his first job on the *Courier*.

Lawrence D. Hogan, biographer of the Associated Negro Press (ANP) and its founder, Claude Barnett, records Prattis's work on that black news agency, noting that he did many of the agency's editorial tasks and also wrote major news stories from the field, serving as Barnett's main assistant.

ANP work was not his first journalism, however. A Philadelphian, he entered the field in 1910 on the *Michigan State News*. Two years later he became a reporter for the Chicago *Defender* and then its city editor.

Hogan tells the story of what happened when Prattis discovered that the paper's janitor was being paid twenty-five dollars a week whereas he was receiving twenty dollars. When he protested to Robert S. Abbott, the publisher, he was fired. This treatment did not discourage him from continuing as a newsman, although he had been on the *Defender* staff for eleven years. It was then that Barnett hired him for the ANP. He was its news editor for a dozen years. From the news agency he moved to the New York *Amsterdam News*, remaining a year. During that time the paper was struck by the news staff. Prattis did not join the strike.

He moved to his fourth news job when he joined the *Courier* staff as city editor in 1936. In four years he was executive editor. He was promoted again in 1956 to full editorship of the paper, by then one of the leading black publications of the nation. While on the *Courier* he wrote a column he called "The Horizon." He retired in 1962.

Other Journalists and Papers

Douglass, Du Bois, Abbott, Garvey, Trotter, Fortune, Vann—these were among the effective men in black journalism by the end of the first century of its existence. Until another two decades had passed there would be none who made the same national impact. But there were other important black publications and publishers in the early 1900s. Among the papers were the St. Louis *Argus*, the *Informer* papers of the Southwest, the Kansas City (Missouri) *Call*, the Buffalo *Star*, and the Norfolk *Journal and Guide*. And the New York *Amsterdam News*, among other papers begun before the turn of the century, went into the forefront by the 1940s.

Among the publishers of that time who carried on their work into the 1960s was Carter W. Wesley of the *Informer* group. When Lincoln University gave two of its citations of merit in 1960, one went to Wesley for his work as head of black papers in two Texas cities: the Houston *Informer* and the Dallas *Express*. Born in 1892, Wesley was both a lawyer and publisher and a founder of the National Newspaper Publishers Association. In law he specialized in civil rights cases, one leading to the Supreme Court decision permitting blacks to vote in primaries.

About ten years his senior was Chester Arthur Franklin, identified with the black press for fifty-seven years. He founded the Kansas City *Call* when he was thirty-eight, but he already had been in publishing for twenty-one years. When he was seventeen he began by running the Denver *Star*, earlier called the *Statesman*. At his death in 1955 the *Call* was one of the larger papers and still is a leading weekly. A distinguishing feature of the *Call* under Franklin was its avoidance of sensationalism; frequently its front page had no crime stories.

Another lawyer-publisher was Andrew J. Smitherman, but unlike Wesley he has received little attention. He was a versatile publisher in the Southwest and East. His specialty in law was criminal trials. His first papers were published in Tulsa, Oklahoma, a daily as well as a weekly. Both, as well as his home, were lost in race riots in 1921. Smitherman began another paper in Springfield, Massachusetts. Then in 1925 he moved to Buffalo, New York, at first working for other black papers, but the satisfaction of ownership was missed, so he borrowed one hundred dollars and in 1932 founded the Buffalo *Star*, later called the *Empire Star*, and remained its editor and publisher for twenty-nine years. At his death in 1961 the white press in Buffalo credited him with having founded the nation's first black daily, but several such papers of that frequency had been published before Smitherman was born in 1885.[28] The *Star* ceased soon after his death.

Joseph E. Mitchell and the St. Louis *Argus*

The life story of many an editor or publisher of a black newspaper is that he began life in poverty. Joseph E. Mitchell did not. His widow relates that his father was a successful contractor and mechanic who also operated a cotton gin and sawmill.

His homestead was stocked with numerous animals.

Mitchell was an Alabamian. He went to the Philippines in 1898 with the U.S. Army. In 1904, having married, he and his wife moved to St. Louis. The Ku Klux Klan (KKK) was making trouble for blacks in his state. He did odd jobs while attending school and later at Douglas College.

He became manager of an insurance firm that issued a newspaper-type house publication, his first taste of journalism. He helped produce it. The work whetted his interest, so much so that he was inspired to start an insurance business trade publication at first. But gradually he "discovered that his real mission in life was to start a newspaper which would serve the whole community of St. Louis in a big way," his widow (his second wife, Edwina Mitchell) wrote in *Crusading Black Journalist*, her biography of him.

Thus, in 1912, the St. Louis *Argus* was born as a five-column tabloid weekly. Mitchell was editor and publisher. The printing was done nearby, in those days for thirty-five dollars.

A major objective, Edwina Mitchell explains, "was to organize for political action." Much of the work was done by Mitchell's relatives. But he also hired graduates of such early schools of journalism as those at the Universities of Michigan and Ohio and Lincoln at Jefferson City, Missouri.

The *Argus* was no instantaneous success, however. In fact, it was a liability to its publisher for its first four years. During those early days it attacked Jim Crowism, the KKK brutalities against blacks, segregation, and denial of civil liberties. Mitchell led a movement in 1919 to form the Citizens' Liberty League to see that blacks were elected to public office and selected for Republican party committees. Some results were obtained with these objectives and other aims within a year.

Mrs. Mitchell reports that her husband experienced at least one physical attack upon him and severe financial trouble. By 1933 he had become a Democrat. By 1944 he was a presidential elector. By this time he also had remarried. The first Mrs. Mitchell had died in late 1938.

Meanwhile the *Argus* fought for certain improvements, such as winning the right of blacks to use public parks, helping get a second high school for them, fighting to make a hospital accept black nurses, and attacking the University of Missouri for rejecting black applicants. Mrs. Mitchell reproduces some of the editorials in the biography. Most would still be suitable now, revealing that not enough progress has been made in certain areas.

In time the paper acquired its own three-story building in St. Louis. Mitchell won recognition from numerous local organizations with which he had been associated, such as the Missouri State Board of Education, an orphanage, and the YMCA.

In his later years and posthumously Mitchell was honored by the Lincoln University journalism faculty, which paid him tribute in 1949 for his thirty-five years' editorship of the paper, his service to the National Newspaper Publishers Association, and the education of young people. The Baltimore *Afro-American* in 1950 called him dean of the active newspapermen of the Southwest. In 1954 Lincoln dedicated its journalism building to him posthumously.

Mitchell suffered from neuralgia. Gradually in the 1940s his health deteriorated, and in ten years he had to retire from active management of his paper. He died in an infirmary in 1952.

The *Argus*'s circulation and advertising revenue have grown. The plant was improved, and finally moved to a larger building. Thirty-five years after Joseph E. Mitchell's death, the paper still is in the hands of the Mitchell family. Dr. Eugene N. Mitchell is president, publisher, and chairman of the board. J. Orval Mitchell is vice-president and vice-chairman of the board. It is a newsy and well-planned paper but most of its writers, editorialists included, are given to composing long magazine-like articles. Color is used on page one, making it a generally attractive front page.

The *Amsterdam News*

With certain individuals, publishing was only one of their activities; we already have encountered several lawyers. Others ran real estate firms, were doctors, bankers, or politicians; a few were diplomats. These connections indicate that especially in the early years of this century publishing was not lucrative, newspapers and magazines receiving neither enough advertising nor circulation revenue. But it also may indicate that successful businessmen were not putting their primary effort into publishing or perhaps were unaware that it takes certain talents and abilities different from those of the more widely followed occupations, such as real estate and banking.

Medical men were involved, as one was in the publishing of the New York *Amsterdam News*. James H. Anderson, who began the paper in 1909, was not a physician. He wanted to start a weekly and evidently used the name of the street on which he lived for its title. James Booker, author of a brief history of the paper, wrote that Anderson had "a dream in mind, $10 in his pocket, six sheets of paper and two pencils" when he put out the first copy. Despite its owner's weak finances, it continued. It has had several owners since, including two physicians who purchased it in 1936. They were Dr. Philip M. H. Savory and Dr. Clelan Bethany Powell. Dr. Powell diversified his business activities by running as well the Victory Mutual Life Insurance Company, a photoengraving firm called Rapid Reproduction, and other enterprises. Dr. Powell's partner died in 1965; until 1971 he was owner and publisher, operating several other businesses in addition to the paper. After the paper's sale he remained as editor and publisher emeritus.[29]

For a time the paper was a semiweekly, tabloid on one day a week, a standard-size sheet on the other. That policy was followed in 1945, when it was meeting competition from Adam Clayton Powell's *People's Voice* and the New York *Age*. It was moved by this strong competition as well to sensationalize the black community's news, but ran what have been called sedate editorials in the midst of accounts of brutal murders, stabbings, and sex crimes. Significantly, perhaps, it outlasted both rivals and today is one of the leading weeklies (see Chapter 5).

The Youngs in Norfolk

The story is that when P. Bernard Young went to work in 1907 for what now is known as the Norfolk *Journal and Guide*, it was the fraternal organ of the Knights of Gideon. Its circulation was 500, it was six years old, and called the *Lodge Journal and Guide*. He got the job because one day the editor did not appear, and Young wrote an editorial. As a result he was made associate editor, and in 1910 bought it and converted it into a general black newspaper.[30]

The Young family ran it for many years thereafter, and served the black press by holding office in the national organization of publishers and by placing the *Journal and Guide* on a par with the large national newspapers.

Plummer Bernard Young, the founder, who preferred simply to sign himself P. B. Young, was a North Carolinian. He ran the paper from 1910, when he was twenty-six, until his death in 1962. A son,

3.5. P. B. Young, founder of the leading weekly the Norfolk (Virginia) *Journal and Guide.*

Thomas White Young, holder of law and bachelor's degrees from Ohio State University, succeeded his father, after working two years as a war correspondent. But in 1967, after having served as editor and publisher only five years, he died. Like many other publishers, he had interests as well in banking and insurance.

The weekly, although until recent years somewhat more conservative in its policies than other major papers, was never silent about the black citizen's place in wartime, but at the same time supported the wars without pretending that blacks were faring better at home. the *Journal and Guide* also has the reputation of avoiding ultrasensationalism more than most of the medium-size or large black papers.

In the late 1980s the paper is newsy, belying its age. Its publisher is Brenda H. Andrews, whose deep interest in the black press expresses itself in historical articles about that journalism for other publications and in the nature of her own weekly.

It carries many short news stories originating in Norfolk, Portsmouth, Virginia Beach, Suffolk, and other parts of the Peninsula territory. The editorial and op-ed pages offer several locally written special opinion articles on current topics including one by Milton A. Reid, publisher emeritus. It carries foreign news of special interest to black readers. Two supplements appear, each once a month: *Dawn* and the *Black College Sports Review.*

Impact of World War I

Several more papers and entrepreneurs must be noted, especially since they are influential. One is the Oklahoma City *Black Dispatch*, a weekly begun in 1915. It got its unusual name, according to its onetime editor and publisher, Roscoe Dunjee, "as a result of an effort to dignify a slur." There was an Oklahoma expression, "That's black despatch gossip." But, he went on to say to his interviewer, "the influence of this statement is very damaging to the integrity and self-respect of the race. All of this has developed a psychology among Negroes that their color is a curse and that there is something evil in their peculiar pigmentation. It is my contention that Negroes should be proud to say, 'I am a black man.'" In saying this Dunjee anticipated the popular expression, "Black is beautiful."[31]

Four years later another paper important today was founded, the Kansas City *Call*, and in 1934, one more major weekly, the Los Angeles *Sentinel* (see Chapter 4).

Many editors and publishers were confronted with a dilemma when the United States entered World War I. American black citizens had little enthusiasm for the conflict, an attitude reflected in the leading publications. Too much for some editors was the contradiction of expecting blacks to fight to save a democracy they did not experience. Most cynical were the socialist and other left-of-center magazines. The Chicago *Defender*, the New York *Age*, the Washington *Bee*, the Baltimore *Afro-American*, and the Norfolk *Journal and Guide* pointed up the irony of the situation in editorials and cartoons. But they concluded that at the same time that the American black should be treated more fairly by the military it was essential that the United States and its allies overcome the enemy, for if they did not the black as well as the white on the American continent would suffer. The *Bee* said editorially:

> But the Negro is willing today to take up arms and defend the American flag; he stands ready to uphold the hands of the President; he stands ready to defend the country and his President against this cruel and unjust oppression. His mother, sister, brother and children are being burned at the stake and yet the American flag is his emblem and which he stands ready to defend. In all the battles the Negro soldier has proved his loyalty and today he is the only true American at whom the finger of scorn cannot be pointed.[32]

Such attitudes naturally led to accusations of sedition by the super-patriots. The Department of Justice placed charges of disloyalty particularly upon the leftist magazines. The effect upon the publications was to stimulate interest in their content and to win the loyalty of readers, who realized that the publications were fighting the battle for them.[33]

A Note on Discrimination

The black press, serving a people with a long history of being the butt of racial discrimination, has been the victim of discrimination as well. During the nineteenth century, especially in the years before the Civil War, it faced the problem of interference with distribution and the right of blacks to read their own publications. In the twentieth century, the discrimination sometimes has been more subtle, depriving publications of advertisers, interfering with their distribution, and ignoring their existence as a force in society.

In the first quarter of the century publishers encountered the problem of suppression. Detweiler records not only the raids on publication offices by the KKK and other hooded hoodlums and the cancellation of advertising by white merchants but also the passage of laws forbidding dissemination of the publications. The Mississippi legislature in 1920 passed "An act to make it a misdemeanor to print or publish or circulate printed or published appeals or presentations of arguments or suggestions favoring social equality or marriage between the white and Negro races."[34] The year before, the Chicago *Defender* had printed this dispatch, from Yazoo City, Mississippi: "Threatening her with death unless she stopped acting as agent for newspapers published by people of her Race, Miss Pauline Willis was compelled to leave town."[35] And in 1920, a black minister who distributed copies of the *Crisis*, the NAACP magazine, on a train in the same state, was mobbed, put in jail, and then on a chain gang when he asked for police protection. The lieutenant governor and the governor both refused to intervene.

Mississippi was not alone. A Somerville, Tennessee, paper printed, on February 7, 1919, this account: "White people of this city have been issued an order that no 'colored newspapers' must be circulated in this town, but that every 'darkey,' the petition read, must read The Falcon, a local white paper edited by a confederate veteran. The whites stated this step was being taken in order 'to keep the "nigger" from getting besides himself, and to keep him in his place.' "[36]

More than twenty years later Conrad reported that the Chicago *Defender* was concerned, for it was being suppressed in the South. It often was taken off the newsstands and halted at the post office.[37]

Such incidents were more likely to occur as the number of papers and magazines continued to mount and because the black press was the only one reporting the news of black America; except for crime there was almost no news of it in the white press. Pride in his study uncovered the fact that in one year—1902—almost one hundred newspapers were launched, beginning a long period of growth in numbers, for about fourteen hundred were founded between that year and 1950.

A traveling exhibit, some of its 150 pieces drawn from the life of the U.S. black people, including their press, began touring the nation in 1987 from its center in Washington, D.C. It was to be on the road until 1991.

The exhibit is part of the personal, seven-hundred-item collection of Prof. Charles E. Simmons, a Howard University School of Communications faculty member. He was a reporter for the Associated Press and other agencies and has written for various publications.

3.6. Charles E. Simmons of Howard University and his 1987–91 traveling historical exhibit on racism and the First Amendment.

Black newspapers, slave papers, racist signs once in public places, and numerous other items that portray blacks or show racist practices of general publications are in the historical exhibit, which is keyed to the celebration of the bicentennial of the Constitution. Sponsoring it are the office of the director of the Armour J. Blackburn Center of the university and the School of Communications. Professor Simmons also directs the Capital Feature Service.

World War II and After

The years between the two world wars saw the strengthening of some papers and the decline of others, particularly in the late twenties and early thirties, when the economic depression had its effect. As usual it was the financially weak, not necessarily the least competent, that went bankrupt. But capable management did help the strong papers to become stronger, as did the beginning of the trend toward formation of chains and groups.

The most important newspaper founded between the conflicts was the Atlanta *World*, established in 1928 as a weekly. Within two years it became a semiweekly and by another year a triweekly, and finally a daily in 1932. It now is one of three daily papers (see Chapter 5). It was the period, also, when several major serious magazines were launched: *Opportunity, Negro History Bulletin*, and *Journal of Negro Education* among them.

When the country entered World War II the publications that took a stand were accused of defeatism because they said black fighting men should be as well treated as white, just as others before them in the previous global conflict were charged with being seditious. Federal government efforts were made to quiet such papers as the *California Eagle* and the Pittsburgh *Courier*. What was considered unacceptable was no more than objection to what the publications considered undemocratic processes. The press was admittedly biased and made no pretensions of objectivity when it came to the need for equitable treatment of blacks.

After the war the black publications continued their demand for civil liberties, a policy which brought upon them new criticism, that of being leftist and even communist. One of the most vituperative critics was Westbrook Pegler, the sportswriter and later syndicated columnist. The black papers "in their obvious, inflammatory bias in the treatment of news resemble such one-sided publications as the Communist *Daily Worker* and Coughlin's *Social Justice,*" he wrote.[1]

Some years after the war *Ebony* magazine examined the executives at the head of twenty-three leading papers, including some of those accused of disloyalty; most of them are being published still and retain their leadership. "Far from being parlor pinks," the magazine said, "most Negro publishers are arch-conservatives in their thinking on every public issue with one exception—the race problem. The owners of the biggest newspapers have but two main missions—to promote racial unity and to make money."[2]

By the early and mid-1940s owners of black publications had to face not only the threat of war but also a rising enthusiasm for integration of the races, particularly in the world of education. The latter was a threat in one sense: blacks might drift away from their own press. On the issue of integration, despite the effect on circulation it could have in the long run, there was largely enthusiasm within the world of black journalism. The skeptics were mainly the more nationalistic black journalists, either remnants of the Garvey days or others concerned about the purity of the race. The large national papers were hopeful, reporting progress, editorializing, and carrying cartoons encouraging the idea of equality of some degree, certainly in education and job opportunities. But a few saw an outcome that would at least greatly weaken the black press. Among these was John H. Johnson, who in two decades was to become the head of a large and successful journalistic enterprise. He foresaw a decline in the press as a result of integration. He did not fear this result, but others did. There were dark forecasts about the disappearance of the press which created discomfort and argument (see Chapter 16). As it turned out, the fears were unnecessary but not illogical.

The rising interest and activity to bring about racial integration was a signal to editors and publishers that they must adjust their policies by reaching out for more black readers. A handful of whites joined some staffs; a few black magazines were put on newsstands that had not displayed them before. Existing quietly alongside the national papers and consumer magazines were a number of scholarly journals accustomed to subsidized living: *Journal of Negro History, Journal of Negro Education, Phylon*, and the *Crisis* among the better known. They were not directly dependent on commercial support.

By 1947, two years after the end of the war, several papers hit their highest circulation figures. By 1969 many had lost 50 to 75 percent of that circulation.

Sengstacke and Others

American white journalism has had its emperors and empires: Luce of Time Inc., within whose giant firm were magazines at first, then broadcasting stations and books; Hearst, father and son, heads of a huge combination of newspapers, magazines, news services, and film companies; Newhouse, head of a conglomerate of printed and electronic journalism enterprises; and Lord Thomson and Rupert Murdoch, both acquiring scores of publications all over the world.

Proportionately, perhaps, black journalism has had just as many with what might be called the Murphy papers (the *Afro-Americans*) and the Scott papers (Atlanta and other *Worlds* as well as some not called *World*) and, largest of all, the Sengstacke Newspapers, which cover a large territory through various *Couriers* and *Defenders* (see Chapter 5). These are the publishers who saw the circulation rises and drops and the gradual rise of advertising volume and revenue to compensate.

John H. Sengstacke's relationship to the Abbott-Sengstacke family already has been recounted. When his uncle, Robert Sengstacke Abbott, selected him for responsibility in the organization he may not have foreseen the extent to which the empire would grow in the period after the first World War, minor as some of the publications in the group are today.

Sengstacke is a modest publisher, a model of neat appearance. Comparatively few mentions of him appear in his papers. He is a graying, low-voiced man who has been a quiet leader among black publishers; has twice served as president of their national organization; still heads the large advertising representatives firm, Amalgamated Publishers, Inc.; and serves on various committees within the industry.

He was born in Savannah in 1912 and attended grade school in the Sengstackes's town of Woodville, Georgia. He first went to Knox Institute, then to Hampton Institute (now Hampton University), from which he received a bachelor's degree, and next did graduate work at

4.1. John H. Sengstacke, publisher of Chicago *Defender* and other papers and leader of several publishing and advertising organizations.

Ohio State University. Ottley reports that during his college days Sengstacke wrote his Uncle Robert what many a neophyte journalist still tells parents and friends: "I am reading books on journalism, newspaper work, and taking a course in advertising. I am going to do some research work on the topic, 'Problems Confronting the Advertising Managers of Negro Newspapers.' "[3]

His first job was on the *Times* of Woodville, a paper his uncle's father had established and which Alexander Sengstacke, John's father, later renamed the *West End Post*. Young Sengstacke did various jobs — printing, advertising, and editorial.

After being at Ohio State he joined his uncle's firm in 1934, and has been in the organization ever since. In his early days at the Chicago *Defender* he studied at the Chicago School of Printing and also at Northwestern University, where he took business administration courses, applying what he learned to the *Defender* operations. In time he became a vice-president and treasurer of the paper and then general manager. Ottley reports that Sengstacke put the paper on a steady financial keel and developed the chain of which it now is the center.

By and large his has been a financially successful tenure at the Robert S. Abbott Publishing Company, still the name of the publishing house. Robert A. Sengstacke is president of the Sengstacke Enterprises.

Not every venture has been a success; few big publishing firms do not misfire now and then. He started a news and picture magazine, *Headlines*, in 1944 and made Louis E. Martin its editor and publisher and Frederick D. Sengstacke business manager. Small in format at first, it became newsmagazine-size, was renamed *Headlines and Pictures*, edited in New York, and at one time had a circulation of 35,000. It ceased in 1946, the white newsmagazines being preferred.

Powell and *People's Voice*

Among the other editors was one who smothered his journalism activity in politics and marital as well as political troubles: Adam Clayton Powell, Jr. The principal journalistic work of the controversial churchman and congressman was as editor of *People's Voice*, begun in 1942 in New York. While he was in that post Powell explained why he became a journalist as well as a churchman and politician. He had four reasons: from grade school years on he wanted to write; he wished to use the press to correct what he considered the false ideas held about the American black people; he wished to raise a militant voice in behalf of the black society; and he desired to employ the press as an educational force with the "new" black citizen aroused to demanding more democracy for his race.[4]

Chuck Stone, after he left the editor's desk of the Chicago *Defender*, observed that "Powell's weekly columns in *People's Voice* when re-read in the light of today's 'Black Power' militancy clearly anticipated these developments. Any one of those columns can stand alone today as a 'call to rally under the banner of blackness.' "[5] Stone also said that the paper, for tough, uncompromising militancy, brilliant editorial writing, and exciting layout "has rarely been matched." It was this toughness that earned some animosity for it. The paper began to run Richard Wright's novel, *Native Son*, now a classic of American literature, but so many readers protested that only four installments were printed. One objection was to the profanity in the realistic novel of poverty and crime in Chicago's black community, an objection which seems quaint today in view of the language in many a modern novel. Powell also invited criticism because he seemed to be timing the introduction of legislation in Washington, after his election in 1944, so that his paper got the story first.[6]

As he did during his career as representative of his Harlem constituency, Powell through his paper battled in behalf of the black people, which appears to be the main reason why, despite personal activities frowned upon by blacks as well as whites—luxurious living, intemperate language, boastfulness, failure to appear in the House or attend committee meetings—he continued to hold his power. Powell died in 1972.

People's Voice was a tabloid weekly, somewhat imitative of *PM*, an adless daily in New York, but it sold space. Powell was not its only editor to gain national attention: so did Doxey A. Wilkerson, executive editor in 1945. Two years later Wilkerson left to become editor of the New York *Daily Worker*, the American Communist party paper. When he departed Wilkerson said that the tabloid "is cowering before the witch hunters." It was playing, he said, the role of Uncle Tom to foes of the black people. But by then Powell had withdrawn and the paper was being directed by Denton J. Brooks, Jr., earlier of the Chicago *Defender*, and Max Yergan, once in charge of the Council on African Affairs. The new publishers placed *People's Voice* in support of Ben Davis, Jr., a black Communist party leader. This policy brought suspicion upon it as being subversive. It ran into financial difficulties and ceased in 1947.[7]

The late James Baldwin, in his appraisal of the black press, published in 1948, found *People's Voice* "pretty limited" in its coverage, and its politics murky. But its exploitations of prominent blacks he considered pathetic, for the paper printed every detail of their lives it could uncover. He said the paper was full of warnings, appeals, and open letters to the government.[8]

Newman and Martin

When Gordon Parks, photographer, novelist, and man of many other talents, was insolvent in Minneapolis early in his career, trying to make a go of it in photojournalism, it was Cecil E. Newman who helped him. Newman gave him the somewhat unsuitable job of circulation manager but also the suitable one of official cameraman. Newman, editor and publisher of the Minneapolis *Spokesman*, at first printed Parks's pictures to get the young man's work before the public, for he was unable to pay him because the paper was in serious financial trouble. Parks paints a graphic picture of Newman and his paper's setting at the time, the late 1930s, in his book, *A Choice of Weapons*.[9]

"Cecil was a small, brown-skinned man of perpetual motion and tremendous spirit," he wrote. In a cramped and disordered office Newman had to write the editorial, the sports, society, and general news and try to keep up with his bills. He could give his few employees little money, so he gave them what Parks calls "titles . . . of Herculean stature."

Times were better for Newman three decades later, but he had to engage in varied journalism activities first. Born in 1903, he entered publishing with the *Twin City Herald* of Minneapolis from 1927 to 1934. For a year during the same period he also published *Timely Digest*, a magazine. In 1934 he became editor and publisher of the *Spokesman* as well as the St. Paul *Recorder*. He served on many government bodies, such as the Citizen's Advisory Committee on Civil Rights of the Department of Agriculture, and was active in various groups, including the United Negro College Fund. He was cited by Lincoln University in 1957 for his journalism and civic activity.

Almost as widely known in the world of Democratic party politics as in black journalism, Louis E. Martin helped establish the *Michigan Chronicle* in the 1930s in Detroit, developing it into one of the major large weeklies. It now is part of the Sengstacke Newspaper empire.

Martin was appointed deputy chairman of the Democratic National Committee. He returned to the newspaper business in 1969. For a number of years he wrote a column, "The Big Parade," for his papers and for a few others outside the group. In it he commented on current problems of concern to the black citizenry, sometimes relying on an alter ego, one Dr. S. O. Onabanjo, "my learned Nigerian friend," to make his points. A graduate of the University of Michigan, Martin was a native of Shelbyville, Tennessee, where he was born in 1912. In recent years and until 1987 he was on the staff of Howard University.

Johnson and His Empire

A major development after World War II was the building not only of newspaper empires but also of large magazine companies (see Chapter 7). Head of the most ambitious of these firms is John Harold Johnson, who presides over the Johnson Publishing Company.

Johnson is bouncy and a bit bumptious. He likes to tell stories, and has a shouting laugh. One incident he enjoys recounting occurred some years ago.

He was driving his car—one fitting to a man of his high income—on one of Chicago's major boulevards one day when he was stopped by a white policeman.

"Boy, does your boss know you're out in his car," the cop asked, suspiciously.

"He sure does," Johnson answered.

"Well, you'd better get it back to him soon as you can," he was warned.

"Sure will," the millionaire publisher of *Ebony* and other magazines assured him, and drove off.[10]

The success story of John H. Johnson probably is one of the few that is at all widely known about black publishers. It is a narrative that would have delighted Horatio Alger but it distresses both the blacks and whites who oppose the present American economic order. Johnson represents economic success gained through use of all the procedures and methods embedded in the private initiative, private ownership system so characteristic of business in western society. He began with a pittance. After overcoming setbacks he persisted until today his company is one of the largest in the industry, regardless of color. In addition to publishing, he also owns cosmetic and insurance firms. He clearly has a vested interest in the U.S. financial system and apologizes not at all for it.

Johnson told a *Fortune* magazine writer, for an article about him and his enterprises, that his aim always has been to get himself into a position where he would own the building, not burn it down. "I don't want to destroy the system—I want to get into it." he added.[11] And it is indeed a substantial building that he maintains.

The Johnson saga began when he and his mother went from rural Arkansas to visit the Chicago World's Fair of 1933. Like many other visitors, they decided to stay, the elder Johnson having died when the future publisher was six. They lived on relief for a time. But, as the *Fortune* writer reported it, in 1936 John Johnson, the student, gave a talk on "America's Challenge to Youth" at the annual honors convocation at DuSable High School, and was heard by Harry H. Pace, president of the Supreme Life Insurance Company. Pace encouraged Johnson to go on to college. He liked to help ambitious and talented black youths; another he befriended was Paul Robeson, whose later political views must have distressed him. He gave young Johnson a part-time job. The future owner of *Ebony* attended the University of

Chicago at the same time. At the insurance company offices he met various young black businesspeople.

One day he was asked to work on the firm's house magazine. After becoming its editor he conceived the idea of a magazine containing articles of interest to the black population and about black citizens. Pace encouraged him, urging him to try to make a go of it without his help but said he could be turned to, as a last resort. Bank loans for black businessmen were much harder to get in those days than now.

The new publisher mortgaged his mother's furniture for five hundred dollars, so he could pay for his first direct mail advertising about his magazine, *Negro Digest* (later renamed *Black World*). That letter, sent in 1942, offered subscriptions at two dollars each and brought 3,000 subscribers. A first issue of 5,000 copies did not sell out. For one matter, distributors did not believe that the newsstands could dispose of a magazine of solely black appeal, a not unreasonable view in those days and still shared by many a newsstand operator. So Johnson persuaded thirty friends to ask for the magazines at the stands and thus create a demand. He then bought from the dealers copies not sold. The second issue did not require such artificial sales stimulation.[12]

Circulation climbed steadily, helped partly by publication of a series called "If I were a Negro," containing pieces by Mrs. Eleanor Roosevelt, Norman Thomas, Marshall Field, Edward G. Robinson, and other whites. Some issues hit as much as 150,000 circulation, a remarkable figure for any black periodical of serious type and unusual even for a white periodical of the kind.

His first venture a success, Johnson now was ready to consider another, a black version of *Life*. In 1945 *Ebony* was born with the intention of emphasizing the bright side of black life and reporting success by black people in almost any endeavor.

The value of imagination and of luck was proved by what happened in the magazine's early years, as A. James Reichley tells it in *Fortune*. Johnson wrote letters to presidents of various large corporations, seeking entrée so he could sell *Ebony* as an idea and as an advertising medium. Presidents of black firms of any sort were not, at that time, accepted by white corporation counterparts, so Johnson received no encouragement. And black businessmen prepared to spend money on advertising were few and reluctant. Johnson's letter, however, did at last bring one appointment, this with Commander Eugene McDonald, president of Zenith, the radio set manufacturing firm. The commander, an Arctic explorer as well as a leading business executive, once had known Matthew Henson, the black explorer who worked closely with Admiral Peary in the 1909 journey to the North Pole. The publisher knew of the McDonald-Henson friendship and brought with him on his call a copy of the biography of Henson that had been autographed for the commander. As a result of this rapport, McDonald saw to it that the Zenith Corporation bought advertising space in *Ebony*. It became the Johnson firm's first big account.[13]

Ebony went through a temporary decline to rise to new strength, and the rest of the Johnson empire was built gradually by the launching of *Jet, Ebony Man, Ebony Jr!, Tan Confessions, Hue, Ebony International*, and *Copper Romance. Negro Digest* was temporarily discontinued, and the last five were not successful ventures, for varying reasons. Johnson's method always has been to put out magazines with formulas and formats that have been used, often successfully, by white publishers with primarily white readers. His *Negro Digest* was suggestive of the *Reader's Digest; Ebony* is like *Life; Jet* much like a long-defunct miniature magazine, *Quick; Tan*, superseded in 1971 by *Black Stars*, had much in common with *True Confessions*. Even his later *Ebony International* was in concept like *Life International*. Such imitativeness is normal in the publications world. Walter Goodman, writing in 1968, noted that Johnson, in his first years in mass journalism, declined to become "all hot and bothered about the race questions." He quotes the publisher as saying that the monthly picture magazine would "mirror the happier side of Negro life." The big money earned by entertainment figures and the lavish lives of some of them were played up, for example.[14] This philosophy *Ebony* has had until recent years; it was modified in the later 1960s from a somewhat Pollyanna-ish view to one of a more strident demand for the righting of wrongs against the race. The struggle for equality with rights finally has led Johnson to realize, apparently, that doing what whites strive to do in the world of business or entertainment perhaps is not the acme of accomplishment for people in the black race.

Perhaps because he smarted from criticism that he was too much concerned with making money and not enough interested in providing talented black writers with an outlet or with being an influence on the serious black citizens, Johnson revived *Negro Digest* just ten years after he had discontinued it. As the civil rights movement gained strength and the philosophy of black power, with its many interpretations and applications, could not be ignored by either whites or blacks, *Negro Digest* began carrying articles with such titles as "Negro Rights and the American Future." Promoting that magazine, which now began attacking white power as expressed through White Citizens' Councils and the like, the Johnson institutional advertising said:

> For more than 100 years, a native-bred philosophy not very dif-
> ferent from Herr Hitler's has been preached in this country. With the
> upward thrust of the civil rights movement, this racist philosophy gains
> more strident voices. And these enemies of humanity are aided,
> perhaps unwittingly, by those whites who admonish Negro citizens to
> "go slow" and to be "more responsible" in the push for full and equal
> rights, as if Negroes had not gone slowly for a century and as if it is not
> precisely white America's disdain of its responsibility which has
> brought the nation to this terrible movement. The enemies of Negro
> rights are both numerous and powerful, and many of them heard the
> cadences of Herr Schicklgruber's marching spirit and are hypnotized.[15]

By fall 1965, *Ebony* was carrying articles by such outstanding
liberal-minded blacks as Martin Luther King, Jr., Carl T. Rowan, and
Kenneth Clark, in a number significantly devoted to the theme of "the
white man's burden." Johnson began to give hard looks, often sym-
pathetically, at the actions of rebellious black people, particularly
youth. But the magazine did not lose its determination to tell success
stories and spoke primarily to the middle-class black family which
wants to be socially and financially successful. *Negro Digest* was discontinued, but with considerable protest from its staff and readers.

The Other New Magazines

John Johnson's early success with *Negro Di-
gest* naturally led to the rise of competitors. One, the *Negro*, was
similar in formula, but not so fortunate. Its publisher was not able to
revive it once it had died. *Ebony* quickly inspired competition: *Color,
Our World*, and *Sepia* came close to its formula but all have since
disappeared. Others, such as *Spotlighter*, which preceded *Ebony* by a
year, were more cheaply produced but fell away after a few months or
a year.

The post–World War II period also was one of establishment of a
wide variety of magazines and of more small community papers. In
the 1950s the larger papers were dropping back in circulation, the loss
in sales revenue offset somewhat by the slightly increased success in
selling advertising space. While not startlingly great, it was a reflection of somewhat better financial conditions for the American people,

in which some blacks shared, and the first signs of impact of the developing civil rights movement, reflected in the New York–issued magazine, *Freedom*.

The specialized magazine and newspaper, although not new in black journalistic history, was by the 1960s a part of the general trend toward publishing periodicals dealing with special interests. There rose such titles as *Soul*, an entertainment paper, and *Pride*, a community magazine. The hairdressing salons had two: *Black Beauty* and *Beauty Trade*. The separatist churchmen brought out *Impact*. In the realm of literary and idea publications arose *Freedomways*.

What developed into the circulation leader of all publications for black readers was launched in 1965: *Tuesday*, a magazine supplement inserted in white newspapers in cities with large black populations. Within five years it had nearly two million circulation and was attracting a number of major advertisers (see Chapter 7). But it, too, did not survive insufficient advertising revenue. A women's service magazine, free of the confession tone, came forth in *New Lady*. It was shelved for a time and resumed again with new funding late in the decade. *Urban West* was a combination general discussion, fashion, and job opportunity magazine. Early in the 1950s, when the more general *Sepia* was founded, the same firm in Texas brought out three more or less similar confession-romance monthlies, *Bronze Thrills*, *Hep*, and *Jive*, and in 1971 added *Soul Confessions*. Most are in the black magazine cemetery.

The Muslim and Panther Papers

Although they were not conventional commercial newspapers, but actually quasi magazines, *Muhammad Speaks* and the *Black Panther*, two comparatively recent additions to the nationally distributed black newspapers, had major attention in the 1960s and 1970s. *Muhammad Speaks* shot to the lead in circulation over all other black newspapers (but not magazines), achieving the highest figure in the newspaper press' history, around 600,000 according to the publishers. *Black Panther*, with only one-sixth of the Nation of Islam weekly's sales, nevertheless was able to note a larger circulation than any of the individual commercial publications, having by 1970 reached about 100,000 every week.

Both papers were tabloid-size and spokesmen for groups within the black society. They were not standard, major newspapers to be linked or equated with the *Afro* or the Chicago *Defender*. They were organs of groups and cause or advocacy journals. Depending upon one's social and political outlook, they may be considered papers whose aim was a sharp, perhaps even revolutionary, change in the form of government of the United States. In the *Black Panther*, at least, such change was apparently to be achieved through the use of force; many an issue contains pictures of guns on almost every page, including photographs of the party leaders carrying weapons, presumably only for self-defense. Nothing was said in the party's ten-point platform and program about how its ends were to be met, for the emphasis was all on the demands, which were typified by these quotations printed in every issue:

> We want freedom. We want power to determine the destiny of our Black Community. We want full employment for our people. We want an end to the robbery by the CAPITALIST of our Black Community. We want decent housing, fit for shelter of human beings. We want education for our people that exposes them to the true nature of this decadent American society. We want education that teaches us our true history and our role in the present-day society. We want all black men to be exempt from military service. We want an immediate end to POLICE BRUTALITY and MURDER of black people. We want freedom for all black men held in federal, state, county and city prisons and jails.

Muhammad Speaks became *Bilalian News*, the name change explained by the movement as part of the change in terminology adopted by the Nation of Islam. It was so called to honor Bilal, a black Ethiopian slave and the first high priest. But this title did not preserve the paper. The organization for which it spoke has a new voice, *Muslim Journal*, of relatively small circulation.

Today's Major Newspapers

Publishers assembled at annual conventions and other gatherings have discussed the possibility of launching a national black weekly. Some of the entrepreneurs already consider their weeklies and semiweeklies national and the publishers of the three black dailies believe that they qualify.

On close examination it is obvious that none of these papers is national either in distribution or content. Support for this special press comes largely from the communities composed mainly of black citizens, much as the foreign language press has its strength in the areas where persons formerly of certain countries abroad or descended from citizens of such countries tend to live.

This practice automatically rules out many other areas that may have only a small number of potential readers. The black dailies have wide but thin distribution over the nation. The black semiweeklies give major coverage in those cities where their papers have editions. The weeklies, which are the great majority of the black newspapers, are divided into two groups: the independents, which exist in just one locality, and the chains or groups, which appear sometimes under different names although usually with some linking identification, as do the *Afro-American* and the *Post*. The latter give strong regional coverage, as they often exist in a single large state or in a group of small adjacent states. But none of these papers provides national coverage or even readership. (See Table 5.1.)

A national newspaper requires a large staff which, in the case of these papers, would need to be stationed in New York, Chicago, Los Angeles, Dallas, Detroit, Washington, St. Louis, and other cities with large black populations.

TABLE 5.1. Number of black newspapers of all frequencies in the United States in 1986, indicating those with most publications

Total in 1986: 266					
States with largest number:					
California	46	New York	18	Georgia	16
South Carolina	27	Illinois	17	Louisiana	10
Florida	21	Texas	17		

Sources: Membership list, National Newspaper Publishers Association, 1987; Client list, Amalgamated Publishers, Inc., 1987; *Editor & Publisher International Year Book,* 1987; *Gale Directory of Publications,* 1987; *Standard Rate and Data Service,* 1987–1988.

Notes: California's strong lead can be explained by the fact that four of the largest chains are published in and cover mainly California towns and cities. This list makes no claim to completeness since a number of publishers belong to no association or other organization that would list them; thus the total is likely to be more than the total shown.

There is debate over whether the United States has a national daily newspaper regardless of race or special subject matter. Sometimes the New York *Times* and the *Wall Street Journal* are referred to as national dailies. In the mid-1980s came a new contender for the honor: *U.S.A. Today.* It has wide distribution and offers news from many segments of the nation, is filled with highly compressed accounts, and wherever possible conveys the news through diagrams, charts, and tables.

Newsmagazines, such as *Time* and *Newsweek,* come closer to being national news publications than the newspapers; similarly *Jet,* the black newsweekly, with a circulation of nearly 800,000, reaches widely into the black population. Like its counterparts in nonblack journalism, *Jet* covers little in depth, even less than they do because it is physically so small.

Earlier in this century numerous papers sought national distribution and readership, especially in the days when they had reached the peaks of their circulation. But as they suffered a sharp falloff in sales most contented themselves with area distribution or became part of a group or chain.

Groups and Chains

The newspaper groups or chains[1] have several advantages in unification, including the possibility for uniform policies, greater purchasing power, more circulation to offer advertisers, larger opportunities for staff members, and wider use of editorial matter. The disadvantages are the possible lack of independence for local executives (especially editors and writers), elimination of competition, possible reduction in news coverage and variety of editorial opinions, and weakening of job opportunities for staff members.

The combinations existing in 1987 numbered eleven, with forty-six papers, mostly weeklies, among them. They are most numerous in California, which has the *Wave, Post, Observer*, and Metro *Reporter* Groups. Maryland has the *Afro-Americans*, Atlanta the Scott Syndicate, and Hartford, Connecticut, the *Inquirer* Group. Chicago has two: the *Citizen* Group and the Sengstacke (or *Defender*) Group. In Louisiana is the *Community Leader* Group, in South Carolina the Black News Group, and in Ohio the Cleveland *Call and Post* chain.

5.1. The *Post* chain in California.

Characteristics of Major Papers

Robert D. Bontrager, in a 1969 study of the use of black publications in a single community, selected five general characteristics of black newspapers, limiting himself, he pointed out, to those "most generally mentioned by scholars." These usually are the weeklies discussed in this chapter.

"Negro newspapers," he wrote, "are protest-oriented; are typically urban weeklies; are supplementary in the 'white' daily press; tend to be sensational; and have a high mortality rate."[2]

Although many of his observations are based on conditions of the 1940s and 1950s, all but one of Bontrager's list of characteristics still are accurately ascribed. The exception is the quality of sensationalism. Possibly these papers are sensational by comparison with general publications in the same cities, but by comparison with black papers in the 1920s to 1950s this press has toned down considerably. Because streamers and banners are used generously on front pages and tabloid size is increasingly popular the black papers often look more sensational than they are in fact.

The older papers, as already noted, were protest-oriented in their earliest days, but they were protesting about human slavery, brutal treatment of men, women, and children, and lynchings. Today the protests are over such matters as the failure of white groups to hire blacks for jobs they could hold, physical mistreatment by police and civilian groups, and discrimination in educational opportunities and housing. The national papers now look more like big city dailies than urban weeklies, although the small weeklies fit the description just as before. More than ever the black paper is the second one in a household. And, among the smaller papers, the mortality rate has been high but it has not touched a major weekly in recent years.

Another characteristic, buried perhaps in Bontrager's point about the urban nature of these papers, is that they are more and more stressing local news, a consequence of backing off from issuing papers for coast-to-coast distribution. This policy resulted from the need to carry news that the general press cannot accommodate, making it more certain that the black reader would continue to be loyal to his own papers. The desire for such local strength is supported by the circulation figures of the few papers that issue local and national editions.

Vignettes of Individual Papers

The *National Leader*

The United States did not succeed in having a national daily newspaper until *U.S.A. Today* was founded in 1982. Before that a number of papers attempted to acquire sufficient circulation and influence to be so designated, but they fell short in one way or another. Foremost among them were the New York *Times* and the *Wall Street Journal*, then the largest circulating dailies in the nation. Another New York paper, the *Daily News*, has thought of itself as national, but the copies sold in the hinterlands were little more than collections of comics and feature stories, with a minimum of news. Although truly national and even international in scope, the *Christian Science Monitor* did not qualify because its circulation is so small and because it publishes five times a week.

These papers attempted to publish in cities outside the one in which they originated. But this did not make for truly same-day national appearance on the stands or on doorsteps. Geography was the obstacle. Unlike England, it was impossible to have a paper on every breakfast table throughout a nation so large as the United States.

U.S.A. Today's publishers achieved national circulation by using the latest technology available to the wealthy Gannett Company, an enormous communications complex involving many different kinds of media. The firm also had the resources to withstand a five-year deficit running into the millions. Furthermore, it printed the paper in full color and presented as much content as possible in the form of charts, tables, diagrams, and pictures, and capsulized much of the news. At first it commanded little advertising,but as circulation passed the first millions the accounts mounted.

In that same year, 1982, a group of black journalists and leaders of organizations seeking to help black people launched a newspaper intended to give the black population a national weekly. Called the *National Leader*, and with six hundred thousand dollars in capital, it was run by Claude Lewis and Ragan A. Henry. Lewis, an experienced journalist of national reputation, was editor and publisher, and Henry, an attorney, was owner. Henry had tried to buy the Philadelphia *Tribune* several years before when it was encountering financial difficulties. When its owners would not sell he decided on a venture of his own, basing it in Philadelphia.

The serious weekly, well written and printed, newsy looking and readable, was the first national black newspaper for black readers. It was wholly devoted to a national outlook and was not a modified version of a city weekly put on the national market.

In two years it had failed. The factors against its success were the same as existed with all black publications since *Freedom's Journal*: not enough subscribers, insufficient advertising, and too expensive an area to cover even once a week.

High in quality as it was, it drew only 40,000 subscribers. Advertisers made the usual explanations. They could reach many of the same readers through the local black press. In cities with well-educated black residents these readers were more readily reached in the local white dailies.[3]

Midway through the *National Leader*'s second year, trying to avoid its being closed, Henry and Lewis issued it monthly. But early in 1985 the owner had to give up. *Editor & Publisher* quoted Ragan Henry as saying, "the *National Leader* has been 100 percent supported by me, and I am not in a position to do it anymore. When we started there were seventeen investors. At the end there was only one—me."

The historical background of some of the older major papers was related in Chapter 3. Events, however, have changed the nature of some of these papers in recent years. It is important to examine them as they were in the late 1970s and the 1980s.

The Chicago *Defender*

The mother hen of the Sengstacke papers, a chain sometimes described by its enemies as an octopus, this four-day tabloid strongly resembles the New York *Daily News* in its typography and in its variety of feature content. For fifty years a standard-size paper, the *Defender* turned tabloid in 1956. Conceiving of itself as an important source of national news about black America, as indeed it is, the *Defender* carries United Press International (UPI) copy, but much more Chicago area and midwestern news of special interest to its readers and not often to be found in the general press. Its editorial page is moderate in its political position and liberal on certain problems affecting the lives of blacks, such as housing, equality in employment opportunities, and education.

Some of the editorial campaigns staged by the *Defender*'s editors include successfully persuading the Coca-Cola management to abandon a national beauty contest because blacks and other nonwhites were not admitted to the competition. The paper accused U.S. Army officials of seeking to discourage blacks from enlisting for fear, as the

Defender saw it, that blacks would dominate this branch of the military establishment. Years before the concern shown in the mid-1980s about the lack of black managers among the leaders of various major sports aggregations, the *Defender*'s sports editor was calling for black managers or third base coaches.

The weekly national edition, more so than the daily, tends to carry greater quantities of editorialized and publicity copy, particularly in special supplements, such as career guides, wherein every college or business buying space also is discussed in editorial copy

5.2. A trio of powerful weeklies.

obviously emanating from the institution's publicity or public relations department. The regular pages of one issue, for example, carried a three-quarter column story about an oil company and its education plans, including considerable promotion of the company as such; it also offered, in the middle of an otherwise newsy page, a clearly promotional story about grass (the kind walked on, not smoked), coming from an acoustical firm. Finally, hardly exceptional in American journalism are the many columns devoted to publicity for and gossip about entertainers.

The paper carries about 30 percent advertising copy. Its circulation in 1987 was 27,611 for the daily (Monday through Thursday) and 32,519 for the Saturday edition.

The Atlanta *Daily World*

This paper is a family venture like the *Defender*, long identified with the Scott family. As a daily, it is the older of the two, having been made into a daily in 1932, whereas the *Defender* did not go on that schedule until 1956.

The Scott who founded it was William Alexander, who, like Abbott, decided to start his publication in a depression. The *World* first appeared in 1928. Scott was not destined to remain with it long, for he was assassinated in 1934 at age thirty-one. By then, however, he had developed something of a journalistic empire and was engaged in real estate as well. He had also contributed a plan of having in another city a staff that gathered news for a local paper printed in the home city, in this instance Atlanta.

The Scott in charge thereafter was Cornelius A. Scott, a Mississippian born in 1908, and a former student at both Morehouse and Kansas universities. Under his direction the *World* has been consistently conservative on political issues. Lomax, in one of his books some years ago, called the *World* "the one exception" among the papers that generally have supported the black revolt. He labels it "highly-respected, rock-ribbed Republican" and notes that in 1960 it carried a double-column editorial asking, "Is This Type of Action Necessary in This Case?" in which it criticized students who had organized an economic boycott of white merchants who refused to hire blacks as anything but menials, although their shops were in the black neighborhoods.[4]

A standard-size paper, it is at the heart of the Scott group. Much of its content therefore appears in other papers as well, including editorials, columns, and some news stories. The editorials frequently are on national rather than local issues.

The *World* has been the training ground for numerous black journalists who have gone on to prominence as writers and editors of other newspapers as well as magazines; some are known for their work as publicists. The paper was issued daily in normal times. Frequency was cut during a 1969-1970 strike. It appears to have little news, but that is an erroneous conclusion, for its four copies a week should be matched against one issue of a weekly by each of the other Atlanta black papers. It has maintained a fixed circulation of from 20,000 to 30,000 daily for a number of years. This four-day schedule, however, makes its claim of being a daily weak, as dailies usually are published at least six days a week.

The *Afro-American*

When the American Society of Journalism School Administrators made its annual award to a newspaper or magazine in 1969, it went for the first time to a black publication; the award had been given annually since 1946. It went to the *Afro-American*: "In recognition of the distinguished record of a newspaper which has served a predominantly black community and which has actively engaged in community service." The paper received nearly three times the vote of the second choice.

The strong vote for this paper, one of the few semiweeklies in black journalism, was earned not only by the headquarters edition but also by four others. The Murphy family ran the corporation for many years. All its papers are standard- or broadsheet-size. Like most other leaders, the *Afro* contains much to read, although its copy is more closely edited and its pages more carefully planned and coordinated than those of many of its rivals, if not as well printed. It gives considerably more coverage to foreign, especially African, news. Substantial stories received from UPI and its own staffers and correspondents report such major events in other countries as changes in government, new policies, and conflicts between them; the discrimination against blacks in Africa is emphasized.

Afro editorial pages are crammed with reading matter and cartoons, often offering as many as six editorials, supplemented by signed columns. The paper also allots far more space to letters than usually is found in black papers, although with so many editions it probably receives more as well. Service and opinion columns appear on the page opposite editorial. Because of its various regional or city editions space is given in the national version to news from those areas. This regional news is supplemented with correspondence from

Atlanta, Detroit, and other cities with large black populations. Society and sports news occupy what seems like excessive space, although church and other special news is not slighted.

The tendency to keep a paper in a family is again illustrated by
this group. In 1986 it was managed by a member of the fourth generation of Murphys. John H. Murphy III retired in that year as president
of the company after forty-nine years in office, serving also as chairman of the board in the preceding twenty-five years. His successor as
president was Frances M. Draper, a granddaughter of the late Carl
Murphy. Her management team consisted of Arthur Murphy and
John Oliver. Another member of the family, George Murphy, Jr., at
one time editor of the Washington edition, died in 1987. He had
begun his career with this group of papers in the 1920s on the matrix
edition in Baltimore.

The New York *Daily Challenge*

The youngest of the three black dailies, the
Challenge, is unlike its companions in various ways. It is a tabloid, as
is the Chicago *Defender*, but the Atlanta *Daily World* is a broadsheet.
Much local news, some of it routine, appears in the Chicago and
Atlanta dailies. The quantity of local news in the daily papers in one
week is considerable. The chief difference with the *Challenge* is that it
avoids most routine stories and offers New York area news of greater
importance in more detail.

The New York paper, if the copies of the final edition are typical,
does not take editorial positions. The publisher, Thomas H. Watkins,
Jr., has a boxed column which is mainly factual and is concerned with
such matters as housing grants, with no judgments expressed. Opinion columns are not used (a policy shared with the *World*).

Human interest stories are rare, for the *Challenge* concentrates
on significant news, although it has space for entertainment and
fashion stories and pictures that are purely promotional. Sports news
fills three or four pages.

The paper carries two regular pages that are in contrast to the
serious tone of most others in an issue. One contains astrological
predictions and games for children; the other is called "Numbers and
Games." The latter is possibly the most popular portion of the paper.

The *Challenge*, which is affiliated with another black newspaper,
the weekly New York *Recorder*, was founded in 1972, with Watkins as
publisher. The offices are in the Bedford-Stuyvesant neighborhood of
Brooklyn. Its circulation is by far the highest among the dailies,

reaching more than 46,000 in 1986. Circulation is partly paid and partly free.

The New York *Amsterdam News*, in covering the 1972 press conference held in connection with the issue of the first edition of the *Challenge*, quoted Watkins as saying, "This is the opportunity Black people here have wished for too many years. We can no longer afford to wait until seven days to read about what is transpiring in major Black communities."

The New York *Amsterdam News*

The *Amsterdam*, as it is often called, is one of the most widely known and oldest of the major black newspapers of the nation. It also has been one of the most troubled in its history, especially in recent decades.

Since 1963 it has had a contract with the American Newspaper Guild (ANG), the first of its kind in black journalism. The ANG is a labor union of editorial and other nontypographical employees. Strikes have occurred several times. The paper is also unusual because its circulation is attested to by the Audit Bureau of Circulations (ABC), the leading agency for such verification. Although a few other papers are able to meet the requirements of the ABC, many are circulated free (sometimes called controlled circulation) or are certified by agencies other than the ABC.

From 1936 to 1971 the paper was run and owned by Dr. C. B. Powell, a physician deeply involved as well with insurance, funeral, and loan services businesses. In 1971 he sold the paper to an all-black group that included Percy E. Sutton, then Manhattan Borough president, and Clarence B. Jones, an officer of a major stockbrokerage firm and an attorney. They paid $2 million for it. Jones became publisher and the largest stockholder. In 1972 James L. Hicks was appointed executive editor, a position he also held between 1955 and 1966. He remained until 1977, then edited the New York *Voice*. He died in 1986.

By 1975 Sutton had sold his stock, which was only second in amount to that held by Jones, in the midst of statements that he had too much control over the paper or that he was being blamed for political positions which he did not hold but which the paper did. That same year dissension broke out, there were financial difficulties, and various editors and reporters resigned. The crusades in which the paper had been engaging were tempered and more space than earlier was given to gossip and political promotion. But there also was better

5.3. Other large regional weeklies (in 1988 the Miami *Times* became a broadsheet).

coverage of such news as weddings and obituaries, neglected by the large white dailies of the city.

Until 1979 the *Amsterdam* had been a standard- or broadsheet-size weekly. That year it became a tabloid; new editors promised to print more interpretive copy similar in type to that found in the nation's newsmagazines, a policy now followed in cities of heavy competition by other black papers or the regular white press. Internal disputes continued, however.

A major strike hit the paper in 1983, when thirty-eight employees walked off the job because management officials tried to stem reported heavy losses by instituting a shorter work week and announcing salary cuts. The strike went on for months, benefiting the paper's rivals in New York.

The main fight in the later 1980s has been against the city administration, with front page editorials to support the campaign. The *Amsterdam News* continues to sell considerable advertising space, especially in the classified sections, where as many as five or six pages will be crowded with small ads. Although some of the other large weeklies or semiweeklies have almost totally abolished the sale of space to palm readers, spiritualists, and astrologers, the *Amsterdam News* is heavy with such accounts.

Once a paper with many columns, it now uses such outside writers sparingly. Today a Saturday tabloid, it runs color as background for the page one flag or nameplate. It remains a large paper but actually not as big as it seems, since it is the equivalent of a twenty-four-page standard-size publication.

W. A. Tatum was chairman of the board, chief executive officer, and editor in chief in the late 1980s.

The *New Pittsburgh Courier*

The *New Pittsburgh Courier* was not always called that. The *New* is a relatively recent addition, intended to let the world know that the paper has been reborn. Originally it was a strongly crusading weekly, known for its disputatious writers and its uncompromising devotion to the improvement of the condition of the black people of the United States.

It still is a champion of theirs, but a portion of the battle having been won and progress having been made in other campaigns, it no longer is as inflammatory as it was in its first thirty years.

The *Courier* was not one of the Sengstacke papers (the publisher of such leading publications as the Chicago *Defender* and the *Michigan Chronicle*) most of its life. The *Courier* was alone for many years and fought its battles under its own power. James Baldwin, the late novelist and a close observer of the black press, considered the *Courier* the only black paper worthy of unqualified praise forty years ago. He considered it a "high class paper" and "the best of the lot."

From the standpoint of broader coverage the *Courier* is a better newspaper, if a less influential one. It is generous in its allotment of space to local news and features and to material in departmentalized pages. Photographs are numerous and usually well printed. Publicity enters its columns as it does with virtually all papers, regardless of racial origin.

The *Courier*, like the big papers of Chicago, New York, Philadelphia, Baltimore, and Atlanta, is a historically important one commanding attention because of the tradition behind it. Since the publication of a biography of Robert L. Vann, cofounder of the paper in 1910, his influence is better realized. Not since his time (he died in 1940) has the paper had among its writers such provocative and stimulating authors as George S. Schuyler, P. L. Prattis, Benjamin E. Mays, Bayard Rustin, Roy Wilkins, and Vann himself.

Its circulation once was in six figures but today is only a fragment of that (30,000). This results from the same causes that explain the losses of its fellow pioneers: television as a substitute for reading along with other entertainments such as sports and movies, the rising cost of operations, and the continued unwillingness of enough advertisers to invest in such papers.

The Cleveland *Call and Post*

Armistead S. Pride, in expressing pungent opinions of the leading black papers in an article, once described the *Call and Post* as a paper that "provides bread-and-butter coverage." It is this concern for local news that has kept it a leading black weekly. At times the handling of such news has bordered on the sensational. Here are a few sample headlines: a five-column two-liner, "Three Men Killed/In Love Triangle"; and the main streamer over the flag, "Nationalists, Pastors Meet on Terror Rumors."

Editorially it has kept an eye on the local scene more than some of the other medium-size papers; these often are elaborate and far more thorough than the usual opinion writing in these weeklies. Local columnists are featured as well as national writers. Much of the reputation for excellent coverage comes from the extensive society, club, women's, and entertainment pages and the generous use of pictures on them. Typographically the *Call and Post* is among the more modern papers, with a somewhat streamlined makeup for its standard-size pages.

Whether it is because of the deaths of its two noted leaders, publisher and editor William O. Walker, and his right-hand man, managing editor Charles Loeb, the Cleveland paper seems not as carefully planned and made-up as it used to be, although typographically it is improved, especially on page one, which is neater and cleaner. Spiritualism and fortune-telling ads continue to be accepted.

The Philadelphia *Tribune*

A semiweekly, the *Tribune* celebrated its one hundredth anniversary in 1984. It is the oldest continuously published black general newspaper in the United States. Unquestionably one of the major papers, it is of professional quality, with an attractively planned front page. It provides detailed news coverage, the stories closely edited as a rule; often this reporting crowds the paper with many short news accounts. So many varieties of headline sizes and types are used that the pages beyond the first are not always easy to penetrate. It has standard-size pages.

Society, sports, and youth materials supplement the several pages of general local news, as does copy from syndicates. The editorial policy is hard-hitting but moderate in tone. The *Tribune* reflects the views of its late publisher E. Washington Rhodes, who believed that such newspapers should crusade for black rights. It has established various programs to aid blacks in the Philadelphia area.

The Norfolk *Journal and Guide*

Color generally has little place in the national papers, but the Norfolk *Journal and Guide* does use a tint in its nameplate on the front page and occasionally in advertising in its home edition. It is therefore a quickly recognizable paper just as the *New Pittsburgh Courier* is easily spotted by the tinted stock for the wraparound pages. Like most of its peers, the *Journal and Guide* is standard-size. It is newsy. A reader may sometimes be confused by the many small and large headlines, but must be impressed with the paper's tone of bursting with information.

The *Journal and Guide* carries much locally generated news as well as wire copy from UPI and correspondence from numerous small midsouthern towns. Pictures are used generously, but, as in so many papers, too often they are of heads, of two persons shaking hands, or of a line of people facing the camera. Special features, in which the black newspaper often is weak because of lack of staff, are more numerous in this paper than usual, and are concerned with individuals as well as with group activities.

The Miami *Times*

This highly successful weekly is a paper that has been in the same family for many years. It was founded by H. S. Sigismund Reeves. Since his time it has been run by Garth Reeves, Sr.,

Garth Reeves, Jr., and Rachel J. Reeves. Ms. Reeves, the publisher's daughter, is executive editor and now generally in charge.

In many ways the *Times* is extraordinary beyond its use of the latest equipment. It has more editorial copy than most weeklies. In 1988 it was running to thirty-six broadsheet pages each week. It is so orderly in makeup and loaded with so much reading matter yet so easily read that it is a model for others in black journalism. It goes full color every week and considers itself the first such paper to follow that policy.

The opinion pages carry from three to six editorials and another three to six op-ed columns, half by syndicated writers such as William Raspberry, Norman Hill, and Chuck Stone. Editorial opinions are forthright and well written, as is most of the editorial copy in the paper.

The *Times* also is one of the few papers whose circulation is verified by the ABC; in 1988, it went beyond 27,000 copies, an increase since the year before.

A thirty-six-page issue carries around seventeen pages of mostly local but some national ads. About one-third of a page of ads is for

5.4. Midwestern and southern leaders.

spiritualists. Full-page copy for local grocery stores and car show-rooms appears frequently.

In 1987 the management installed in the front office a new Unisys computer and went on line with Pro-MACS software. This installation gave the paper the latest technology in ad billing, circulation, general ledger, and accounts operations.

Publisher Garth C. Reeves, Sr., a 1940 graduate in printing of Florida A. & M. University (FAMU), has gone through the ranks of the paper in the past half-century. Several organizations have honored him for his work in behalf of his race.

Reeves has served on the board of directors of several black colleges. In 1987 FAMU benefited when Reeves and the Knight Foundation made major contributions to a campaign to establish a million-dollar Garth C. Reeves, Sr., Eminent Scholar Chair in Journalism and Graphic Arts at his alma mater. The campaign was to receive a matching grant from the state to complete the million.

The Indianapolis *Recorder*

Another city weekly approaching its one hundredth anniversary is the standard-size Indianapolis *Recorder*. Known for decades for its devotion to covering the news of the Indiana metropolis, it maintains its reputation, sometimes dramatically.

Its respect for news is shared with its liking for many pictures. When in 1987 an Air Force pilot left his plane as it was about to crash and it struck a large hotel near the city's airport, the *Recorder* ran two page-one stories with jumps and two pictures. Inside were five more photos, all the work of a staff photographer.

Even more fully reported, in a manner reminiscent of Robert S. Abbott during the early days of the Chicago *Defender*, was the story of a local teenager shot while in police custody in a car. The circumstances of his death by gunshot were unusual, for his hands were cuffed behind his back, no finger marks were on the gun, and he was shot in the temple. The first-day coverage beginning under a streamer on the first page included an editorial, two news stories, and a related picture. Inside was a picture of the teenager and an interview with his mother, as well as a statement calling for an investigation signed by the head of the NAACP in Indianapolis. The next week there was a follow-up.

A Saturday weekly, with an ABC circulation of more than 11,000, it offers considerable reading matter as well as a comparatively heavy advertising budget. The percentage in two 1987 issues ran to sixty in one and fifty in another.

The editorial and op-ed pages present a half-dozen columns and long editorials by staff or guest writers. Original feature stories, dozens of short news accounts, a poetry corner, a comic strip that is comic and not soap opera, a half-page of letters (some overlong), two pages of sports, several of lifestyle and society, three of church material, and one of business also appear. Out of tone with other content is an astrology column; obvious publicity stories are used as well.

Founded in 1895 by George P. Stewart, Sr., it remained in the Stewart family when he died in 1924. The publisher in 1987 was George J. Thompson and the editor Eunice Trotter. The paper has a staff of six editors, two general assignment reports, and eight on the business side.

Major Papers and Their Stance

The position a black paper or a chain or group of such papers should take in the racial situation of today is one of the major problems facing owners and publishers (see Chapter 12). Here it is enough to note that the large newspapers that support the ideal of justice for black citizens in all matters are impatient, both with the white community and with the tactics of violent militants. Those that are cautious, noncommittal, or silent have experienced circulation problems. The highest circulations of all were held by the two papers that took strong stands.

The competition from the white press insofar as that press has stepped up its coverage of the more prominent racial news and issues of the day, and the rising popularity of several black magazines of national distribution, such as *Ebony* and *Jet*, have pushed the major papers somewhat out of the race to cover countrywide racial stories and caused them to bear down harder on the local scene.

In 1970, writing about the major newspapers, L. F. Palmer, Jr., said that "the end of the national black newspaper is clearly in sight."[5] He was supported in this view by John Jordan, then acting publisher of the Norfolk *Journal and Guide*, who was quoted as saying: "We can't afford field men any longer, and transportation is too complicated and expensive. It is virtually impossible to provide adequate coverage of the national scene anyway." Palmer also pointed to the statement of an unnamed black editor in Chicago who observed that the four black-oriented radio stations there reached more listeners in an hour than the black paper had readers in a month. The support for such a general statement was not made clear. Nor does the statement compare the depth of attention for radio versus newspeople. On the other hand, minds can be made up and action taken quickly through the impact of broadcasts in contrast to the slower effects of reading newspapers.

Fifteen years later, however, the black major papers are still in business, although some have been weakened.

The Black Daily

In writing about the newspapers serving a group of citizens which for years has constituted about 10 percent of their country's population, one would expect to be able to report that there are many papers that come off the press from five to seven times a week. But today only three daily newspapers are being published. A few black papers have gained attention as dailies over the years, but the daily has been a losing investment for most black publishers.

With around 1,750 dailies for whites, including several for the business and other specialized worlds, the few for black readers is surprising but understandable. In the history of this press there has been no time when more than three or four dailies were issued in the same period. More than fifty have been attempted but today there are only the Chicago *Defender*, the Atlanta *Daily World* and the New York *Daily Challenge*. Perhaps the black society in America does not want or need more than two or three such dailies. But this is a physically large country; white papers, although their coverage of black citizens and their activities and interests has improved, still handle only the more obvious stories and, in many communities, do not cover even those.

Pride, the historian of the black newspaper, reported in 1950 that forty-five black dailies had been published in the preceding century, of which he had been able to identify forty-four.[6] Such papers naturally were issued in communities with large black populations. New Orleans had seen several efforts, as did Dayton, Ohio, and Washington, D.C.; others were founded in Cairo, Illinois; Knoxville, Tennessee; Roanoke, Virginia; Newport News, Virginia; New York City; and Muskogee, Oklahoma. Since 1950 a few more have been attempted; all but one are gone.

An early daily usually considered the first was the New Orleans

Tribune. It began as a triweekly in 1864 but soon was converted into a six-day daily. Published in both English and French, it also was known as *La Tribune de la Nouvelle Orleans.* Because it was the voice of the state's Republican party it was considered influential. Allan Morrison, of *Ebony*'s staff, has recorded that it campaigned for weekly wages for ex-slaves; was highly critical of certain Southern representatives in Congress; asked for the ballot for freedmen; and foresaw persecution of blacks when Federal troops were withdrawn from the state. It was too early, perhaps, for a crusading paper to succeed in New Orleans, and its owner, Dr. Louis Charles Roundanez, a physician, had to suspend its publication in 1868; he revived it but it ceased permanently in 1896.

5.5. The black dailies of the 1980s.

Reasons for Failure

Black dailies fail mainly for economic reasons. Raising sufficient capital is one problem, making a sufficient profit to meet the always increasing costs is an even more formidable one. Until recent years profits were difficult if not impossible to make because of the comparatively low literacy rate and the small incomes of black readers. Advertising income could not absorb costs; circulation income, while high, had a ceiling. These obstacles have existed for years, and only now are lessening. That they persist, even if slightly less overwhelming for some papers, is all the more to be regretted because by now more well trained and able writers, advertising personnel, and others needed for staffs might be attracted if there were more dailies offering adequate salaries.

Chuck (C. Sumner) Stone, who was editor in chief of the Chicago *Daily Defender*, once advised the National Newspaper Publishers Association members to "go daily" because "as long as all Negro newspapers are weeklies, we can never compete as equals in a society controlled by daily newspapers." This advice was logical, but it did not show how to finance such dailies.[7]

In addition to Stone's motive there also is, in a day of electronic journalism, the need to communicate more often with readers than weekly or even semiweekly. Not only to provide information unobtainable elsewhere but also to set before readers points of view rarely found in the general press, a strong daily press for blacks is desirable.

The way publishers sometimes move into the costly area of daily black journalism may explain the failures as being more than economic. At times it is merely well meaning but inexperienced activity. This point is illustrated by the Washington *Daily Sun*, brought out in the national capital in 1968. Eugene Melvin Garner, a Washington lawyer, published it first on October 30 as a morning daily tabloid. It became the city's only black daily. Clearly Washington is a rich market, for the population is predominantly black. If a black daily can be sustained in any American city, it would seem to be in Washington. The *Sun* sold for seven cents a copy. Within less than two months it was showing signs of hasty production. Changed to standard size, it was far from comparable to the other black daily papers of the country or its semiweekly competitor, the *Afro-American*. Some editorials obviously were no more than news releases. Numerous technical errors appeared: pages were misnumbered, headlines garbled. Almost all headlines, where there were any, were in typewriter capitals; only front page streamers were easily read. The *Sun* was produced by offset. When not carefully used that method can produce an amateurish-looking paper. The entire edition offered six pages. UPI and Negro Press International copy was used but little original material appeared except on page one. Almost no hard news was reported on inside pages; advertising occupied one page.

It was no surprise, then, when the *Sun* soon set permanently.

A few publishers have started papers or continued some well established national ones as semiweeklies. Both the Washington and Baltimore editions of the *Afro-American* come out twice a week; the Philadelphia *Tribune* goes to its readers every Tuesday and Friday.

But for all its life the American black newspaper press has been essentially a weekly type of journalism, made up largely of separate, independent papers. A successful daily is an exceptional publication. Publishers now appear to be more interested in groups and chains of papers.

Local Newspaper Voices

The black newspaper is tiny so far as circulation is concerned. Even one of the major weeklies or semiweeklies, any of the trio of dailies and of the few monthly papers is a pygmy by comparison with the standard press of the United States or of many of the world's other nations.

One Japanese daily has a circulation of more than eight million; another has in excess of seven million every day. One Soviet paper has eleven million, another ten million, and two others have eight million each. One British paper has nearly four million every day, another five million.

Not even the largest U.S. daily of general circulation is in the running with these European and Asian papers so far as distribution is concerned. What is more, the European and Asian figures are for paid circulation; the huge numbers claimed by Soviet publications are somewhat suspect because government pressure is used to enhance distribution, which often is free.

The largest U.S. paper, the *Wall Street Journal*, hovers around two million copies a day, in a nation vastly larger than the United Kingdom or Japan. Two others, the New York *Times* and the New York *Daily News*, are slightly under that figure. For a time one black paper was into the six figure list, the now defunct *Mohammed Speaks* (later called the *Bilalian*), which did reach 600,000, but it was suspect because its distributors often had to eat their unsold copies, as the expression goes in the newspaper business; i.e., pay for the unsold copies.

But even if there was a black paper today that sold or even gave away a half million copies it would hardly be comparable to these multimillion sheets in other nations. The largest papers in black journalism are those formed into groups (see Chapter 1).

There seems little point, however, in carrying comparisons any further, for circulations have been decreasing among the black papers in recent years even while the black population is growing in numbers and literacy (the ability to read and write) is nearly total in the population over age twenty.[1] The strength of the black press is in the moderate-size local papers, of which there are more than two hundred. They are locally owned, independent, and sometimes equal some of the chains or groups in circulation size and perhaps in local political and social influence as well, because they are of local family ownership and have managers who are from the community. Circulations of 3,000 to 15,000 are commonplace among these papers.

The black newspaper, then, is for the most part a local voice, with mainly a local outreach, for even the national newspapers have their core circulations in the communities from which they spring, issuing city and other localized editions separate from those for wider distribution. A good many retain the tone of personal journalism so common in the nineteenth century in the press as a whole. For in some towns and cities the black community newspaper office, like the newspaper building of the country village of the past, is the gathering or meeting place for black residents. The readers bring their problems to the proprietor. This practice is especially common among black people because many have nowhere else to go. A church or club may provide a haven, but such institutions are not often prepared to advise on such practical matters as taxes. If the owner wishes, the paper can crusade for its readers, for he knows many personally.

At the same time they discharge this social function, the small papers nevertheless are business operations. For many years they have been speaking out loudly for the liberties due black citizens. Such leadership has been accentuated in recent decades, chiefly because of the increased interest in the life and culture of the black American citizens by both blacks and whites. What the early papers said is becoming better known because of the attempts made in recent years by the microfilm makers to recall from long forgotten files some of the early publications. The historians someday may have a better idea of the black life of the nineteenth and twentieth centuries by reading the black papers, large and small, now being preserved far better than they were. An anonymous prophet wrote in 1955:

> Negro editors may not know it as a body, but it is one of the
> inescapable truths of our time that the Negro weeklies of today will be

prized possessions of the future and will be religiously sought out for the record of the Negro's thinking, his movements in a flexible society, and his manner of encountering a rebuff. The editor may go unheralded and unrewarded in this hour but the perennial monument to his name is a carefully preserved . . . file of his daily labors.[2]

The Mélange of Formats

Future researchers will find a mélange of formats, styles of writing, and viewpoints when they examine the community weeklies that exist in the shadows of the larger papers. They will learn that in Texas, for instance, in the 1960s there existed a group of vigorous if not always well-produced papers, some energetic in aims, other clumsily written and edited, and still others sedate and substantial in their news coverage. Clustered near major cities in other states, weeklies will turn up, some commercial, some mere political tracts. In Chicago *Defender* territory, for example, the historian will find several small papers covering news of the black residents in the suburban towns.

The rationale for many a community paper was described by Lesley Kimber, at one time publisher of the Fresno *California Advocate*. His paper, with a circulation of 8,000, was established in 1968 "to bring out the positive things," he told a Sigma Delta Chi group. The white papers, he said, print only such black news as crime rates in the black community. Further, he said, "financially, the paper has been a disaster but it has been a gratifying experience to see how the people of West Fresno have responded to our efforts."[3]

The publishers of these papers, devoted as they are to being local voices, were encouraged to launch their publications by the improvement in living conditions of some of their potential readers after the 1960s. Both employment and income were up for the black population.

But a larger audience is no guarantee of publishing stability. The publication must win the support of enough of that audience to survive. For a time it appeared that the black press was headed for serious problems of survival (see Chapter 4), but since the civil rights movement and the black revolution against many white institutions, several of the small local voices have gained strength and have been joined by dozens of newcomers.

The importance of these local voices is impressed on the white community by such incidents as the effective boycotting by black citizens of institutions in their neighborhoods which they believe treat them unfairly, in which activities they usually are aided by their own papers. One example was described at length by D. Parke Gibson, a prominent black public relations and advertising man. Philadelphia residents conducted a campaign, which he called an economic withdrawal, against various oil companies and food chains. Gibson noted that "the consumer campaigns . . . received little, if any, publicity in the white-oriented media." But they did receive wide exposure in the black media. Finally, one of the white papers, the *Evening Bulletin* (now defunct), was chosen for "selective patronage" because it had no black truck drivers or blacks "employed in any numbers in sensitive positions behind a desk in the editorial or business department." It took seven weeks, but the company complied by hiring blacks.[4]

Involvement or cooperation with such activities increases the element of danger in publishing a black community paper. Although black journalism never has been exactly a placid occupation, it is free in these times of the sorts of hazards which haunted the early publishers, whose plants were burned or who themselves were murdered.

Policies of Local Papers

Some local papers have their credos and platforms just as do the larger nationals like the Chicago *Defender* and the *Afro-American*. They express aims similar to those of other local voices, such as these:

Madison (Wisconsin) *Sun*: "From rising to setting sun — all over the world, our policy is truth, righteousness, justice and charity for all."

The Orlando (Florida) *Times*: "Looking at the World from a Black Perspective."

The St. Louis *Argus* and the Miami *Times* both run The Black Press Creed:

> The Black Press believes that America can best lead the world away from racial and national antagonism when it affords to every person, regardless of race, color or creed, their human and legal rights.

Hating no person, and fearing no person, the Black press strives to help every person in the firm belief that all are hurt as long as anyone is held back.

The Charlotte (North Carolina) *Post*: "The Voice of the Black Community."

The Portland (Oregon) *Scanner*: "No Other Can Speak for Us."

Norfolk (Virginia) *Journal and Guide*: "Dedicated to the cause of the people . . . no good cause shall lack a champion and evil shall not thrive unopposed."

The Washington (D.C.) *New Observer*: "Covering the News Today for a Better Tomorrow."

Tallahassee (Florida) *Capital Outlook*: "Your Community Weekly Newspaper." The slogan that has lived longest, however, is that of the nation's first black newspaper: *Freedom's Journal*. With Biblical words, it reads: "Righteousness Exalteth a Nation."

It may not be unduly cynical to observe, however, that, as with certain white papers that announce such policies, they are violated in some instances, simply perhaps because newspapers are products of the fallible human mind. The fidelity to their ideals may also be a matter of interpretation. A certain white Mississippi paper, for example, applied its aims in its editorials in ways which, from another point of view, can be considered inconsistent with them. It editorializes against northerners coming to the South to take part in civil rights activities, and called school integration hopeless several years before the federal government actions of 1970 appeared to be canceling gains toward educational integration. Black power was called, in 1968, "just another part of the scheme to widen and continue to promote hatred in the minds and hearts of Negroes toward white people and is lock, stock, and barrel a part of the communist scheme for using the Negro in its revolutionary plan to overthrow the present government."[5]

Life and Death

Small papers are born in large numbers; most die, but a few continue here and there in their own modest formats. Among the new, smaller standard or commercial papers, i.e., the weeklies or biweeklies that seek to be community news organs and not shrill street-corner political papers, a number have survived. They exhibit a briskness of tone and a forthrightness of attitude and policy. Because of them it is possible to say that a new force has been added to the small city black press. It may be the result of a greater push toward commercial success but it also has been in the direction of providing for opinions not so often heard in this journalism since the nineteenth-century days of strong protest.

The experiences of owners show that keeping new papers alive is a serious problem. It is virtually impossible without heavy political, academic, or other financial support that must be available for several years or until the paper catches on sufficiently to acquire the revenue needed for survival from advertising. New papers sometimes are launched with the expectation that the recent desire to make black enterprises succeed will shorten the waiting and operating loss period, but this assumption requires management abilities that are not always available.

Owners of chains can absorb losses when buying or starting papers for as much as a year or two while the older, companion papers carry the burden of the start-up.

If *Freedom's Journal* were to be revived today, with slavery gone and material conditions better (even if not satisfactory by any means), it would not last perhaps even the short time it did. The successful and influential black local voices are those that seek not only to arouse their readers to do something about the injustices of the day, but also are service papers that give readers a substantial budget of news and facts that support opinions.

The Conventional Weeklies

The quasi-revolutionary paper that existed in the 1960s and 1970s is virtually gone. But still with us is the more or less conventional paper unfavored with advertising, ill-supported by readers (perhaps for lack of money), published where there may not even be enough possible readers or produced by an owner seeking influence in a community.

Often papers combine these circumstances and outlive them. In Rochester, New York, is a bimonthly, *Frederick Douglass Voice*, once the Rochester *Voice*. Douglass, it will be recalled, published the *North Star* and *Frederick Douglass' Paper* from that city. This present-day publication asserts its intention of carrying on in his tradition. The story of its life is that of so many other small black papers, past and present. Most of the time after 1934, when it was founded, its owner, Howard Coles, has done other kinds of work for a living. Circulation is 2,000 per issue in a city with a sixty-five thousand black population.

Vignettes of Individual Papers

Descriptions and evaluations of certain papers in this local voice group are even more essential for an understanding of them than for the major newspapers. The big papers have received some attention elsewhere, but these local voices have won little notice from commentators on the black press. Because it is necessary to be selective, many worthy publications have been passed over in what follows. The papers included are considered representative by the author. To provide geographical balance, they have been selected from different areas of the nation. These also will reflect some of the local variations in journalistic fashions and black concerns.

The *East Side News*

Big cities usually have small neighborhood newspapers, variously called shoppers, throwaways, and community papers. Most are free and must exist, consequently, on their advertising revenue.

They are enormously different in quality. Usually they publish publicity releases unashamedly and do little or no original reporting. They do not seek to compete with but merely to supplement the regular daily or weekly papers of their cities. They are useful for their many classified ads of garage sales and various services.

The world of black journalism also has such papers. They are of varying degrees of quality. Some of the larger weeklies dubbing themselves community papers give most of their circulation away, a sensible procedure since it is costly to keep records and make collections. They face the drawback, however, that advertisers are not convinced of the value of their circulation, knowing that they can reach some of the black readers through the standard local dailies and weeklies. And readers receiving a publication without paying for it tend to think less of it than one they pay for.

Cleveland, Ohio, has the powerful *Call and Post*, a veteran weekly with editions as well in Columbus and Cincinnati. The Cleveland version has a circulation of more than 40,000, verified by the Audit Bureau of Circulations (ABC).

The city also has a weekly community paper of 10,000 free circulation called the *East Side News*. It is distributed to homes in more than a dozen neighborhoods or towns on the east side. The paper is one of ten of the community type joined in the Neighborhood Community Press Association of Greater Cleveland. They have united to make it easier to sell space, a sort of small scale Amalgamated Newspapers, Inc., which serves the *Call and Post* and many of the other large black papers, giving them access to national advertising.

6.1. Prominent community newspapers.

6.2. Harry Alexander, the late publisher, Cleveland *Call and Post* (left) and Ulysses Glen, publisher, Cleveland *East Side News.*

East Side News was founded as a biweekly in 1980 by five men, including Ulysses Glen, who was named publisher from the outset. Glen long had the ambition to have such a paper and has developed it from a throwaway to a constantly insecure community publication carrying some news not found even in the dominating and professional black weekly, the *Call and Post.* Glen was a professional boxer at one time, became a teacher at Cuyahoga Community College, earned a master's degree in journalism from Kent State University, and then launched the paper.

Since August 1984, it has been a weekly. Standard-size, with seven columns, it carries considerable local news. A small amount of it is sports, cooking, and entertainment; there also are columns devoted to health, religion, and other specialties. Crime news is played down and as usual in such papers, publicity releases and obvious puffery are printed, most of it harmless. All advertising is local and occupies about 30 percent of each issue. Editorials are not in the content. Photographs, while essentially mug shots, sometimes are of action. Occasional features deal with activities of the NAACP and other groups; these come largely from public relations offices.

The *East Side News* can be characterized as essentially a paper containing neighborhood news but not interested in exerting a strong political influence.

The Cleveland *Crime Reporter*

Another Cleveland community paper has a completely different aim than other local voices. It is the Cleveland *Crime Reporter*, a free monthly tabloid devoted to reporting crime news and supporting police efforts to decrease criminal activity in the city.

Some typical headlines: "Children left alone in roach-infested house, mother jailed"; "Woman, 81, knocked from wheelchair, beaten and robbed by two burglars"; "Lone gunman sneaks into victim's unlocked car, kidnaps and robs him."

A half-page headed "Burglars" reports more than a dozen accounts. Almost all of another page is given to somewhat longer crime stories under the heading "Domestic Violence." On the last page of this 12-page paper are twenty photographs, half of them of black men and women, all wanted criminals. The Cleveland Crime Stoppers organization in a full-page announcement offers "up to $2,000 in cash for information leading to the arrest . . . of these suspected felons."

More advertisements may occupy three to four pages an issue, placed by anti-crime organizations, legal advisers, bail services, and sellers of burglar alarm systems.

The paper was founded in June 1988, by Eric J. Brewer, a Cleveland journalist who for two years had published the Cleveland *Independent*, an orthodox black weekly. Brewer published *Clique* in East Cleveland in 1979, then joined the Cleveland *Press*, a large daily, as a reporter. In a year he was released to be active in the Guardian Angels patrol movement. He also worked as national publicity director for a record company. Brewer later brought out a social services paper, the *Urban News*, which is still being published. Twice during this period he was on the staff of the large black weekly the Cleveland *Call and Post*.

The Cleveland *Independent*'s finances were unsteady during its first two years. For a time it was dormant, but revived in 1987 only to be temporarily discontinued, Brewer said in March 1988, because his time and money were needed to make the *Crime Reporter* more stable.

The *Crime Reporter*, its publisher said after four issues were published, soon brought about several arrests. It is said to have reached a readership of 100,000 in its 25,000 press run.

Some of Cleveland's downtown businesspeople, according to Brent Larkin, a Cleveland *Plain Dealer* commentator, are not enthusiastic about the paper, noting that downtown crime has decreased in recent years and the paper gives an incorrect impression of conditions.

The paper prints crime stories involving persons of all races. Brewer has said of his philosophy of publishing: "My methodology, to some, might appear a bit unorthodox. Many people in this field believe that you work one thing and keep it going until something breaks for you. I believe in experimenting with ideas. If one doesn't work, try another. To me, publishing is not different than the recording industry or the motion picture industry (I've worked in both). You keep going until you get a 'hit.' "

Competitive Atlanta

One of the most competitive black newspaper cities is Atlanta. As the white papers, two large dailies, drew closer by combining their business operations, the black publications multiplied. This deep South metropolis has one of the nation's three dailies, the *World*; two weeklies, the *Inquirer* and the *Voice*; a monthly, the *Tribune*; and another, the *People's Crusader*.

The *Tribune* has a controlled circulation of 32,000 and was founded in 1987. The *People's Crusader*, with 5,000 circulation, was founded in 1970. Both the *Voice* and the *Inquirer* are pre-1970.

The Atlanta *Inquirer* grew out of reaction to the conservative *World*. A group of students and teachers founded it in 1960. It became a crusader, so much so that the late Louis E. Lomax, the black author and journalist, credited it with persuading hospitals that once were all-white to change the policy of not allowing black doctors to practice. Vigorous in writing tone, appearance, and policy, the *Inquirer* uses the slogan, "To seek out the Truth and report it without fear or favor."

The Atlanta *Voice*, begun in 1965, has a strong editorial page stance, relying often on sarcasm. Space is provided for syndicated columns as well as for local writers; these balance the *World*'s viewpoint. The *Voice* provides the usual entertainment, sports, and other such pages. It has a combined paid and free circulation of 50,000.

It may appear that a city able to support five black papers must be in more need of such a press to help solve its racial problems than most other cities. That is not the situation in Atlanta, which has the reputation of being moderate in its racial attitudes. It is not a city teeming with efforts to solve its racial problems that has no black press. It is a rigid and unprogressive city that lacks vigorous black papers. When little hope for reform appears possible a publisher fears that he will not obtain support for a local journalistic voice.

Other City Weeklies

Like Atlanta, Milwaukee has a lively black weekly press, and perhaps for the same reasons: a bold civil rights movement has joined both black and white portions of the population and considerable news has come from their actions. In the early 1960s as many as five black publications were issued, four newspapers and one magazine: the Milwaukee *Courier*, the *Greater Milwaukee Star*, the *Gazette*, the *Sepian*, and *Echo* magazine. By the end of the 1960s both *Gazette* and *Sepian* were gone and in another fifteen years only the *Courier* and *Star* survived, joined by the *Community Journal*, a weekly founded in 1976 with a verified circulation of 39,431, more than the circulations of its rivals combined.

St. Louis's best known paper is the long-published *Argus*, a solid, news-centered paper founded in 1912. It is crammed with local coverage, considerable free publicity for one black enterprise or another, special features, and columns. All this copy tends to run heavy; that is, to be solid with type with little attempt to help the reader through the large amounts of material. Two decades ago it was selling 50 to 60 percent of its space to advertisers, today it's from 30 to 35 percent. Circulation remains small. A substantial paper, for years it has made a point of running interpretative material on racial issues. Its front page is somewhat flamboyant and is kept bright with color blocks.

Not as old as the *Argus*, but still among the older papers of the Midwest, is the St. Louis *American*, founded in 1928. Issues run to twenty or twenty-four pages, with 50 to 60 percent of the space sold to advertisers. Page width is about one-fifth narrower than two decades ago. It is a tidy, well-planned paper, vastly better in production than it was in 1970. It is typographically pleasant and readable.

The *American* belongs to the Associated Press and uses dispatches from Africa or from U.S. news areas of special interest to black readers. Church news occupies two pages. Crime is covered, but is kept from one-half a column to one-half a page. Some classified ads are run free. There are no spiritualism or palmistry ads.

The St. Louis *Evening Whirl*, founded in 1964, and the St. Louis *People's Guide*, begun four years later, both have modest circulations both free and paid, between 3,000 and 4,000, according to a publisher's statement.

The West Coast Scene

Professor Jack Lyle of the University of California faculty has made one of the few studies of black community journalism.[6] His book, *The News in Megalopolis*, consists of about one-third background on the news media, mainly newspapers in the United States in general, and two-thirds examination of the total press in Los Angeles. In the chapter titled "The Negro and the News Media" he points out that Los Angeles has within it not only geographic communities but also communities of "interest" or "mutual identification." Ethnic groups are included here.

"The Negro's community is very apt to be both geographic and ethnic," he observes, and goes on to say that the "prejudice-enforced relationship of geography to ethnic group is a growing source of tension."[7] As ethnic groups break out of geographic isolation, therefore, the whites object to the arrival of blacks in their territory.

To comprehend the Lyle report we should know that at the time (1966) more than a half-million black citizens were living in Los Angeles County, most of them in the largely black areas which he describes as "the southern quadrant of the central city which includes the Watts area." At the time he was writing the bulk of his book, he said, there were three weeklies for the black readers of the area, the *California Eagle*, the *Sentinel*, and the *Herald-Dispatch*. On record for the time, however, were the *News* and a fifth, *United Pictorial Review*, the latter described as a controlled circulation publication of about 70,000. These Lyle does not mention. The three he discusses were somewhat different papers; their characteristics are described. But the *Eagle* was suspended later the same year after an unsuccessful attempt to maintain it when Loren Miller, a national NAACP officer and lawyer, was appointed to a judgeship and had to sell the paper. The new owners could not make it go. A full-size weekly, with much attention to civil rights coverage, it generally supported Democratic party candidates. It had 27,000 circulation.

The *Herald-Dispatch*, founded in 1952, is a considerably different type of paper, judging by reports on it, for at that time it was much in the news despite a small circulation of then only 3,100. Lyle writes that much of its content bordered on racism, that there has been an off and on relationship with the Black Muslims. It has sporadically attacked the black "establishment" (meaning the NAACP, the Urban League, and other groups) and labeled them as Uncle Tomish. It generally endorsed Republican candidates at the time. In summer 1964, its offices were bombed by persons still unidentified. A paper of standard-size, it mixed objective news reporting and writing with editorializing, according to Lyle's report on it at his time of writing. He also noted it was carelessly prepared, with many unprofessional practices, such as lack of proofreading. Today it has a circulation of 19,000, controlled.

The *Sentinel* he reports to be the dominant paper in both circulation and size, and perhaps the only profitable one. On the first two points it still is outstanding. It is in four sections, with from forty-eight to fifty-six pages, and has an ABC circulation of 25,225. Considerable advertising and fifty or more pages a week were characteristic earlier. Its 1966 circulation was 39,811; after a slight loss for a few years it was up to 41,482, audited by ABC, by 1970, confirming Lyle's point about its dominance. A moderate paper, although strongly outspoken on civil rights, it supported the Democratic party and in Lyle's opinion was professional in its techniques, having as its editor a professionally trained newsman. Founded in 1934 by the editor, who also was publisher and owner, it today stresses local crime as well as political news at the local and national levels. The owner-editor, the late Leon H. Washington, Jr., received his original experience on the onetime rival, the *California Eagle*. Ruth Washington now is publisher.

Frederic C. Coonradt, lecturer at the School of Journalism at the University of Southern California, analyzed the coverage of the Watts riots of August 1965 by two black newspapers and one black radio station in Los Angeles (the *Sentinel* and *Herald-Dispatch* and KGF). He concluded that the three media "seem to be, in their separate ways, more mirrors of the thinking of various elements of that community than leaders in the community's thinking."[8] The *Sentinel*'s attitude in the crisis was "impatient, perhaps, but not violent," he added.

In 1971 the late Chester L. Washington, publisher of two Los Angeles community papers, *Central News* and *Southwest News*, announced purchase of five new weeklies for "approximately $1 million": *Southwest Wave, Southwest Wave Star, Southwest Topics Wave, Southside Journal*, and *Southwestern Sun*. The combined circulation, to be "well over 200,000," would make the group the nation's largest among the small weeklies.

Today, with the group expanded to thirteen papers, all of either free or controlled circulation, the Wave group is the largest black combination in the nation. The circulations range from 10,000 to more than 30,000 each; much of the content is repeated in the regional or neighborhood editions. The papers are *Southeast Wave-Star, Southside Journal Wave, Southwestern Sun Wave, Southwest News Wave, Southwest Topics News, Southwest Wave, Tribune News Wave, Angeles Mesa Wave,* Culver City/Marina Del Ray *Wave,* Hawthorne *Wave,* West Chester *Wave, Central News,* and Inglewood *Wave.*

The combined circulations well exceed the 200,000 figure announced at the time of the purchase of the original five weeklies.

Los Angeles is not alone in publishing influential California black papers. San Francisco and environs have several substantial groups, including the San Francisco *Post* and the rival *Sun-Reporter* and four other *Post*s in Richmond, Berkeley, Oakland, and the Seaside *Post News-Sentinel.* These make up a group whose 124,000 circulation is sold as a whole.

Begun almost half a century ago, the tabloid *Sun-Reporter* is a generously illustrated paper run by Dr. Carlton B. Goodlett, a leader in black newspaper journalism. Strong on editorials and other opinion writing, the *Sun-Reporter* is noted for its fair policies and willingness to voice dissent. Its ABC-audited circulation of around 10,000 a week has held steady in recent years. It carries two pages of classified ads, including some for palmists. Crime is played down and local black organizational and cultural activities emphasized.

In Detroit and Kansas City

Another paper serving a large black population is the *Michigan Chronicle* of Detroit, a weekly with a circulation of about 25,000 according to the ABC. One of the Sengstacke publications, it exists in a city which has a larger percentage of black inhabitants than New York, Chicago, Philadelphia, and Kansas City. Because its circulation is so heavily concentrated locally, it emphasizes Detroit events but includes material, such as columns found in other papers of the Sengstacke chain, not obtainable from nearby rivals by readers. Standard in size, it is a physically big paper because of its heavy advertising schedule.

Also reflecting local interests is the Kansas City *Call,* a weekly which gives an unusual amount of space to religious news, as generally is true of papers in Missouri and other Southwestern and Southern states, regardless of color. Printed by offset and standard-size, it is strong on local stories but tends to de-emphasize national news. Local topics are treated often in the editorial pages, a practice that over the years has given it the reputation of being a fighting paper.

The Portland Papers

The two weeklies published in Portland, Oregon, serve as illustrations of certain types of publications that appear in U.S. communities. These papers are the *Skanner* and the Portland *Observer*, both about the same age and circulation size yet sufficiently different otherwise to be able to survive.

The *Skanner*, like its name, is an unusual paper somewhat in the way that the Washington *New Observer* is different from the standard black community weekly. It, too, is a tabloid, running at times to forty-eight pages. The *Skanner* does better in selling advertising, however. Typical issues show that fifty percent of its space in a special career issue was sold. And it did even better in the body of the paper. It has 10,500 circulation, according to the publisher's statement of 1986.

A husband and wife team founded the paper in 1975. Bernie and Bobbie Dore Foster divide the main titles. She is editor and he publisher. Bernie Foster had worked on a Seattle black paper before settling in Portland to handle the business side of the *Skanner*. He also had acquired experience at the white Seattle *Times*, a large daily, and had taken communications courses at the University of Washington.

He explained to the editor of *Focus*, a Portland printing and graphics paper, that one of the main reasons he and Mrs. Foster started the paper was that "every time I'd look (at local newspapers or television) I'd see blacks handcuffed for robberies, or blacks in confrontations with police. There were no role models for the kinds of things black people did, no positive images I could see. Our role was to say, 'You can' and 'You have made a significant contribution to America.'"

The Fosters see no conflict with the *Observer*. Instead they think the papers complement each other.

The somewhat older *Observer* — by five years — has a larger circulation, most of which is paid while the *Skanner's* is controlled. And the *Observer* carries more vigorous opinions to its readers.

It is run by Albert Williams. Brian White, editor of *Focus*, writing about the black press of Portland in 1987, reported that Williams came to Portland the week before the Watts riots in Los Angeles where he then was living. "He had $30, knew only one person in

Portland, and was uncertain about how he was going to make a living," White related.

Williams had no luck getting work in Portland in 1965, but tried again the following year. He began selling free-lance photographs to a black paper owned by a white publisher, apparently the *Northwest Clarion Defender*, in Portland. This contact with journalism aroused

6.3. The two weeklies of Portland, Oregon.

his interest in newspaper work. He began selling ad space for the paper.

Meantime the *Observer* had been founded in 1970 by Alfred Lee Henderson, using the slogan, "The Only Newspaper in the Whole Wide World That Really Cares About People." Thin and amateurish, it was a weekly running six or eight pages and selling for a dime. It also was outspoken, as it still is.

Williams became a man of all work for the paper, with the title now of general manager. Henderson continues as editor and publisher and serves also as a national officer of a black church denomination in Tennessee. The company's legal name since the beginning has been the Exie Publishing Company; and it produces another black publication, a magazine called *Job Trends*, which is inserted in subscription copies of the paper but is also sold on certain newsstands for job hunters.

Responsibility for the magazine also falls to Williams, who has a hand in most production aspects of both publications. He made statements to Brian White that show his point of view on community journalism for black readers: "We try to provide the black community with good, up-to-date truthful news. We're not afraid to tackle anyone. If we feel that the *Oregonian* [the Portland general daily] or any other newspaper prints something that's unfair to the community, we cover it. We look at the Portland police department and investigate problems we see." He added: "I print things the way I feel. I have a habit sometimes of putting my message in a headline."[9]

The Washington Papers

The Washington *Afro-American and Tribune*, Washington *Informer*, Washington *New Observer*, and Washington *Sun*—these are the main newspapers originating in Washington, D.C., aimed specifically at the large black population of the nation's capital, almost 500,000.

All four of the black papers are twenty or more years old; one, the *Afro-American and Tribune*, originated in 1932. Considering the size and importance of the District of Columbia the circulations are small, together reaching about 90,000. Only one paper, the *Afro-American*, has an ABC verification. That paper also comes out twice weekly, the others once a week.

These figures indicate, even allowing for the accepted practice of counting four readers to each copy, an indifference to the black press and the preference for the white-owned. A further consideration is that three of these four papers are given away, even if selectively, as "controlled" implies. It also should be noted that the white Washington *Post* has a circulation of more than 700,000 daily; the Washington *Times*, 80,000. These figures may be multiplied by four or five to indicate readership size rather than sales of copies.

The *Afro* is a combination of a local weekly, a journal of opinion, and a newsmagazine. It offers many columns, some locally written. Here and there is a feature, such as one about a black woman astronaut. An astrology/numerology column appears regularly. It might be placed not far from a magazine-like article on aging. A news story could be datelined Africa. Other soft stories might be "The Oldest Black Church in America," or "The Push Button Society." The staff is particularly eager to use pictures and in some issues has two full pages of ones taken at meetings or parties. One issue in 1987 included a supplement distributed at a conference of the Congressional Black Caucus Foundation, with twelve pages of material related to the session, organization history, and membership.

Six to seven pages of local and national ads appear in a sixteen-page issue. About a half-page of ad space goes to palm readers.

The Washington *New Observer* fits itself into this scene with a pattern different from that of its rivals. It ignores the formula often urged on editors of black papers: go for the news. It leaves that to its three rivals and offers what they do not provide so generously: timeless features, human interest, and many pictures.

West Indies Publications

Some black publications are giving considerable space to the black citizens of the West Indies and other areas in the Caribbean. Some seek advertising and circulation there, others wish to bring news to former residents of those areas. Two such publications are *Class*, a magazine and *Carib News*, a paper.

Aggressive publicity offices in some of the islands send news and feature copy free to mainland black publications, with a consequently larger coverage of certain areas.

Editors can phone or write tourism offices for news releases, but must be reminded that such offices will not supply hard news but mainly releases about new hotels and other attractions. Any local travel agency can supply the latest addresses of the tourism agencies for the West Indies in general, or for such islands as Barbados, Jamaica, and Tobago.

Campus Local Voices

Like local voices within local voices, several dozen newspapers are issued at black colleges and universities and generally owned by the institution. W. E. B. Du Bois in his days at Fisk edited that university's paper, and many another black journalist who became a professional broke into the field of journalism through such a publication.

Some of the better known papers issued on black college campuses include *Voice of the Wildcats* of Bethune-Cookman College, the *Famuan* (formerly the *Florida State A. & M. News*), *AUC Digest* of Atlanta University, the *Lincolnian* at Lincoln University (Pennsylvania), and the *New Voice* at Hampton University. As will be noted in the biographies of black journalists, several of the more prominent did their first journalistic work on their college papers (see Chapter 10).

In many ways typical of these generally orthodox papers is the *Famuan*, for like college publications everywhere it takes a critical attitude toward the institution's administration and deals with national topics, but lacks the bitterness of the black paper on a white campus. And, like its white counterparts, it now is less of a bulletin board than it was several decades ago and to some extent given more to opinion than informative journalism.

The *Famuan* serves as an open forum for the campus at Tallahassee, but it does not have easy going, for it lacks paid advertising and depends upon university subsidy.

Many of these papers are tabloids. Unless, as few do, they have a substantial journalism program in the curriculum they are likely to be amateurishly written and edited. Nevertheless, they give students an outlet and a measure of experience.

What is recent in campus journalism is the black paper for black students who study at white colleges or universities. Usually such a campus already is served by a university-sponsored paper, but at a few the black student groups have wanted their own publications.

6.4. Typical college papers.

In at least one instance — Wayne State University — black students gained control of the paper intended for all students. *South End* was the official daily serving a campus population then of about thirty-three thousand, of which 11 percent was black in 1969. During its first year under black editors, beginning in 1967, and in a second year with a predominantly black executive staff, the paper became vigorously militant. One slogan was: "Year of the Heroic Guerrilla."[10]

Among the earliest of the independent, black campus papers at white institutions was *Blackout*, published by the Legion of Black Collegians at Missouri, in fall 1969. The Legion, asserting that there have been "no news media representative of black opinion," that there " is now an urgent need for consolidation," and that "Blacks comprise one of the largest minorities on campus," set up a newspaper committee to produce *Blackout*. Although unprepossessing physically, if its first issue was typical, its purpose was clear enough. Duplicated on legal-size sheets, it sold for ten cents. Poorly reproduced, most of the line drawings were hardly discernible, and some of the text was obscure as well. The paper contained little news, and as to be expected with any advocacy publication, a maximum of opinion. Two stories had news value. The rest was subjective pieces or literary materials. One of the latter was on the Black Panthers. Several were critical of the university, one beginning: "The University of Missouri, alias 'Little Dixie,' is a society of racism." The literary content — a book review, a list of new black books, and several poems — occupied three pages.

The *Vindicator* was published in early 1970 as an eight-page tabloid financed by the Cleveland State University Student Affairs Committee. It served a campus of thirteen thousand, of whom three hundred were black. Its reason for existence, its editor explained to the Cleveland *Plain Dealer*, was that "there is no other now-existing student publication that has included the black life style in its scope of news coverage." Another statement by its editor, Ronald E. Kisner, shows that black students, like many white ones, overrated the college publication as a training ground. He told the *Plain Dealer*: "There is a great demand for black journalists. I see the *Vindicator* as a vehicle through which interested students could get basic training in journalism and then go into professional media."[11]

Black Voice, a semimonthly tabloid published irregularly since 1968 at Syracuse University, began as a duplicated newsletter; since 1970 it has been printed offset. Some years it emphasizes news events, offers a news feature or two, poetry, and photographs; others it goes in for controversial articles and modern artwork in photography and drawing. It has a strong separatist tone in its content. Its editors want it to be a communication medium for black students alone.

Newsletters as Local Voices

Newsletters are local voices mainly in the sense that they provide information and opinions that cannot reasonably be thought the responsibility of a standard commercial newspaper in a community of any size, whatever the race or ownership.

Newsletters are the journalism of individuals, companies, clubs, and other aggregations of humans. Existing by the thousands, they carry content of interest only to a relatively small circle of readers.

At the University of Michigan, for example, is *Caas*, a newsletter issued by the Center for Afro-American and African Studies there. Now in its fourth year, it runs to sixteen pages, comes out quarterly, and contains internal news and reports on the work of the Center. A similar publication, issued by the Center for Afro-American Studies at the University of California at Los Angeles, is in its tenth year and comes out twice annually.

Howard University in Washington, D.C., an outstanding predominantly black institution, each Monday during the academic year distributes to its various schools and colleges copies of the *Capstone*. A concise, cleanly printed, four-page, 8½-by-11-inch publication, it offers news from all parts of the campus.

A combination newsletter and house publication is a fancifully titled four-pager called *Sistahs*, with a subtitle, *The Bulletin for Black Corporate Women*. Issued from Altadena, California, it is a product of Jenesis Public Relations agency, costs thirty dollars a year, and comes out every other week. Its format matches its title in originality. It prints editorials, short news stories relating to the place of black women in the work world, pen and ink sketches, and verse related to the central topic, reports of meetings, and advice on various professional opportunities for black women.

The sheer size of the United States makes newsletters essential. If the Los Angeles papers, whether for the majority or a minority, should carry the content of the newsletters being issued in that city each day, their editions would be as unwieldy as the big Sunday papers of New York, Chicago, and any other major metropolis. Readers would ignore much of what would be in those papers except the few columns about their own clubs, business, or whatever human unit they belong to.

Many newsletters are vertical; that is, they report the news of a single group in a given community. It might be the small, 8-by-10-inch paper of one branch of the NAACP. If it is published for the employees of a single firm, like the offices of a magazine publishing company, it goes up and down in the building in its coverage of news of those employees and of the company's programs or progress.

Other newsletters are horizontal. In other words, they cut across the field, giving readers news of similar activities in various other parts of the nation. An example is the *Network*, a publication of black communicators in the Southeast. Its headquarters is in Atlanta but it has contributors in Charlotte, North Carolina, New Orleans, Memphis, and other cities. It deals with the way blacks are portrayed in media advertising, gives news of a forthcoming National Association of Black Journalists national convention, and describes the work of an anti-Klan network.

Clearly horizontal is the *Parent's Notebook*, with a newsletter format but mainly educational guidance content. The editor, Aminisha Weusi, describes her paper as "The Newsletter for Effective Black Parents." Now in its second year, it runs to eight pages, is published monthly in Brooklyn, and sells for ten dollars a year. The editor has studied journalism and writes for *Essence* and other black publications and is herself the mother of seven children.

Vertical newsletters usually are free; functional newsletters of this type, having mailing costs, usually charge unless subsidized by an organization.

The Black Magazines— the Front-runners

Magazines of any kind generally are divided into two broad groups: consumer and specialized. The first are the large-circulation periodicals of broad appeal, aimed at anyone who can read and containing something for almost anyone. The others are magazines that deal with all kinds of special interests—cats and Caterpillar tractors, music and the milk industry, plumbing and party-making. In a twilight zone between them are magazines that, while somewhat specialized, make such a mass appeal that they belong with the consumer group; among these are the newsmagazines, women's and men's publications, and the shelter periodicals for home lovers.

The black magazine industry has the same divisions. Although numerically there are relatively few in any area, the patterns are the same. It is made up of a dozen or so consumer books (magazine industry people talk of these publications as books), such as *Ebony, Jet, Essence*, and *Players*; several more in the twilight zone, like *Excel* and *American Visions*; and about fifty that are truly specialized and are dealt with separately in the next chapter.

The front-runners occupy that position not necessarily because they are better as magazines but chiefly because, being generally consumer-aimed, they have larger circulations, more advertising revenue and volume, or broader influence than the others. Furthermore, there is reason to say that the modern black magazine of general circulation

7.1. Four of the front-runners among black magazines.

is coming to symbolize the black press, whereas in the past black journalism was dominated by the newspaper. But newspaper distribution, slightly improved as it has been in the late 1970s and early 1980s by the creation of more papers rather than the rise in circulation of the established ones, is overshadowed by the steady growth of the magazines.

Yet the story of the black consumer magazine has been one of success for only a few, and those in relatively recent times. Beginning with the *Colored American* in 1900 failures were frequent until recent decades (see Chapters 2 and 4). For a time such magazines as *Bronze World, Color, Our World*, and the *Urbanite* hoped to stay in the consumer field but failed. Some clues to their failure are to be found in the story of one of the longer-lasting, *Our World*. Expensively produced, lavish with tinted inks and printed on high quality paper, it was a rival monthly to *Color* and *Ebony* when it was begun in 1946. Subtitled *The Picture Magazine for the Whole Family*, it attempted to penetrate the black market.[1] It evidently hoped to ride on the popularity of the then white leaders, *Life* and *Look*, but too little of that popularity rubbed off.

Nevertheless, *Our World* managed to reach a circulation of 251,599 in 1952, an achievement for a magazine of the sort today and even more so for one of that time. But as with various white magazines that reached high circulations (the original *Coronet* and all the Crowell-Collier publications attained boxcar figures running into the millions but failed nevertheless) it is possible to have too much circulation. Such a situation comes about when too many copies must be printed and distributed in ratio to the advertising revenue and circulation earnings collected. And in 1955 *Our World* went bankrupt, having lost 100,000 circulation as well as precious advertising accounts because it could not sell more space.[2] A brief effort to salvage it failed.

Another attempt at a general consumer magazine was the *Urbanite*. *Life*-size but otherwise not *Life*-like, it was issued monthly for nearly a year in 1961 from New York. Announced as a magazine aimed at comparatively affluent blacks with fifty-two hundred to fifteen thousand dollar incomes, it attracted quality advertising—book clubs, cigarettes, and record players—but not enough. Contributors were among the best known writers at the time, such as the authors James Baldwin, John O. Kellens, and John A. Williams, and the playwright Lorraine Hansberry. John Ciardi, poet and teacher, also wrote for it, one of the few white writers to appear. Evidently the economically elite group was too small or not interested in the intellectual fare the *Urbanite* offered.

The story of the black consumer magazines in the past two decades has been largely one of frequent experiment and frequent failure. As in the industry in general, the successful magazines, by and large, are the specialists. Although a majority of the consumer books launched fail, that is the story of such journalism in the economic order. If financial stability cannot be found in the business system it must be obtained by subsidy. That method of financing a publication goes on alongside the risky commercial ventures.

American journalistic history has been filled with hopeful entrepreneurs, eager special pleaders, and idealists. The years from 1965 to the later 1980s illustrated that historical theme dramatically. Here are the names of some of the consumer or quasi-consumer magazines that have gone out of existence; all but five were launched between those years: *Black American, Black Creation, Black Laughter, Black Sports, Black Stars, Black Theater, Ebony Jr!, Encore, Everybody, First World, Freedomways, Hep, Jive, Liberator, Main Man, Modern Black Men, Negro Braille, New Foundations, New Lady, Relevant, Sepia, Soul Confessions, Soul Illustrated, Soul Sounds, Tuesday*, and *Urban West*.

Although usually classified as newspapers, *Muhammad Speaks* and the *Black Panther* had important qualities that categorize them as magazines. Produced on newsprint, they contained far more opinion than news, a characteristic of magazines (with such notable exceptions as newsmagazines). In makeup and layout they had a magazine, not a newspaper, appearance. If they can be accepted as quasi magazines, their cessation should be noted in the preceding group as serious losses because of their function as tools for manipulating public opinion. *Bilalian News*, successor to *Muhammad Speaks*, also failed.

There were others of these twenty-nine publications that were significant losses to the black press force, such as *Encore*, which gave space to temperate but forceful ideas about the life and work of American black citizens; *Freedomways*, which was doing the same and also publishing literary research; *New Lady*, which offered women something more than fashion advice; and *Tuesday*, which reached thousands of white readers since it was distributed by white standard newspapers as a supplement and dealt with important aspects of American black life.

A Dominant Company

Dominating the general magazine field of black journalism is one company which issues two of the largest circulating periodicals and has made several other ventures into the magazine world. (See also Chapter 4.) This firm is the Johnson Publishing Company with headquarters in Chicago.

The *Ebony* Story

The Johnson output is led by *Ebony*, a picture monthly usually containing about 160 pages. Like the original *Life* and *Look*, it offers considerable text in addition to numerous pictures, and thus is not merely a photo collection for riffling. For many years it was oversize and much like *Life* in format. Since 1968 it has been in the select group of around sixty U.S. magazines that have more than one million circulation (there are approximately twenty thousand U.S. magazines of all types).

The first Johnson magazine, *Negro Digest*, was begun in 1942. It did well enough to encourage John H. Johnson, its publisher, to attempt *Ebony*, which was born in 1945 with the intention of emphasizing the bright side of black life and reporting successes by black people in any endeavor. It had this philosophy until the late 1960s, when the struggle for the righting of wrongs against the black race in America demanded its cooperation more heartily. At the beginning *Ebony* was a mild, moderate picture monthly. Then, to boost newsstand sales, it was changed into a somewhat sensational publication. Sexy articles, cheesecake pictures, and other come-ons shot the circulation to a half-million. But its success did not last, for an economic recession hit the country in 1954, cutting the circulation by 20 percent. Moderation again became the tone, to get the book back into black homes.

Johnson wanted his magazine in those homes, for without such an audience it is difficult to obtain much advertising. With the content changed, *Ebony* then was able to add a substantial home circulation. By 1987 its circulation was 1,703,019. This circulation has enabled it to obtain many advertising accounts of a type vital to consumer publications.

With the rise in black militancy and the impression upon the black society made by groups such as the Black Nationalists and the Black Panther party, *Ebony* became more outspoken in behalf of

7.2. A trio of the leading figures among major magazine editors and publishers.

more rapid improvements in the living conditions, educational opportunities, and vocational acceptance of blacks. The change — still not enough to convince the would-be revolutionaries who prefer *Black News* — was reflected in articles such as "How Racists Use 'Science' to Degrade Black People," by Carl T. Rowan, and editorials such as one against no-knock drug raids. The extremists did not see these articles as clearly as they saw an editorial warning blacks against being lured into violence to bring about their revolutionary aims. They were disdainful, also, of the success stories in each issue.

Walter Goodman quotes an unnamed New York photographer who is "particularly scornful of 'all those flukey jobs they write about, like the cat at IBM who's making seventy-five hundred dollars a year. What the hell are they telling me, man? Everybody *knows* if he was white he'd be making twelve thousand.' "[3] A comparison of issues two decades apart, however, shows that in the later 1980s room had been made for more aggressive writing in behalf of the race.

In assuming their changed position, the editors ran into new sorts of trouble. A reader in Isle of Palm, South Carolina, wrote: "I'd like to protest the insults I receive every time I read it. Not an issue goes by but that you refer to the Caucasian race in the most insulting terms . . . Whitey, Charley and Honkie." The writer goes on to say that he feels "we are all Americans, not black, white, yellow or red," and accuses *Ebony* of preaching bigotry and violence.[4]

A Canadian reader called the magazine discriminatory because whites were excluded from it. "For you to be proud that you are a black man is just as wrong as for me to be proud I am a white man. We are men," he wrote, adding: "You are the ones now giving importance to the colouring of the skin, the very crime you condemn the whites for."[5]

But *Ebony* went on, gaining in circulation steadily at a time when some of the largest white magazines were cutting theirs for economy reasons.

Jet and Ebony Man

The other magazines from the Johnson firm in the late 1980s are *Jet*, a peppy, pocket-size weekly, lighter in advertising volume than *Ebony* but long on news nuggets that sometimes are original coverage and always tightly written; and *EM — Ebony Man*, the latest venture.

Jet was modeled after the midget or less-than-pocket size of the original Cowles magazine, *Quick*, and remained about four inches by six inches in size until 1970, when it was enlarged to roughly five by eight inches. At founding it sold for fifteen cents a week. Ben Burns, then executive editor of *Ebony*, added the editorship of *Jet*. Edward T. Clayton, associate editor of *Ebony*, was made managing editor of the new little book. Owner Johnson explained its function: "to provide Negroes with a convenient-sized magazine summarizing the week's biggest Negro news in a well-organized, easy-to-read format. . . ."

Jet was not, as sometimes thought, the first black newsmagazine. In 1925 appeared a *Time*-size one with the unlikely name of *Heebie Jeebies*. Published in Chicago, it had departments but also some fiction. P. L. Prattis, a widely known black editor, was its president and editor. It may have been the first.[6]

During the recession period of the later 1950s *Jet* lost heavily in newsstand sales, although it had the benefit of more exposure than either *Negro Digest* or *Tan*. But it came back. The early issues carried sensational titles ("Ten Ways to a Mink Coat") and this tone has been maintained, as in an article headed "One of the Sexiest Men Alive, Says Miles Davis' New Bride." Along with such copy have gone hard hitting crusades against injustices to which blacks have been subjected. Alfred Balk has pointed out that *Jet* brought the Emmett Till and Montgomery bus boycott stories before the country and "it probably saved Jimmy Wilson's life by publicizing the now famous $1.95 theft case."[7]

Robert E. Johnson (not related to the owner, John H. Johnson), an editor whose brisk personality is reflected in the magazine's punchy style, has seen *Jet*'s circulation reach 790,279 by the later 1980s. But Johnson is most proud of the exclusive articles he runs, stories overlooked or ignored by the white press. At a meeting of the Chicago Headline Club in 1969, for example, he asked the members of the audience of eighty-five to raise their hands if they had heard or read the statement made by President Lyndon B. Johnson in 1968 about the report of the National Advisory Commission on Civil Disorders, known familiarly as the "Kerner report." In March of that year the president, at a White House conference with members of the National Newspaper Publishers Association, had said: "I think that the most important thing in the report is the conclusion that it reaches about the cause of our problems in this country evolving primarily from white racism." He also said: "I think it's the most important report that has been made to me since I've been President."[8]

Only one member of the audience raised a hand; there was a sprinkling of black journalists in the group but the only hand was that of a white. Bob Johnson's point was that here was an important statement by the president, especially in view of the accusations against him of silence concerning the report, and it had been overlooked or ignored by the white press.

Onetime members of the Johnson magazine family and now discontinued are *Tan* (originally named *Tan Confessions*); *Black Stars*, successor to *Tan* and an entertainment magazine; *Black World*, issued after the pioneering *Negro Digest* was halted; and *Hue*, like *Jet* in size and shape, a monthly. *Hue* was to provide a place for copy left over from the others. Another motive was to see if money could be made with still another pocket-size newsstand periodical. It emphasized entertainment world doings of the black society, reached 150,000 circulation, and then went weekly. But like the early experience of *Jet*, the new little magazine never commanded enough advertising, its size preventing it from using standard plates. It also brought in too little circulation revenue. The newsstand diseases that hit most large magazines in the 1950s and 1960s brought about its demise. Another unsuccessful Johnson publication was aimed at Africa, *Ebony International*, intended for English-reading Africans. It lasted only a few issues, running into political and ideological complications as well as high production and distribution costs.

When the Johnson firm discontinued *Black World* in 1976 protests far in excess of the influence and circulation of the magazine were heard. *Black World* had replaced *Negro Digest*, the first Johnson magazine. *Negro Digest* was discontinued once before, in 1951, but revived a decade later.

In its second existence it was a literary magazine, given to serious political and social problem articles as well as to poetry and fiction, all by black authors, many among the leading writers of the nation. Hoyt Fuller was editor. Unlike most publications of its genre it paid for manuscripts. A decade later the name was changed to *Black World*.

The digest-size magazine was philosophically out of step with the other Johnson magazines, giving attention to social concerns and literary forms that they did not.

But *Black World* made no money. And the Johnson company decided, in the words attributed to the company's circulation manager, that *Black World* would be around "only as long as it pays its freight bill." The bill was unpaid in 1976 and the publication taken out of production.

Consequently numerous prominent black writers met as a group with John H. Johnson that year to express what the Hartford *In-*

quirer called their outrage at the closing. The publisher did not restore the magazine, however, and seemed to exacerbate the situation by announcing the publication instead of a new magazine, *Fashion Fair*, a quarterly.

For twelve years, beginning in 1973, black children had their own magazine from the Johnson presses: *Ebony Jr!* Color printing was used generously and the quality of the artwork and editorial copy was high. It existed in a field of successful periodicals for children of all ages and races. But like such journalism in general, despite a top of 100,000 in circulation *Ebony Jr!* could not command advertising, and circulation began to decline. The magazine was dependent upon circulation revenue so it was withdrawn in 1985. That same year *Ebony Man* was begun as a well-printed magazine aimed at the up-and-coming black professional beginning to find a place in management, home ownership, higher education, and other areas of interest to men seeking career success.

The Johnson enterprises include far more than magazine publishing: Fashion Fair Cosmetics; the first black-owned radio station in Chicago, WJPC-AM; the "Ebony/Jet Showcase," a syndicated television program; and Supreme Beauty Products, a hair care products company.

The Johnson firm has a hand, as well, in *Essence* magazine, for the publisher bought 20 percent of the stock of Essence Communications in the mid-1980s. That did not, however, give him a place on the board of directors.

For years the Johnson Publishing Company ranked first on the *Black Enterprise* magazine annual list of "The Big Ten in Black-Owned Business." On the 1987 list (covering 1986) it ranked above Motown Industries and eight other black enterprises. But in mid-1987 the Johnson firm was suddenly displaced as number one by the TLC Group, Inc., which until it bought the Beatrice International Food Company had been ranked sixth.

The Good Magazines and *Tuesday*

Sometimes thought of as competitors for the Johnson magazines, those of the Good Publishing Company in Fort Worth, Texas, were barely a shadow compared with the ones published in Chicago. The idea of competition came about because the flagship magazine of the group, *Sepia*, was *Life*-magazine-size, as was *Ebony* in the 1960s. Both *Ebony* and *Sepia* were picture periodicals, among the few black magazines that could find a place on news-stands. But there the resemblance stopped. *Sepia* was not as well printed or edited, nor did it command the advertising volume or circulation of the rival.

This difference may have come about because the Good firm, owned by a white publisher, George Levitan, directed a staff that produced several magazines from one office. In addition to *Sepia* were *Hep, Jive, Soul Confessions*, and *Bronze Thrills*, designed on the confession or fan magazine formula. Eventually *Bronze Thrills* and *Jive* were sold to a New York firm and live on still as mixtures of personal problem, personality worship, and confession magazines. The others ceased.

For some years newspapers had a colorful supplement called *Tuesday*. Launched in 1965, it was reported to have achieved a circulation of two million. It was a monthly supplement to white newspapers in large cities that had substantial circulation among black citizens. Another magazine of this type, *Tuesday at Home*, was also distributed for a time in the same manner. Although it was original in concept and of high quality content, the publisher, W. Leonard Evans, Jr., was unable to find sufficient advertising support.

Magazines for Women

For a time there was a revival of interest in magazines for black women, bearing such names as *New Lady, Essence, Elegant*, and the latter's younger companion, *Eleganteen*.

New Lady, clearly a women's service periodical of the *Good Housekeeping* variety, was begun originally in 1966 in California. It managed to produce three issues, and then was suspended because of inadequate financing. Three years later, with the help of the Ford Foundation and Opportunity Through Ownership, each of which provided loans of seventy thousand dollars, it was revived. Staff members visited the offices of *McCall's* and *Redbook* for briefing on their duties; Select Magazines, a distributor, undertook to put it on the stands in nearly one hundred localities. Early in 1970 its executives reported a paid circulation of 100,000, obtained through the efforts of various organizations, such as the National Council of Negro

Women, National Association of Negro Business and Professional Women's Clubs, and youth groups and sororities.

The theory behind the formula was expressed by Warner Beckett, the publisher, who came to his post with public relations and marketing experience. "Our magazine attempts to fill a void for the black woman," he told an interviewer at the Los Angeles *Times*. "All of the other popular women's magazines are edited for the Caucasian woman." Beckett believed that the black woman had her own special needs and was a special individual. About 80 percent of the staff was black. Few of the top editorial staffers had professional journalism experience or training. The editor was a former mail carrier, the managing editor had been a free-lance writer and once worked on a black weekly community newspaper. Copy was accepted regardless of the race of the writer.

The magazine's content, offered in an eight-by-ten-inch format, in general was in the familiar patterns of women's magazines—a few short stories, a children's page, articles and departments on fashion, cooking, medicine, personal care, dieting, and like topics, and personality pieces about successful black women, therefore offering what editors like to call an opportunity for reader identification. Editorials were not used. After a few issues articles dealt with racial subjects, the views of Rap Brown or the viewpoints of black activists on campus or of other rebels, perhaps in answer to a reaction represented by a letter to the magazine saying:

"Your magazine is 'nice.' How come you don't tell it like it really is, that the black people are starving and losing their lives in the streets every day. I don't see anything about the Panthers or their activities and why don't you use Kathleen Cleaver for a new black lady. Your black lady doesn't even have a natural. Black people are involved in the serious struggle to live every day. That's what you should be printing."[9]

Advertising, slim in the first year but expected to pick up, was from major firms advertising beverages, floor coverings, bakery products, and household supplies. Such accounts are in strong contrast to the other magazines aimed at black women except the newer *Essence*.

Technically the magazine was better produced than all the others except *Essence*. Fashion and food materials were in full color. The fiction, however, was much like the shallowest in the white women's magazines. Black characters used language the reader of *New Lady* presumably abandoned long ago, if she ever spoke that way. Artwork did not match the photography in quality. Much of the major copy was staff written, perhaps for reasons of economy and because high quality material by and about the interests of blacks was difficult to find. *New Lady*, like all others not of the romance or confession type, succumbed to high costs. Only *Essence* was able to make the grade.

The most glamour-filled black magazine on the market in 1968 was conceived when a white executive of the Shearson, Hammill firm of Wall Street brokers encouraged a trio of young black businessmen to launch *Essence*. After considerable delay raising $1.5 million (part of the backing coming from Playboy Enterprises), and after being briefed by various New York magazine publishing people at Time Inc., *Psychology Today, New York,* and *Newsweek,* as well as advertising executives, the entrepreneurs were in business. They were Cecil Hollingsworth, who had a graphics consulting firm; Ed Lewis, a financial planner for the First National City Bank at the time; and Jonathan Blount, an advertising salesman for the New Jersey Bell Telephone Company. All were in their twenties at the time the magazine was launched. Blount left the firm in 1971.

Essence was launched in spring 1970 with considerable advance publicity. *Time* and *Newsweek, New York,* the trade press, and NBC's "Today" show helped launch it. With Gordon Parks, the photojournalist, novelist, music composer, and cinema producer as editorial director, it began with a formula of providing handsome color photographs of fashions and food, numerous articles on current black issues, some aimed particularly at women (the problem of black men sometimes preferring white women, for instance), fiction, and departments of the sort common to white women's magazines— home, recipes, and personal care.

Newsmagazine-size but looking larger because of its many bled pictures, *Essence* then was an odd combination of defiance of the capitalist order ("Cornell in Crisis" is sympathetic enough with the black students to disturb persons who remember the photograph of the armed young men leaving a campus building) and advertisements for some of the symbols of decadence—cosmetics and expensive clothing.

Ida Lewis, an early editor in chief, was a free-lance writer for ten years before joining the magazine, contributing to *Life, L'Express,* and other French publications while living in France for five years. During the NBC program Lewis was asked about the magazine's audience. She replied that 7.5 million black women between the ages of eighteen and thirty-four were potential readers. The name was chosen out of hundreds of possibilities because black is the essence of all color. Lewis resigned in 1971; Marcia Gillespie succeeded her and in turn has been succeeded by three more.

Before the editorship settled down there was internal dissension, which the magazine survived. It was over ownership. In 1977, a group led by Parks brought legal action. Lewis and Smith rode out the storm and *Essence* became one of the financial successes of black journalism, in 1987 having more than 800,000 circulation. By then it had considerably altered its formula, particularly under the editorship of Susan L. Taylor (see Chapter 10). Its advertising sales also mounted. It took a clue from *Ebony* and has a national traveling fashion show.

The business department also began issuing what it called an Essence Style catalog, thus entering the direct mail market. In the mid-1980s the magazine produced "Essence—The Television Program," a weekly show hosted by editor in chief Taylor. The magazine became much more down to earth, less sophisticated, and more alert to problems in the lives of black women at many social and economic levels. It still is colorful and high in graphic quality, but it gives space to articles on AIDS, on "The Mis-education of Our Children," on religion, on "Economics and You," among many others.

Several years before there was much public attention to the problem of AIDS, *Essence* examined it, probably the first magazine for women to do so. Other issues—unemployment, poverty, treatment of male prisoners, and drug addiction—have been faced by the magazine.

Magazines for Men

During the years that publishers were seeking successful formulas for magazines for black women they also, with less energy and enthusiasm, were searching for the way to win male readers for magazines for black men. None, however, has gained permanence, certainly nothing comparable to that of *Essence*. The only consistently issued book is *Players*, the black reader's version of *Playboy*, classified among the girlie or skin publications. *Players*, published in Los Angeles since 1973, has 206,474 monthly circulation.

Publishers have attempted to reach what they consider a higher level of readers than those interested in the flesh magazines. They try chiefly perhaps because the readers of the latter may not be as well educated or as well employed. Magazines that give attention to the arts, professional problems, fashions, and careers must be expensively printed and able to sell considerable advertising space. Such ventures as *Main Man* and *Modern Black Men* were not able to convince advertising agencies that to reach the black male market it was necessary to go beyond *Ebony*.

EM—Ebony Man is John H. Johnson's candidate for success in this field. His nominee is handsomely printed and timely in its content. In its third year by 1988, at first it was somewhat unsteady because of staff changes in the advertising department. Its eye appeal is strong, with generous use of color and articles dealing with various types of problems and interests of black male readers. It is too early to know its future. Alfred R. Fornay is executive editor and has his offices in New York rather than Chicago, the mother city of most Johnson ventures.

The macho magazines for and about black athletes, despite the prowess and success of the black football, baseball, and basketball stars, have not fared well. *Black Sports* survived for a few years, as did *Black Tennis*. After all, when *Sports Illustrated* and other veterans of sports journalism tell the stories of the black athletes there is little left for the separate magazine on black sports to cover. Nevertheless, in 1988 a new attempt was made with *Black Sports World*.

The Response

What is the reception for these black consumer magazines? Are they preferred to white periodicals? If so, which are preferred and why? Little research has been undertaken to answer these and many similar questions. The few studies reported are perhaps of less significance than they might ordinarily be because the climate of opinion within the black society in America is both confused and rapidly changing.

A thesis written at West Virginia University recorded the results of an attempt to "investigate the use patterns, and to some extent, the effects of the mass media on the residents of a metropolitan Negro ghetto."[10] The research tool used primarily was a public opinion survey based on a questionnaire and personal interview with one hundred black residents of Pittsburgh, Pennsylvania, in 1967. The researcher learned that *Ebony* was read by most of the persons interviewed and received by more than one-third of those taking a magazine. Two-thirds of the respondents received other magazines; none received a weekly newsmagazine.

Part of a report by Dr. Jack Lyle on the media in Los Angeles indicated that most of his respondents read some magazine regularly, with a median number of three. *Ebony* led the list of black magazines. The only other black periodical scoring substantially was *Jet*.[11]

Two later studies made at Syracuse University in 1969, one a master's thesis and the other a doctoral dissertation, produced similar information about two different groups of black residents of Syracuse (see Chapter 15).[12]

The two Syracuse studies and that of Allen indicated that broadcasting received far more attention from the groups of respondents than did printed matter.

Such studies, while their purposes and findings go far beyond the matter of response to black magazines, since they deal also with the black newspaper and the accessibility of black and white publications to readers in this ethnic group, and many other aspects, help to explain why *Ebony*'s circulation is so much larger than that of any other publication issued by black publishers. *Ebony*'s dominance also explains its selection for more intensive study than any other current black magazine. Research was conducted into it, for example, by a graduate student at the University of Michigan in 1967, which resulted in a careful in-depth analysis. Paul M. Hirsch was concerned with the nature of the magazine's readers. He wrote: "It has been suggested, throughout this paper, that the Negro middle class consists of several factions which disagree over a variety of questions . . . in short, our study of *Ebony* as been a study of within-class differences." He also discussed the magazine's "editorial ambivalence and occasional self-contradiction," which he believed came about in an attempt to "please all segments of its audience."[13]

Vignettes of Other Front-runners

American Visions

Positioned above its flag *American Visions* carries the subtitle *The Magazine of Afro-American Culture*. Between its covers are articles about historic quilts made in Mississippi, biographies of notable musicians, artists, and scientists, and pieces about hypertension among Afro-Americans. Reports appear about black families. All copy is well supplied with color and black-and-white photographs.

It is a serious magazine, free of the hype and promotional tone of some other periodicals for the same audience. It is never strident.

Technically, *American Visions* is on the fringe of black journalism. Its owners are not predominantly black. It is supported mainly by the Smithsonian Institution of Washington, D.C., Rutgers University in New Brunswick, New Jersey, and the Philip Graham Fund of the Washington *Post*. The publishing firm is the Vision Institute, a nonprofit group formed by the Smithsonian in 1983. On other tests of racial control, however, the magazine qualifies. Its staff is largely blacks; its editor in chief is a black historian. And its material is about blacks and is aimed at black Americans.[14]

Gary A. Puckrein, the editor in chief and publisher, conceived the idea of the magazine four years before it was published, a period during which much time was used raising money for its start in 1985. His intended audience was upscale blacks. It began as and remains a bimonthly.

A magazine of its quality might expect advertising support comparable to that accorded *Black Collegian, Ebony, Essence*, and *Black Enterprise*. While it has some of the characteristics of these front-runners and some of the same rich accounts, the advertisers seem unappreciative of the buying power of its readers and the attractiveness of a well-printed magazine.

Dr. Puckrein's vision for the magazine comes from his career as a historian. His degrees, all in history, are from Brown and California State universities. Before becoming an associate professor of history at Rutgers beginning in 1982, he had been on the Rutgers faculty for two years as a teaching assistant and associate, and as an assistant professor for four years. He has taught at two other colleges. Active in various professional associations, he has lectured on historical topics, and contributed to a number of historical and professional journals. He had had no editing or publishing experience when he became head of *American Visions*.

Magazines on the national publishing scene of the United States that emphasize cultural interests have not been known for their longevity or financial success; witness the scores of small literary and arts magazines with a few hundred circulation, virtually no advertising, and a persistent deficit.

From the commercial world there are comparable examples in

the *Atlantic Monthly* and *Harper's* magazines which have managed to survive, in both instances for more than a century and a half, but with diminishing influence in the last third of their existence.

How well *American Visions* fits into the black press scene is undetermined three years after its founding. If the audience it looks to for support responds it may go on, resented perhaps by some of the commercially oriented publishers who receive no subsidies.

Black Enterprise

Like magazines in general, those issued for the black consumer tend to be more attractive physically than are the newspapers. Some black newspaper publishers and editors bristle at this statement, but it cannot be denied, whatever the race of the publishers. Nor can it be refuted when applied to another newspaper rival — broadcasting.

By having less frequent publication dates, the ability to use color printing in both reading matter and advertising, and high quality printing stock, the consumer magazines for black readers especially are superior. They can attain more circulation and advertising revenue than the newspapers, almost all of which are for general consumers.

No black newspaper exceeds 100,000 circulation, and those that nearly reach it are publishers of chains or groups. Much of the circulation is not verified by official auditing firms. Many papers list the circulation figures that come from the publisher's statement, which to some advertisers does not appear the most scientific form of auditing. Others use controlled circulation as their distribution method, also somewhat cautiously accepted by advertisers, since there is no assurance of the number and quality of the reading. The predominance of even numbers in the reports from newspapers (seen in listings like the *Gale Directory*) raises questions about the reliability of the counting and verifying.

On the other hand, the weekly, semiweekly, and daily newspapers (there are three dailies and a few twice-a-week papers) reach their readers far more often than do the monthly or quarterly magazines. Presumably by repetition alone the newspaper reading matter and advertising has a greater impact when it comes to influencing public opinion and creating living patterns. To this point must be added the fact that to some extent there is an aura provided by a publication, whatever its format and frequency. A reader may accept or believe a publication because of its age, its proven dependability on other occasions, or its habitual presence in a household.

Black Enterprise not only has a paid circulation verified by the Audit Bureau of Circulations (ABC), the leading agency in the verifying business, but also has an aura induced by its handsome appearance, its generous use of color, the high quality of its advertising, and the successful formula for its editorial matter, such as the general use of authorities on subjects as writers.

It is one of the originally specialized magazines that has gone beyond its specialty, business. At first Earl G. Graves, its founder, deliberately sought to reach the traditional businesspeople of his race with strictly business-oriented content. But he soon realized that he would be of greater service by seeking also to satisfy other interests that would be acceptable under his magazine's title for the millions of American blacks. He also realized that he should try to reach not only the small business operators but also the big entrepreneurs. He did not stop even there. He knew the general consumer and attracted some of them with articles covering vital economic interests — personal investments, solutions to the unemployment problems that hit blacks more than most other minorities, and scientific and other non-business developments that in the long run have some effect upon the business world.

In mid-1980 issues, for instance, there appeared articles on seven black men and women under age forty whom "experts and colleagues" had tagged "among the best in their respective professions."[15]

Other pieces had these titles: under science/technology, "Reaching Beyond the Outer Limits"; on politics, "Whole Wheat," about Representative Alan Wheat; under health, the story of Dr. Adlie Hamer, "Historian with a Mission."

The June 1987 issue ran to 352 pages. It offered twenty-five major articles, a dozen departments, and scores of original photographs and drawings and full-page advertisements from top advertisers, almost all the latter in color. Much of the advertising copy also was to be seen in the *New Yorker, Travel and Leisure, Town & Country*, the *New York Times Magazine*, or *Smithsonian*. The advertisements alone fill 170 pages and were inserted by Rolls Royce, Lincoln, and other car makers; Marriott Hotels; Polaroid cameras; Godiva chocolates; and Merrill Lynch, the financial house.

This story of the success of a magazine is one that would fit *Black Enterprise*'s editorial formula perfectly. It is a reflection of the magazine's founder, Earl G. Graves. He started it in 1970. Within ten months he announced that it was making a profit, which it has done ever since. In the mid-1980s it ranked among the one hundred most successful black businesses.

Its first editor was Lawrence Patrick Patterson. Patterson, generally called Pat, was an enthusiastic, forceful young executive who brought considerable journalistic experience to the magazine. He had been a reporter for the big Long Island daily, *Newsday*, then editor of the New York *Courier*, a black weekly, after which he became managing editor of the Manhattan *Tribune*. He graduated from the journalism department at New York University. When Graves listed himself as both publisher and editor of the magazine, Pat became editor at large, an enigmatic title.

Over the years since 1970 the magazine has been able to reach not only black businesspeople but also general businesses seeking to win the black population market, now estimated to be worth $100 billion. More than any other black magazine *Black Enterprise* enables nonblacks to understand the black population. This black/white audience explains the large circulation figure of 234,760 by 1987.

As long ago as 1972 the magazine began research of its own market possibilities. Its editors had found that little investigation had been done by the black media in this area. They wanted to discover the buying patterns of the potential audience, how they differed from those of nonblacks, and what advertising copy was most effective.[16]

The most consulted issue of each year is the one containing the *Black Enterprise* "List of 100 Top Black Businesses," a compilation begun in the magazine's second year.[17] The table is based on sales in millions of dollars.

Black Enterprise, as a result, is promoted with care. One outcome of the research was to persuade several airlines to include it in their magazine racks, the publications offered readers from the aisles. Another was to allocate some of its press run to be given, under a controlled circulation plan, to large corporations of any race.

The *Black Collegian*

The black college student is likely to be aware of this magazine even if he or she has no interest in *Ebony* or *Essence* or any of the other high circulation periodicals. The *Black Collegian* can play a part in a student's career, so he or she turns to it in the junior or senior college year.

A glance at the table of contents of several issues can explain why. Here are the titles of some articles published in 1986 and 1987: "The Top 100 Employers and the Majors in Demand 1986–87," "How to Begin the Job-Search Process in Your Chosen Field," "How to Get into Grad School," "Wanted: Top Research Scholars," "The Robots

7.3. The *Black Collegian* is widely circulated on college campuses.

are Here—and Working," "Why Afrikana History?" and "Developing Confidence in Job Interviews."

Surrounding these and other practical treatments of the job situation are articles or departments on topics having no relation to employment or careers, such as one on the black family, another on Paul Robeson, or an overview of the top fifteen college football teams.

This material runs in issues of from 100–140 pages, with color printing on high quality paper, and a generally smart and professional appearance.

The *Black Collegian* was founded in 1970 by Preston J. Edwards, the publisher still, with headquarters in New Orleans. It has reached a mainly controlled but audited circulation of about 122,000. Its advertising volume is greater than that of most such specialized magazines, running from 40 percent to 50 percent, and much of it is from prestigious accounts.

Black Family

When Frank C. Kent took over *Black Family* magazine in 1986 he described a philosophy for it which had six major points. At least the first was an especially original concept.[18]

1. The essence of it is in these passages: "Within our ranks [of black Americans] every color of mankind is represented. With this in mind, *Black Family* will not focus on black Americans as a minority group within a white country. That shouldn't be what any black American is about. Those who think of themselves as a minority will also tend to think of themselves as second-class citizens. . . . *Black Family* views black Americans as 'part of the majority.' We are first and foremost Americans. The United States is our country. We were born here."

2. "*Black Family* aims to set its sights on black American success stories."

3. "*Black Family* strongly supports the idea that as more and more blacks move up the ladder of success, they have an obligation to help the others struggling to succeed."

4. "*Black Family* believes that we must give strong support to black institutions which have been the tower of strength in our communities. . . . The black church is our rock. The black college has been our key."

5. "*Black Family* believes that our national black leadership must seriously begin to deal with a national crisis in our black communities. We must find ways to end the ever increasing 'black on black' crimewave. In particular, we must let it be known that we will no longer tolerate or excuse crimes perpetrated against defenceless senior citizens by disrespectful and cowardly black youth. We believe our social workers and other professionals, who understandably are looking for the underlying root causes . . . must stop apologizing for young black criminals."

6. "Finally, *Black Family* believes that the American system of free enterprise is the best economic system for this country, and therefore the best economic system for black Americans."

The magazine was founded in 1980 by Dr. Mary Ellen Strong, with headquarters in Chicago, and published under the name Black Family Publications. When Kent, who also is editor, acquired it he moved it to Reston, Virginia.

It continued to use color in editorial and advertising matter and carry articles on education, health, fitness, food, and various family topics. By 1987 the publisher's statement of circulation was 200,000; ABC verification had been applied for. In 1986 the magazine was running to fifty-six pages plus covers each issue.

Typographically it had more appeal than in its earlier existence. Bled covers, more attractive design, and easily read blurbs gave it more strength, as did the emphasis on personalities.

In 1988 it was temporarily suspended. The formula was not working well enough.

Dawn—Newspaper Magazine Supplement

Magazines distributed with newspapers are not new in U.S. journalism history. Some successful ones appeared early in the twentieth century; a few eventually gained independent and successful publication.

Usually associated with Sunday newspapers, these magazines have been attached to black papers on other days, since most are midweeklies. *Dawn* is one of the most hardy of the lot.

Founded in 1973 by the Afro-American Newspapers, a major chain of semiweeklies consisting of five editions for as many large cities or areas, *Dawn* has made its way into other papers as well.

In its early years it was typical of the color supplements of the time: a short tabloid measuring 11-by-12½ inches, on newsprint, most of it in color, with health articles, features on black topics, and personality sketches. Cigarette and other ads filled 50 percent of the space. Editorial views were not expressed; some letters were run. *Dawn* was in competition with *Tuesday* and *Tuesday at Home* (although the latter two were placed mainly in white-owned big city papers), the *Amalgamated Pictorial Supplement*, and *National Scene*. It was a thoroughly conventional publication in 1973. Perhaps for that reason it did what few of the others accomplished: it survived.

In the later 1980s it is a far more impressive publication, even though physically smaller and more like a standard magazine than a newspaper supplement. It measures 8½-by-11 inches, is on much better quality stock, and the color printing is vastly improved. So are typography and layout, which were amateurish in the early years. Physically it is more changed than it is in content.

The usual astrological page appears, one page each is devoted to cooking and personalities, and an occasional two-page serious article on some feature topic. Its subjects remain homely and innocuous.

The Modern *Crisis*

Exceeded in age only by the religious black press, the *Crisis* remains a force for the same reasons that such publications as the *Christian Recorder* and the *Star of Zion* do, within a more limited circle of readers This sustaining power comes from the religious loyalty and zeal behind its publication.

Since its founding in 1910 the *Crisis* not only has reflected the activities of its owner, the National Association for the Advancement of Colored People (NAACP—an organization name long unsuitable but so loaded with tradition it resists change), but also has chronicled much of the history of the black race in the nation.

The *Crisis* is far more than a house organ for its sponsors, for it has published literary work as well as general articles on public affairs. For a time it carried the subtitle *A Record of the Darker Races*.

The version of the 1980s is in what is called newsmagazine-size, uses color printing on the front and back covers and on certain advertising pages. The sale of space for advertising is in itself a drastic change in policy, made necessary by the inability to increase the subsidy.

The anniversary issues produced almost every decade since mid-century (and on other significant occasions in black history) are filled with material of historic importance—excerpts from editorials, special articles and poetry in early numbers, and new articles on current issues. So important has the *Crisis* been in its time that its first seventy years of issues appear in a reprint edition.

The seventieth anniversary, for example, was observed by publishing two issues devoted to the occasion, one in November and the other in December 1980. Each was more than 110 pages in length and supported by more advertisers than the regular issues.

Articles on different aspects of black society were contributed in November by Benjamin Quarles, James D. Anderson, Clarence Mitchell, Henry F. Winslow, Sr., Robert W. McDonnell, and other prominent scholars, authors, and staff. The December number was an anthology from past issues, with preliminary essays and excerpts written by other leading contributors, including Paul Giddings, Pat Patterson, and Broadus N. Butler. G. Gerald Fraser of the New York *Times* staff contributed a history of the *Crisis*, covering its first seventy years.

A more typical issue may contain six to eight articles on miscellaneous subjects, one or two poems, an editorial, book, dance, and concert reviews, and reports on NAACP activity. Some characteristic titles: "The Growth of Suicide Among Black Americans," "Why Aren't Inner City Students Learning English?" and "Memphis' Crisis in Education."

The magazine is published by Benjamin L. Hooks, the executive director of the NAACP. Its editor, only the sixth in nearly eighty years, is Fred Beauford. His predecessors were all major leaders

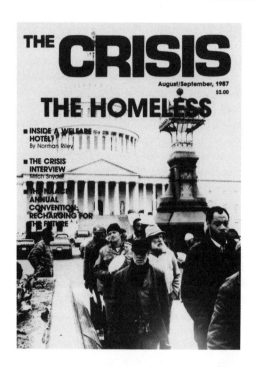

7.4. Founded by W. E. B. Du Bois and long the voice of the NAACP, the *Crisis* is an important opinion-maker.

among American black citizens, beginning in 1910–1934 with Dr. Du Bois, the founder. Roy Wilkins served for the next fifteen years, then James W. Ivy was editor for a similar span. Henry Lee Moon was in the editorial chair from 1967 to 1974; that year Warren Marr II took over.

Several of these editors were professional journalists. Wilkins and Moon were experienced newsmen. Wilkins had worked on the Kansas City *Call*, still a prominent black weekly, eventually becoming its managing editor. Moon had rich experience in the black press, including service on the Cleveland *Call*, Cleveland *Herald*, New York *Amsterdam News*, and the Chicago *Defender*. He also wrote for national magazines and was author of various books.

By 1982 the *Crisis* editorial management changed, with Chester A. Higgins, Sr., as editorial director. The magazine was calling attention to Ronald Reagan's presidential actions. Benjamin Hooks, the publisher, as well as various writers for the magazine, expressed dissatisfaction with what they considered the Reagan administration's "openly abandoned traditional civil rights enforcement, among other policies of similar nature."[19]

Maybelle Ward, who had been assistant editor for a decade, by

1984 was editorial director, the first woman to reach so high a post on the magazine during its long history. Advertising volume was mounting. The June/July issue of 1984, sixty pages long, carried twenty-eight ads, mostly full-size, for Coca-Cola, ITT, General Foods, Sears, the Equitable, Delta Airlines, and other prime accounts.

But all has not been constantly smooth for the *Crisis* in the past two decades. In early 1971 Stephen Spottswood, president of the publishing company that issues it, called on the readers to "Save the *Crisis*." By fall 1988 it was proud to have 350,000 subscribers. From then on the circulation climbed, keyed as it was to membership, since the magazine could not be bought on newsstands. The climb was in part the result of modernization—brisker editing and coverage of more timely topics and setting a subscription fee to be paid by members and nonmembers alike.

Profiles of Two Editors

Fred Beauford

Fred Beauford, the *Crisis*'s editor beginning in the mid-1980s, brought considerable professional journalism and public relations experience to the magazine. Like Chester Higgins, who served as editorial director for three years, he had both magazine and public relations experience. He also had taught at three universities in those areas.

He had been founder and editor of *Neworld Magazine*, whose subtitle was *The Multi-cultural Magazine of the Arts*, and editor of *Black Creation*, one of the more substantial periodicals devoted to what is called the black arts. His background included being public relations coordinator for James Booker Associates, public relations coordinator and staff writer for the Edward Windsor Wright Corporation, and public relations director of the Los Angeles (Inner City) Cultural Center, the second largest in the city. He taught, either as an adjunct visiting professor or lecturer at his alma mater, New York University, and at the University of California, Berkeley, and University of Southern California.

Beauford's entire background is reflected in the mid-1980s issues of the *Crisis*. In the decade or so before he became editor it had become a somewhat general magazine as well as an internal publication for the NAACP. The house organ function is still being performed, but in a more limited and crisper manner.

The frequent historical or philosophical articles have been dropped in favor of such vigorous subjects as homelessness, welfare hotel living, the KKK in Georgia, the work of black cooperatives, and the problems of black public colleges.

Space now is devoted regularly to the arts, including music, dance, books, film, and painting. Letters, poetry, and reports from Washington and the NAACP branches continue to appear.

The policy of selling space for advertising remains. From a fourth to a third of the space is being used by various large corporations and some institutional advertisers, including beverage, tobacco, and several service firms.

Circulation has increased, the magazine reports, and in the late 1980s stood at 350,000.

Earl G. Graves

Enterprise has been the key word in the business life of Earl G. Graves, founder, publisher, and editor of *Black Enterprise*, the business magazine for the black population in the United States.

Enterprise not only is in the name of the magazine but also in Graves's life so far. He learned his Horatio Alger–like aims early. At age five, the story goes, he earned $150 selling Christmas cards.

He was born in Brooklyn in 1935. When he attended Morgan State College in Baltimore, Maryland, he majored in economics. He went out for track both in high school and college and made the dean's list at Morgan State. He paid his tuition by working as a lifeguard summers on New York beaches and running campus businesses of the usual kinds, such as a snack food service and gardening. After graduation and military service he became a narcotics agent for the Federal Treasury Department. From that job he turned to selling real estate in New York.

Graves's next activity, working for Senator Robert F. Kennedy as an administrative assistant, began in 1966. That lasted until Kennedy's assassination in 1968. Among other Alger-like lessons he learned from this experience, he says, was that "anything can be done once you make up your mind to get on with the work."

Ever since then he has owned his own business enterprises, which by 1987 had amounted to five separate ones, all bearing his name. Before them he set up a management counseling firm that advised businesspeople on urban affairs and economic development. Earl G. Graves Ltd. has five subsidiaries: EGG Dallas Broadcasting, Inc., operating KHVN-AM and KDLZ-FM; the Earl G. Graves Marketing and Research Co., Inc.; the Earl G. Graves Development Co.; the Minority Business Information Institute; and the Earl G. Graves Publishing Co., Inc.

Like many publishers, Graves gives time to several special groups, such as the board of governors of the corporate fund for the Performing Arts at the Kennedy Center in Washington, the board of trustees at Tuskegee University, and the trustees at the American Museum of Natural History and the Planetarium Authority. He has been active for many years in scouting and has held the third highest office in the organization.

His views sometimes are not exactly what one might expect from a publisher with this conventional background. When the two hundredth anniversary of the U.S. Constitution was celebrated in 1987, Graves published an editorial in *Black Enterprise* in which he advanced ideas far from conservative and anything but accepting of the current conditions of blacks in the United States.

> May 17, 1954. It was one of the most momentous days in judicial history. In its landmark decision of *Brown vs. Board of Education* the Supreme Court declared segregation in the nation's schools as unconstitutional. Not only did the ruling open up all classrooms to America's children, it paved the way for a series of social reforms in the following 20 years that would protect the constitutional rights of blacks across all social and class lines.
>
> Since its inception 200 years ago, the Constitution has provided black Americans with a framework in which to fight for civil rights, whether it be the abolition of slavery or access to public facilities. In assessing the value of the Constitution, Justice Thurgood Marshall, the only black to sit on the Supreme Court, said: "The government was defective from the start, requiring several amendments, a civil war and momentous social transformation to attain constitutional government and its respect for individual freedoms and human rights we hold as fundamental today."
>
> His assertion rings true. The framers of the Constitution deemed that a black man counted for three-fifths of a person, and for the century that followed we were denied our right to citizenship and full participation in mainstream society. The measure of freedom that we enjoy today took the efforts of courageous men and women who fought fierce legal and political battles, endured economic hardships and forfeited their lives.
>
> Government is still rife with imperfection and the Constitution continues to grow in importance as black America is besieged with challenges that threaten to subvert economic, political and social prog-

ress. In recent years the Supreme Court has made a series of inconsistent rulings regarding affirmative action programs and quota systems. Discriminatory electoral practices still hinder many blacks from exercising their right to vote. Thousands of black youths continue to receive inadequate education, and as a result, they will wind up as unemployable and nonproductive adults.

We must continue to fight for our rights as we have for the past 200 years, especially in affirmative action. As Eleanor Holmes Norton, former chairperson of the Equal Employment Opportunity Commission, wrote: "The major peril of affirmative action is not that we see an outright judicial rejection of the decisions on record. The danger lies in the scraping, trimming and chipping away that could reduce the potency of [affirmative action] decisions as they are interpreted in future cases."[20]

The Black Magazines— the Specialists

Name a human special interest and at least one magazine is available for it, whether it may be ecology or entomology, space travel or slenderizing. At least this is so in the United States.

Publications usually feed interests and respond to them. Such a policy exists in black publishing, but it is restricted by the racial differences or special circumstances. Blacks do not need a magazine of their own when their special interest is mining or gardening. But they do need their own in areas where they are physically different, have cultural differences from the nonblacks, cannot obtain white services, have been forced into their own groups, or have special problems of little interest to nonblacks and so not worth much space in the white journal.

Black business, for example, supports three periodicals for black beauty salon operators. The special reasons are clear enough. Until recently black women did not have the services of white establishments in certain areas, and still do not in some places, partly because of prejudice and partly because white operators were not trained to handle their hair. Enough women patronize the black-operated beauty parlors to support a trade press. Whenever for some reason a large number of blacks could not join whites in an activity they developed publications of their own—there are or have been journals for black

doctors, dentists, lawyers, journalists, religionists, and other professionals.

Some specialized black periodicals came into being because of
prejudice. Black society's more substantial house organs, sometimes
confusingly called industrial publications, come from insurance companies. Black firms were founded because white companies refused
policies to blacks on various bases, such as uncollectibility of premiums or greater risk because of the way many blacks had to live
(their dwellings being more vulnerable to fire). Thus a black agency
logically issues its own magazine for its clients or its agents.

The black specialized periodical (it sometimes has newspaper format but magazine content and vice versa; the majority are magazines,
but both types are included in this chapter) is most often a scholarly,
political, or literary journal, an organ of an organization, or a business publication. The rest are no less specialized but simply fewer in
number.

The militant or radical spirit so strong in the United States in the
late 1960s and early 1970s gave rise to several new publications, some
of such wide following and impact that they were of national significance. But most of the special interest publications go on in their
small circles, known only to their little groups of readers albeit influential among them, as has been the way of such periodicals for
many years. And if the readers influenced are themselves key individuals in society the outreach of this specialized black press is important. When Roi Ottley wrote about the black press in *Common
Ground* magazine in 1943 he said he knew of 239 religious, fraternal,
literary, labor, school, fashion, picture, and theatrical periodicals. To
these he apparently added what he called quality publications, specifically naming *Phylon*, the *Crisis, Opportunity*, and the *Journal of
Negro History*.

The variety, if not the number, is as great as ever. Many of the
239 are no more, but the staying power of the specialized books is
greater, on the whole, than that of the consumer type. No consumer
book is as old as many of the specialized. The argument can be made
that numerous special interest publications are subsidized to keep
them alive, whereas the consumer periodical usually must make its
own way financially. That is true, but subsidizers sometimes tire of
steady losses, so there is an element of uncertainty as well for the
publishers and editors of the specialized magazine.

The Major Specialized Journals

Usually because of their long service, certain magazines in this group stand out as influential and significant. Out of any list of those existing in the 1980s should be selected *Black Scholar* and the *Journal of Negro Education*. Several more which have not been as favored with noted editors or as many distinguished contributors deserve attention as well: the *Review of Black Political Economy*, the *Urban League Review*, and the *Western Journal of Black Studies*, for example.

Usually a publication serving as an organ of a group is looked upon by the public as less than authentic journalism, not to be equated with a commercial magazine. Somehow it seems to be less than professional as journalism. To be sure, many organization publications are amateurish propositions. A reflection of this attitude is in the wariness of advertisers, who cite it, among other reasons, for not buying space. A number of periodicals serve as examples in the white world's journalism. The well-written and edited *Junior League*, the *Rotarian*, the *Jaycee*, and the *Kiwanis* magazines are not lush with advertisements. Only a few organization publications have been able to override the handicap. *National Geographic* is one; *Boy's Life* is another.

In the same situation is the black world's journalism. *Western Journal of Black Studies,* for instance, is not on the newsstands, is financed by institutions and organizations, and has been unable to command advertising revenue of consequence. Yet it and others like it have published some of the best literary and scholarly work in black journalism.

Public Affairs and Literary Magazines

The dissenting spirit, violent and nonviolent alike, turned to the magazine no less than to the newspaper as an outlet. Carolyn Gerald, a Philadelphia poet and free-lance writer, reported in 1969 that she could list as many as thirty "revolutionary" journals which appeared (almost none survived) between 1966 and 1969. She divided them into types: a) those with local contributors and readers; b) those produced on college campuses by black student groups; and c) those which have appealed or seek to appeal to the black community as a whole.[1] *Soulbook, Black Dialogue*, and the *Journal of Black Poetry* were cited. Those three she considered magazines of the black literature, written by and for blacks, noncommercial, irregular in publication frequency, carrying only a little advertising, and possessing overlapping editorial boards.

Black Dialogue, Gerald wrote, "provides a good study in the growth and development" of a revolutionary journal. It was begun in 1965 by a group of students at San Francisco State College. In the years since it apparently has come out four or six times a year and offered political writings, illustrations, and literary work of increasing breadth, dealing with national as well as local issues. *Soulbook* is described as more militant than *Black Dialogue*. It subtitled itself the *Quarterly Journal of Revolutionary Afro-America*, also was begun in 1965, and likewise on the West Coast, at Berkeley. It, too, published poems and short stories as well as political and cultural articles. Gerald cited as its theme "throwing off the shackles" and the call to arms for the revolution.[2]

Also a mid-1960s product, the *Journal of Black Poetry* differed in that it was concerned with one literary form supplemented with illustrations. But the revolutionary aim came through. Tributes to Malcolm X and to revolutionary heroes abounded.

Although almost all such revolutionary journals are unknown to the great majority of black and white citizens and appear to be of interest only to a small minority, Gerald was of the view that "they are an important index of the measure and meaning of the sixties." They exist, she thinks, "as one manifestation of that intense looking inward to see what we really wanted." She may be right, if one remembers the place in literary and journalistic history occupied today by the *Masses* and various other small literary and political magazines of the first half of this century.

Black Theatre, which Gerald mentions only in a note, reflected the black revolution as seen by the dramatist. Subtitled *A Periodical of the Black Theatre Movement*, it was eight-by-ten inches and printed on low quality stock. Issued by the New Lafayette Theatre of New York and edited by the theatre's director, Ed Bullins, it first appeared in 1968. Its scope was broader than the stage, however, for it carried poetry and line drawings. Interviews with LeRoi Jones and others, an article by Bullins rejected by the New York *Times* as well as a radio interview with him and another black theater playwright which never was aired, appeared.

A handsome, new, and expensive scholarly magazine came from San Francisco in 1969 not long after Dr. Nathan Hare, director of black studies at San Francisco State College, resigned from his post. Dr. Hare, joined by Robert Chrisman, also formerly of the college faculty, late that year brought out the *Black Scholar* to be devoted to "Black Studies and Research." They announced that its issues had within their pages "the most weighty and meaningful black thought we could summon." Thirty persons lent their names as contributing and advisory editors, including Lerone Bennett, Ossie Davis, Vincent Harding, Chuck Stone, Carlton Goodlett, Alvin F. Pouissant, and John O. Killens.

The magazine's intention, under Hare as publisher and Chrisman as editor, was to be issued monthly and, according to *Newsweek*, it sought "to unite the black intellectual and the street radical." Its first few issues contained considerable rhetoric as well as evidences of scholarship, revolutionary aims, and doctrinaire opinions. Early issues contained such articles as Earl Conrad on Harriet Tubman, Shirley Chisholm on "Racism and Anti-Feminism" and Robert Staples on "The Myth of the Black Matriarchy," a few poems, and drawings.

The *Black Scholar* is among the few magazines from the late 1960s and early 1970s for intellectual readers. Robert Chrisman, who served as editor in the founding year of 1970, still had that responsibility in 1987, only the title has been enlarged to editor in chief. It is published in Oakland instead of San Francisco, and its publishing body is the Black World Foundation. It is published six times a year. Its content tends to be thematic, on such topics as the black family. This small magazine has had great tenacity and is to be found in many university and city libraries.

Four years earlier, at Harvard, the Association of African and African-American Students launched a quarterly, *Harvard Journal of Afro-American Affairs*, which until 1969 turned out to be an annual.

The *Black Politician* was a quarterly founded in 1969. Its purpose was to fill "a need in the classroom and among the public for a single authoritative reference source on the political tendings in the black community. . . ." Published by the Center on Urban and Minority Affairs in Berkeley, it was edited by Mervyn M. Dymally, a state senator from Los Angeles. Early issues announced that the *Black Politician* would be bipartisan and cover "the full spectrum of political thought now current in the black community." No revolutionary fervor was detectable in the first few issues. One article was about American Indians, describing their conditions candidly, another on President Nixon and the American blacks, written by a White House research assistant. The magazine ceased in the mid-1970s.

Few black magazines have attempted to duplicate the formula

and general format of the journals of opinion of general appeal, such as the *Nation*, the *New Republic, Commonweal*, or *National Review*. One that did was the *Liberator*, a monthly founded by Daniel H. Watts, an architect. Like one of its counterparts, the *Nation*, which for a decade was banned in New York City schools because of supposedly anti-Catholic articles, the *Liberator* was embroiled in controversy, although of a different order. On one occasion both Ossie Davis and the late James Baldwin resigned from its editorial board, charging anti-Semitism. Made up along opinion magazine lines, with editorials, articles, poetry, and reviews, it had the same modest following as what are called, inaccurately, the butcher-paper weeklies. Much of its readership was from the revolution-minded. Typically it obtained little advertising. The *Liberator* used photographs, unusual for such publications, and these plus the occasional artwork gave it a livelier appearance than its sober articles promised.

Watts has been quoted as saying that he became so aggravated with both the white and black press in their handling of black news that he began the *Liberator* as a "voice of the Afro-American. The white press," he went on to say, "constantly covers only one side of the Negro community—that of degradation. Financially well-off Negroes are rarely given exposure by white media." Watts commented about the black press as well, as his views echo those of other critics (see Chapter 15). The black newspapers might serve the race better if they went out of business, he once said, because they do not give the true picture of events within the black community.

In the *Liberator*, the use of literary material not usually found in the general magazines of similar formula, like the *Progressive* (also a monthly), has provided one more outlet for the black creative writer. Until lately such writers have had few places in which to publish short stories and poems about what goes on within the black society. The *Liberator* included fiction but did not present itself as a magazine of literature, only as one charged with offering opinions. Black journalism has few entirely literary publications, a genre that has gone out of fashion on the larger publishing scene. Usually poems, novellas, and plays are printed alongside current affairs articles.

Uptown Beat, a quarterly issued by the East Harlem Writing Center in New York, qualified as a literary publication that came from the grass roots as did *Echo*, a Milwaukee community publication, for both printed drawings and creative writing by members of writing and art workshops. Begun in 1968, *Uptown Beat* gave space to new writers and artists and provided opportunities for designers. Since it lacked outside support, it did not pay contributors; the editorial and production duties were performed by volunteers or done at cost. A somewhat unusual aspect was that much of the content first was exhibited on bulletin boards of community centers and theaters. Like *Echo*, it was affiliated with a workshop, one started in 1967 by Gayle Greene, a writer and teacher. Much of the magazine's content was drawn from the workshop, but some copy was contributed by writers in Europe and Africa.

Bearing the subtitle *Quarterly Review of the Negro Freedom Movement*, *Freedomways* grew out of the efforts for freedom from injustice and discrimination that reached a peak during World War II and soon thereafter. It continued because of such activities as the bus boycotts of the mid-1950s in Montgomery, Tallahassee, and other cities; the student sit-ins; and the work of the Congress of Racial Equality (CORE), NAACP, the National Urban League, the Southern Christian Leadership Council, and many other groups. First published in early 1961, it remained a quarterly of distinguished but not stodgy format until 1985. Like the typical scholarly and literary magazine published anywhere in the world that has not been underwritten by a government, a foundation, or a millionaire, *Freedomways* always had been in need of dollars. It continued to appear only because of the devotion of a small group of people who believed it deserved to live.

Shirley Graham, the late widow of W. E. B. Du Bois and herself a writer, was its first editor. Working with her was Esther Jackson, managing editor from the beginning. During the years 1961–1966, according to a summary by staff member Ernest Kaiser, the magazine introduced many black writers of poetry, short stories, and articles. It was, as it continued to be, deeply concerned with racial events, issues, and problems in and outside the United States. Certain black leaders were featured, such as Louis E. Burnham, onetime editor of *Freedom* and an associate editor of the general weekly, *Guardian*, as well as a public speaker and organizer. Du Bois, whom Kaiser has called the godfather of the magazine, also was written about considerably in *Freedomways*; the magazine became something of a repository for new material about him. Particular attention was given to Africa and to the black people of Latin America and the Caribbean. Much of the fourth issue of 1969 was devoted to the native American as another American minority group.

Kaiser, a contributing editor, evaluated the magazine thus: "Over its first five years, the evidence is overwhelming that *Freedomways* has done a tremendous, almost unbelievable job as a critical review, a stimulus and direction-giver of the freedom movement and as a publishing outlet for young and developing and reputable unknown writers." He also found shortcomings. Not enough such writers were published, "the language of the magazine is too sanitary, not earthy enough as a fighting people's organ," and there was not much humor.[3]

Still abiding by the formula expressed in its first issue, it gained a circulation of about 7,000 and carried a few pages of advertising, depending for its income on various sources — benefit concerts, theater parties, house parties, individual contributions, sales of greeting cards, art, books, and other materials. "Occasionally," an editor reported, "we receive a legacy or an editor receives a foundation grant for a special issue."[4] But the magazine suffered a loss in 1970 of the sort that can knock one of these literary–cultural affairs magazines out of existence. *Freedomways* suffered twenty-five thousand dollars in damages when a fire burned the building, part of which had been used in the magazine's greeting card business and for its mailing service. The magazine could not afford to pay the insurance premiums.

This disaster did not discourage loyal supporters. *Freedomways* continued for another fifteen years, publishing work by new and established writers, commenting through them on the issues of the times. But in 1985 the financial burden became too heavy, and the editors announced the magazine's end.

The black press published its first bookazine or magabook (a regularly issued periodical bound like a paperback book) in 1970 when *Amistad* was launched as a literary–cultural affairs publication. Although it published material that could just as readily have appeared in *Freedomways* or *Black World*, it depended upon its paperback book format to get into black studies classes; it was issued infrequently (semiannually) to serve as a textbook. Its professional backing was somewhat unusual. Random House, a major white-owned book firm, published *Amistad* through its paperback subsidiary, Vintage Books, and also undertook to distribute it. One of *Amistad*'s coeditors was Charles F. Harris, a Random House senior editor, the other the late John A. Williams, the novelist.

Robert Bernstein, Random House president, explained at the magazine's launching that it hoped to become a quarterly and that it "will be a great step forward in helping black people to know and understand more about themselves and in helping white people know and understand more about blacks."[5] The editors agreed and added a practical angle. In the first issue they said: "The word *Amistad* means friendship in Spanish. The Amistad Mutiny of 1839 stands for revolt, self-determination, justice and freedom. With these meanings always firmly in mind, we have designed this publication primarily for use in college courses in literature, history, sociology, psychology, education, political science and government, and the arts."

Exceeding three hundred pages, its first issue carried articles by Vincent Harding, professor of history and sociology at Atlanta University; C. L. R. James, visiting professor of political science at Northwestern and other universities; and Calvin C. Hernton, an essayist. These and other contributions dealt with James Baldwin, black history and the slave trade, and Southern white writers. The fiction consisted of three short stories, two by George Davis and Oliver Jackman, recording first person experience, and one by Ishmail Reed, whose unusual approach may be judged by the title of his, "D Hexorcism of Noxon D Awful."

A clue to the magazine's racial attitude came in a statement by Williams, when asked if it would be open to white writers. "We'll handle white, black and pink writers if they deal with the problems of the black or third world," he answered. "We feel they're all linked."[6]

Amistad was discontinued in the 1970s.

Callaloo

A literary magazine that has been kept alive since its founding in 1966 at Baton Rouge, Louisiana, is *Callaloo*. A quarterly, the size of the usual scholarly journal, it is subtitled *A Journal of Afro-American and African Arts and Letters*.

It is published by the Johns Hopkins University Press and sponsored by the University of Virginia, so the purity of its blackness is in doubt. Charles H. Rowell, of the University of Kentucky at Lexington's Department of English, is editor.

One of the 1987 issues was devoted to the work of Nicolas Guillen, a Cuban poet. It was a substantial issue of 206 pages with numerous black-and-white illustrations and reproductions of Guillen's verse.

The Scholarly Journals

To some extent magazines in the political and cultural affairs group also are scholarly, some more than others. Certainly *Freedomways*, with its strong emphasis on history, thanks to John Henrik Clarke, once its chief associate editor, offered results of important scholarly work. And *Black World*, which for so many years under its old name of *Negro Digest* was much broader in its appeal, printed scholarly work along with the hortatory and argumentative.[7] In recent years a number of new scholarly journals have appeared, some lasting only a few quarters.

The *African Scholar*, a quarterly that considered itself a "Journal of Research and Analysis" and was published in Washington, appeared in the late 1960s. A quarter of a century earlier had come the *Negro Quarterly*, from the Negro Publishing Society of America, Inc., in New York. First issued in spring 1942, it carried articles concerning "The Negro Author and His Publisher," by Sterling A. Brown; "Negro Education and the War," by Doxey A. Wilkerson, the black newsman and editor once connected with the New York newspaper *People's Voice*; and "Slavocracy's System of Control," by Herbert Aptheker, who in the 1980s is assuming a position as an authority on black history from a Marxist viewpoint. The magazine did not continue.

But by no means did all of the scholarly journals go the same path. Certain of these serious magazines of research and theory have had a greater longevity than any group in black journalism with the exception of the religious and fraternal and for the same reasons: they are subsidized by organizations and often go automatically to those who hold membership. The better known are the *Journal of Negro Education, Black American Literature Forum*, the *Journal of Black Psychology*, the *Journal of Black Studies, Phylon*, the *Review of Black Political Economy*, and the *Negro Educational Review*.

Patrons of a large public or college library who wander among the shelves that hold current periodicals soon are struck by the sameness of the scholarly journals of the various disciplines, particularly in the social sciences. The black journals of this type, except for the word *Negro* in some titles, are not immediately recognizable as different from the majority because the familiar scholarly journal format is followed. Since they usually are subsidized and need not compete on the newsstands with such glamour books as *Black Tress* and *Right On!*, their covers often carry their table of contents or little more than the logotype plus a few titles and the symbol of the association sponsoring them. Inside are from one hundred to three hundred pages of solid type, with article titles breaking the bleak pages or a poem filling an empty space at the end of an article. News notes and book reviews give the last few pages a little more variety. Devoted readers, college professors, researchers, or independent scholars are not disturbed by the blandness. They want the ideas and facts, not entertainment. They would resent pictures, jokes, and the other ingredients of the typical newsstand magazine for robbing them of material needed for their thinking, research, and writing. Furthermore, such a journal provides an outlet for publications by black college faculty members, who are subject to the "publish or perish" tradition as much as any white teacher, perhaps even more, since the black college has had to fight for recognition. As with the white journals, not all the contributions are equally important and some are insignificant. In view of the lack of systematic study of black history and culture in the United States, however, these scholarly journals sometimes are the only sources available.

When W. E. B. Du Bois returned to Atlanta University to teach, after having made his imprint on American magazine journalism with the *Crisis* and other periodicals, he founded *Phylon*, in 1940. When he left the university to go to New York, the combination scholarly and literary quarterly was edited by Dr. Ira D. A. Reid from 1944 to 1948 and by Dr. Mozell C. Hill, both heads of the sociology department at Atlanta. Often the power of these journals comes from such department heads.

Phylon still comes from Atlanta University. Subtitled *A Review of Race and Culture*, it takes a more thoroughly scholarly approach than the purely literary and cultural affairs periodicals. A typical issue will carry several literary, biographical, or social articles or book reviews, a short story, and a small amount of advertising. As do such intellectual publications as a rule, it has a circulation hovering around 2,000. It has not been accepted fully as an orthodox scholarly journal partly, no doubt, because of its mixed formula. A journal that concentrates on one subject, such as religion, education, or history, can make a solid place for itself as an authoritative medium. But one that publishes fiction, long suspect among scholars outside the foreign language and English departments, and also is hospitable to scholarly writings in any discipline is a non-conformist. Yet *Phylon* has endeared itself to many black scholars and writers for giving them an outlet for their work. It is edited by Wilbur H. Watson. In the late 1980s it was off its publication schedule by a year.

Representative of the strictly orthodox journals was the *Journal of Negro History*, to which new attention was directed after the 1960s because of the intensified interest in the history of the race. And with it came heightened attention for the life of the man responsible for this major serious journal, Carter Goodwin Woodson. Long considered the foremost authority on the black society in America, Dr. Woodson founded the *Journal* in 1916. Published continuously until

1983 as a quarterly, it came from the Association for the Study of Negro Life and History in Washington, and had a circulation of 4,600. Intended for the advanced scholar, it sought to carry out the Woodson view that the American black people have not been accorded their correct place in U.S. history. Traditional in format, it carried articles on such subjects as "The Canadian Negro," on various historical figures, including many not dealt with elsewhere, news of prominent black persons of historical importance, book reviews, and a small amount of advertising, about 5 percent of the content. William M. Brewer was editor until his death in 1970. The halt in its publication came about because of the financial difficulties of the Association for the Study of Negro Life and History. A related publication, *Negro History Bulletin*, also is in limbo.

Carter Woodson was a Virginian, born in 1875. He worked in the mines of West Virginia while attending high school, then went to Berea College. On completing the bachelor's degree work he taught and was principal of a black high school in Huntington, West Virginia. Later he became dean of the college of liberal arts at Howard University and at West Virginia State College. Woodson originated Negro History Week, wrote various books and monographs on black history, and founded the *Journal*. The annual history week is intended to popularize black history and correct earlier concepts. The black press in general assists by printing special columns and features, photographs of familiar black heroes, and editorials recalling the race's heritage.

A less elaborate publication than the *Journal* was the *Negro History Bulletin*. It sought to appeal to students. Established in 1937, it was issued for eight months of the year in a more popular format than the *Journal*, carried illustrated historical and biographical articles, book reviews, news of association branches, and a little advertising. In 1969 its circulation was 8,070. The late Dr. Charles H. Wesley, successor to Woodson as association head, author of numerous historical works, and retired president of Central State, was editor.

Called an "interdisciplinary quarterly of the black world," *Black Academy Review* was first published in Buffalo, New York, in mid-1970, a neat, sixty-eight-page collection of six literary and historical articles and a book review. It was one of the enterprises of the Black Academy Press, Inc., primarily a publisher of books on black affairs and of black literature. Dr. S. Okechukwu Mezu, a Nigerian who taught at the State University of New York at Buffalo, both headed the firm and edited the magazine, a well-printed periodical of serious intent. Dr. Mezu, a poet and novelist educated at Georgetown and Johns Hopkins, directed the university's African Studies Department.

The Trade Journals

The black population of the United States has had little need for most of the magazines and newspapers usually lumped under the term trade, technical, or business publications. Having been mainly farm or industrial workers until recent years, and kept to menial jobs, they had little use for the technical content or the materials intended for business executives that one usually finds in these publications, which now are for the most part magazines and number about 3,000. But there have been exceptions. Where blacks have been able to go into businesses of their own, publishers have moved in with a service publication. And as black enterprise grows more will follow, although those activities that well-established white-owned publications cannot satisfy are the only ones likely to need their own publications. Over the years such papers and magazines have been launched. Few have survived; these have been mainly for two occupations: beauty shop operating and tavern and bar owning. The black newspaper press for a time had its own trade publication, but *PEP* went out when hard times came in the 1950s.

Reported available in the 1980s was a handful that included *Beauty Trade, Black Beauty, Negro Traveler/Conventioneer*, and *Financial Independence Money Management* of Washington, D.C., which claimed a circulation of 100,000. The first two are intended for beauty salon operators. Their content is similar to that of white periodicals in the field—heavily illustrated articles on new hair styles, reports of beauticians' conventions, and features on individuals or establishments. Not as lush with advertising as their white counterparts, these magazines nevertheless sell more space than do many other black publications, except the national newspapers and a few consumer periodicals.

When he was a steward on a New York Central parlor car in 1944, Clarence M. Markham, Jr., began a magazine he called *Negro Traveler*. Once he had been a railroad news agency manager and thought a monthly concerned with the blacks working in transportation might help improve their status and morale. The publication was developed into a 75,000 controlled circulation monthly going to black travel agencies, offices planning conventions and conferences, and restaurants and taverns. The editorial content provides coverage of large conventions, guides to hotels and restaurants, and listings of nationwide events. Of the business publications for blacks available, a magazine of this type should have a future others might not obtain, with some black Americans now in a better financial position to go on cruises, transatlantic plane trips, or journeys by car within the United States. The market for such a public has been neglected by white publications and only touched on by a few general circulation black publications. Byron E. Lewis, Jr., president of Uniworld Group, Inc., a black marketing, advertising, and public relations concern, told a travel conference in 1969 that $540 million to $600 million of the income of black Americans is spent on travel. Approximately half of this is spent by about eight hundred thousand persons who attend at least one convention each year. Lewis estimated that if each spent three hundred dollars, the expenditure on conventions for travel alone would reach $240 million.

Equal Opportunity was a monthly for minority college students, published in New York by an interracial staff headed by Alfred Duckett, a black journalist and publicist, and John R. Miller III, white and a former Procter & Gamble sales manager. Launched in 1970 for use by colleges, public and other libraries, and minority community groups, its main aim, according to the publishing firm, was to bridge "the vital communication gap" between black students and corporations.

Another monthly reported to be helping black and other minority group members obtain employment information was *Contact*. Content included facts about job opportunities among the magazine's advertisers. A controlled circulation of 50,000 was listed.

Late in 1969 plans were announced for *Black Enterprise*, "designed to advise and encourage the development of black entrepreneurs," as publicity releases described it. (See Chapter 7 for more details.)

The other side of the coin of the business press is the labor press. It has taken black workers many years to be accepted by white labor unions. They have few unions of their own. An outstanding organization has been that of the Sleeping Car Porters, of which the moving spirit for many years was A. Philip Randolph, whose earlier career in journalism included coeditorship of an outspoken prolabor magazine early in the century, the *Messenger*. He served for years as editor of the *Journal* of the porters' union, which had been preceded by the *Pullman Porters' Review*, publisher of fiction and other general material as well as news of members.

Industrial Publications

Often associated with the trade, business, and technical publications are the house organs, or, as their editors prefer they be called, the industrial or corporate publications. Printed for free distribution within a company for its staff and employees or outside the firm for its customers, dealers, and friends, these magazines, which the majority are, in the United States alone number about ten thousand. This specialized journalism manifests itself in the black business world as well, particularly in that large area, insurance. Bearing such names as *Whetstone* and *Ulico*, these are internals for individual companies. Usually they are eight-by-ten inches in size, sixteen or twenty-four pages, use only spot color, and devote themselves to news of the business—coverage of meetings, personnel news, executive messages, speeches, and features on people. They carry only institutional advertising.

George W. Lee, the late editor of the Atlanta Life Insurance Company's magazine, *Vision*, on the other hand was free to editorialize on black affairs, perhaps because he was a vice-president as well. A quarterly that began in 1968, *Vision* carried primarily material about people. It used more color printing than is usually seen in these magazines.

Editors of these numerous but often little-appreciated newspapers and magazines, whether for black or white readers, generally have comparatively little professional journalism background or training; their experience more often is in advertising, public relations, or printing, if they have any communications background of any sort. The situation is changing as more journalism school graduates enter this specialized area and as more working journalists from the general field turn to house publications, trade magazines, and professional journals.

One of the black editors with more than the usual professional background was Murray J. Marvin, editor of *Whetstone*, magazine of the North Carolina Life Insurance Company. He was a reporter and art editor for several black weeklies and formerly edited the *Pilot*, the business magazine issued by the National Insurance Association. He also edited for the North Carolina Company the *Hot Line*, a semimonthly home office–duplicated newsletter. A few black firms have had newsletters or small newspapers to serve as their house publications.

Like many other similar small magazines and papers, those in this category suffer from lack of trained staff. Page after page carries pictures of stiffly posed figures; other pages are solid with speech copy. Yet they play a part in shaping public opinion about the institution that issues them, because the general press, even the black, has no room for such detailed copy.

Related to these papers and magazines is printed matter not ordinarily thought of as a form of journalism but rather of printing. These are the special publications, some regularly issued by companies for one or more of their publics. Included are annual reports, promotional leaflets, and special-purpose brochures. Often the editors and writers for the house magazine are called upon to produce such printed material. These materials are public relations tools with some of the aims of the regularly issued external house publications.

Magazines about Religion

The black religious press comes almost entirely from the black organized churches. A few newsletters and magazines are issued by black churchmen from within the white denominational world or by blacks from black and white churches who have their own organization. White denominations, Catholic and Protestant, sponsor periodicals for blacks and even have black staffers producing them, but they are white in ownership and origin.

Among the older of these is a mission magazine, *Josephite Harvest* of Baltimore. Black Catholics are so few in the United States they perhaps could not support their own journal. The *Josephite Harvest* provides for a segment of Roman Catholicism that is affiliated with the Josephite Fathers, an order known as the Society of Saint Joseph of Sacred Heart. The magazine, at one time called the *Colored Harvest*, has a mission objective. "The Josephites are an American Society of priests and brothers who labor to bring the Gospel to all men and to work for the full incorporation of the Negro into the Church and into the society of man," reads a statement on an early contents page. A quarterly, it is almost a picture magazine because of its heavy use of photographs supplemented by drawings. Articles describe interracial religious activities and the problems of black men and women who are the objective of the missionary activities.

Message, a Seventh-Day Adventist magazine issued eight times a year, has somewhat similar objectives and content, but more variety

8.1. A Roman Catholic (top) and a Muslim publication.

in its fare, with room for poetry, editorials, and regular departments on topics this denomination is particularly interested in, such as health and food. Published by the church's house, Southern Publishing Association in Hagerstown, Maryland, *Message* has 120,000 circulation and uses high quality printing, including color, possibly be-

8.2. Four black magazines of religion.

cause the denomination is one of the most advanced of religious bodies in employing the printing press to further its cause. It is entirely nonfiction, for the policy of all Seventh-Day Adventist publications is not to print fiction. It is white-owned.

What might be considered the genuinely black religious publications are those from the black denominations such as the National Baptist Convention, U.S.A., the National Baptist Convention of America, the African Methodist Episcopal Church Zion, and the African Methodist Episcopal Church. Like the press, the church has been a major influence among American black citizens. Its magazines and newspapers have given them a sense of security and hope. They have helped unite the people, and like other black media, have given them a sense of identity as well. When the churches turned to the printing presses in the nineteenth century the combination was powerful; because they could obtain subsidy for their journals the publications were among the longest lived.

8.3. These publications are among the oldest in black journalism.

One of the oldest extant black publications of any format is the *Star of Zion*, official paper of the African Methodist Episcopal Church Zion. Founded in 1876, it still is issued from Charlotte, North Carolina, with a paid circulation of about 7,500. This tabloid carries news of individual congregations, changes in personnel, general church notices, and reports on conventions and other meetings. It is published every Thursday.

Somewhat like the *Star of Zion* in appearance but more a newspaper in format is the *African Methodist Episcopal Christian Recorder*, official organ of the African Methodist Episcopal denomination. Dr. B. J. Nolen, once editor, considered it "America's Oldest Negro Weekly Newspaper."[8] A 1987 copy carries in its first page folio line notice that it is Volume 136, Number 23. A *Christian Recorder* is listed by Mott, the leading historian of American journalism, as existing from 1852–1931 in this denomination.[9] The present version is a weekly; in content it is like the *Star of Zion*. Its circulation is 7,500. The African Methodist Episcopal Church also claims the oldest magazine issued by and for black people in America.[10] This is the *A.M.E. Church Review*, published in Nashville, Tennessee. A publication of that name from the denomination was founded in Philadelphia in 1884, with B. T. Tanner, at one time editor of the *Christian Recorder*, as its editor. Mott records that it ended in 1936,[11] yet a paper of that name is being published still.

The Fraternal Publications

One of the more important national newspapers, the *Journal and Guide* of Norfolk, Virginia, was created out of a fraternal organ (see Chapter 4). Such fraternal groups—the Masons and Odd Fellows are examples of one segment, college fraternities are another—have published journals for many years, a few going back to the nineteenth century. At one time there was a *Fraternal Advocate* in Chicago that served various orders as well as insurance and labor groups with news of each other's doings.[12]

The *Pyramid*, begun in 1942, is the quarterly magazine serving members of a freemason's group officially known as the Ancient Egyptian Arabic Order Nobles Mystic Shrine of North and South America and Its Jurisdictions. Newsmagazine-size, it reports on the order's activities and promotes its interests, such as the annual convention and trips abroad. Its 1986 circulation was 35,000.

Today each of the larger black college fraternal groups, four fraternities and four sororities, has a publication of some kind, generally issued quarterly. They go to alumni and present members of active chapters chiefly in the black colleges or to campuses where segregation has created black fraternities and sororities.

Community Magazines

Nearly all black community publications are in newspaper form. Here and there one encounters a publisher who prefers the magazine format, either to have something different to offer in a city where black newspapers exist, or in a place where such newspapers have usually failed. But it is an expensive formula and format, as the experiences of some publishers in recent years indicate.

The Milwaukee periodical, *Echo*, and the one in Syracuse, New York, *Around the Town*, had financial troubles for lack of support from enough advertisers or angels. *Echo* depended for financing indirectly on the Milwaukee Inner City Arts Council, which received its money from the state for nearly three years until October 1969. The council maintained the Echo Writers' Workshop, and three other arts groups; the magazine was related to the workshop. The projects went out with only sparse funding. The publication was edited by Virginia Williams, who, about the time of the loss of funding, was appointed editor of publications by the Milwaukee school board, although she continued to edit the magazine. The magazine had some returns from advertising sales but not enough to meet all the costs of a monthly printed on high quality paper whose staff believed that the art work, short stories, and other content should be paid for; it was produced in the workshops conducted as part of the general project. Although *Echo* took no official editorial positions, its contributors often spoke out clearly for the freedoms they believed black people deserved. The magazine, eight-by-ten inches in size and running often to forty-eight pages, sold for five dollars a year and appeared, comparatively, to have considerable advertising support, but its rate was low and the quantity was not enough.

Around the Town, published for Syracuse, was issued for about six months in 1969 and 1970, and had more of a local touch than *Echo* but was much like it physically. It was suspended, the publisher planning to revive it as an all-state magazine, a novel formula seeking to capitalize on the fact that New York has four cities with large black populations: New York, Buffalo, Rochester, and Syracuse. As a community periodical it contained more news and straight journalistic material than *Echo*, but was illustrated also with photographs. Some material was obtained with the aid of university journalism students and of townspeople. Cornelious Loftin, its publisher, said when he began the magazine that he hoped it would reflect the life of the black community. It was to give the black people of the area some identity, some motivation. But it was difficult to reach the audience, now formed into small groups as a result of urban renewal or dispersed to distant parts of the city and a few suburbs.

about . . . time

All categories of black press publications have one characteristic in common. There are a relatively small number of highly profitable or strongly influential members. Somewhat more numerous are those than can be placed in the middle ground of fairly stable organizations. The rest, depending upon the medium (newspaper or magazine), barely manage to survive.

For every success (*Jet* or *Essence*) are a dozen other magazines that fail or barely attain stability. For every Los Angeles *Sentinel* or Chicago *Defender* are scores of small-town newspapers that have disappeared or must fight to stay in business, always at the mercy of general economic conditions.

That is the story, as well, of the black radio stations. Black-owned television broadcasting is still too small for such division. The situation is in microcosm that of the world of communications in general in the United States, regardless of the race of the owners.

In other words, publishers or stations not subsidized by churches, colleges, or other nonprofit institutions or by businesses issuing publications for public relations purposes have a difficult time.

The city or community magazine for black readers in particular is highly vulnerable because the magazine is not the type of journalism that fills the gap of insufficient news coverage or of in-depth writing. It is the community weekly newspaper in the large cities that tries to do both jobs and usually provides hard news but offers little penetrating writing of features and articles.

But Rochester, New York, ever since 1972 has had a monthly city magazine called *about . . . time* aimed at black citizens. It is a story in itself.

It was founded in a city which has an important place in U.S. black journalism, for it was there that Frederick Douglass launched his *North Star*, a newspaper later merged with another and renamed *Frederick Douglass' Paper*. There still exists in Rochester a black weekly, the *Frederick Douglass Voice*, begun in 1934.

The original formula for *about . . . time* was explained by its editor, Carolyne S. Blount. She wrote that the magazine was intended for the pubic at large "in an endeavor . . . to provide you with entertainment, information and other items to serve the best interests of the Black community of Monroe County and surrounding areas. Our goal is to present the material, deal with the issues and be responsive to our readers."[13]

The first official issue was dated December 1972. The corporation had been founded the preceding May. As a journalistic product it was amateurish. Most of the photographs were poorly reproduced and the original copy for the pictures was often equally inexpert, consisting of heads and shoulders, full figures, or groups of persons crowded into too small a space. The typography was blatant and the

8.4. A Rochester, New York, community magazine.

writing often more promotional than informative and factually impartial. Advertising occupied a fourth of the space in the thirty-eight-page issue.

In spite of such defects *about . . . time* (from the beginning the editors have insisted upon use of the lower case in the title) had a characteristic that is imperative for a local publication. It exhibited a sincere interest in the concerns of the black society in general and in the people of the city and the geographical area in particular.

In the period between Volume 1, Number 1 and Volume 15, Number 5, the magazine has improved steadily. Photographs are now clear and sharp and fewer mug shots or too obviously posed pictures are used. Considerable original copy is offered readers; some of it is intended to educate them. The biographical sketches, historical accounts, and most other contents are inherently attractive in writing and presentation. Advertising in 1987 occupied more than a third of each issue in a forty-six-page magazine. The space buyers now include banks, colleges, grocers, and other local enterprises as well as such firms as Xerox, 7UP, and Budweiser.

This improvement in general advertising volume is impressive for a magazine of its size in the third largest city in New York State. But increased volume in space sales is not always a sound basis for measuring success. Rates may be set too low, bills may not all be collectible, costs of production may increase too rapidly, and a changing economy may harm as well as help a publishing business. At some point *about . . . time* did begin to offer general printing services and continues to do so, much as do the small weeklies, or country newspapers as they once were called, across the nation.

James M. Blount became publisher and president of the firm, succeeding the founder, James J. Jackson. James Blount and Carolyne S. Blount were the chief stockholders and became the owners.

The changes in graphics, writing, and scope evolved gradually. So did the topics covered by the writers and editors. Here are some of the subjects dealt with by the magazine a decade or more after it was started: "The Lady is a Champ: Gloria Peck, Boxing Coach and Referee"; "Story of a People: Where Are We Now?"; "A Reflection of Shadows: Another View of Claude Brown's *Promised Land*" (an interview with Brown); "Appreciating the Arts Locally"; "On Prejudice: America, Let Me In"; "Parenting: Changes in Family Structure"; "Reagan Administration Tries to Hide Success of WIC Program"; "Is Student Action Dead?"; and "An Empty Stocking."

If one looks over the issues of *about . . . time* it soon becomes evident that someone on the staff is a book lover. From the first issue on there have been articles based on books, reviews of books, interviews with authors, both local and visiting, and occasional book lists.

In the now historic first issue is a piece called "Read a Good Book," which lists twenty "Gift Books for Children," works of Arno Bontemps, John Oliver Killens, Langston Hughes, and others. There also is an emphasis on black history in the magazine.

This desire to alert readers to certain books and authors and to the readers' heritage can be credited mainly to Carolyne S. Blount, who was a librarian before she became editor of *about . . . time*. Her background includes study at Virginia State University and Drexel Institute of Technology, with a degree from each.

Like her magazine, Blount has won awards. In 1987 she was corecipient of the Rochester Women in Communications, Inc. (WICI) annual Matrix Award. Her magazine since 1983 has won several honors, including the Howard Coles Communication Award in 1983 and 1985 as well as the WICI Special Communications Award.

In 1987 the magazine's circulation was 24,300. More than 95 percent of the circulation is paid, the owners reported that year. That is a publisher's figure.

When asked to account for the magazine's ability to survive when there was so much mortality among black periodicals, Blount explained that "basically the key to our survival has been 'cost control management.' We have had to constantly analyze marketing conditions that would favor our future expansion. But to this point, remaining small has been a key factor in our longevity. I cannot overstress the personal sacrifices made by the owners and the commitment/belief in the integrity of the black press as an absolutely necessary instrument for documenting black history/success."

Blount also thinks that the editorial approach is a factor in the survival. "Editorially, our publication has been 'issue' oriented, even when doing stories on local folk, and we have managed to blend national/international and local/regional topics to match the issues."[14]

Clubdate

Clubdate is a city magazine for Cleveland, Ohio, but intended for the black citizens alone. Founded in 1979, it is subtitled *Magazine of the Good Life in Cleveland, U.S.A.* and appears quarterly.

It highlights the doings and accomplishments of Cleveland's black citizens in sports, business, entertainment, and the professions.

Other articles are on welfare and black people, family problems, professions in the Cleveland area, personalities in the professional world, black social activities, and biographical or personality pieces on local figures. Attention also is given to food, the arts, shopping, travel, and question and answer pieces on topics in the news, such as AIDS. Madelyne B. Blunt, publisher and editor, writes the editorials.

Magazines of this type can supplement the white newspapers as well as the black. As one staff member put it: "We feel there is much in the black community which has not been covered by the regular press in the past and are seeking to fill the void with a somewhat sophisticated and quality magazine. . . . In the past, the black press had tended to be somewhat slanted, amateurish, unsophisticated and militant. We feel this has had appeal for only one segment of the black population. . . . This seems to be a growing market, especially in light of the fact that more and more blacks are finally getting recognition in the professional areas and are moving up, proportionately, in the economic levels."

The world of black journalism, despite the wealth of publications whose history and characteristics preoccupy this book, has had few publications about itself. One of the most useful but least pretentious

8.5. A community magazine for Cleveland, Ohio.

was the *Lincoln Journalism Newsletter*, begun in 1944 and lasting until 1957. It was duplicated, on business letter-size paper, and issued monthly, running from eight to twenty pages a time, with jaunty little cartoons to break up pages. Changes in publications and activities of editors, publishers, reporters, and other staff people were recorded. It called attention to new journalism books, courses, and other black journalism news; entered the controversies about the black press; and generally kept an eye on developments. During most of its life it was edited and largely written by Armistead S. Pride, chairman of the department of journalism at Lincoln University in Missouri. That university also for a time produced *PEP*, monthly organ of the National Newspaper Publishers Association (NNPA), a pocket-size printed magazine containing news somewhat on the order of the *Newsletter* but supplemented with photographs. NNPA also at one time had *Dateline*, a quarterly. Both ceased when financial conditions became difficult in the 1950s.

Today no regularly issued publication serves black journalism as a whole, but a group of Californians working on publications in the San Francisco Bay area brought out a monthly beginning in 1969, the *Ball and Chain Review*. It contained articles and cartoons relating the position of black journalists in the country then. Among titles in the early issues were "Plight and Promise of Black Journalism," "Press Parodies Propaganda," and "White Liberalism vs. A Black Reporter." Some contributions tackled more general matters, such as relations between black and white police officials.

Although most of *Ball and Chain Review* was devoted to blacks on white media, the black press received some attention. One of the most important recent assessments of the press was the report of an interview with Hoyt Fuller, editor of *Black World*, in which he was critical of the press, saying that the analysis of E. Franklin Frazier, the black sociologist, is still valid and that the papers are not fulfilling their role.

The *Media Woman* is an annual magazine published by the National Association of Media Women, Inc.; the New York chapter also issues a quarterly newsletter.

The *NABJ Journal* is a quarterly published by the National Association of Black Journalists in Philadelphia. In newsprint, it is a sixteen-page tabloid with news of the job situation, personals of members, news of the organization, features, and coverage of conventions.

Another Specialty

Magazines and papers aimed at special age groups have their own scope. It is a small assembly, mostly of magazines, for readers of any race, the more successful being for older men and women. Black journalism has ventured only slightly into this kind of magazine publishing.

Black Teen is a magazine for young black people, founded in 1986 by a publishing firm in New York City with the unusual name of Go-Stylish Publishing Co., Inc. Printed on low-grade stock, it uses both black-and-white and color illustrations and runs to seventy pages of material. A monthly, it appears to concentrate on show business stars.

Although apparently intended for persons over twenty years of age, there is a group of magazines read eagerly by teenagers. They appear to be popular but remain secretive about their circulation figures. One of these is *Black Romance*. Between those two words in the logo is another, in smaller type: *Intimacy*. Among the articles plugged on the cover are: "My Sexual Daydreams In The Classroom Had Me Ripe for Seduction," and "Seduced by Drugs and Sex Into A World of Evil." Most bear this tone. But there also is one called "Some Jazzy New Hats for This Fall" in the fashion tips department.

Right On! is found more often on newsstands than most black periodicals except *Ebony* and *Essence*. Its concept is built heavily around personalities from the world of black musical groups, movie and television productions, and sportsdom. The advertising is for cosmetics, hair preparations, and books for teens.

Fresh, founded in 1984, is of the confession genre, out of Los Angeles. Also of that appeal is *Secrets*, a Macfadden monthly and therefore white-owned. A magazine of that name was produced from 1936 on, but a 1987 issue is listed as one in Volume 15. *Secrets* makes a strong appeal to black readers. Most articles and stories as well as photographs have black characters.

What Is in the Black Press?

Black publications sit for their own portraits week by week and month by month merely by what they put in their columns. Here and there, in the first eight chapters of this book and in sections following this one, are indications of what is in the pages of the black newspapers and magazines of the United States. A closer examination of their content, however, may give deeper understanding of the role of that press.

The more honest, courageous, and professionally competent the press the more nearly accurate the representation of its audience will be. Whether the black press of this time faithfully reports the lifestyle of the Afro-American is a question still without a scientific answer. Undoubtedly it mirrors the activities and interests of some of the people some of the time. But as with most segments of the American press, there is little depth to the portrayal. The newspapers, as usual, devote their space largely to the transient, fleeting news. They must do so, for the most part, for what happens periodically is the essence of journalism. Most of the magazines are specialized and therefore exist in compartments, meeting the needs of only portions of the black population.

Parochial as the press may be, it is much less so today than it was in the 1920s, when Frederick Detweiler devoted a chapter in his book to its content. He noted that much of the country correspondence began: "Please allow me space in your paper," an unprofessional touch no longer encountered. The folksy tone of much copy was an exaggeration of the informality of small newspaper journalism in gen-

Lynch Story, the Protest Story aimed at Jim Crowism, and the Integration Story. For a few years after 1956 the Black Power Story, the Separatism Story, and the Black Revolution Story were popular, but by 1985 were rarely seen.

The Achievement Story has been a staple of black communication for years and today is prime copy everywhere. This popularity is the result of blacks now having more opportunity for achievement. The nature of the accomplishment has changed somewhat since 1956. Then it was achievement along the lines of white accomplishment — earning much money, being accepted by whites, having possessions and ease. Today it also is achievement of a more socially conscious nature — leadership in power groups, in the arts, in the sports and entertainment worlds, and in social action.

Next in Pride's group was the Negro Angled Story: news of blacks taking part in white news events, but covering only the black participation. This type continues to appear.

The Gossip Story is a staple of all journalism: personal news of such great importance that it is put into the regular news columns, such as weddings and other social news beyond the routine. This story also has persisted, but now is written with greater dignity.

To Pride's list can be added the African Story. With the intensified interest in that continent in the 1970s, for a few years some American blacks tried to identify themselves with the land of their forefathers by wearing African garments, studying African languages, singing African music, learning African native dances, and visiting the continent, sometimes settling there permanently. News from Africa or reports of visits there by prominent or local blacks can be found in both newspapers and magazines. The back-to-Africa movement has subsided somewhat.

The Kinds of Content

Undoubtedly most editors and publishers would affirm that their readers look to the press to find out "what really went on" when a news story about blacks breaks, even though it may be covered by the white media. And unquestionably they must turn to their own press for details about the vast majority of events occurring in their ranks. Such information is the stuff of black journalism. Elizabeth Murphy Moss, for years an officer of the *Afro-*

only the black members of a mixed theatrical cast, a discussion of why black women resent black men dating white women, or a collection of recipes for food especially liked by blacks.

Most dramatic is the difference in emphasis. In general news with a black angle much more detail is included. The news is played differently; it is on the angle. For instance, the St. Louis *Sentinel* put an eight-column streamer, two lines deep in 90-point type, on a story about Governor Lester Maddox of Georgia calling a certain black congressman a baboon and giving away ax handles in the House restaurant in Washington. It is unlikely that any white paper gave this story comparable play. It was big in other black weeklies as well. Similarly, the *Afro-American* devoted a full half-page, with six pictures, to the story about a model agency director who sued Time Inc. for three million dollars for ignoring her firm in a *Life* article about such black agencies and giving space, instead, to a white-owned one.

The story of the natural death of some accomplished or locally influential black citizen receives far bigger play in the black publication than the white; furthermore, the deaths of blacks who were not extraordinary often receive no space in the white. As with so much other black news, the black publication is the only outlet for it, even black broadcasting having limited news gathering resources and restricted time for news.

Biased News

One tradition in American journalism to which black journalists usually have assented even though it is a white standard, at least in theory, is that of separation, so far as possible, of facts and opinions. The opinions are expected to remain in the editorials so the reader knows they are the paper's official voice. Or they are supposedly under the bylines of writers, assuring the readers that they are the writer's views and can be discounted or accepted from knowledge of the responsibility and reliability of the writers. In practice, however, there is considerable violation. *Considerable*, however, is a comparative. American publications are spotless in this matter when compared to those of many other nations. But when held up to an ideal situation they are far from being free of bias. The policy of a publication, the views and prejudices of editors and owners, or its poor organization can result in opinions straying off the editorial pages and out of signed columns into what is thought to be factual only: the news columns.

In the days when the black press was mainly a protest organ and not a commercial venture it had no pretense of objectivity in it. Virtually everything in the early paper was propaganda for a cause, a practice inherent in protest. Today, however, most of the general black press is commercial and sets itself forth as fulfilling the traditional functions of newspapers and magazines: to bring readers facts and opinions, with a minimum of mixing. By its slogans and credos, the press has the agreement with its readers that it will be honest and keep facts and what someone thinks about them apart and recognizable for what each is.

Neither the black nor the white press succeeds. It perhaps is a matter of degree. The black press, particularly the newspaper, crusades more than does the white, having more to crusade for, and having a tradition of being campaigners. Thus, having embarked on crusades, it is likely that the fervor of campaigning will rub off on the presumably objective news stories. Journalists have several ways of breaking faith with the reader in this matter of attempting to tell the whole truth and nothing but the truth. One way is to use emotion-laden words in what supposedly is a straight news story and thus influence the reader. The black press has its practicers of the system. For instance, the Milwaukee *Courier* once began a news story this way: "Advanced methods of police methodology, seventh district style, saw a young Blackman handcuffed and thrown to the floor of a police wagon early Sunday morning following a speeding arrest." Late in the account appears this: "Milwaukee's finest, he said, graciously offered him a wet paper towel at the seventh district to wipe his bloodied nose."[8] The first eight words of the opening paragraph and use of *finest* and *graciously* later, in an anonymous story, are chosen by a reporter intending not to present facts only to the readers. There also was a conscious attempt to prejudice them. What is described is perhaps the way the reporter saw it but it is not necessarily telling it like it is — or was. If the events are as reported they can be described by witnesses or the victim quoted directly.

Such angled writing is to be expected in the ultramilitant publications, for they make no pretense of telling it like it is but only of telling it like the way they think it is (or want it to be or to be seen). Often it is the result of neophyte reporters and editors being given freedom to write as they wish without supervision of their copy before publication.

Not reporting the whole story or a story at all is the second way in which deliberately or innocently a publication controls or establishes opinion with facts. Leaving out what the owners or editors do not want publicized — or what the reporter or writer anticipates is not desired — is a common procedure in all journalism. Only the readers who have been on the inside of a story, perhaps themselves played a part in the news event, can be aware of the omissions. More often, perhaps, the deletions occur because the staff is too small to cover an event, especially if it is a complex happening reported by the white press. The black viewpoint on a major conflict within the black community or in the public schools of a large city is not easy for a community paper's staff to obtain. It takes several trained reporters to cover such a story, and since the basic facts usually are known already via the white media, including radio and television, it does not seem practical to neglect everything else, which might be necessary in covering the story fully. The existence of many factions within the racial community also increases the difficulties.

The third manner in which editors and publishers consciously or unconsciously try to influence the reader to their viewpoint is by the way they position and dress the news. Putting material on the first page is accepted as the way to tell the reader that the executives of the paper think it important or significant. It may or may not have high reader interest, but the editors want it to have.

Thus another Milwaukee black weekly, the tabloid *Greater Milwaukee Star*, put on its first page one week a story with a full-width headline reading, in inch-high letters: "PASTOR HITS RACIST HEADLINES." It was a three-quarter column story about a local minister attacking the Milwaukee *Journal*, the large white daily, for using what he called "racist headlines." The whole account was largely the text of a letter the minister had sent to the *Journal*, but the reader was not told if the letter was printed. The *Journal*, it appears, had used a headline reading: "YORTY DEFEATS NEGRO IN L.A. MAYOR RACE." The minister objected to the head because it pointed out the race of the mayor's unsuccessful opponent. Without arguing the point he made, a reader might wonder, however, if this out-of-town story was the major news of the week of interest to most black citizens of the area of Wisconsin covered by the paper, since they can read the white paper for themselves, and many do. Several stories inside the *Star* dealt with housing and other important subjects affecting the daily lives of Milwaukee's black citizens.

On the editorial page of the paper, furthermore, was another attack on the white daily. It would seem, then, that opposition to the white papers was then a part of the *Star*'s policy.[9]

In the world of journalism, regardless of creed, color, or politics, there are publishers or owners who like to gratify their egos. The *Impartial Citizen* of Syracuse, New York, is a bimonthly newspaper that for years has faithfully reported even the most trivial honors conferred on the publisher, Robert S. Pritchard. This black publication has three rivals in the city. Typical is a late 1980s issue which contains six separate photographs of the publisher printed on four pages of the paper, as well as three articles of an eighth to a quarter page in size about his appointment to committees, one a temporary chairmanship for a special event.

Such information long ago ceased to be news in the city. The publisher needs to hear what members of his own race say about his egocentrism. It might be more palatable if the paper really covered the area, but propaganda is strong in it and hard news weak. It has managed to get official advertising, however, with the subsequent necessity for businesspeople to keep an eye on it and on the insatiable thirst for fame of the publisher.

Putting in What Sells

Newspapers and magazines that fail to publish what readers will read disappear. Their readers and advertisers decrease in number. Not even a subsidy can save any but the smallest. The black press realized this truism of publishing in the United States, since it is a secondary press. The front page headline in a newspaper or the front-of-the-book articles or stories in a magazine are depended upon to pull in readers. Until recent years the streamers or banners on black papers dealt with crime. Now likely as not they are concerned just as often with some racial issue. A group of Syracuse University students noted that for twenty-five weeks the national edition of the Baltimore *Afro-American* gave its page-one streamer to a crime story but that crime had little place elsewhere in the paper. Elizabeth Murphy Moss explained why:

> What we do here is attempt to strike the best possible balance each week, without resorting to what we would agree to as sensationalism.
> This becomes a bit tougher and somewhat a mixed bag when you consider some of the factors which may not immediately be apparent in

comparing a national paper and a local paper, particularly a daily publication.

First, we are a second (or otherwise) paper. Second, some of the stories used which have crime appearances actually gain their prominence because of their civil rights context (examples: the one about white snipers using the gun of a police chief to fire on black protesters, and the one about South-Africa type arrests being used to arrest Mississippi students). The same is true of some of the crime appearance stories involving such groups as the Panthers and personalities like H. Rap Brown.

It also would be useful, from our point of view, if your team considered that the AFRO considers it a responsibility to play up on front page as many civil or human rights stories as possible. When an editor leans heavily in one direction as a service, then it sometimes becomes necessary to lean in another direction to balance off the interests of the newspaper's readers.[10]

The *Afro-American* uses more or less similar page-one makeup in its various editions. It consists of a streamer and several spread heads. But few other black papers appear to have any such journalistic formula. With the majority one week the main heading is sensational; another week, if there is a streamer or banner line at all, it is on more or less routine news. Such formulaless editing tends to play the news with the emphasis it may deserve instead of forcing a story into a prominence it ought not be given, as in the instance of the story of the letter sent to the Milwaukee *Journal.*

The Credo of the Black Press

Even if printing credos and platforms, as some black publications still do, were not a practice left over from an earlier day, when such statements were common, the policy would be worth noting because the aims of such statements are peculiar to this group of publications. The credos of some smaller papers appear in Chapter 6.

Found over the years in or near the editorial columns of the *Louisiana Weekly* of New Orleans, the *Weekly Bulletin* of Sarasota, Florida, and other papers is a statement resembling this:

The Negro Press believes that America can best lead the world from racial and national antagonism when it accords to every man regardless of his race, creed or color, his human and legal rights. Hating no man, fearing no man — the Negro Press strives to help every man in the firm belief that all men are hurt as long as anyone is held back.

The platform of the Chicago *Defender*, under Robert S. Abbott, was longer in his time than it is today. The present-day statement offers seven points which are a substantial goal for any publication:

1. Racial prejudice world-wide must be destroyed.
2. Racially unrestricted membership in all unions.
3. Equal employment opportunities in all jobs, public and private.
4. True representation in all United States police forces.
5. Complete cessation of all school segregation.
6. Establishment of open occupancy in all American housing.
7. Federal intervention to protect civil rights in all instances where civil rights compliance at the state level breaks down.

The *Afro-American* Newspaper chain used to carry on its editorial pages, above and below its name on the masthead, three statements. The first, from Martin Luther King, Jr.:

Let us not seek to satisfy our thirst for freedom by drinking from the cup of hate and bitterness.

The second, part of it a biblical paraphrase, was written by the late Carl Murphy, son of the founder, and declares:

May we let our light so shine that it will illuminate that which is good and beautiful, and magnify our Father which is in heaven. May we stand strong and firm against despair, falsehood, rudeness, hatred, pessimism and prejudice.

Perhaps the most famous *Afro-American* statement of policy was that written by its founder, John H. Murphy, in 1920, and reproduced regularly since in the chain. That credo says:

I measure a newspaper not in buildings, equipment and employees — those are trimmings.

A newspaper succeeds because its management believes in itself, in God and in the present generation. It must always ask itself —

Whether it has kept faith with the common people;

Whether it has no other goal except to see that their liberties are preserved and their future assured;

Whether it is fighting to get rid of slums, to provide jobs for everybody;

Whether it stays out of politics except to expose corruption and condemn injustice, race prejudice and the cowardice of compromise.

The AFRO-AMERICAN must become a bi-weekly, then a tri-weekly, and eventually, when advertising warrants, a daily.

It has always had a loyal constituency who believe it honest, decent and progressive. It is that kind of newspaper now and I hope it never changes.

The presence of such credos and platforms serves as a commitment of the paper to publish news and other information that will sustain the promises or aims of the platform. The *Defender*'s earlier version of its first goal, "the obliteration of American race prejudice," logically would mean recognition of the existence of black prejudice against whites or yellow peoples. America's black people, in the late 1960s and early 1970s, were exposed to many popular slogans, such as "power to the people," "right on," and "tell it like it is." During the years that they were popular, these expressions as least served as rhetorical counterbalance.

Humor in the Press

If this book gives the impression that the black press contains no relieving humor and no light touches it is a reflection principally of the newspapers; the magazines are considerably less sober. The papers overflow with news of racial conflict, columnar musings on the internal problems of the race, reports of activities, doleful editorials, and great quantities of promotion materials for entertainment and sports personalities on various business enterprises. The black newspaper is a clear denial of that stereotype of the American black citizens: always cheerful, singing no matter what their adversities or how badly rejected by others.

Their press is not altogether long-faced, but it is close. It hardly has had reason to be other, but for the psychological effect perhaps it needs more balance. A little effort is made. Some newspapers have one or two humorous comic strips or panel cartoons. Occasionally a columnist tries a quip; noted elsewhere was Louis E. Martin's character, Dr. S. O. Onabanjo, long popular in the Sengstacke papers. One can read through scores of black papers from many parts of the nation and not once encounter what the newspaper business calls "a bright," i.e., a brief, human interest story, or a humorous incident in the news. Here and there some editor or publisher prints bits of wry wisdom. ("Be careful what you say in front of children, they are like blotters, they soak it all in and get it backwards" appeared in the San Francisco *Sun-Reporter*.)

Black magazines do far better, having more time and being more of a target for free-lance writers. Cartoons do much to keep the balance: full pages, as in *Ebony*, share space with single panels and strips; an occasional piece of funny fiction appears in the community magazines. *Jet*, always breezy in its style, squeezes quips into some of its departments; *Essence* is giving space to entire satirically or ironically humorous articles.

Turner's "Wee Pals"

Examples of humor in the black press are found in comic strips and panel cartoons. Some portray racially integrated characters, others black figures only. Both magazines and newspapers print such work by black artists; some also have found their way into the white press. One of the most successful is Morrie Turner's strip, "Wee Pals." It goes beyond the usual integrated characters, for the small children who populate it include Americans of Oriental descent. "The main purpose of 'Wee Pals' is to entertain," Turner has explained. "Then, I like to poke some gentle fun at adult black and white prejudices and misconceptions. Deep down is a signal to Americans that black and white children get along together famously until they learn about prejudices from adults." He went on to say that he tries to use his comic art to call attention to the goodwill in the world and how it might be applied to the adult society.[11]

Turner, who has won awards from the National Conference of Christians and Jews and the B'nai Brith Anti-Defamation League for his work, developed "Wee Pals" from an earlier strip, "Dinky Fellas." It was used by several large white and two black papers and then taken by North America Syndicate, an experience that white cartoonists also have had before their work gained wide attention.

Son of a Pullman car porter, Turner began serious cartooning during World War II, when he was with the all-black 477th Bomber Group of the U.S. Army Air Force. He drew panels and strips for GI publications. After leaving the service he worked for eleven years as a clerk in Oakland, California, to support his family. Meanwhile, he free-lanced his cartoons to *True, Argosy, Better Homes and Gardens, Extension,* and *Black World* magazines and the *Defender*. Impressed and inspired by Charles Schulz and his "Peanuts" strip, Turner at first had all black characters. He later included white, Native American, and Oriental-American children. He was drawing the cartoon for the black weekly in Berkeley when Lewis A. Little, president and general manager of the Register and Tribune Syndicate, spotted it. The "Wee Pals" strip has appeared in *Stars and Stripes*, the military paper. Turner reported a mainly negative response at first, some GIs thinking it antiblack and others having an antiblack reaction and demanding it be stopped. He attempted to make his social points and still be entertaining, a difficult combination. His own social philosophy, belief in nonviolence, was arrived at following the assassination of Dr. Martin Luther King, Jr.

Surprisingly few black strips (strips by and about blacks) appear in the black press itself, probably because the papers cannot afford the cost of original work.

Ollie Harrington

The world of white journalism has had its Dave Breger, Bill Mauldin, and Herblock. The world of black journalism also has had cartoonists, some of them syndicated, who were popular, perhaps for different reasons. Breger reflected the views of the white rank and file soldier during World War II and the ordinary citizen in peacetime. Mauldin similarly drew wry cartoons about the thoughts of the man in the trenches or on the march and after the war pointed up in panels the ironies of current situations. Herbert L. Block, also a white artist, has been more concerned with the injustices suffered by America's black people than any other cartoonist who had access to large numbers of editorial pages in white publications, and sometimes bitterly limned their condition.

The black cartoonists are fewer in number, for if black journalism has barely been a living for many years, the career of a black cartoonist is even less promising, unless like the late E. Simms Campbell he manages to break into the big white magazine field, as Campbell did with *Esquire, Playboy*, and the *New Yorker*.

The one cartoonist that older black readers knew, if they were conscious of any who produced drawings for their papers, was Oliver "Ollie" Harrington, who labeled his feature "Bootsie." The drawings, which appeared in the *New Pittsburgh Courier*, portrayed some of the ironies of black life, but with a caustic humor. In one, for example, a little girl says to other black children playing outside a tenement: "I think I messed up in the civics class and ain't gonna git promoted this term. The teacher, Miss McCharles, been saying we be spreading freedom all over the world. Then I opens by big fat mouth and asked when it would git to Georgia and Florida . . . and Harlem!"

Harrington recalled the origin of his popular feature. He temporarily, in 1936, was replacing the regular cartoonist of the New York *Amsterdam News*, receiving seven dollars a week for his work. "After awhile a rather well-fed but soulful character emerged and crept into each drawing." The atmosphere was provided by Harlem, where Harrington lived. The character was named "Bootsie" by Ted Poston, then city editor of the *Amsterdam News* and for many years thereafter a noted black reporter for the white New York *Post*.[12]

Harrington went far beyond the single-character drawing: his panels tackled subjects of the day. His cartoons were largely realistic, edged with caricature. A panel typical of those poking fun at whites showed scientists at dinner. The white scholars along the table were takeoffs on the academic types to be seen among full professors in science departments. The bald chairman standing beside the elderly black visiting speaker says to him: "Doctor Jenkins, before you read us your paper on inter-stellar gravitational tensions in thermonuclear propulsion, would you sing us a spiritual?" His lime-flavored humor was not restricted to his drawings but also appeared in his writing. Telling, for example, of restaurants in New York "where the greys wouldn't panic if a member appeared and ordered a meal," he adds: "But it would take a strong constitution to pass off the ground glass and other delicate spices they were apt to drop into that particular serving."[13]

Another cartoonist who gained attention was Robert Brown, who signed his work "Buck" Brown. He regularly contributed a humorous panel drawing, "Fumbanks Tecumseh McShane," to *Tuesday*; it also appeared in *Esquire* and other national magazines. "Fumbanks" was a black who usually was in a humorous situation with his black employer; he was not bright and his boss despaired of him.

What Is Not in the Press

Black journals usually content themselves with editorials asking for cooperation between blacks and Jews in the efforts to bring about particular social reforms of common importance. Now and then one encounters a departure from this policy, as when the New York *Amsterdam News* published a story to the effect that "Jews control New York City's top jobs." The article, based on a survey whose source was not disclosed, brought condemnation from Protestant and Jewish organizations. Fearful perhaps of handling material about other minorities as clumsily as the white press has handled news of themselves at times, black publishers move cautiously in the area.

Also not often in the black publication, especially the newspaper, is coverage of events that lack a racial angle. Since the black paper is a second paper, this is entirely logical. Furthermore, it would be impossible for even the most financially substantial large black dailies and weeklies to duplicate—if it were necessary—what appears in the white papers in the same community, although in numerous American cities that are ill-served by one paper or two under the same ownership it would be beneficial if a black daily entered the scene and provided needed competition.

To the confirmed haters of blacks what is in the black press is either frightening or ridiculous. They see with fear the call in a few publications to a campaign to attack the police and stories in most others of the proud social and artistic accomplishments of some blacks, daring to equate themselves with whites.

But to other outsiders, those nonblacks who are not beset with suspicion, discovering what is in the black press is an exciting experience. They turn the pages of a big national weekly crammed with news of the many activities and interests of black people, or look at the increasingly successful consumer magazines, with their professional appearance, and are impressed. Another world opens before the reader when he has empathy for black America.

The time may come when the ethnic minorities will find it advantageous to work together in operating their publications. In a few instances that is done by black papers, such as the Portland (Oregon) *Skanner* and the Washington *New Observer*, that print material of interest to Hispanics. One California chain, the Post newspapers, issues a papers, *El Mundo*, for Latinos. Physically it is much like the local weeklies published by this firm in a half-dozen cities.

The Modern
Black Journalist

Stanley Roberts, while Washington Bureau chief for the Pittsburgh *Courier*, several times scored beats, but his best known exploit was in getting an interview with General Douglas MacArthur when all other reporters had failed. MacArthur had just returned to the United States from the Orient and was at the Waldorf-Astoria Hotel in New York City but refused to see newsmen. Roberts sent word to the general calling his attention to a situation overlooked by other reporters; some black papers were calling the general a supremacist and putting on him the blame for unjust treatment of blacks and for army segregation.

MacArthur called Roberts to his room and gave him a reply, denying the accusation and making a statement about black troops. "They didn't send me enough of them," he told Roberts. That led not only to a two-part article in the *Courier* but also to a piece about Roberts in both *Time* and the New York *Times*.[1]

This incident is an instance of a black reporter having an advantage over a white one in that he is more likely to be informed on the concerns of his particular ethnic group, and has a natural interest that white reporters are unlikely to possess. It is an argument for including black journalists on white staffs.

But the typical journalist working in the world of black journalism has gained little notice outside of his own small circle. When *Time* published its informative special issue on April 6, 1970, called "Black America 1970" it devoted its "Press" section to the black journalist. Most of the four columns were about the place of blacks on white publications, news agency and broadcasting staffs, and restricted to seven newsmen then working for white-owned media. These were Carl T. Rowan, William Raspberry, Thomas A. Johnson, Lem Tucker, L. F. Palmer, Jr., William Drummond, and Ray Rogers. Black journalists on black-owned publications serving the black readers, however, received no attention beyond one sentence. The paragraph devoted to black publications merely recorded that the New York *Amsterdam News* was the largest paper, that the *Afro* chain then had 87,600 circulation and that *Muhammad Speaks* had 400,000 circulation. *Ebony, Jet*, and *Negro Digest* were mentioned but *Tan* overlooked in the listing of Johnson publications. Thus would the general public as well as the uninformed black citizen gain the idea that the black press per se is of little consequence, with no black journalists of its own worth mention, and gain no idea of its size and extent.[2]

A few months before, the results of the work of two researchers, who had polled the NAACP's state conference and key branch presidents concerning black persons, were announced. They were asked whom they considered the ten most outstanding blacks, dead and living, and to say why they selected their first choice. Three among the first twenty-five of the living and two among the first twenty-five of the dead had some identification with journalism. Roy Wilkins was ranked second, A. Philip Randolph fifth, and Adam Clayton Powell ninth in the first group. Among the deceased W. E. B. Du Bois was second on the list and Frederick Douglass third. It should be noted that no living practicing journalist was named in the first twenty-five, for Wilkins's journalism, all in the past except for his syndicated column, was not what made him known to the public so much as his work as secretary of the NAACP; Randolph had not been thought of as a journalist for many years; and Powell's journalism had not been full time since the 1940s and he had written only sporadically thereafter. But a few others beyond the first twenty-five among those who are dead were named as journalists, including Martin R. Delaney, who assisted Douglass; Samuel E. Cornish, cofounder of the first black newspaper in America; John B. Russwurm, his partner; William Monroe Trotter of the Boston *Guardian*; and T. T. Fortune of the New York *Age*. Carter Goodwin Woodson, founder of the *Journal of Negro History*, and Marcus Garvey also were on the list. Among the then living mentioned beyond the first twenty-five were John H. Johnson, owner of *Ebony* and other magazines, Carl T. Rowan, Andrew T. Hatcher, and Louis E. Lomax.[3] The activities of most of these men are discussed in this and other chapters. No female journalists were included.

That black journalists deserve more than the short shrift they were given then is evident from the records, sparse as they are, of their performance. They scored their scoops on the war fronts as well as under more placid conditions, and often against handicaps white writers rarely experience, especially in those parts of the nation (but less so outside the United States) where they had not been admitted to certain hotels, clubs, and restaurants.[4] These obstacles are fewer today than ever before. But they still exist, as is known by black newsmen covering racial demonstrations and disorders who are mistaken for demonstrators and treated as protesters sometimes are treated.

The black journalists in the United States are reporters, writers, editors, and other journalistic staff members of black or white (or other minority) newspapers, magazines, news agencies, or in the journalistic end of broadcasting. They are not publishers, advertising people, or those in circulation or production, for these are identified with such other occupations as administration, management, selling, and printing, although they are closely enough related so that these services are dealt with briefly in this book.

The number of black journalists on white media is small, judging by the few clues we have thus far. Pride in 1968 published a figure of 175 blacks on white daily newspapers.[5] Columbia University, the same year, released results of a survey made jointly by the *Columbia Journalism Review* and the Anti-Defamation League of B'nai Brith. It showed that 4.1 percent of all media workers were black. Replies were received from news publications and stations only; thus numerous general magazines were not included. About 44 percent of the 388 units responded. Magazines handling news had hired the largest proportion of blacks, 5.1 percent. Newspapers were next with 4.7 percent; radio-TV last with 2.7.[6] A good many gaps in the survey may have skewed the results, since several major newspapers, one of the two national news agencies, and three newsmagazines refused to provide facts. The American Society of Newspaper Editors survey in 1987 produced these figures: black reporters and editors on white-owned newspapers, 3.5%, and black journalists in television, 13%.

These surveys produced figures that undoubtedly are low, considering the omissions and the changes that have taken place, for the push within the journalism and communications industries to obtain black talent and the increase in training recruits should have raised the percentages. The number still must be small, however, since there are about 1,780 white dailies and around 10,000 papers of other frequencies, and approximately 20,000 magazines of all kinds.

Black Job or White Job?

Although the concern of this book is mainly with the journalists working on media issued by and for blacks, at this juncture it is appropriate to consider the merits of working for a black publication or a white one, from the viewpoint of the man or woman who might be attached to one or the other. A case can be made for each.

Factors that the white-skinned journalist does not think of, for he need not, enter into this problem for black journalists. Will they be assigned to cover black news only, or write articles on black topics alone? Will they be used as the house blacks, victims of tokenism? Will they lose status with friends or family by going to a white publication instead of a black, or vice versa? Do they feel guilty by going to better-paying jobs on white publications when they know that black papers and magazines are seeking staff but usually cannot pay as well? Do they fear inability to keep up with the competition on white publication staffs? Are their chances of promotion on white papers or magazines limited by race? Will they change their minds after first working on black magazines or at black radio stations? Will they be able to go to white media without loss of status or salary? Is the experience on a black medium inferior and professionally injurious? And perhaps the most important question of all: On which publications can they be of most service (if they want to put it in such high-minded terms) to their race, country, mankind?

These are among the many questions that arise. Often they can be settled only in individual instances by assessing the experiences of others, although what others have done is not an absolute guide. Luck, being on the right spot at the proper time, the ever-present "in" provided by friends, and changes in policies of publications in a rapidly altering racial situation all can be more important than is realized. The vocational problem of the black journalist simply is more acute than that of the white. The latter has many factors to weigh in making decisions about what kind of journalism to engage in, and even, in rare instances, whether the black press is perhaps the best place to be, considering goals and ideals.

An examination of the careers of some black journalists should indicate what can be accomplished. Some have shown that the matter is not simply one of working on a black publication or a white one only but of working, at different times, on both. The decision is made out of necessity, perhaps; nothing else may be around to do.

When Virginia W. Williams, copublisher and editor of *Echo*, a black community magazine in Milwaukee, wrote a special series of articles for the white Milwaukee *Journal* while she was in Europe, she reported on what she had learned about race prejudice against blacks. Were these articles more effective in combating prejudice or gaining understanding of blacks than they would have been had they appeared in *Echo*, read mainly by blacks and with an infinitely smaller circulation than the *Journal*? Or would they have been equally effective?

Easy answers to such questions do not exist, for only an expensive and elaborate research program would reveal them. But the black journalist must weigh such experiences, and, being within the black community, can perhaps guess at answers.

The conditions of black journalists on black media, as we have seen in the history of the publications, usually have been inferior to that of the white on general media. Salary has been lower, facilities unequal, security little. The few black publications that provide pleasant work surroundings, job stability, and salaries at all commensurate with those of white offices are the exception. Walter White, at one time executive secretary of the NAACP, summarized the status of the black journalist in 1948, when he wrote:

> In many ways the establishment and rise of the Negro press in America has been a miracle in journalism. Until quite recently no Negro could obtain employment as a reporter, editor, or craftsman on any white daily newspaper or magazine. The Negro thereby had been denied the opportunity to learn the newspaper trade by working at it.[7]

He noted that a few blacks had been graduated from schools of journalism up to then and that more were taking courses as opportunities on both the black and white press increased. "But as a rule," he wrote, "the Negro newspaperman has had to establish his own practices and standards and the results have not always been uniformly good."

The situation improved in the four decades thereafter, black journalists having been accepted, even sought after, in the offices of many white media and needed more than ever by their own press. More are attending schools and departments of journalism and communication; others are being trained in short courses and workshops. But in the whole picture they are a small minority and rarely admitted to executive rank in the white press world.

As in the past, some black journalists continue to work for the black papers and periodicals, either out of pride in blackness, a desire to see black journalism gain in influence, or because they merely feel more at home among blacks than among whites. Others go right to the white press, some from an unrelated occupation, others by shifting out of the black journalism sphere.

The Uncommon Backgrounds

Generalizations about the careers and backgrounds of the better-known black journalists are not easy to make. Some attended colleges; some preferred newspapers to magazines, some the reverse. Some chose the world of white journalism, others the black. Counting which did which is meaningless because studies to obtain such facts reliably have not been made, either of a representative group, if such there be, or the total of journalists. Both studies would be incomplete scientifically because the records of journalists are difficult to obtain; even some of recent years are unavailable, for the publications for which they worked often are not on file anywhere and office records of staffs have been lost in mergers, fires, and careless disposal.

A useful source is denied observers of the black press and black journalists: the autobiographies, biographies, and books of reminiscence so often written by white journalists, editors, publishers, and others connected with the communications industry. Such books are among the richest portions of the literature of American journalism, of vastly higher quality and importance than the hundreds of novels and volumes of verse about journalism published over the years which ordinarily constitute the body of strictly literary material about an occupation or profession. Yet of the many scores of such life stories, few are substantially about black journalists. Included are one on Robert S. Abbott, a half-dozen about Frederick Douglass, five about W. E. B. Du Bois, three about Marcus Garvey, two on Booker T. Washington, two on George Schuyler, the same number on Carl Rowan, James Weldon Johnson, and Martin R. Delaney, and one each on John Russwurm, William Monroe Trotter, T. Thomas Fortune, Robert L. Vann, Claude Barnett, Enoch Waters, J. E. Mitchell, Cecil E. Newman, Gordon Parks, Roy Wilkins, Roger Wilkins, and John H. Johnson. There are also brief sketches in I. G. Penn's history covering the nineteenth century and in modern encyclopedias.[8]

This list constitutes the extent of the biographical source material in print form to this writing. Here and there are life story publications, few of them in readily seen magazines and newspapers. The scarcity of information about these journalists makes all the more valuable that which exists concerning those of recent years and the present. (See Bibliography.)

Ambitious authors seeking subjects for new biographies might find that the following men and women have lived lives of adventure, courage, intellectual activity, or extraordinary business or journalistic acumen: Samuel E. Cornish, John H. Sengstacke, Earl G. Graves, William O. Walker, P. Bernard Young, Ted Poston, Lewis E. Martin, Charlayne Hunter-Gault, Ethel L. Payne, Era Bell Thompson, Dan Burley, C. Sumner Stone, and John H. Murphy, Sr.

These and other biographies are unwritten not because of great racial prejudice but because sales cannot be depended upon to finance them, promoting them is costly in a nation the size of the United States, and the natural readers, the black Americans, often cannot afford such books.

The Careers of Black Journalists

At the risk of seeming to offer an abridged Who's Who in Black Journalism, an up-to-date volume that indeed would be useful, this section briefly tells the stories of a few black journalists who have gained public attention, often national awards, for their work. And, at a further risk, that of offending those omitted, or their families, it should be noted that this account makes no pretense of being a directory or catalog but seeks mainly to give the reader unfamiliar with these journalists an idea of their work and accomplishments.

Some of the men and women accounted for here have worked only for black media; these are emphasized, since their careers are more directly relevant to this book's scope than are the professional activities of those associated mainly with white publications and stations. But both are here. We begin with several who are no longer alive but who worked in a period beyond the years covered by the strictly historical chapters; they should not be passed over.

One was Allan Morrison, who died at fifty-one in 1968 while New York editor of *Ebony*. A Canadian, he had been the first black correspondent for the European edition of *Stars and Stripes*, the GI newspaper. After the war he edited the Harlem weekly, *People's Voice*, then joined the Johnson Publishing Company in 1947. He also did radio work while with *Ebony*.

Another *Ebony* staffer was a most versatile black journalist — Dan Burley, who died in 1963 when he was fifty-four. A Chicagoan originally, his first journalistic work was as a teenager with the Chicago *Defender*, and then, as either reporter or editor, he followed the tradition of the old-time tramp newspaperman who moved from publication to publication. His stops were at the New York *Amsterdam News*, of which he became managing editor; the New York *Age, Ebony, Jet, Tan*, an early version of *Muhammad Speaks*, and the *Crusader*. At his death he was publishing the *Owl* in Chicago. Burley had a variety of interests and talents. He not only was a skillful newsman and editor but also a composer of popular music, a critic, sportswriter, and promoter of sports and entertainment events.

The War Correspondents

Stanley Roberts, who got the MacArthur story related earlier, was only one of numerous war and peacetime correspondents. Several dozen others served in the two world wars, the Korean War, and the Vietnam War. Their experiences in general were those of white writers entering the battle zones. Most lived to return to their home offices. One who did not was Albert L. Hinton, lost at sea in 1950 when a C-47 transport plane he boarded in Japan went down while he was on his way to cover the Korean War. Hinton was working for the Norfolk *Journal and Guide* but also filing to other papers in the National Newspaper Publishers Association (NNPA) pool. He had been with the *Journal and Guide* for twenty years. Others, some no longer alive, included Philip Dunbar, Roi Ottley, Fletcher Martin, John Jordan, Enoch P. Waters, Ollie Harrington, Francis Yancey, Ollie Stewart, Walter White, Art Carter, Lem Graves, L. Alex Wilson, and James Hicks.

Ollie Stewart worked as foreign correspondent for the *Afro-American*, writing stories with a racial angle from abroad, such as a report from Augsburg, Germany, on the persistence of discrimination against black military personnel in the U.S. Army. Enoch Waters wrote from overseas for the Chicago *Defender*. Thomas Sancton, a onetime editor of the *New Republic*, singled out Waters in a series about wartime race problems, saying, "By any standards, he is a first-rate reporter."

ENOCH WATERS. Although Enoch R. Waters is included here as a war correspondent, he was far more than that, effective as he was at the assignment.

One of the few black newspaper workers who left an adequate record of his life,[9] Waters is remembered best for his connections with the Chicago *Defender*, since 1956 one of the few black daily newspapers of the nation, and for his editorship of the only significant black news service, Associated Negro Press (ANP).

He began his career in journalism as a boy, working part-time for the Philadelphia *Tribune*, still a major paper, and then briefly for the Norfolk *Journal and Guide*, an important black weekly. He did not get along well with the *Journal and Guide* publisher and moved on to the Chicago *Defender*, where he held many of the staff jobs during his quarter century with the paper. He became its World War II correspondent, one of the few black writers accredited to the corps, and served for three years in the Pacific theater. He left the paper in 1957 to edit the ANP.

Waters introduces into his recollections not only many of his encounters with little known or famous news and feature sources, but also with his colleagues at the papers where he worked and the views he held on various matters relating to the black people in the United States.

His book, because of his death, stops before his work with the Department of Health, Education, and Welfare in Washington. What stands out in his career is his moderation and courage when he immersed himself in journalism. He fought for the betterment of his race and was smeared, as so many others of any race have been, as a traitor to his country because he asked for the righting of wrongs.

William Worthy

"I have consistently maintained that all citizens have the right to go to any country that will admit them, and that newsmen in particular should not be prohibited by the U.S. government from traveling wherever news is breaking."[10] These are the words of William Worthy when he was a foreign correspondent for the Baltimore *Afro-American*. The statement is not merely a theory of freedom of the press or freedom of movement in a democracy because Worthy accepted it and followed it in his work as a journalist. He defied the restrictions placed upon citizens and journalists alike; not once, but several times.

In 1956–57, for six weeks, he went behind the Bamboo Curtain to the People's Republic of China for his paper as well as for the New York *Evening Post* and for the Columbia Broadcasting System (CBS). The U.S. State Department had banned such travel, but Worthy made the trip. On his return to the United States Worthy's passport was revoked. CBS, meanwhile, had killed some of his reports at the behest of the State Department.[11]

The Baltimore *Afro-American* stood firmly behind its correspondent. Raymond H. Boone, then the *Afro*'s editor, said, "We're not a newspaper that goes along with American foreign policy, right or wrong. We're for what's right and just. We're proud of Mr. Worthy and his courage."[12]

It was not until eleven years later that the correspondent recovered his passport. He went on with his travels just the same as if he had one.

In 1961 he went to Cuba, entering from Mexico. He wrote about the Cuban revolution. As a result he was prosecuted the next year under the McCarran-Walter Immigration Act; he was convicted and sentenced to a year's probation and three month's imprisonment. The conviction was reversed by a court of appeals.

Three years later he went to Cambodia, lacking a passport but with substitute papers that were accepted.

In 1980 he went to Iran and wrote about conditions there for the *Afro* as well as for CBS. He was the first American correspondent allowed into Iran after U.S. correspondents were ousted by the government.

While he was in China Worthy was on a leave of absence from Harvard University, where he was studying as a Nieman Fellow, a plan under which professional journalists could do special study in any specialty they desired. On his return from the Orient he resumed these studies in Cambridge.

Samuel F. Yette

Samuel F. Yette became known not only for his career in several communications areas but also for his suit against *Newsweek* in 1977. The details of this suit indicate the complexities that exist in newsrooms when the usual problems of management involve people of different races.[13]

Yette's experience during his four years on the newsweekly in its Washington bureau offices and the consequences of his bringing suit demonstrate problems of adjustment by both new employees and employers when different races are involved. In this case, Yette charged that he was called names, was made the butt of racial jokes, had to cover unsatisfactory assignments, and, after he had published a book on racism in the United States, denied assignments and finally discharged.

The magazine, on the other hand, denied the charges, cited instances where it had helped promote the book and its author, and affirmed that the reporter had not done his work satisfactorily.

The legal handling of Yette's case began when he brought his complaints to the Commission on Human Rights of the District of Columbia. The commission decided that there had been racial discrimination against Yette by *Newsweek* and awarded him one thousand dollars as "reasonable counsel fees." It also ruled that *Newsweek* must establish an employment policy, "maintain an affirmative action program," and report regularly to the Human Rights offices on the program.

The magazine took the case to the District of Columbia Court of Appeals, which reversed the decision of the Commission on Human Rights. Yette, a decade later, wrote of what he considered to be "the true significance of the case. . . . It is the danger of the First Amendment being misused to deprive the public and individuals of certain other constitutional rights. In my case against *Newsweek*, it was the position taken by *Newsweek* that its First Amendment right to publish both preempted my right to do so, and also superceded any rights I might have against racial discrimination under the Fifth and 14th Amendments and subsequent legislation pursuant thereto."[14]

Yette's interest in journalism took him through graduate study at Indiana University, where he earned a master's degree in that subject.

Before going to *Newsweek*, Yette had worked in several different areas of communications. He had an interest in photojournalism that began in 1956, when he and Gordon Parks (see Parks biography in this chapter) did a photographic series for *Life* magazine on segregation. His newspaper experience includes staff positions on the *Afro-American* papers, and the Dayton (Ohio) *Journal Herald*. He also worked for *Ebony*.

This work was followed by a position as executive secretary of the Peace Corps. His next post was with the Office of Economic Opportunity. He went to *Newsweek* as a correspondent in 1968. His complaint against the magazine, filed in 1977, came after the publication of his book, *The Choice: The Issue of Black Survival in America*. In 1972 he joined the faculty of the School of Communication at Howard University. During and following his teaching he continued his photojournalism free-lancing. In 1977 he was one of a quintet of journalists invited to the People's Republic of China. He also practiced his photojournalism in the USSR. When the Southern Christian Leadership Conference peace mission met in Lebanon in 1979 he was the only journalist allowed to accompany it. He now provides photo service to publications and organizations, and heads Cottage Books, a publishing company with offices in Silver Springs, Maryland. One of the books the company has published is *Washington and Two Marches, 1963–1983*, written by Yette with his son, Frederick Walton Yette.

Nunn and Rowan

A good many others gained attention during peacetime years, fighting another kind of battle. William G. Nunn, Sr., was on the Pittsburgh *Courier* staff for forty-four years, in the later years as managing editor. He left the staff in 1963. During his tenure the paper campaigned for integration of blacks in the military and in major league baseball. A son of the same name later held his father's post on the *New Pittsburgh Courier*.

Carl T. Rowan is perhaps the best known of all present-day black reporters; he has had one of the most extraordinary careers among these journalists. It has included work not only as a newsman, columnist, magazine and book writer but also as a U.S. diplomat, military man, and government official. When he was nineteen he became a naval officer. This appointment took place during World War II, for he was born in Tennessee in 1925. Rowan was one of the first fifteen blacks in U.S. history to become an officer in the navy. After the war he attended the School of Journalism at the University of Minnesota; earlier he had studied at Tennessee State University, Washburn University, and Oberlin College, receiving a bachelor's degree from the latter. At Minnesota he earned a master's.

From study he went to the Minneapolis *Tribune* staff, at first as a copy editor for that large white daily and then as a reporter and foreign correspondent from 1950 to 1961. His series of articles on conditions abroad and at home brought him to the attention of President John F. Kennedy, who in 1961 appointed him deputy assistant secretary of state for public affairs and a member of the U.S. delegation to the United Nations. Two years later he was named U.S. ambassador to Finland, for the liberal social attitudes of all the Scandinavian countries usually have made them receptive to nonwhite diplomats. While in that post he was the youngest U.S. envoy. The next year President Lyndon B. Johnson recalled him; he then suc-

10.1. Carl Rowan, the columnist, being sworn in as a U.S. ambassador.

ceeded Edward R. Murrow as director of the U.S. Information Agency. This appointment made him the first black to sit in the president's cabinet sessions as well as those of the Security Council of the United Nations.

Rowan left public service to become a daily Washington columnist writing for Publishers-Hall Syndicate. More than one hundred papers use his column, which deals with national and international affairs. At the same time he contributes to national magazines and to date has written four books. His honorary degrees and awards are more numerous than those of most other American journalists of any race.

The Alex Haley Story

Alex Haley is one of the few living black journalists who has been the subject of two biographies.

No black journalist had ever written anything that achieved as great a financial and popular reading success as that which came in

1976 to Haley, up to then a magazine article free-lance and publicity writer. But after his book *Roots* was published it took only two years for it to achieve a sale of 4.3 million copies, gross $5 million for its author, be reprinted in twenty-three languages, and be the basis for two miniseries on television which had enormous audiences. It also brought him a special Pulitzer prize.

The book had unexpected consequences and Haley had unanticipated problems as an author.

Alex Haley is a journalist who comes from a small town in rural Tennessee named Henning. He was born in the North, however, into a poor Ithaca, New York, family, August 14, 1921. After graduation from high school at fifteen, he went on to study for a year at Alcorn Agricultural and Mechanical College and then transferred to Elizabeth City State Teachers College in North Carolina, remaining a year. He dropped out to join the Coast Guard. By then he was seventeen and became a cook on an ammunition ship.

Some of his fellow seamen began asking him to write their letters home. This work led him to try free-lance journalism by sending articles to U.S. magazines, which led to his promotion to public relations officer. When Haley left the Coast Guard in 1959 he ranked as Chief Journalist.

Determined to have a free-lance writer's career, he settled in New York. As do most independent writers, he had to struggle for acceptance. After some time, assignments and sales began to come from such major popular magazines as *Reader's Digest* and *Playboy*. When the latter assigned him to interview Malcolm X, Haley was on the road to success. He and Malcolm X wrote *The Autobiography of Malcolm X*. Several million copies were sold and it became a classic in the literature about the lives of black Americans.

Haley then became interested in writing about his own ancestors, believing that knowing where they came from would stimulate blacks to pride in heritage. The investigation into his ancestry led to the successful *Roots*, accepted as a nonfiction book. Into it he poured traveling, endless interviewing, and pleas for financial support. When finally published it became a leading best-seller, far beyond even the Malcolm X book, and Haley became a millionaire. He used his earnings unselfishly, giving away much of them.[15]

But there was to be another chapter in the saga of Alex Haley.

In April 1977, the *Sunday Times* of London, England, one of the world's leading newspapers, printed an article asserting the factual basis of *Roots* was questionable, apparently because Haley had been duped by one of his major sources in Africa. He also was accused of inventing some of the supposedly factual information.

Haley had explained in the book's preface that "most of the dialogue and most of the incidents are of necessity a novelized amalgam of what I know took place, together with what my researching led me to: a plausible belief of what took place."

The *Sunday Times*'s reporter had gone to Africa and visited the site of Haley's investigation. He found no substantiation for some of Haley's claims. The New York *Times* interviewed several historians at Harvard and Yale universities and found that some of the scholars thought the errors to be unimportant but others agreed with the *Sunday Times* writer, Mark Ottaway, and the paper's judgment about the accuracy of the book.

Haley announced that he was flying to London to debate the *Times* reporter. But the American journalist withdrew from the encounter. Haley is reported instead to have "castigated" Ottoway in radio broadcasts.

Haley's troubles were not yet over. Harold Courlander, an American author who wrote a slavery novel called *The African*, sued Haley for plagiarism in late 1977. Passages from the novel and from *Roots* were presented together as examples of copying.

This incident was the second such in Haley's career. He had been the defendant in an earlier suit for plagiarism filed by Margaret Walker, a recognized author who wrote a novel entitled *Jubilee*. Her suit was unsuccessful however. Courlander did better. Haley's contention was that he had never read *The African*, that his book was offered as a "symbolic truth," and that some friend may have passed along to him material from the novel without his (Haley's) knowledge.[16]

The judge in the case recommended an out-of-court settlement and it ended in that manner, Courlander getting five hundred thousand dollars in damages and Haley acknowledging and regretting that "various materials from *The African* by Harold Courlander found their way" into his book, *Roots*.

Haley went on to publish another version of his book and to set up a foundation named for the principal character in his book, Kunta Kinte.

An important consequence of the suits was the attention they drew to the question of how true-to-fact fiction must be, the validity of a fictionized account sold as a factual record, and the merit in Haley's statement that he had written what he called "faction."

Walter Goodman of the New York *Times* editorial staff, writing about "Fact, Faction, or Symbol?" made two major points that journalists, black or any other color, are expected to consider. He wrote:

> Does it matter if, as seems to be the case, "Roots" is filled with inaccuracies? For the tens of millions who were moved by the book and by the unprecedentedly popular television version, probably none of the recent criticisms of Alex Haley's work count for much. Americans, white and black, responded to the appeal of the saga of Kunta Kinte's journey from his home in Africa to slavery in America, and they found inspiration in a black author's search for his ancestors and the heritage of his people.

And

> Valuable and significant as "Roots" is, the distinction between a disciplined work of history and pseudo-history or "faction" is still of consequence—to the historian who has the standards of his craft to uphold and to the general reader for whom a "true story" evokes a special emotional response. "Symbolic truth" is not a good synonym for want of truth.[17]

Undaunted, Haley went on to publish a novella, *A Different Kind of Christmas,* and the script of a drama, *Roots: The Gift,* shown in 1988 on a network.

Wilkins, Holman, and Others

Roy Wilkins, the NAACP executive director, may not be thought of as a black journalist. Yet he had considerable practical experience in the profession and for years wrote a regular column appearing in dozens of papers. Wilkins's first journalism work was in college, while majoring in sociology at the University of Minnesota. He edited the *Minnesota Daily.* When he graduated in 1923 he went to work for the Kansas City *Call,* a leading midwestern black weekly, eventually becoming managing editor. Even then he was a columnist, with one for the *Call* named "Talking It Over." He left black journalism to be assistant NAACP secretary in 1931. Three years later he added the editorship of the *Crisis* to his duties and kept it for fifteen years. He also wrote a syndicated column, "Along the Way" or simply "Roy Wilkins's Column" or "Roy Wilkins."

One of the earliest of the modern black journalists to join a white daily staff was Ben Holman. He was a 1952 graduate of the University of Kentucky when he became a Chicago *Daily News* reporter, then was drafted and spent two years in the army. He returned to the paper as a reporter. Once while on an assignment he disguised himself as a Black Muslim to write a series on that group. He became director of Community Relations Service of the Department of Justice and counseled organizers of several regional conferences to bring together black and white journalists and publishers to consider race news coverage.

A successor to Wilkins as editor of the *Crisis*, James W. Ivy was on both black and white publication staffs. He joined the NAACP as an editorial assistant in 1943. Earlier he had been a Virginia high school and Hampton University teacher. Born at Danville, Virginia, he studied at Virginia Union University and New York University. Ivy left the *Crisis* to serve as managing editor of *Common Sense*, a liberal white magazine of public affairs; his background for that post was his work in the late 1920s with the controversial black periodical, *Messenger*, as book review editor. When he returned to the NAACP magazine it was to be managing editor.

Another man who was on both specialized and general publications was Roi Ottley, the biographer of Robert S. Abbott, founder of the Chicago *Defender*. After studying at the University of Michigan, St. Bonaventure University, and St. John's Law School, Ottley became a World War II correspondent for the unusual, adless, New York white paper *PM*, owned by Marshall Field. All its reporters signed their stories. Ottley also was on *Liberty*, a onetime competitor of *Collier's* and other mass magazines. After the war he joined the Pittsburgh *Courier* as a special correspondent. While in Europe for the white publications he emphasized the roles of black people in both war and peace. He covered more than thirty thousand miles and continued traveling when he went to the *Courier* staff. He already had published a highly successful book, his first, *New World A'Coming*; later he published *Black Oddysey, No Green Pastures*, and *The Lonely Warrior*, the Abbott biography.

Photojournalist-Editor-Cinema Producer

Certainly one of the most versatile of all U.S. journalists, regardless of race, is Gordon Parks. For he not only has been recognized as one of the best photographers and photojournalists of the country but he also is known as novelist, poet, cinema producer, movie writer and director, music composer, magazine editor, and author.

Parks decided to become a photographer, he relates in an autobiographical book, *A Choice of Weapons*, when he stopped in at a Chicago movie house one day in 1937. Then he was a Pullman car waiter, newly impressed with the power of a picture after seeing many paintings at the Chicago Art Institute. At the theater he saw newsreel films of the Japanese bombing the U.S. gunboat *Panay*. When the film was over, Norman Alley, the photographer who had taken the pictures, came on stage to talk about his experiences.

"I sat through another show," Parks recalled, "and even before I left the theatre I had made up my mind I was going to become a photographer." He was reminded by the pictures of those in magazines he had seen long before of poverty in the Southwest, taken by Arthur Rothstein, Carl Mydans, Ben Shahn, and others working for Roy Stryker of the Farm Security Administration (FSA) during the depression years of the early 1930s.

When his train run ended at Seattle, he relates, he immediately tried to buy a camera. He was appalled at the high cost of equipment. Finally he bought a secondhand one for $12.50, in a pawnshop. While shooting his first rolls of film he fell off a Puget Sound wharf and had to be pulled out. But the photographs were undamaged and so good, in fact, that the camera shop where he bought the film exhibited them. From then on he went everywhere experimenting with his new-found art as widely as his money would let him.

The St. Paul *Pioneer Press*, a large white daily in Minnesota (the other end of his run) printed some of his pictures; later the Minneapolis *Spokesman and Recorder*, a black weekly, ran Parks's work regularly on its front page, although neither paper paid him. But it put him into practical journalism, for he went to work as combination circulation manager and official photographer for the weekly, which bought him a press camera. But, Parks admits, he was not much of a salesman. Having to earn a living forced him back to railway work on the Chicago & North Western as a porter. He took pictures on the run between Chicago and the Twin Cities and continued his study of paintings in art galleries. "I read every book on art and photography I could afford," he later wrote.

When one day Bernard Hoffman, a *Life* cameraman, boarded Parks's train, he questioned him for hours about the profession. By persistence, he got a chance to do fashion photography for an exclusive St. Paul store, nearly bobbled the assignment but came through with the needed films. After some delay because he had to move to Chicago, he soon was making a fair living with his camera there. At times he earned as much as $150 a day, a fabulous amount for the time, but there were some idle days. He continued to take fashion pictures and portraits of wealthy women, but he also spent some of his time exposing film in the Chicago ghetto districts; the photographs of people in those neighborhoods and living under similar conditions elsewhere have become his specialty since.

When Parks was awarded a year's Rosenwald Fellowship of two hundred dollars a month he decided to apply to the FSA, whose photographers earlier had so much impressed and inspired him. Under Stryker he was a trainee in Washington early in 1942, the World War II days having come. There he learned lessons not only in photography as an art but also about his reactions to race prejudice. The human compassion of the noted white photographers with whom he snapped pictures side by side kept him from being totally antagonistic toward whites. From the FSA he went to the Office of War Information staff and later to the Standard Oil Company of New Jersey.

Life's photo staff accepted Parks in 1949; he thus joined a cluster of some of the country's most famous photojournalists. He took many memorable pictures and series of photographs for the weekly until he became interested in book writing and motion picture making. His first book appeared in 1963, *The Learning Tree*, an autobiographical novel. Two years later came the partial autobiography, *A Choice of Weapons*, in which he explains not only his background but also his view that through his art he can fight the battle for his race better than by the use of more conventional weapons. Some of his poetry and color photographs appeared in 1968 in *A Poet and His Camera*. His writing, like his photography, is clear and realistic.

As the first U.S. black to produce and direct a full-length film for a major studio, Warner Brothers-Seven Arts, Parks in 1969 completed a cinema version of *The Learning Tree*. He also wrote the music, a symphony in three movements, although he never had music lessons. This experience led him to form his own motion picture producing firm. His most recent work in journalism was as editorial director of *Essence*, a magazine for black women (see Chapter 7).

Why did Parks choose photojournalism, poetry, music, and cinema? His answer was quoted by *Jet* in 1969: "This leads me into bigotry and discrimination and all the indignities that black people have suffered here in the United States. And that leads me back to why I chose a camera. Why I have chosen the film. Why I have chosen poetry and music to fight these particular things. I think that these have been more effective than the more violent weapons such as the gun, the knife, the club or other weapons that you might use."

Parks's background was not what one might expect in so sensitive and artistic a writer and photographer. Born in 1912 in Kansas, he

10.2. George S. Schuyler, Pittsburgh *Courier* writer and controversial journalist.

was the fifteenth child in his family. When his mother died fifteen years later he was sent to Minnesota to live in its slums, where he lived for fifteen years more, disappointed at not getting a college education but reading widely on his own and studying by himself the techniques of artists whose work was to be seen in nearby galleries and museums.

Conservative Spokesman

One black journalist who was listed in *Who's Who in America* was George S. Schuyler, long identified with the Pittsburgh *Courier*. Discussing the writing and writers in the black press, Thomas Sancton, writing in the *New Republic*, said that in his opinion Schuyler "is about the best."[18] This praise from a widely respected white newsman and liberal magazine editor may seem unusual, for Schuyler espoused ultraconservative political and social views for much of his journalistic life and it biased his work. Sancton wrote his opinion while Schuyler was moving from one social philosophy to another and may not, therefore, have realized the extent of the journalist's and columnist's eventual political change. It is not, however, that Schuyler was so ardent a conservative; it is that his viewpoint warped his work. It would have had the same effect had he held to directly opposite beliefs, such as he had in youth, and strained everything he saw through them.

A Rhode Islander born in 1895, Schuyler was a journalist from the time he was twenty-eight. He was assistant editor, then managing editor, of the *Messenger*, the gadfly magazine then considered radical, edited by A. Philip Randolph and Chandler Owen. He edited *National News* briefly in 1932, then went to the NAACP's publicity department. From 1937 to 1944 he was business manager of the *Crisis*. In the latter year he returned to the Pittsburgh *Courier* until 1964, having worked there on and off previously. On the *Courier* he was a special correspondent in South Africa, the West Indies, French West Africa, and the Dominican Republic. At the same time he edited *National News* for a year and worked for the white press as a special correspondent in Liberia for the New York *Evening Post*. In 1953 he became a columnist, writing regularly until 1962. In 1960 he also began work as a foreign correspondent once more, this time for the North American Newspaper Alliance (NANA), a white syndicate, in Nigeria, Portugal, and East Africa, meanwhile doing other writing for NANA.

So energetic and prolific a writer as Schuyler also turned to books and articles as outlets for his work. He was author of three volumes, two of them novels, and contributed to numerous magazines, the articles tracing the changes in his views over the years. In early days he wrote for the *Nation, Plain Talk, Common Ground, World Tomorrow*, and *Americas*, all white, and what can be called liberal publications. He did not neglect the black press, for his byline also was in *Opportunity, Negro Digest*, and the *Crisis*. But in the fifties and sixties his work appeared, when in magazines, in the rightist periodicals, socially and politically: *Freeman, National Review, Human Events*, and *American Opinion*, the latter the John Birch Society magazine. All were white-owned.

In 1953 he was cited by Lincoln University for his performance in journalism. Fifteen years later he had come to represent ultrareactionaryism to the militants among the nation's blacks. He documented his position in a straightforward autobiography, *Black and Conservative*. Whatever one thought about his social outlook, his writing style and use of irony and wit in making his points marked him as outstanding among black editorialists. Sancton called him "a clear and vivid writer," adding: "Sometimes he writes with a mordant sarcasm, but he does not let it unbalance the order of his ideas. And he hammers what seems to me the soundest line of all: that the Negroes' natural friend, and natural ally, is the white worker, and that the two should strive for a unity of purpose in the labor movement." From this comment it is obvious that Sancton was writing in the early 1940s when white labor was identified with the hardships some of which the black society still has not overcome.

During Marcus Garvey's day Schuyler was skeptical about the man who has been called the black Moses, chiefly because he sought to lead the black man out of his misery with various somewhat grandiose plans. When Garvey founded a new church body, the African Orthodox Church, and wrote that God was black, Schuyler commented: "Last summer Marcus accused the Deity of being a Negro. No wonder the luck went against him!"[19]

Schuyler, less productive as the 1970s began, nevertheless was still in view. *American Opinion* at that time carried a picture of him on its cover and a tribute to his social philosophy inside. He retained his philosophical position, still the obverse of his views early in the century. Both his wife and daughter died before he did, on August 31, 1977, in New York at age 82. George Goodman, Jr., the New York *Times* reporter who wrote his obituary, accurately described him as "a major black author and the first black journalist to attain national prominence with the acidic bite of his ideas."

The Black Sportswriters

A. S. "Doc" Young, himself a sportswriter, has told the stories of some other journalists of the black press world in an *Ebony* article. He includes such sportswriters as Brad Pye, Jr., Frank A. "Fay" Young, Bill Nunn, Sr., Bill Nunn, Jr., Wendell Smith, Chester L. Washington, Eric "Red" Roberts, Abie Robinson, and Sam Lacy. The two Nunns, Smith, and Robinson all worked for the Pittsburgh *Courier*; Robinson was on two papers, the *California Eagle* and the Los Angeles *Sentinel*.

RUST AND SIMS. Black talk-show hosts covering the sports world have gained large followings, particularly in heavily populated New York City areas. Two of these were Art Rust, Jr., and Dave Sims, who were at the top of a group of five such program stars during the mid-1980s and represented by sports columnists as rivals.

Rust, the older of the two, not only had a five-day evening program on WABC radio but also had a column in the New York *Daily*

News. Sims, in his midthirties, was with WABC, on the Madison Square Garden cable network, and part of the sports team on WABC-TV.

Rust, a native New Yorker, went to Long Island University. In 1987 he led in sports broadcast journalism by having 437,000 listeners nightly, or about half again as many as the next largest host, Sims, who recorded 227,000. The sportswriters in the area had various explanations for Rust's popularity, usually noting that his obvious enjoyment of his role had a good deal to do with it. Bruce Chadwick, a veteran reporter at the New York *Daily News*, writing about Rust and Sims, quoted Rust: "It gives me a chance to educate people, to be an historian, to be a sociologist."

Rust also touched on race problems, saying to one caller: "You want to know why blacks aren't managers and owners? Hey, it's not just sports, it's racism, my friend, and I talk about it." He also was quoted as saying, "I love my callers. I've gone to their weddings. . . . You can't get me out of this job with a stick of dynamite."

Sims, twenty-five years younger than Rust and a Philadelphian educated at Bethany College, West Virginia, where he was a communications major, also enjoyed the job. "It's a perfect format," he told Chadwick. "You interview guests and you talk to callers. You argue, you agree. . . . It's the perfect job."

Sims brought a strong background of journalism experience to the job. He was a sportswriter for the New York *Daily News* (Rust's paper) and also was a sports producer, reporter, and anchor at KYW-TV in Philadelphia. He was sports editor before that at Satellite News Channel in Stamford, Connecticut.

SAM LACY. Another popular sportswriter, considered the dean of the beat, is Samuel H. Lacy, who was eighty-four in 1987 and still on the job. He was one of the speakers in that year at the first Black Press Hall of Fame sessions in Baltimore.

Baltimore has been the scene of his work for decades, for he has been sports editor of the Baltimore *Afro-American* since 1943.

Henry Scarupa of the Baltimore *Sun* wrote just before Lacy's appearance at the black press celebration that "The *Afro* sportswriter is perhaps the best known for his role in helping break the race barrier in major league baseball."[20]

Scarupa said that Lacy insisted that black baseball players were the equal of white athletes. In Lacy's writings he steadily urged team owners to integrate their outfits. It was in part because of his crusading that Jackie Robinson signed with the Brooklyn Dodgers in 1947.

He supported Robinson during the star's early years as the only black in professional baseball.

Lacy and another black sportswriter, Wendell Smith of the Pittsburgh *Courier*, stayed in the inferior hotels where Robinson was segregated and like Robinson were turned away from southern ball parks' main entrances because of their color. Lacy suffered such treatment at other times.

He became the first black member of the Baseball Writers Association. Since then he has had various awards, among them: first black person enshrined in the Media Hall of Fame, in 1984; "Man of the Year" selection in 1985 by the Washington Pigskin Club; and representation in the Black Athletes Hall of Fame in Las Vegas. Concerned about the careers of young black athletes, he continues to travel to college campuses to speak to students in schools and departments of journalism.

Writing in *Dawn*, the magazine supplement to numerous black papers, Lacy credits the black press for much of the removal of prejudice against blacks in sports, both professional and amateur.

Lacy's sportswriting career began in high school and college. His first professional job was on radio in Washington, D.C. He went on to the Washington *Tribune*, the Chicago *Defender*, and the *Afro*. WBAL-TV, Baltimore, hired him as a sports commentator from 1968 to 1978.

First Black TV Newsman

Faced with competition the white journalist does not have to confront, the black newswriter or magazinist has found that versatility or intense specialization is an asset. A number of the journalists mentioned so far in this chapter have possessed one quality or the other. Louis E. Lomax, who broke a precedent when he became the first black newsman on television, was another who had various talents. A Georgian, born in 1922, he came from a family of teachers and writers. At Augusta's Paine College he began his journalism by becoming editor of the *Paineite*, the college paper. His first professional journalism was with the Baltimore *Afro-American*. He continued his formal education by attending American University in Washington for graduate work. This study led to a faculty post at Georgia State College in Savannah, where he taught philosophy. He did further graduate work at Yale.

Lomax returned to journalism as a staff writer for the Chicago *American*, later called Chicago *Today*, a large white daily. It was in

1958 that he went into television, at WNTA-TV, New York, and was the first black newsman for what was then a fairly new medium. He continued writing by contributing articles to such major magazines as *Harper's, Nation*, and *New Republic*. Three years later he published his first book, *The Reluctant African*. It brought him the Anisfield Wolf-*Saturday Review* Award for 1961. He also wrote *To Kill a Black Man, When the Word is Given, The Black Revolt*, and *Thailand*. His television work was writing and producing as well as handling news. With Mike Wallace he wrote and produced a program called "The Hate That Hate Produced." He also was associate producer of a prizewinning documentary, "Walk in My Shoes," seen on American Broadcasting Company stations. At his death in 1970 in an automobile accident he was professor of humanities and social sciences at Hofstra University.

The Washington Scene

Louis R. Lautier broke into the news himself in 1947 when he became the center of a case in which, because of his race, he was refused admission to the Congressional Press Gallery in Washington, an area for reporters covering Congress. This and other media galleries are operated under rules adopted by the standing committee of correspondents whose members are elected by the newsmen. Reporters whose credentials have not been approved by the committee cannot sit in the gallery. Lautier was turned down ostensibly on grounds other than race but fought the case out and was recognized. The National Press Club, which for years has occupied two floors at the top of the National Press Building in the national capital, also held out against admitting not only black journalists but female applicants as well. Lautier gained admission in 1955; the stricture against women was dropped in 1970. It was the restrictive attitude which led to formation of the Capital Press Club by black journalists working in Washington. Both men and women of any race are accepted.

Lautier worked for the NNPA in the days when it ran a news service for its member papers; he also was on the staff of the Atlanta *Daily World*. He won a Willkie Award for Journalism as a result of his successful fight to gain admission to the press gallery.

Chuck Stone

As will have been noted by now, most black journalists who have attained some degree of public recognition had accumulated journalism experience before attaining their topmost positions. But Charles Sumner Stone, Jr., better known as Chuck Stone, appears not to have had any such preliminary preparation. Yet before he was forty he had been the top editor of three major national black newspapers: New York *Age*, the Washington edition of the *Afro-American*, and the Chicago *Defender*. During his ten years in black news work Stone won two awards and then moved on to organization and government committee public information activity.

A St. Louisian, born there in 1924, Stone went to New England for his first college degree and then to the Midwest for his second. From Wesleyan University he received an A.B. in 1948; from the University of Chicago a master of arts degree in sociology three years later. From 1956 to 1958 he was employed by the Cooperative for American Relief to Everywhere (CARE), the first year in India, Egypt, and Gaza and the next as an educational consultant in the United States. In 1958 he went to *Age* as editor; in 1960 moved to the Washington paper; in another three years to the Chicago daily. He won a first prize from the NNPA for the best column of 1960 and was named for an Outstanding Newsman of the Year award the next year.

Stone left journalism for the tangential field of public information, becoming executive assistant for the committee of education and labor of the U.S. Congress, public information director and vice-chairman of the National Conference on Black Power, and a member of the steering committee of the Black United Front, Washington. In early 1970 he became director of educational opportunity projects, Educational Testing Service, Princeton, New Jersey. During 1969–70 he appeared every few weeks on NBC's "Today" program as a commentator on racial problems. He withdrew from the program in 1970, saying that he was unable to communicate with "white America" and reported receiving antagonistic mail.[21] Stone is author or editor of five books: *Tell It Like It Is, Black Political Power in America, Contemporary Black Thought* (editor), and *The Best of the Black Scholar* (editor). He published *King Strut*, a novel, in 1970.

The list of Stone's awards and special activities is huge. His two main jobs are professor of English (journalism) at the University of Delaware and senior editor and columnist for the Philadelphia *Daily News*. He also is active in the National Association of Black Journalists, of which he was a founding member and first president. He fulfills special lectureships frequently, some in government and others in communications groups. Wilberforce University gave him an honorary doctorate in 1977.

His column, called simply "Chuck Stone," is syndicated nationally, but he is known for the fact that he is more than a columnist. He has undertaken a certain crusade, the objective of which is to aid criminals and their families who come to him for help and fair treatment by police departments. By 1987, according to the *Wall Street Journal*, forty-two criminals had turned themselves in to him, assured that they would get fairer treatment from the authorities. He refuses to help rapists. He is convinced, however, that many black criminals have reason to fear being beaten by police.

William Gordon

Also active in government service was William Gordon, a senior officer of the U.S. Information Agency (USIA) in Washington, who had as one of his duties writing a weekly column on civil rights for distribution to the media in other countries and to the Department of State's agencies abroad. Since the citizens of other nations, especially those with nonwhite populations, watch race-related events in the United States closely, Gordon was in a vital and sensitive position.

Gordon's journalistic experience before joining USIA was extensive. His first work came in 1947, after he had received his A.B. from LeMoyne College. He was a copy boy at New York *PM*, the adless daily. He became an editorial clerk there before serving for a few months late in 1948 as a special assignments reporter for the New York *Star*, another white paper that tried to stay in New York after *PM* failed. During most of 1949 he was city editor of the Newark (New Jersey) *Herald News*, but moved from there to the Atlanta *Daily World*, the great training ground so many black journalists have used. For nearly a decade there he was associate and then managing editor.

During 1958–59 Gordon was an Ogden Reid International Journalism Fellow in Africa, remaining on that continent for five years more, leaving then for government service, at first as branch public affairs officer in Enugu, Nigeria, and then chief information officer at Lagos in the same country. He was assigned to Sweden in 1964 as director of the U.S. Information Service (USIS) in Stockholm for two years. He did graduate work at Columbia and New York universities, in 1949 receiving a master's degree in economics, the subject of his undergraduate major. In 1952–53 he was a Nieman Fellow at Harvard. Gordon served, in 1969–70, as Kemper Knapp visiting professor in the School of Journalism at the University of Wisconsin, a post for which he also had preparation, since he had taught journalism and other subjects at Morris Brown College and Cannon Theological Seminary in Atlanta while on the black daily there.

William J. Raspberry

A Washington *Post* columnist since 1966, William J. Raspberry has become widely known and received numerous awards for his concern about urban affairs and race relations.

He did not begin in journalism as a columnist, however. His first job was a part-time one at the Indianapolis *Recorder*, a leading black weekly, while he was a student at Indiana Central College: he was a reporter, photographer, and proofreader. Eventually he was made managing editor, but soon was drafted. In the Army he was an information officer in Washington, D.C. There he observed the major white daily the Washington *Post*.

On being discharged from military service he applied at the *Post* and got a beginner's job despite his practical experience at the *Recorder*. He was assigned to the obit desk. But he went on the familiar route of covering police, courthouse, and general assignments. Then he was offered the "Potomac Watch" column, but refused it. He changed his mind when he realized that he could deal with material of close interest to black readers as well as general topics. It was all columning from then on. The column, which bears his name, is syndicated nationally by the Washington Post Writers Group and received by wire or mail twice weekly.

Among his awards: Capital Press Club named him "Journalist of the Year" in 1965; Lincoln University in Missouri, the Federal Bar Association, and the Washington unit of the Newspaper Guild added other honors.

John Henrik Clarke, Scholarly Journalist

An entirely different experience has been that of John Henrik Clarke, whose journalism has been combined with historical scholarship despite early lack of formal education. He has been identified with five black publications. Born in 1915 in Union Springs, Alabama, he grew up in the textile mill city of Columbus, Georgia, one of nine children. His boyhood is a familiar one of being in poverty, learning to read sooner than others in the family, and being expected to accomplish much. Even at grammar school he was interested in history and was an eager reader of books, magazines, and newspapers.

During Clarke's two-faceted career he contributed short stories to many U.S. and foreign publications. Creative writing attracted him early; he went to New York in 1933 to study at the League of American Writers School and at Columbia University. He also became interested in the writing of poetry and contributed verse as well as articles and criticism to numerous publications. Some of his tales have been on the "distinction" list in *Best American Short Stories*, an annual compilation.

Clarke's publication connections include being cofounder and fiction editor of *Harlem Quarterly*, book review editor of the *Negro History Bulletin*, and associate editor of *Freedomways*. He has been a feature writer for the Pittsburgh *Courier* and the Ghana *Evening News*. His articles have appeared in numerous other black periodicals.

Like most scholarly journalists, he has had a hand in book writing and editing, largely the latter, editing several volumes of black literature, such as *American Negro Short Stories* and *Tales from Harlem*, as well as books on Harlem or leading black figures, including Malcolm X, Garvey, and Du Bois.

He is on the Urban Leadership training program faculty. His devotion to black history, in which he has taught classes at Hunter, Cornell, and Columbia, began when he was told that the black people had no history. One day he saw an essay by Arthur H. Schomburg about the black man's past. He sought out Schomburg (now best known for the branch of the New York Public Library in Harlem bearing his name, a center for study of black history and culture), who told Clarke to "study the history of your oppressor" and to understand the history of his people.

Clarke is known for his work in the somewhat controversial 108-part CBS television series, "Black Heritage, A History of Afro-Americans," in 1968. He coordinated it and was a member of the committee that developed the program and gave some of the lectures. Subsequently he began editing a twenty-volume illustrated work based on the series.

Carlton B. Goodlett

Among the nine black journalists honored in 1987 at the first Black Hall of Fame of the Press celebration in Baltimore was Carlton B. Goodlett, publisher of the *Sun-Reporter* newspaper chain in California. The remaining eight were such stalwarts of the press as Russwurm, Cornish, Douglass, John H. Murphy, Sr., Christopher J. Perry, John H. Sengstacke, and John H. Johnson. Only Goodlett, Sengstacke, and Johnson were alive at the time.

It was not the first press group honor for Goodlett that year; shortly before, the West Coast Black Publishers Association saluted him not only as a publisher but also for his work in the areas of social justice and world peace.

Goodlett is both an M.D. and a Ph.D. in psychology. More important, perhaps, is that during his forty years as a newspaper editor and publisher he has taken a place as one of the foremost social activists in black publishing.

His original career intention was to be a teacher of psychology, in which he had a bachelor's degree from Howard University and a doctor of philosophy from the University of California. In fact, he became a member of the psychology faculty at Virginia State University. As many doctors of psychology and psychiatry have done, he decided to add work for a medical degree to his education and training, and obtained the M.D. degree at Meharry Medical School. He opened a medical office in 1945 in San Francisco.

However, he saw greater possibilities in journalism for the idealism expressed in the Hippocratic Oath than in medical work. In 1948 he and a dental colleague, Daniel A. Collins, became copublishers of two local black weeklies: the *Sun* and the *Reporter*, which they combined. In 1987 Goodlett was publisher not only of the *Sun-Reporter* but also of the Metro Group, seven black papers in Berkeley, Oakland, Richmond, and other cities. He has served as president of the NNPA and headed the San Francisco NAACP.

His other activities include serving since 1963 with the World Peace Council Presidium. He addressed the council at its meeting in Poland. The *Sun-Reporter* was one of the first black papers to oppose the Vietnam War and strongly supported nuclear disarmament. His confidence in the black press was indicated in an article he wrote in 1977: "With blacks distributed over the vast American landscape . . . who will send the alarm to man the defenses? Of course, the only black-owned communications medium, the Black Press!"

William O. Walker

"Newspapering is one of the most rewarding things that has ever happened to me. Where else could a black boy out of Selma, Alabama, get to visit with the president and travel around the world?" These are the words of William O. Walker, for many years editor and publisher of the Cleveland *Call and Post*, one of the most successful black weeklies in the United States.

His career, though a long one (he died in 1981 at age eighty-five), is quickly enough summarized. He was born in Selma in 1896. He attended Wilberforce University but his degree came from Oberlin Business College. From college he went to the Pittsburgh *Courier*, long a leading black weekly, as a reporter, soon becoming its city editor. After four years on the *Courier* he moved to the Norfolk *Journal and Guide* in Virginia.

By 1932 he decided to try to rehabilitate the Cleveland *Call and Post*, then almost defunct. His salary was thirty-five dollars weekly but he was allowed to hire staffers. One of these was Charles H. Loeb, who later became prominent in black journalism in his own right as managing editor of the *Call and Post*, seeing it through the days of expansion to include editions in Columbus and Cincinnati.

Walker was no dogmatist. He worked for help to the poor, for the civil rights of blacks, and was pragmatic in his methods. When there was discrimination he accepted the help of questionable local businesspeople to right the wrong. He voted for conservative politicians while at the same time supporting causes they would not champion, for he needed their help on other social problems.

His paper, while it fought for black rights, sometimes was criticized for its sensationalism and its advertising of fortune-tellers. If he was to keep the weekly alive, he believed he had to interest and hold readers. "The sheep graze where the grass is," an obituary writer quoted him as saying. "If the department stores advertised in the *Call and Post* I wouldn't have to go to the fortune tellers and the nightclubs."

Ted Poston

As a reporter for thirty-three years for the New York *Post*, a standard daily, Ted Poston not only was one of the first black journalists to be hired by the city's major dailies but also proved that a black journalist could handle general stories. He scored many news beats in his time.

His first job on the *Post* was as a stringer, but he wanted to work full-time on the paper. When in 1937 he asked the city editor to hire him full-time, he was told to get an exclusive story. If he did, he would be taken on the staff. After he left the building, wondering how he could get such a story, he saw a man being attacked on the street, covered the event, and was hired.

He got exclusive interviews with Wendell L. Willkie, Huey Long, and other political leaders. He covered trials and civil rights activities in the South, eluding the Ku Klux Klan to do so.

His full name was Theodore Roosevelt Augustus Major Poston

and he was born in 1906 in Kentucky. A graduate of what is now Tennessee State University, he worked as a dining car waiter before becoming a free-lance writer. His journalism led him to Germany and the Soviet Union. He then worked for the New York *Contender*, a black newspaper no longer issued, and the Pittsburgh *Courier* and the New York *Amsterdam News*, two of the outstanding black papers in the United States. Poston was active in the American Newspaper Guild; he lost his job on the *Amsterdam News* for his leadership in establishing a Guild unit at the paper.

During his career he won Polk, Broun, and other awards and citations from numerous organizations, not only for his journalism but also for his work in defense of civil rights.

He died in 1974 after retiring to write an autobiography, which he began but did not complete.

Other Types of Experience

Henry Lee Moon and George M. Daniels illustrate other types of experience. Moon was director of public relations for the NAACP and editor of its magazine, the *Crisis*. He had a labor union connection before he went to the association. He was assistant to the director of the political action committee of the Congress of Industrial Organizations. Moon also was among the journalism school–trained black journalists. His bachelor of arts degree was earned at Howard. The next year, 1923–24, he attended Ohio State and received a bachelor's degree in journalism as well. Seventeen years later he took courses in public relations and public administration at American University.

In the meantime he was a journalist, from 1926 to 1931 as editor of the Tuskegee *Messenger* and assistant to the press relations secretary of Tuskegee Institute. Then he went to the staffs of the Cleveland *Call*, Cleveland *Herald*, and the New York *Amsterdam News*, all black weeklies. He covered the organizing meeting of the World Federation of Trade Unions in London in 1945 for the Chicago *Defender*. His experience also included six years, 1938–44, as regional racial relations adviser with the Federal Public Housing Authority. More recently he was for six years a member of the board of directors of the Joint Queensview Housing Enterprise and for another period on the boards of the United Housing Foundation and the National Housing Conference. Moon then did considerable magazine writing, having contributed articles to the *Nation*, the *New Republic, Saturday Review, New Leader, Phylon, Opportunity*, and the *Crisis* as well as the New York *Times*, New York *Post*, and the London *Tribune*.

He died in 1985, aged eighty-four, and is remembered for his long term of service to the NAACP (1948–74).

Public relations and magazine work have occupied George M. Daniels in his career. The road he followed included editorial positions on a black news agency, a black daily, a black fraternal magazine, and four religious magazines published by a white denomination.

A Drake University and Columbia University graduate with journalism degrees from each, Daniels became a rewrite man and foreign news editor for the Associated Negro Press wire service soon after leaving Drake. He went in 1954 to the Chicago *Defender*. While there he won the Chicago Newspaper Guild's Page One award for "outstanding performance in the field of journalism" and a Chicago Press Club award for general reporting.

He left black journalism to do editorial work for *Together* and the *Christian Advocate*, two large magazines then published by the United Methodist Church. This work led to a move to New York to become associate news director of the General Board of Global Ministries and the Mission Education and Cultivation Program Department (MECPD) of the Methodist denomination. He was made director of Interpretive Services for the latter body in 1968 and remained so for twelve years. He then became executive editor of the *New World Outlook*, also a United Methodist periodical. In addition to his editorial duties he is director of the editorial group for MECPD. For three years he edited the *Sphinx*, the magazine of Alpha Phi Alpha fraternity.

Four books have come from his deep interest and personal experiences in Africa. He wrote *The Church in New Nations, Drums of War*, and *People and Systems: Tanzania* and edited *Southern Africa: A Time for Change*.

The Johnson Ménage

Because of their prestige, the higher salaries they may pay, or for less realistic and tangible reasons, certain publications attract more of the talented journalists than others. The New York *Times* and the *New Yorker* magazine have done so in the world of white journalism. *Ebony* and *Essence* magazines have gained that reputation in black journalism. Some writers and editors came to *Ebony* via the companion magazine *Jet*, as well as those no longer issued: *Hue, Black World, Tan, Ebony Jr!* and *Ebony International*.

All are or were owned by the Johnson Publishing Company in Chicago.

Alex Poinsett, an *Ebony* senior staff editor, specialized in education writing. He won a trophy and a one thousand dollar cash award in the second annual Penney-Missouri magazine competition for his article, "Ghetto Schools, An Educational Wasteland." He won another for his education writing. A journalism graduate of the University of Illinois in 1952, he remained another year to earn his master's degree in philosophy, and then did graduate work in library science at the University of Chicago. He went to the Johnson firm in 1954.

Another award winner in the Johnson ménage is Simeon Booker, a Washington reporter since 1949. Now head of the *Ebony-Jet* bureau in the nation's capital, he also has done national radio and television broadcasts on racial problems and is a commentator for the Washington TV-radio group. Booker, who came from Youngstown, Ohio, attended Virginia Union University and was a Nieman Fellow. Like Poinsett, he won a Wendell Wilkie award for an educational series.

10.3. Simeon Booker, chief of the *Ebony/Jet* bureau in Washington, D.C.

Booker has worked for the Cleveland *Call and Post* as well as the large white Washington *Post*, where he was its first black reporter. He is author of several books. In *Black Man's America* he discusses the black press as well as other black institutions. In *Susie King Taylor* he tells the story of a black nurse. His viewpoint can be gauged by an incident that occurred in 1969 while he was chief of the bureau in Washington. He was invited by the Mayor's Human Relations Commission to speak at its annual dinner in his hometown of Youngstown. But when he was asked to avoid any mention of the city administration and the mayor he left the banquet hall without speaking because he objected to what he considered censorship.[22]

Black photographers and photojournalists who have received recognition for their work are few. One, Moneta Sleet, Jr., brought the Johnson publications a Pulitzer prize in 1969 with his picture of Mrs. Martin Luther King, Jr., and her daughter Bernice, taken at Dr. King's funeral. A staff photographer for *Ebony* since 1955, he had worked behind the camera for five years before that for *Our World*, another black consumer magazine. A Kentuckian, Sleet was born in Owensboro in 1926. He studied at Kentucky State College; after graduation he attended the School of Modern Photography, New York. He also received a master's degree in journalism from New York University and has taught photography at Maryland State College.

In 1986 Sleet had his first major retrospective exhibition, displayed in the New York Public Library. The exhibit, up for seven weeks, was of both black-and-white and color photographs. It was in six parts: Dr. Martin Luther King, Jr., the civil rights movement, Africa, portraits, children, and photo essays.

Sleet told Marsha Jones, in an interview with *about . . . time* magazine, that people who wish photojournalism careers need to employ discipline when they are trying to capture the essence of their subjects. "You have to develop the discipline to block out everything but you, the camera, and the subject. And you develop the tenacity to stick with it," he said.

Photography has not led many black journalists into the field but it was a factor for Herbert Nipson, who became executive editor of *Ebony*. He was a photographer for the *Daily Iowan* in Iowa City and a writer-photographer-stringer for the Cedar Rapids *Gazette* before going to *Ebony* in 1949. Nipson came from North Carolina, born in 1916 in Asheville. At age two he moved to Clearfield, Pennsylvania. He went to high school there and then on to Penn State University, where he received a journalism degree in 1940. While there he wrote for the *Penn State Collegian* and two literary publications. After graduation he joined the staff of the *Brown American* magazine in Philadelphia, first as assistant editor, then editor. After military service from 1941 to 1946 he received a master's in fine arts at the University of Iowa. He joined the *Ebony* staff in 1949, became co–managing editor in 1951, managing editor twelve years later, and then executive editor. He retired from that post in 1987.

One of the most scholarly of the Johnson staffers is Lerone Bennett, Jr., associated with the firm since 1953. He is author of a half-dozen books, some widely read because they first ran as *Ebony* articles; several have been used in black studies programs at various colleges and universities. He has become a recognized historian of Black America.

Bennett's study of and writings on black history have not been free of controversy. In 1968 *Ebony* carried an article which startled readers: "Was Abraham Lincoln a White Supremacist?" He concluded that the president had been one and cited the research of white scholars as well as his own investigation in support of the view. His books include *Before the Mayflower*, which traced the history of blacks in America from 1619 to 1966, and *Black Power U.S.A.*, which described the Reconstruction period, a time in history when blacks had considerable power. Several other volumes are on contemporary social problems; another is a biography of Martin Luther King, Jr.

Bennett was born in 1928 in Clarksdale, Mississippi, and graduated from Morehouse College with a degree in economics. He went into full-time journalism from college. At Morehouse he edited the *Maroon Tiger*. As a teenager he had worked on the black papers in Jackson, including the *Mississippi Enterprise*. Like several other Johnson editorial people he is a onetime reporter for the Atlanta *Daily World*. Beginning as a reporter, he had become city editor by 1953. In that year he undertook his first work at the Chicago magazine company, as an *Ebony* associate editor. In 1958 he became senior editor; in 1988 he was named executive editor.

In 1972 Bennett was asked to become chairperson of the new Department of Afro-American Studies at Northwestern University. The move was short-lived. Six years later he received an award for his historical work from the American Academy and Institute of Arts and Letters.

Pointsett, Booker, and Bennett are among the writers and editors on the Johnson magazine staffs who have received considerable public recognition. Other, younger men and women have had less spectacular success with their work but should not be overlooked. A dozen other names could be added, for these magazines have been published since the 1940s and 1950s. Other present or recent staff members who have played important parts within the organization are Robert E. Johnson (not related to the owner), executive editor of *Jet*; Hans J. Massaquoit, managing editor of *Ebony*; Hoyt W. Fuller, former managing editor of *Black World*; and Phyllis Garland, former New York editor of *Ebony*.

Robert Johnson's original intention was to become a lawyer, but journalism interfered with his plan. An Alabamian by birth, he gave journalism a start in his life before the law had an opportunity by being editor of *Trail Blazer*, the Westfield High School paper in Birmingham. This work threw him into association with the paper's faculty adviser, a history teacher who also was managing editor of the Birmingham *World*, a black weekly. That led to two jobs, as cub reporter and salesman. When Johnson attended Morehouse College, still planning a law career, like Bennett he edited the *Maroon Tiger*. He added editing of the yearbook, *The Torch*. World War II and the navy interrupted his college work but not his journalism, for in the service he was assigned to be a reporter for the *Masthead*, a San Francisco naval base weekly. He was ordered to do this work because the paper's editor had published an antiblack joke and it was thought that giving him the black news beat would allay the criticism that had resulted from printing the joke. In the year he was on the naval paper Johnson went from reporter to managing editor. The law career was as far away as ever, but not forgotten.

Next the Twelfth Naval District Press Association selected Johnson to be a war correspondent. He interviewed sailors for stories to be sent to their hometown press, going to the Hawaiian Islands, Okinawa, and the Philippines on these assignments. His naval journalism experience covered more than three years. When he was discharged in 1946 he attempted to continue his law plans. But he still lacked two undergraduate college years, so he returned to Morehouse, was graduated in 1948 and went, not to law, but back to journalism by joining the Atlanta *Daily World* staff, covering the standard beats. From reporting sports, police, and courts he became city editor in a year. The law definitely had lost out by 1951, when he took a leave of absence to work on a master's in journalism at the School of Journalism at Syracuse University. After a year, master's in news editorial work safely in hand, he returned to the *World*. While in Atlanta he added free-lance writing to his interests.

Among the publications that took his articles was *Jet*, the small-format newsmagazine of the Johnson firm. Originally he had an offer of full-time work there, but refused it. Later, however, he agreed and became an associate editor in 1953 and successively assistant managing editor, managing editor, executive editor, and associate publisher. He told an interviewer that he has no regrets about having chosen journalism over law.[23] His book, entitled *Bill Cosby: In Words and Pictures,* was published in 1988.

Lester H. Brownlee

In the past, more so even than today, the black journalist had to be versatile. The more journalistic skills he or she possessed—writing, editing, public relations advising, radio newscasting, reporting for any medium, selling, advertising, talk-show hosting on television—the steadier the work and the income and the greater the enjoyment of the experience.

Such has been the career of Lester H. Brownlee, a World War II U.S. Army major but primarily a journalist capable of handling almost any journalistic job and a number involving such related fields as advertising, public relations, journalism teaching, and book authorship.

His present title is professor of journalism at Columbia College in Chicago. He also serves as adviser to the *Columbia Chronicle*, the student newspaper. He joined the Columbia faculty in 1978.

Brownlee attended the University of Wisconsin in Madison for the first three years of his undergraduate education, concluding his bachelor of science degree in journalism at the Medill School of Journalism, Northwestern University, Evanston, Illinois. In another year he had a master's degree in journalism from Medill.

His professional experience indicates a remarkable versatility. Some of the many positions he has held in the communications field are associate editor of *Ebony* magazine for a year; feature writer for the Chicago *Defender*; reporter for the Chicago *Daily News*, a major white daily, for eight years; feature writer for six years on Chicago's *American*, another large white daily; and executive assistant to the publisher of the *Informer* group of black papers in Houston, Texas, for a year.

During the time he was also an advertising manager at the Chicago *Defender*, and a teacher of journalism. Added to all this must be his broadcasting experience: six years as a newsman for WLS-TV, Chicago, education and urban affairs editor of the same station for three years, director of its community affairs for three years, and news director for a year for WBEE radio, Chicago. He also was for four years director of media relations for the Chicago Board of Education. Meantime he was talk-show host for eight Chicago radio or television stations.

His teaching service has been at three institutions: a year as an instructor in journalism at Texas Southern University, Houston, his present post at Columbia, and thirty-one summers as lecturer at Northwestern University's summer institute.

As might be expected, Brownlee also is a book author. He has written six books for children, all published as texts by the Scott, Foresman & Co. firm. He has published more than three hundred articles in nationally circulated magazines. He is listed in a half-dozen *Who's Who*–type directories, and has won numerous professional awards.

The Work of Rudolph Aggrey

Another American black journalist who has had both a journalistic and diplomatic career is Orison Rudolph Aggrey. As he tells about his relationship to the black press:

> That press has been on my mind quite a bit lately. Much of my time in 1986 and early 1987 was spent at Howard University surveying its international activities and making recommendations for enhancing current programs and for developing new academic directions and structures. My survey included Howard's rapidly improving School of Communications. Dr. Orlando Taylor, the dean of the school, requested that I be interviewed for Howard's Black Press Oral History Project. Meanwhile I renewed my acquaintance with Louis Martin, a former special assistant to Presidents Kennedy, Johnson, and Carter. Now Howard's Assistant Vice President for Communication (public relations and information) Louis was editor of the Chicago *Defender* in 1948–49 when I served as *Defender* correspondent in Cleveland. That experience coincided with my year as a general assignment reporter for the Cleveland *Call and Post*. I also received a call from Enoch P. Waters. Enoch was the managing editor who engaged me as a *Defender* stringer. He was one of several able black journalists who had preceded me as editor of the *Hampton Script*, the undergraduate newspaper at Hampton Institute.
>
> In a number of ways I have been close to the black press all of my life. Growing up in North Carolina—fatherless from the age of one— as a child I waited anxiously for each week's edition of the Baltimore *Afro-American* and Norfolk *Journal and Guide*. My mother bought these two papers faithfully. My aunt, who lived with us during the summer and school holidays, contributed the Pittsburgh *Courier*. At

Livingstonc Collcgc across thc street from our home, where both my parents had taught earlier, the librarian encouraged me to read the Chicago *Defender*, the New York *Amsterdam News*, and the New York *Age*, as well as the *Carolina Times*. S. W. Garlington, a sociology professor at Livingstone, founded the short-lived *Salisbury Citizen*, a local black weekly and we talked often of the Black press. We were to renew our acquaintance in New York during 1949–50 when Garlington was managing editor of the *Amsterdam News*.

As an undergraduate at Hampton, 1942–46, I was a student assistant in the Office of Public Relations and read nearly all of the black publications. I assisted reporters and editors who came to the campus for important events. Some of them asked me to write occasional articles for their publications and honored me with a byline. Hampton students were proud of the fact that the publishers of the *Defender* and the *Journal and Guide* as well as the editor of the *Afro-American*, the *Courier*, the Kansas City *Call*, and the Philadelphia *Tribune* were Hampton graduates.

After three years in Syracuse and Cleveland, I moved to New York where I worked as a publicity aide for the United Negro College Fund's national headquarters, did special assignments for *Our World* magazine, and took French courses at night at Brooklyn College. I spent many Saturdays with friends from Hampton who were then employed by *Ebony*, the *Amsterdam News, Our World*, and the *People's Voice*. I met Claude Barnett, the head of the Associated Negro Press, who asked me to do special articles over the years and encouraged me to consider the foreign service as a career. I took time off to knock on the doors of all the dailies and newsmagazines in New York as well as several trade publications in the New York/New Jersey area. Each had one black editorial employee at the time and considered that quota filled. I had similar experiences earlier in Cleveland. The only offer I received from a daily came after an interview in Providence, but that was after I had made a commitment to the foreign service.[24]

His foreign service career extended over thirty-three years in Africa, Europe, and the United States. It was highlighted by missions as Ambassador to Senegal and The Gambia (1973–77) and to Romania (1977–81). Before the ambassadorial assignments Aggrey directed the Department of State's Office of West African Affairs.

Beginning in 1951, he held a variety of information, cultural, and public affairs positions in American missions in Nigeria, France, Zaire, and in the United States. Subsequently, at USIA headquarters in Washington he served as chief of the Voice of America's French Branch and as program manager of the Motion Picture and Television Service.

Aggrey retired from the Department of State in 1984 with the senior foreign service rank of career minister. He was self-employed as a consultant until his appointment in September 1987 as director of the Patricia Roberts Harris Public Affairs Program at Howard University.

And Many, Many More

Among other black journalists known within the profession was Layhmond Robinson, who was with the New York *Times* as a reporter and WABC-TV, New York, as a correspondent; in public relations work for the National Urban League; and in 1970 named chief information officer of the New York City hospital system.

Martin D. Richardson, who was connected with various papers, at one time was managing editor of the Boston *Chronicle* but worked mainly on the black Cleveland *Call and Post*. William I. Gibson has held top posts on the *Afro-American*, including managing editorship of the Washington edition. The late Clifford Wesley Mackay was with two of the country's black dailies. On the Chicago *Defender* he was theatrical editor, on the Atlanta *Daily World* managing editor. He also was editor in chief of the *Afro-American*.

Another *World* man, Stanley Scott, a member of the family connected with the paper for many years, left it because he wanted to cover more than the black community. For a while he was with the NAACP, but then became a radio reporter for WINS, New York, where he covered other than black assignments. He was one of the first black reporters with United Press International, to which he went from his family's paper. In 1970 Scott won the Russwurm Award of the National Urban League for "sustained excellence in interpreting, analyzing and reporting of the news" and his "use of the immense power of the press in advocating equality for all in the best American traditions."

Scott went on in 1971 to become a White House official, serving during President Gerald Ford's term as special assistant for minority affairs. His next post was as assistant administrator for Africa of the Agency for International Development, beginning in 1975. He left government employment in 1977 to be vice-president for public affairs for Philip Morris, U.S.A., in New York City, later becoming director of corporate public affairs, his post in 1987.

Other prominent journalists include Moses J. Newson, executive editor of the Baltimore *Afro-American*; Claude Lewis, formerly of

Newsweek and the New York *Herald Tribune* and an NBC commentator following that; Jesse H. Walker, executive editor, New York *Amsterdam News*; Louis E. Martin, editor in chief, Sengstacke Newspapers; John Pittman, writer and editor for both black and white papers; Rudolph A. Pyatt, Jr., Washington correspondent, Charleston (South Carolina) *News* and *Courier*; Ernest Dunbar, senior editor, *Look*, the once strong rival for *Life*; and Lutrelle F. Palmer, Chicago *Daily News* reporter and war correspondent.

Some from the past who worked mainly on white publications were Orrin Evans of the Philadelphia *Record* and the Philadelphia *Tribune*, the first a white paper and now defunct, the second still one of the major black papers; Horace Cayton and Joseph Bibb, both of the Chicago *Sun-Times* when it was only the Chicago *Sun*; Edgar T. Rouzzeau, of the now departed great New York daily, the *Herald Tribune*; George Anthony Moore, the Cleveland *Press*; Earl Brown, *Life* magazine staff man and later active in New York City political life; Frank Harriott, of New York *PM*; Eugene Gordon, New York *Daily Worker*; and Michael Carter, Brooklyn *Daily Eagle*.

Les Payne

Les Payne is best known to the newspaper readers of the nation for the column bearing his name. The Los Angeles *Times* Syndicate sends it to a dozen major U.S. dailies. It was running only in the Long Island daily *Newsday*, where it started, for the first five years. *Newsday* now puts it in an edition for New York City.

Payne, whose main job is as assistant managing editor of *Newsday* for domestic and foreign news, has been an international reporter during his career, covering many stories in Africa, Haiti, and other news hot-spots.

He has become known for his vigorously written personal opinions on politicians, government people, and others who outrage him by what he considers their racial prejudice. In a mid-1980s column he attacked Alexander Haig, former general and ex–secretary of state. After bringing up Haig's assumption that he was in control at the White House the day President Reagan was shot, Payne quoted from Haig's writings. They boasted of his great fitness for public office and the lack of appreciation he encountered from certain other leaders in the Reagan administration. Payne cited racist remarks attributed to Haig by other writers.

Payne is an Alabamian, born in 1941 to a poor family. He attended the University of Connecticut after his family moved north. After completing six years in military service, he worked for *Newsday* as a reporter. In that job he was assigned to stories in Turkey, Rhodesia (now Zimbabwe), and Uganda and shared in a Pulitzer prize. Later he also covered news in South Africa and Haiti.

Many of his columns present the black point of view on events and are blunt and outspoken. He told an interviewer, David Astor, writing in *Editor & Publisher* magazine, that he informs "people about a point of view they don't usually get."

Clarence Page

In the late 1960s and early 1970s there were more opportunities for black journalists in all media because radio, television, newspapers, and magazines were under pressure to give them a chance.

One of the young writers who took advantage of the opening doors was Clarence Page, an Ohioan born in 1947. He chose to work in the white media after receiving a degree in journalism at Ohio University, where he was the only black student in his specialty.

His first work in the press was as a free-lancer in photojournalism, a path followed by many journalists. He worked independently for the Middleton (Ohio) *Journal* and the Cincinnati *Enquirer*.

At graduation in 1969 he had five job offers. He took the one from the Chicago *Tribune*, and was one of two black reporters on its staff. He worked at the *Tribune* as a reporter and then as assistant city editor. He shared in a Pulitzer prize for reporting in 1972 and in 1976 won a Beck award for overseas reporting in South Africa.

Page left the *Tribune* in 1980 for another area of communications: television. Beginning as director of the community affairs department of WBBM-TV, a Chicago CBS affiliate, he wrote and hosted shows and wrote documentaries for the next two years. Then he became a reporter and a planning editor for two years. But having learned the differences in the media and what he could do best, he went back to print journalism.

Returning to the *Tribune* in 1984, Page became a member of its editorial board and writer of a signed column. By 1987 the column was appearing twice a week. Then it was picked up for syndication by the Tribune Media Service; by fall of that year twenty-five papers were buying it.

He writes about public affairs. He told Tricia Drevets, an *Editor & Publisher* interviewer, that he tries to go beyond policies and the makers of policy to examine the impact of the policies.

Like a good many young journalists, he had wanted since he was a free-lancer to have his own column. He accomplished this, despite his race (some observers might say because of it), in the highly competitive area of general, or establishment, communication.[25]

Thomas A. Johnson

One of the leading reporters on the New York *Times* staff, Thomas A. Johnson once wrote in defense of the black journalist who chooses to work for the white rather than the black media. He saw no need to insist upon one or the other. The aim, he said, should be to work where the greatest good can be done for the black race.[26] He has covered stories for his paper in many parts of the world and won awards for his writing. He is a strong advocate for training of young black men and women for the field of journalism.

Robert C. Maynard

Another black journalist, who is editor of an important white daily and also its publisher, is nationally known in U.S. journalism and serves on many industry committees as well as in activities remote from journalism. This is Robert C. Maynard, head of the Oakland *Tribune* in California since 1982.

Maynard got his start in journalism when he was only sixteen, working for the New York *Age*, a prominent weekly in its time. He moved into white journalism from there, going to the York (Pennsylvania) *Gazette and Daily* as a reporter for that leading politically and socially liberal paper. He later joined the staff of the Washington *Post*, the largest daily in the national capital, as a reporter, national correspondent, ombudsman, and editorial writer.

The Oakland daily was nearly defunct when Maynard bought it from the Gannett chain for $22 million and revived it.[27] Maynard has a controlling interest. Five years after he acquired it difficulties had to be faced with new financial problems and what Maynard called restructuring was necessary. As with so many other papers, expenses were outrunning income, even though that income was higher than in previous years.[28]

One of Maynard's goals has been to increase the number of blacks and other minorities in both printed and electronic journalism, especially at major white publications and broadcasting companies. He has served as codirector of a minority journalists' program at

Columbia University's School of Journalism and also established the Institute for Journalism Education at the University of California, Berkeley, whose purpose is to help develop careers for minority journalists.

Black Journalists in White Journalism

In the past four decades more black reporters have worked on the nonblack press than ever before. From the view of the black journalist there are not enough still, nor do enough rise into executive posts. But there has been progress. The biographical sketches appearing here are some proof of that. Other men and women have been recognized in other books and in newspaper and magazine articles.

Mentioned only briefly here are a half-dozen more:

Warren Brown, long identified with journalism in New Orleans, worked on Long Island *Newsday* as a summer intern while studying for his journalism degree at Columbia University. Before going to the *States-Item* in New Orleans in 1970 he had a stint at the New York *Times* as a news clerk.

Vernon D. Jarrett, an outspoken, somewhat controversial columnist for the Chicago *Sun-Times* and a commentator on WLS-TV in that city, has a background in black journalism. He worked for both the Pittsburgh *Courier* and the Associated Negro Press before going to the white daily. Jarrett became news himself after the death of Mayor Harold Washington of Chicago in 1987. He made a speech denouncing the supporters of a city councilman from the political opposition to Washington for mayor and in support of another councilman from the pro-Washington group.

William J. Drummond, a reporter for some years for the white-owned Los Angeles *Times*, earned two journalism degrees, one from the University of California, Berkeley, and the other, a master's, from the Columbia University School of Journalism in New York. He started at the Louisville *Courier-Journal,* with the social problems beat. From there he went to the Los Angeles *Times*, still a reporter, but in time the paper's bureau chief in New Delhi, India.

One of the few black journalists to reach the top executive position on a white newspaper is William A. Hilliard of the Portland (Oregon) *Oregonian*, a major Pacific Northwest daily. He began work there in 1952. In ten years he had moved from copy boy to reporter to assistant city editor; he had covered sports, religion, and general assignments and also was picture editor. He went on to become assistant city editor, associate editor, and in the mid-1980s editor in full charge of the paper. Was he a token black, one of the few in high positions? M. L. Stein, author of a book on black people in communications, reported that when Hilliard got his first job at the Portland paper it was because he was black. At that time an effort was being made by white dailies to hire black journalists, and Hilliard got offers. The editor of the *Oregonian* saw a future for him there and his prediction was accurate.

Today's Female Journalists

This report on the black journalists discusses women in a separate section because the relative few who have had an opportunity to be productive writers and editors would be lost in the accounts of the men. Although in black journalism there is somewhat less tendency to give men the job advantages than exist in white newspaper and magazine work, women nevertheless are a small minority. The reasons do not necessarily include sex discrimination. Black women, even more so than black men, have had little chance to obtain journalism training. Opportunities leading to major positions are claimed by men, as in white journalism, because in the past the male was considered to be the family head and financially responsible. Work on black publications, especially newspapers, is more difficult than on white, since the black paper does not have the entrée accorded the white, as a rule. If black journalism is more nearly a man's job than white journalism, women make less progress in it. Nor have many women been interested in journalism as a life's work; they too have heard of the long hours and low salaries.

But the romantic view that some persons have ink instead of blood in their veins exists for black journalism as well, with the result that some women have made a reputation for themselves in this occupation. And in recent years, women's place has become a little larger, with the increase in consumer and specialized black magazines, although the greatest area of growth has been on the white publications. By this time it is clear that the situation is better for the black female journalist.

Until now only a few have had much opportunity to make their skills and views felt. Chapter 2 presents what Penn, the recorder of nineteenth-century black journalism and journalists, had to say about black women journalists. In what follows some of the better-known twentieth-century women are accounted for.

Era Bell Thompson

The title "International Editor" is an unusual one in U.S. journalism. Its meaning is not exactly clear, but it is the designation for a woman who was one of the widely known black journalists of either sex, Era Bell Thompson, a member of the Johnson firm. She occupied this position at *Ebony* and for some years lived up to one sense of it by being international in her travels, particularly in journeys to and from Africa.

Long the senior member of the staff aside from the company's founder, John H. Johnson, Thompson started with these publications in 1947. She began as an editor of the first periodical, *Negro Digest*, and went on to executive positions at *Ebony*, the first woman to become an executive of the firm.

An Iowan born in Des Moines, Thompson spent two years at the

10.4. Era Bell Thompson, for many years international editor at the Johnson magazines.

University of North Dakota, and then completed her bachelor's degree at Morningside College in 1933. During the years 1938–40 she did graduate study at the Medill School of Journalism, Northwestern University. Before putting her journalistic training to work she was a senior interviewer for the U.S. and Illinois employment services. She then was given a general assignment as an associate editor of Johnson's. After her stint with *Negro Digest* she was named co–managing editor of *Ebony*, holding that post from 1951 to 1964. Her world traveling increased in the latter year, when she was made international editor.

Although Thompson went to all continents as a writer, she concentrated on Africa. From there she wrote articles on such subjects as the progress of the new black republics and safaris of black hunters. She was not welcome in South Africa, once spending a night in jail awaiting deportation. On a second attempt to enter that country she was denied a visa.

Like several other Johnson staffers Thompson wrote books. *American Daughter*, an autobiographical work, was written before she went into journalism. She spoke frequently before women's groups, black and white, and was active in various religious, social, and cultural organizations. She also wrote *Africa, Land of My Father* and *White on Black*.

Elizabeth Murphy Moss

Another female journalist identified with a prominent publishing firm was Elizabeth Murphy Moss, of the *Afro-American* newspapers. Moss, who had been a war correspondent as well as managing editor of the Baltimore paper, became vice-president, treasurer, and editorial supervisor of the publishing firm, of which her family was long the owner. She was one of several black women in executive positions on newspapers; in most instances the others have been officers who succeeded their husbands as owners, managers, treasurers, and secretaries after they were widowed.

Ethel L. Payne

Until early 1970 Ethel L. Payne, Washington correspondent of the Sengstacke Newspapers, was the only black newswoman to be assigned to cover the Vietnam War. She spent ten weeks there in 1966–67, writing about the activities of black servicemen from Da Nang to the Mekong Delta. She also sent dispatches from Hong Kong, Korea, Thailand, and Japan. In 1970 she was one of a group of journalists who accompanied the U.S. secretary of state on an Asian tour

War, however, has not been Payne's only assignment. She has covered a wide variety of other stories. Her regular beat included the White House, Capitol Hill, the District of Columbia, and various government agencies. A Chicagoan, and like Thompson a onetime Northwestern journalism student, Payne was one of a group of thirty-five reporters who in 1957 went with then Vice-President and Mrs. Richard M. Nixon to various African and European nations. Earlier she had covered the Asian-African conference at Bandung, Indonesia. She also was sent by her papers to write about the Nigerian civil war in 1969 and the World Council of Churches assembly at Uppsala, Sweden, in 1968.

10.5. Ethel L. Payne (right), longtime Washington correspondent for the Sengstacke Newspapers, with former Rep. Shirley Chisholm (left) at the capitol.

Payne also has had experience in government posts. She has been a consultant to the Special Security Administration and visited twenty-two cities for the Medical Alert Program. As a staff member of the AFL-CIO Committee on Political Education (COPE) in Washington she wrote for and edited its biweekly, *Notes from COPE*. She has worked as well for the Democratic party in Texas and for the national party's Conference of Women. She has won numerous awards for her work, twice being given the newsmen's Newsman Award of the Capital Press Club, of which she became president in 1970. The National Association of Black Women named her the Ida B. Wells Media Woman of the Year. She also was selected in 1978 to be a Ford Foundation Fellow in Educational Journalism.

Describing how she entered journalism in the first place she has said: "My career in journalism began by accident. While I was working in Japan as an Army Service Club hostess, I put down my impressions of life under the Occupation . . . those jottings found their way into the Chicago *Defender* and caused an earthquake in the high command. But for the intervention of Thurgood Marshall, who happened to be in the country on a court-martial case, I would have been cashiered and sent home in chains for allegedly upsetting the morale of the troops. Six months later, I left under my own power and joined the staff of the *Defender*, where I have remained off and on."

Two *Essence* Editors: Marcia Anne Gillespie and Susan L. Taylor

Few nonblack present-day editors of women's magazines are driven by a social conscience. They are far more concerned with serving what they consider to be the traditional needs of women—style, housekeeping, furnishings, health, and cookery. These concerns are a source of advertising, the lifeblood of the expensive, colorful, high-quality paper stock newsstand publication. Social problems—unemployment, racial discrimination, divorce, drug addiction, and other social ills—bring no space-buyers.

The black women's magazine editor, on the other hand, is likely to be especially aware of the problems of black women. Usually she cannot overlook them because her readers will not let her ignore them. *Essence* started out as a conventional magazine, in many ways resembling some of the white women's world front-runners. But as new chief editors were engaged those of social conscience entered the scene and the magazine changed focus gradually. (See Chapter 7.)

Credit for the *Essence* formula of a mixture of the traditional women's fare with that needed by black women goes to two editors,

Marcia Anne Gillespie and Susan L. Taylor.

Gillespie, one of the early editors in chief of *Essence,* had been a writer for Time-Life Books for four years before going to the magazine for black women. She had joined the Time Inc. roster upon graduation from Lake Forest University, where she had majored in American studies.

Gillespie told *Advertising Age* that she left Time Inc. after being assigned to write black history material, which was much to her distaste. "I saw how the Anglo-Saxon view colored all aspects of history. . . . I saw who had power to make changes," she explained.

Gordon Parks, Sr., the noted photographer and author, was editorial director of *Essence.* One of Gillespie's departmental editors was Susan L. Taylor, who was destined to be editor in chief some years later. Taylor was the fashion/beauty editor.

Gillespie is credited with having changed the magazine's focus to some extent. A 1971 issue she edited contains a mixture of the earliest formula and the more socially conscious approach. There was a short story titled "Love Knott" by Anne Crittendon, five items on beauty and two on fashion, an article called "The Explosion of Black Poetry" by Clarence Major, and two under the heading Food and Home, one dealing with African fare. In the departments were pieces on child abuse, heroin on campus, and venereal disease. Mingled with these were travel, entertainment, careers, and health problems.

The editor has been quoted as saying that the magazine in the early 1970s was "the first of a new breed of black magazines . . . with its roots in the black power movement." Gillespie shared her experiences with editors of major magazines for whites at meetings of the American Society of Magazine Editors. She remained in command of the editorial division until 1980, when she resigned to take up freelance writing and teaching. Eight years later she was named executive editor of *Ms,* a white-owned magazine for women.

When Susan L. Taylor assumed the post of editor in chief in 1981, she was thoroughly familiar with the magazine's operation. Hers is an example of learning on the job, for her previous experience had nothing to do with journalism.

She lived in east Harlem and came from a line of black businesswomen, but unlike most prominent editors of today had no college education. She wanted to be an actress and had received small parts on television and in cinema productions. By then she had married, was awaiting a child, and concluded that the stage was not to be her future. After her daughter was born, she began a line of cosmetics. Representing it, she called on *Essence* in 1971. That was the beginning of her editorial work. She became a part-time beauty writer. Within months she was full time. In a year she was also the fashion editor and in 1981 promoted to editor in chief.

Writers about Taylor rhapsodize about her compelling personality and her editorial judgment. Her versatility is admired, and she is praised by writers because of her ability to do her job. She is a company vice-president as well as the chief editor of *Essence* and a host of the *Essence* weekly television program. Her magazine has become a financial success in the same class with *Ebony* and *Black Enterprise*, two other outstanding periodicals in an area of American journalism that is not known for stability.

A strong social conscience is not a common companion of these accomplishments, but Taylor demonstrates it not only in her choice of material for the magazine but also in talks on the lecture circuit. Typical are these quotations:

After reminding her audience—often of young people—of the statistics on black unemployment, poverty, and problems of survival in the economy of the mid-1980s, she has said: "The continuation of the pain in black America is dependent upon what we do today. Blacks in this nation, the underclass, are counting on you . . . to do what you are supposed to do no matter how professional you may become."

She also tells audiences of young college students that they are "the most blessed generation of black people to walk the face of the earth." She supports this statement by observing what they can do in spite of the difficulties still besetting the lives of their people. But she calls the solution of the problems today "a piece of cake . . . compared to where we have come from as black people."

She explained her aims for *Essence*: "I want *Essence* to give readers a clear vision of themselves and their world. I want to help my sisters realize all their opportunities for self-actualization.

"Now more than ever *Essence* must be a light source for black women, a handbook that inspires, affirms and informs us."[29]

At the time in 1988 that Taylor was at the peak of success, newspapers and magazines were carrying an advertisement placed by Fordham University, a large Roman Catholic institution in New York City, concerning its programs for adult students. In it, almost as large as the ad, is a photograph of Susan Taylor, then aged forty-two, taken outside one of the university buildings. Above it was her statement: "I wanted to go back to school for my Bachelor's, but not just anywhere. Manhattan's center of excitement is Lincoln Center—and Fordham is right there." She was in the class of 1989.

Profiles of Other Female Journalists

Among the black women who have served on publications and broadcasting staffs are Dorothy Gilliam, formerly of the Washington *Post* and then at WTTG radio, Washington. She has taught a course on black journalism history at American University, one of the first of its kind. Lena Rivers Smith has been on the staff of the Pittsburgh *Courier*, Kansas City *Call*, and with the *Informer* chain, where she was once managing editor, in Houston. Lucile H. Bluford, managing editor of the *Call*, was cited in 1961 by Lincoln University for her work, by then amounting to a quarter of a century, as a reporter and editor for that weekly. It was her suit against the University of Missouri, recounted elsewhere in this book, that led to establishment of Lincoln's journalism department.

Many black newspapers and a few magazines have on their staffs female writers and editors. Scores are society, women's interest, and religious editors or columnists, few of them working at it full time, however. Among the more familiar names are those of Betty Granger Reid of the New York *Amsterdam News*, Theresa Fambro Hooks of the Chicago *Daily Defender*, Nancy L. Giddens of the Philadelphia *Tribune*, and Toki Schalk Johnson of the Pittsburgh *Courier*. The larger papers have as many as a half-dozen women contributing special departments — society, food, religion, fashions, entertainment, and gossip — in every issue.

Female staffers on magazines, as in other periodicals, have risen to managerial positions of prominence in some instances. The editors of magazines aimed at women usually are women, as are most of the editorial staff members. A few women have risen high in black newspapers as well. One of these was Hazel Garland, who from 1974 to 1977 was editor in chief of the Pittsburgh *Courier*, one of the most prestigious black newspapers. She had various jobs on the paper, including work as a writer and columnist. She served on the Pulitzer Prize selection committee in 1979. She died in 1988, at the age of seventy-five.

Charlayne Hunter-Gault

If there is one black female journalist known widely by the general public it is Charlayne Hunter-Gault because she has been in the news herself. In 1961 she was the first black woman accepted and one of the first two black persons enrolled as a student at the University of Georgia. Her appearance on the campus produced a riot among some of the students. She was not discouraged, however, and obtained her degree in 1963. In 1969 she was the first woman admitted to the Georgia chapter of the Society of Professional Journalists, Sigma Delta Chi, an international professional organization up to then open only to men. She was one of the first two women accepted by that international organization.

Contributing most to her public recognition is her work on the "MacNeil-Lehrer News Hour," a news program on public television. She is a writer and at times serves as anchor. Her title is national correspondent. Among the stories she has covered for the Public Broadcasting Service are those of the 1983 U.S. invasion of Grenada, Admiral Elmo Zumwalt and the use of Agent Orange in Vietnam, and a series on the consequences of apartheid. She has won one Peabody and two Emmy awards and still other honors from *Good Housekeeping*, American Women in Radio and Television, the Newswomen's Club of New York, and various other groups.

She has done comparably important and successful work in print journalism. She was a reporter for the *New Yorker* magazine and a staff member of *Trans-Action* magazine. For eight years she was a New York *Times* reporter, with special responsibility for covering the urban black community.

As a free-lance writer she has contributed to *Ms, Essence, Life*, the *New Leader, Coronet*, and other periodicals.

In an interview with Rochester's black city magazine *about . . . time* Hunter-Gault had advice for black youth interested in a career in communications. "My advice," she said, "is to stay out of journalism schools that don't stress a strong liberal arts background. The who, what, when, where, how, and why formula in journalism will serve you well so long as you have an understanding or a foundation that is rooted in an understanding of the economic, political and social issues and problems in the world."

Marilyn A. Batchelor

Marilyn A. Batchelor represents a group of young men and women who planned careers on prominent black publications (in her instance a leading magazine), but for one reason or another they have been frustrated in that aim.

Some of these young people resigned from the publications that were so long their goals. Others found satisfaction in some other medium owned and managed by blacks. Still others were attracted to white-owned publications, especially those of general interest offering higher salaries and greater chances for recognition than the black newspapers or magazines. Others either would not or could not persist in applying to the kind of publications they preferred.

Batchelor explained her goals, "When I left Syracuse University [where in 1984 she was a magazine major] I initially wanted to join the staff of *Essence* magazine. But, after submitting a few freelance pieces . . . , my dream was crushed when I was not offered a job upon graduation. So, I tried Condé Nast, but with no luck there. I tried my other option. I had quite a few college internships (three) and a couple of part-time reporting jobs (two), so I applied to general newspapers."

She explains why she applied to those papers: "I never wanted to work at a black newspaper because I didn't like the layout, the contents, nor the style of writing." It was black magazines like *Essence* and *Ebony* that caught her interest, as early as in high school.

The job she finally took was on the *Orange County Register*, with a circulation exceeding 300,000. In 1987 she was the only black reporter. There was a black assistant features editor as well.

"My work at the *Register* is equally distributed with a variety of assignments," she wrote. "I am approached like an expert on all black issues in the county and on a national level, which bothers me sometimes because others could be as knowledgeable on some subjects and sometimes are.

"However, I do request to do some issues involving blacks because I know that if I don't do it, it may not get done. And I believe some issues should be covered."

Her interest in the large black magazines continues. Now, however, she would not be content to be on the editorial staff as a writer. "Now," she writes, "I would want to hold a position on the editorial board because of the experience I am acquiring daily."

Although she works on a white-owned newspaper, she continues to read black periodicals. Other evidence of her continuing identification with black journalism is her membership in the National Association of Black Journalists (NABJ). She is a member of the board of directors for the unit in Southern California (NABJSC), for which she also serves as fund-raising chairperson. She is enthusiastic about NABJSC because of what it stands for and what it does (such as giving away more money in college scholarships than any other unit in the regional conference).[30]

E. Fannie Granton

Another noted black female journalist spent her entire journalistic career with one publishing firm. She was E. Fannie Granton, who for nearly a quarter of a century was on the staffs of *Ebony* and *Jet* magazines in the Washington bureau. It was her first journalism work. She remained in it and was a Washington figure until her death.

She became an encyclopedia of facts about Washington people and the capital's many events. Before working for the Johnson Publishing Company she served on the staff of the Washington office of the Urban League. A Virginian, Granton went to high school in Washington and then to Atlanta University for a degree in social work. She also studied law at American University.

Although she joined the *Jet/Ebony* staff as office manager–secretary, she shifted to reporting Washington news and became widely known in the city, especially in the White House. In 1979 more than one thousand Washington friends assembled for an "I Love Fannie" party. Winner of awards from the National Association of Media Women, she was the first black journalist to hold an office in the Washington Press Club, serving several terms as recording secretary. Meanwhile she was an associate editor of *Jet* and assistant editor of *Ebony*.

She died in 1980 at age sixty-six, having asked that, instead of flowers, monetary contributions be made to the Howard University School of Communications. One of its scholarships bears her name.

Pamela M. Johnson

Several female journalists publish black newspapers. Usually they are persons of long experience in the black press or members of families that own papers.

Pamela M. Johnson, publisher of the Gannett-owned Ithaca (New York) *Journal*, is neither long in journalism nor a member of a journalistic family. Born in 1946 in the Midwest, she attended the School of Journalism at the University of Wisconsin in Madison, not sure that journalism was the career for her, so unsure, in fact, that she had a dual major with education so she could teach if she did not make the grade in journalism school. She did obtain the journalism degree, however, and her first job was on the reporting staff of the Chicago *Tribune*.

She then joined the Wisconsin journalism faculty. One of her university assignments was to recruit black students, which she did successfully, the number rising from four to forty. Her academic connection led her to join the faculty of Norfolk State University where she helped to develop a journalism department.

Johnson next took a sabbatical to become an intern at the Gannett paper in Quincy, Massachusetts, the *Patriot-Ledger*. This experience roused an interest in becoming a publisher; Gannett, a white-owned chain, gave her publishing experience at the Bridgewater (New Jersey) *Courier-News*. It then shifted her to the Ithaca *Journal*, as assistant to the publisher. When the publisher resigned a month later she took over his post. The *Journal* is one of the smallest in the huge chain, with an Audit Bureau of Circulations (ABC) circulation of nearly 20,000, but it has won top Gannett awards.

"I think the removal of obstacles for women and blacks in management is going to have to come from the industry," she told interviewer Jane Rhodes.[31] "They're going to have to see that it's in their best interests economically. We formerly approached them with the idea that it is morally right to hire us; now we have to approach them from the standpoint that it is economically right."

Whites in Black Journalism

A look at black journalism in the United States should not fail to note that a few whites have worked for black newspapers and magazines. The motivations of those whites who have gone to black publications are not always clear; few have explained their reasoning. It is not unwarranted to assume that some certainly have done so out of idealism, hoping to assist the race in its fight for just treatment. A few active in this sort of journalistic switch or crossover are noted here.

Ward Caille, for twenty years on the Chicago *Daily News* staff, left that paper when he was night editor to become managing editor of the Chicago *Defender*. Ben Burns was among the early managing editors of *Ebony*. Earl Conrad, a New York newspaperman who also went to the *Defender*, served voluntarily, it has been said. He headed its New York bureau. Conrad wrote frequently for major magazines as well and published a number of books about black life, including *Jim Crow America*, which attracted wide attention in the late 1940s.

A few black newspapers and magazines today carry the work of other white journalists, but usually as outside contributors. With the desire of some blacks not to be dependent upon whites if avoidable, and the clear opposition of certain militants toward any reliance whatsoever upon whites, employment of whites is largely clerical or in highly specialized positions which few blacks are as yet trained to fill.

Press Organizations

The black journalists have a number of organizations of their own. Some belong to the various white-dominated groups, such as the one large labor union, the American Newspaper Guild, or to comparable organizations in the broadcasting field. An increasing number are joining Sigma Delta Chi and Women in Communications, Inc. (WICI), national journalism honoraries, either through college chapters or professional units in the larger cities. They are affiliating also with various associations, also predominantly white, existing in a few specialities, such as the Religious Public Relations Council, the Associated Church Press, and the Religion Newswriters Association.

Four black journalists' groups were united in 1970 into the National Association of Black Media Workers (NABMW) as an outcome of the case of Earl Caldwell, a black correspondent for the New York *Times* in San Francisco who refused to testify before a grand jury investigating the Black Panther party. These included Black Perspective, of New York, which earlier had rallied to Caldwell by hiring a lawyer to help defend him and had affirmed its position on the integrity and freedom of the black reporter; the Black Journalists of the San Francisco Bay Area, publisher of the *Ball and Chain Review*, then one of the few publications on the black press; and similar groups in Chicago and Nashville. NABMW, beginning with fifty members, decided to accept both print and broadcast personnel.[32]

In a message "to the Black Community from Black Journalists" Black Perspective had said:

> We will not be used as spies, informants or undercover agents by anybody.
> We will protect our confidential sources, using every means at our disposal.
> We strongly object to attempts by law inforcement agencies to exploit our blackness.[33]

Among the signers were mainly staffers of white New York publications, broadcasting stations, news services, and book firms, but writers for *Essence, Jet,* and *Ebony* magazines and the *Amsterdam News* and New York *Courier* also were in the list. The *Times* supported Caldwell by hiring a constitutional lawyer to represent him and advising him to refuse to appear with his notes.

The leading group in the late 1980s was the National Association of Black Journalists (see sketch of Chuck Stone, a founder, in this chapter). Another organization was the Afro-American Employees Association of the New York *Times.* The organization at the *Times* was founded by the black employees there "to protect their interest, welfare and security." It charged the New York paper with "a white racist attitude towards black workers," saying that the paper employed about 6,000 persons, of whom about 450 were from minority groups, and that most were service workers and office and clerical help in lower level jobs.[34]

In Washington, black journalists of both sexes, rejected for many years by white organizations, formed their own Capital Press Club in 1944. Black women communicators have an organization of their own, somewhat like WICI (which has had many black women as members but is a predominantly white honorary society) or the white National Federation of Press Women. It is the National Association of Media Women, Inc., begun in 1966. Its aims are to provide members with an opportunity to exchange ideas and experiences, to hold research seminars to find solutions to mutual problems, and to enlist young women in mass communication careers. For a time it published the *Media Woman*, a slick paper magazine. It came out several times a year and now is an annual. Eleven women headed by Rhea Callaway, formerly woman's editor of the New York *Age* and later manager of the Brooklyn edition of the New York *Amsterdam News*, originated the group. She was the first president.

Widening Opportunities

Black journalists today stand nearer the edge of wider acceptance and opportunity than at any time in American journalistic history. The situation is favorable largely by comparison, for they had little acceptance of any sort until recent years. Their own publications were too poor economically to sustain them. The white publications had no interest in black journalists, even repelling them. Those for whom they worked might face humiliation and obstructionism. Jules Witcover, a white Washington correspondent, told of the experience of a black member of the press corps there, who worked for a large black weekly. In his earlier days the black reporter was covering a racial trial in the South. He had to go to the courthouse a day ahead of time to find places where he would be allowed to eat, park a car, and telephone his story back to his paper. On the day of the trial he got up early and put an Out-of-Order sign on a phone booth so he'd have one to use.

"Then, after the morning session, I ran out and called in my story," he told another Washington reporter. It worked the first day, but on the second the operator said: "Aren't you the nigger boy who called yesterday? You just put that phone down." He protested but had to go to another phone.[35]

Training and education also no doubt played a part in the rejection of the black journalists, and now are more than ever important in blacks' new possibilities for service to their people and to themselves. Under today's conditions there is less reason for lack of either to be used in refusing black journalists an opportunity to practice the profession.

Journalism Education and Training

Journalism education and training for a minority include these purposes:

1. To convince people lacking such education and training that it is essential to their future usefulness and happiness.
2. To make available a partial, practical substitute for the time being; i.e., special, short-term training, so that a person can move into the income-producing stage sooner than otherwise.
3. To help people after they have the required education and training to find work in the journalistic areas of their interest.

At the beginning of the 1950s a small number of students studied journalism. Scholarships and special training programs were few. This is not to say that the programs now available are sufficient in value or number, but they far exceed what existed forty years ago.

Two methods are bringing slightly more black people into journalism. One involves offering short courses and workshops for quick imparting of skills, usually but not always elementary. The other makes it easier for blacks to obtain a university journalism education, not by lowering standards but by providing practical help. Variations on these plans exist, including combining them, but in the long run the aims are the same: to train adults or youths who have certain skills and know-how to follow specific procedures and to help young people, especially, in getting a general education that includes a certain amount of professional training. The latter offers studies intended to help develop the mind and ensure that students acquire knowledge beyond the area for which they are being prepared.

The goals of both training and education programs are broader than the vocational.[1] Additional intentions are to enable blacks (as well as members of other ethnic groups) to fit into the economic structure, to be able to compete with the dominant group, to realize their ambitions, to use their talents, to balance their dissatisfactions with society by giving them a stake in it, to win their cooperation in correcting the evils about which they complain, to obtain needed personnel for publishing houses, and, as one major plan explains it, "to challenge and confront the racism so often apparent in many American newspapers, especially Southern newspapers."

Journalism Education for Blacks

As differentiated from training in crash programs or other plans separated from general education, journalism education is not new even for members of minority groups; in the North, black students have been studying journalism since such education began more than half a century ago. Most such degree courses are in white institutions, but they are available in several black or predominantly black universities. Separate courses, in English or other departments, are taught in a number of black colleges and universities, some going back to the 1930s. Lack of interest in journalism as a profession, high tuition costs, inadequate preparation, and unavailability of jobs have kept enrollments of black students low. While a little higher today, they still are out of balance with white enrollments in proportion to the total population and are far short of what the profession could absorb. Attempts to remove these obstacles are being made but far too slowly to solve the immediate problem of adjusting the black student to the white press world, or attracting him or her to work on the black press.

Educators Work for Change

The Association for Education in Journalism (AEJ—it later enlarged its name by adding "and Mass Communication") in 1968 appointed a special committee to perform "the task of ascertaining, stimulating, and coordinating the activities of AEJ members in bringing more blacks and other minority group members into our pipeline." The Ad Hoc Coordinating Committee on Minority Group Education set four goals for AEJ. The goals included seeking five hundred scholarships for minority group members for the 1969–70 academic year; establishing cooperative relationships with more black colleges and junior and community colleges to help them establish communication courses on their own campuses; getting pledges from local media that they will hire minority group members and establish internships for them; and "the incorporation by all schools and departments of mass communication of material on the role of minority groups in America and on the portrayal of that role by the media into existing or new courses."[2]

Although the committee was unable to accomplish these goals in as short a time as it had hoped, it did, judging from its survey of what is being done, discover there were some accomplishments and plans. Financial support of some degree was available specifically, it learned, for at least 250 black students and undoubtedly more than that number because at least twenty-three plans were listed as being "for minority students," and surely would include some black young people. The report also noted that financial assistance then was obtainable for attending short courses or workshops for from 166 to 184 black high school students, 82 to 87 black community residents, plus the number of blacks that would come under the label *minority*. Such support, the report observed, ranged in scope from textbooks to ninety-eight hundred dollars a year.

Professor William R. Stroud, then committee secretary, was somewhat disappointed by the report, believing that many more scholarships, workshops, and other of the aids desired by the committee should be forthcoming. The committee nevertheless made further recommendations for the future, including recruiting of black and white students on a national scale; supplementation by the schools of journalism of their present texts and courses so that they "present an unbiased view of the role of black and other minority groups in America"; indicating "the manner in which minority groups have been or are being portrayed in the mass media"; and helping to "prepare students for work in urban areas." A related recommendation was for AEJ to establish or designate a library to collect materials to be used in fulfilling these purposes.[3] In 1970 the committee became permanent, named the Division of Minorities and Communications. It continued its work and has an important program today.

Performance of the Schools

Slow as the progress appears to be, journalism schools attempt to educate members of minority groups by giving them a sound general education along with training in use of basic journalistic techniques. Some provide opportunities to specialize at the same time. These possibilities are in addition to the scholarships, short courses, workshops, conferences, and other training programs. E. Franklin Frazier, the black sociologist, wrote as long ago as 1955 that "Negro journalists have been recruited on the whole from the inferior, segregated Negro schools, and their outlook has been restricted by the social and mental isolation of the Negro world." But white journalism schools, until recent years, were only just tolerated in both the journalistic and the academic worlds and even today still must defend in some quarters their need for more financial support and equal treatment with other studies. They are among the minority groups of educational institutions, not segregated but at times discriminated against. And if the school or department (more likely only two or three courses) exists in a black college, it is a minority group within such a group.

Whatever the cause, little was taught about black journalism and relatively few black journalists were educated for life and the profession in either black or white college journalism courses, although more of the effective practitioners had such schooling than may generally be realized. And the white press, despite the occasional hiring of a black reporter (rarely a black editor or other executive) was actually blameworthy, doing little either to cover the black community or to give blacks journalistic experience and responsibility.

Two 1968 studies reported by Dr. Edward J. Trayes, of Temple University's School of Communications and Theater, bear on the acceptance of blacks in both classrooms and offices of newspapers and magazines. One study indicated that the percentage of black news executives, deskmen, reporters, and photographers on newspapers in large cities was extremely low. The other study showed that the enrollment of black students was even lower. Of 6,418 juniors and seniors majoring in news-editorial or photojournalism at eighty-three colleges and universities, less than 2 percent were black. About half the schools had no blacks in their degree sequences. Professor Trayes, reporting on an early 1970 survey, found that the proportion of black news-editorial and photojournalism majors — junior and senior undergraduates — had increased more than 50 percent during the preceding year but that the extremely low level of black enrollment persisted in most undergraduate programs. More than 40 percent of the schools studied had no black undergraduate news-editorial or photojournalism majors, he learned.

Simeon Booker, Washington bureau chief for *Ebony* and *Jet*, has said that he often had wondered "why the major journalism schools refuse to recognize the Negro press and do not attempt to improve its quality, as is done among white newspapers and magazines."[4] Some attempts have been and are being made, but there is a fallacy in his assumption about the schools' attempts to improve the white press. They have helped improve it largely in technical matters: writing, layout, desk techniques, marketing. Until the 1980s few have been critical of the white press' coverage, of its ethical standards. Instead they have served, on the whole, as handmaidens, preparing young journalists to serve just as uncritically on it and rarely calling the newspapers and magazines to task for their faults, and virtually never for their neglect of the black world's news and for their unfair treatment of blacks when they did make news. Usually only crime or sports involving blacks found a place in the pages. Contented or indifferent as the schools were about the white press' handling of racial news, the schools hardly would be interested in the black press, although they might have been had they not over the years been so understaffed. Now, however, there are signs of discontent among some journalism educators as well as students with the handmaiden attitude or the view that the major function of the journalism school is to train staff members for publications and stations.

The Black Press Attitude

Nor, for that matter, has the black press, any more than the black college, until recently done much to promote journalism education. In a 144-page tabloid-size vocational supplement published by a major black newspaper, the only mention of journalism education or training — a line in a one-half-page advertisement taken by Lincoln University and a story about its journalism department running a bit over a column — was hardly in proportion to the space for other vocations.

When the author of this book was preparing the present edition in 1987, only a small number of black newspaper and magazine publishers responded to appeals for assistance with information and examples of their publications, despite reminders.

During most of American journalistic history, it has been the practice of some journalists to scoff at journalism education; it is a commonplace experience for a reporter's or editor's son to be discouraged from entering his father's profession, being told it is only an area of low pay, hard work, and few rewards. The press has done little to cover its own news, under the excuse that the general public is uninterested in the internal affairs of journalism, an excuse that might also free the press from the necessity of dealing with what is going on within the profession that not always is pleasant. A casualty of this policy has been journalism education, which rarely is mentioned.

When the black press has printed stories about itself, they have been confined to obituaries of editors and publishers, brief reports of annual conventions, boasts of honors received by owners and publishers, and other self-exploitation. When Negro Newspaper Week and other such promotions were sponsored, they said little about the need for more and better staff by black publications, nor did they urge young people to consider journalism as an occupation. The white press has been similarly neglectful. At that, only some of the larger firms concerned enough about their future personnel send recruiters to schools of journalism. Some recruiters are on the watch for able young nonwhites. With few whites inclined to work on black publications and with few black students enrolled, it would not be practical for even the larger black firms to send emissaries in search of talent, although one or two scouts might be so assigned by the National Newspaper Publishers Association in behalf of the newspapers and magazines that belong to it.

The Education Available

Journalism education is available to the black person who wants it in the environment supposedly most familiar to him, the predominantly black college, as well as in the predominantly white institutions of higher learning.

Although it is not imperative to go to a school of journalism or school of communications to have a career in either area, it helps. Most new employees of newspaper editorial departments have attended such schools, and the majority have received degrees, bachelor's or master's or both and sometimes the Ph.D. in journalism or communications. Radio and television companies also hire staffers from the colleges, but the use of journalism-educated personnel is not so general on magazines. The ideal is for a job-seeker to have both journalism education and training and practical experience, including work on college publications.

The service areas—advertising, circulation, production, and

public relations—hire personnel from schools of management as well as from journalism or communications.

Should the student go beyond the undergraduate degree in the professional school? The bachelor's degree is so commonly held that the owner of that degree is at a disadvantage with someone competing for the same job who brings the master's. Similarly, above the master's level the Ph.D. gives an advantage but is not expected of someone seeking an entry-level job.

The degree alone should not be the focus. Advanced degrees often determine where a person's life is to be spent professionally, so the specialty selected as the field for the degree is important.

Few black journalists are in the general communication fields, especially as members of management. Since editors and publishers now are accustomed to seeing applications from journalism graduates, it will help a black applicant to have a degree from a recognized college or university.

If a teaching career in journalism or communications is the objective, at least five years of sound, full-time practical experience are a minimum to add to the degree work. It should accompany advanced study.

All this preparation may sound formidable, but in these days of available scholarships and fellowships it is more practical than it may seem at first.

Courses and Programs

Two of the early courses directly concerned with black journalism were those at American University in Washington, D.C., and at Syracuse University in Syracuse, New York. They provide good examples for other college and university schools of journalism to follow. The course at American, begun in 1968, was on the "History and Evolution of the Afro-American Press and the Afro-American in the Mass Media" and was taught by Dorothy Gilliam, who had been a black staff member of the white Washington *Post*, a major daily, and later was in broadcasting. The course, which may have been the first ever to deal with the history of black journalism, began with 1827 and went to the 1970s, ending with the related topic, "The Negro and the Mass Media."

Syracuse's course, begun in 1968, included such history, but its major attention was to the contemporary black press and such auxiliaries and competitors as the news services, broadcasting, advertising, circulation, and production, covering most of the chapter topics of this book. (The white teacher is the author of this book.) Black journalists were brought in as guest lecturers, as were white specialists in black journalism.

Discussed at the outset of this book was the validity of the concept of a black press. In this chapter, as part of the examination of the training and education of the black journalist, there should be inquiry into the validity of teaching black press courses, for in some quarters these have been questioned as unnecessary. "Journalism is journalism, whatever the color," sometimes is heard. The more militant blacks attack black history courses in general as being taught only in the perspective of white history. It is true that if the events of white history are the only guideposts such a course is artificial and unrealistic. Related to this charge is another: black subjects when taught by whites cannot be taught adequately because whites do not have—and cannot ever have—the understanding of the black experience and point of view that only black people possess. It is conceivable, however, that an informed white teacher, a professional in two fields, education and journalism, can impart facts and ideas and can direct analysis of such facts and ideas perhaps more successfully than some black teachers who bring an inner understanding of certain aspects but may lack expertise as educators. Furthermore, so few people are available to teach courses in black journalism that the educational world will have to rely on both white and black instructors.

Black studies courses are thought to be an attempt to be popular, especially when taught by whites. White colleges and universities are charged with trying to do what now is wanted, just to placate signtoting, protesting students, after having neglected black subjects for years. Perhaps these accusations once were deserved on some campuses. One might ask, however, at least in the instance of a course on black journalism, whether proposals to teach about that journalism, if made in the past, would have been considered seriously. It is doubtful that they would have been accepted. And perhaps they could not have been in the mood of the time. To begin with, to have done so in the 1940s and 1950s would have been damned as discriminatory, as downright segregationist. It was not so long ago that college admissions offices refused to issue figures about the number of black students accepted or enrolled because they had abandoned taking racial counts. Also, there was not the possibility of support for such courses equal to the small amount existing in the years since 1968, when the first was begun. The climate of opinion was not warm enough, any more than it was at one time for classes in religion journalism, science journalism, or other specialties.

So long as separation thrives, black journalism courses will be useful. And when it is discovered that the subject contains considerable substance, it will continue to be taught, since black journalism has a rich content and a great potential for study, particularly if broadened to include the African background and influence upon that continent.

But the lack of support of the black media is paralleled by insufficient backing for study of black journalism. Consequently, little study and research were being done in the late 1980s.

The experience of Professor Hattie S. Knight with teaching a course on the black press at Hampton University indicates the attitudes and backgrounds of present-day students of this journalism. It corresponds to the experiences of other teachers.

The Hampton course has been offered annually, sometimes twice a year, since 1975. When Professor Knight took it over, enrollment had dropped sharply. She decided to stimulate interest in it, and the enrollment in the seminar has increased, averaging between ten and twenty students.

Professor Knight found that students, in the Hampton case mainly members of the black race, are not much aware of the black newspapers and usually have not read one. They are, she found, more familiar with the magazine circulation leaders, such as *Jet, Essence,* and *Ebony*.

"Once they begin to explore various newspapers, they really develop a deep appreciation for the black press," she says. Through the course "they are challenged to look at earlier editions of *Jet, Ebony, Black World* and *Crisis.*"

"They discover," she says, "that some of the same political, social, and economic conditions pertaining to Black Americans discussed in the earlier magazines are still being discussed in the present-day magazines and newspapers."[5]

Also, as in some other universities, the black students are broadcast media–oriented, Professor Knight explained. "I have students who express a desire to work for the black press, but many cannot afford to work for such publications because of the low pay or because there are so few jobs."

Nevertheless some of the Hampton graduates have joined the staffs of publications and stations. Several have gone to the Norfolk *Journal and Guide,* a leading weekly; another is managing editor of the Washington *Informer*; one has been at *Essence* for five years; one was on the recently discontinued *Ebony Jr!*; one works for the Philadelphia *Tribune*. Several are in black-owned radio. An executive of Sheridan Broadcasting Network is a Hampton graduate. Several other students have worked on black-oriented although white-owned radio stations.

Three of the journalism education programs at predominantly black colleges and universities are described here: those of Florida A. & M., Hampton, and Howard universities. Twice that many more might have been selected and should be considered by anyone seeking such education. Clark, Shaw, Texas Southern, Norfolk State, and Grambling are among other possibilities. Special attention to black journalism is rare in either black or nonblack institutions. Treatment of this special aspect of communications at best is a week or two in a U.S. journalism history course, even in the black colleges.

This sparse concern for the black communications media and their problems and opportunities has several explanations. Colleges cannot offer courses or degree programs for which there is too little demand. Although some black journalism organizations try to arouse interest in black journalism among young people, the efforts are not sufficient to bring enough enrollments in classes. Black publications enterprises are not competitive with those of nonblack businesses.

Would-be students can obtain helpful assistance toward finding a place in journalism, whatever racial group this communication serves, through training programs. These are dealt with at the end of this chapter. Such programs do not presume to give a rounded education; they give practical preparation for lower-level jobs in the different media. But they have led would-be practicing journalists to places of importance—some of these trainees have subsequently obtained college degrees in majors that provide them with specialties to which they can apply the journalism techniques learned in a training program.

Florida A. & M. University

Among the widely known journalism education centers whose faculties encourage blacks is Florida A. & M. University (FAMU) in Tallahassee. Its journalism training and education department was founded in 1974 and has developed into a division of the School of Journalism, Media, and Graphic Arts.

FAMU was the first black school to be accredited. Three sequences—public relations, print journalism, and broadcast journalism—were approved. The school has three divisions: journalism, film and electronic media, and graphic arts. The accreditation was granted by the Council on Accrediting of the Association for Education in Journalism and Mass Communication. In 1988 it was reaccredited for six years.

The school is directed by a dean, to whom report the directors of each division. The school has the necessary modern equipment for its varied practical courses. Its curricula resemble those of the other major schools accredited in the same areas. It has been able to provide these facilities and teaching programs because of support from various sources, including two awards totaling nearly one million dollars from the W. K. Kellogg Foundation.

As with some other black journalism educational plans, its graduates do not often go to the staffs of black media but prefer to work in white communications areas. Nevertheless some black newspapers are benefiting from the program. One FAMU graduate was managing editor of the Orlando (Florida) *Times*, in 1987, another was a reporter for the Daytona (Florida) *Times*, and one was a staffer at the Indianapolis *Reporter*.

One FAMU activity that introduces young black people to the profession of journalism is the summer newspaper workshop for high school students, first offered in 1964. Now a two-week session, it has

11.1. Students of broadcasting in lab at Florida A. & M. University.

more than a dozen sponsors, most of them leading Florida newspapers as well as the Dow Jones Newspaper Fund.

Staffed by School of Journalism and other FAMU faculty as well as members of the working press, the workshops cover the basic newswriting, feature writing, photography, newspaper graphics, and other classes. Students also produce a newspaper for the workshop. The 1987 *Workshopper* was an eight-page tabloid. A special program of this sort is especially important in the effort to direct black persons into the field.

Hampton University

Hampton University in Hampton, Virginia, has been one of the black institutions offering a course on black media per se, through its department of mass media arts. The university describes itself as "the first historically black college in America to establish a degree-granting program in mass media arts." The program was begun in 1967. Three concentrations (sequences) lead to a bachelor's degree: news-editorial, broadcasting (radio/television), and a comprehensive sequence. Hampton students issue a weekly newspaper, the *New Voice*, for the university.

The curriculum includes a wide variety of courses beyond the introductory classes, among them advanced reporting, photojournalism, advertising, media law, graphics, propaganda analysis, public relations, ethics, and various radio-television classes.

Howard University

Situated as it is in Washington, D.C., the School of Communications of Howard University has an ideal location for its programs. The nation's capital is one of the news hubs of the world. Its newspapers, magazines, and broadcasting centers are owned by some of the leading communications firms in the nation.

Founded in 1867, and with a present-day enrollment of more than twelve thousand full-time students, Howard has one of the most elaborate and successful communication schools whatever the nature of the ownership (in this case it is black). It has three departments: Communications Arts and Sciences, Journalism, and Radio, TV, and Film.

The School of Communications is known for its faculty, curriculum, and large body of alumni. It has acquired its reputation even though it was not founded until 1971. The Journalism Department was accredited in 1986 by the Accrediting Council of the Association for Education in Journalism and Mass Communication. Within the department are three areas of study: news-editorial (print journalism), broadcast journalism, and editing and management. Its large battery of courses, as good as if not better than those of most major schools of communication in the United States, provides education and training for persons of any race; its enrollment includes large numbers of students from overseas and from all parts of this country.

The black press is recognized in the curricula. Through the Journalism Department students have access to about thirty courses; the Radio, TV, and Film Department offers an equal number. Many of the courses are fundamental and important to finding and holding a place in print journalism. The class of direct value to understanding the objectives and nature of the black press is the required "History of the Black and White Press," taught in the 1980s by James S. Tinney, associate professor at Howard and coeditor of the book *Issues and Trends in Afro-American Journalism.* A collection of chapters on both print and electronic journalism published in 1980, it helps fill some gaps in this specialized journalism.

Professor Tinney weaves background facts on the black press into the sixteen-week course, not only directly in such topics as "The Abolitionist Press, Rise of the Black Press" and "Major Black Editors of the 20th Century" but also in lectures and readings on "The Press and the Civil Rights Era" and "The Rise of Yellow Journalism in Tandem with the Jazz Age and the Harlem Renaissance."

The special project, a term-paper assignment, is met by either preparing an oral history interview, writing the history of a black newspaper or magazine, writing the history of the press in Africa or a Caribbean country but focusing on one publication published there, or making a content analysis of two or more publications.

The philosophy of the Journalism Department was expressed in a report made in 1985 before the accreditation procedure began. In part it read: "The Howard University Department . . . was born out of the recognition in the 1960s that more minority journalists were needed to bridge the divergent perspectives of black and white America." The results of this aim have been dramatic.

Mark Alleyne, a 1984 magna cum laude graduate of Howard, was on the dean's list each semester while in the journalism program, and won the E. Fannie Granton Scholarship. He declined another to study political science at Howard and opted, instead, to work in the Caribbean, making his home in Barbados, where he was feature editor of *Bajan* magazine. In 1985 he gained another honor: he was selected to be a Rhodes scholar from the British Caribbean in 1986. He was thought to be the first Howard graduate to win this world-famous scholarship to study at Oxford University and may be the first black journalism graduate to do so from any institution.

Although Howard has no comprehensive and complete alumni list — a situation common to universities teaching communications — Howard, like Hampton and several other predominantly black institutions, has impressive partial lists. They include, beginning in 1972, Stephanie Stokes Oliver, who became senior editor, and Curtia Lynn James, associate food editor, *Essence*; Obafemi Oredein, editor of *Sunday Sketch*, Ibadan, Nigeria; Denise Roark, managing editor, Washington *Informer*; Carol Patrick Burrows, assistant professor of mass communications, Hampton University; Trudie Moore, associate editor, *Jet*; John Templeton, editor and general manager, Richmond *Afro-American* and executive editor, Winston-Salem *Chronicle*; and Paul Akomenji, editor, Malawi National News Agency.

Other graduates went to the staffs of white-owned newspapers and magazines. They were reporters and editors on the Washington, D.C. *Times*, Detroit *Free Press*, the *Wall Street Journal, Ms* magazine, Philadelphia *Daily News*, Associated Press wire service, Wilmington (Delaware) *News*, Atlanta *Constitution*, Pensacola *Journal*, *People* magazine, Saginaw (Michigan) *News*, Boca Raton *News*, Rochester (New York) *Times Union*, Dallas *Times*, the New York *Times*, Detroit *News*, and Greensboro (North Carolina) *News and Record*.

Several dozen joined television (mostly white-owned) and radio stations and nonjournalistic organizations to do public relations or publications work, including universities, church denominations, businesses, and government. Usually fifty students are hired each summer to be interns in professional offices. In one recent year, two of the forty-two newspapers and magazines hiring interns, as reported by the Journalism Department, were black: the New York *Amsterdam News* and *Jet* magazine.

A dozen scholarships funds are administered by the Journalism Department for undergraduates; others are available through the general financial aid program.[6]

Lincoln University

The Lincoln University department of communications in Jefferson City, Missouri, for years has been thought of as a strong training and educational center for people interested in black journalism. In recent years the enrollment in the university as a whole has become predominantly nonblack and its communications department puts less emphasis on black communications.

The original reputation existed not only because of special courses but also because of the holdings of black publications and the research done by faculty. The work of the faculty was led by Dr. Armistead S. Pride, at one time director when the unit was called a department of journalism. An additional contribution was publication of a newsletter conveying much news about the black press and black journalists nationally. Awards to leading publications and journalists also were important in the department's work.

In the 1980s efforts were made to enroll more black students at the large, nonblack colleges and universities. These activities have caused enrollments to decrease at some smaller institutions with journalism programs of less breadth and lacking in the financial aid for improvement in faculty size and equipment.

Lincoln now has a department of communications with a faculty of five and stresses journalism and broadcasting. Four undergraduate degrees are offered, two for majors in journalism and two for majors in radio and television broadcasting. Heading the department is Dr. Thomas D. Pawley III, professor of speech and theater, who has been at Lincoln for more than forty-five years.

The attention at Lincoln to black journalism per se occurs in the history of journalism courses, whose teachers have devoted lectures to that journalism which was Dr. Pride's specialty.

Teachers of Journalism

Journalism teachers who are black are primarily on the faculties of black colleges. A few teach in the largely white institutions. The tendency today in those universities is to offer courses on ethnic minorities, grouping Afro-Americans, Asians, Hispanics, and Native Americans.

Black journalism, therefore, comes to the attention of a limited number of students in such colleges who might not otherwise be aware of it as a force in U.S. communications. But inevitably the attention is too slight to equip a person with a sound knowledge of the black press.

There is another aspect of the predominantly black educational institutions: they usually have better library facilities on this subject. They are likely to stock relevant books and to receive black newspapers and magazines. The college also will bring special lecturers from the press, telecommunications, and government areas with this minority.

Included here are brief accounts of a half-dozen black teachers, mainly at predominantly black universities. These scholars are representative of others who might have been selected. The staffs of Clark College's journalism department and of the William Allen White School of Communications at the University of Kansas, for example, include notable and widely experienced teachers of the journalism of the black people of the United States.

Armistead S. Pride

One black teacher, although he had comparatively little practical experience in journalism, for years has been outstanding if not entirely alone in the teaching profession. This pioneer is Armistead Scott Pride of Lincoln University. He was dean or chairperson of its work in journalism education for many years. Born in Washington, D.C., in 1906, Pride also is unusual in that he has the full list of academic degrees: an A.B. from the University of Michigan, an A.M. from the University of Chicago, an M.S. from Northwestern's Medill School of Journalism, and a Ph.D. from Northwestern's English department with a journalism subject dissertation.

Pride's journalistic background is less impressive than his education, but some of the other widely known teachers of the subject have had little practical experience, as for example the internationally noted teacher, administrator, and historian Frank Luther Mott, one of whose histories in journalism won a Pulitzer prize. Pride was city editor of the Lamar (Colorado) *Daily News*, in 1933 and 1934, and at the same time area correspondent for the Associated Press. Earlier, for two years, he was an editor in the department of forms and reproduction of the Massachusetts Geodetic Survey. But the rest is teaching. At first it was English for several years in Southern colleges and at Lincoln, where he was an assistant professor of English in 1937, moving into journalism fully in 1942. In two years he was acting director of the school of journalism, becoming director the next year, dean and full professor in 1947, and remaining as chairperson when journalism was put on a departmental instead of a school basis.

During several leaves of absence he made an international impact. He served as a Fulbright lecturer at Cairo University, as well as at American University, in Egypt. Another year he was at the University of Rome; later at Chungang University in Seoul, Korea. In 1969–70 he was a visiting professor at Temple University.

His major contribution to black journalism in America, aside from educating dozens of students over the years, has been exploring the history of the black newspaper. His doctoral dissertation at Northwestern was an invaluable record and historical account of these papers from the first in 1827 to 1950, when the dissertation was completed. This thorough and careful study is far more than a checklist, for the history in general and that of individual publications are discussed and analyzed.

In addition, Pride has contributed articles on black journalism to the *Nation, Editor & Publisher, Journalism Quarterly*, the *Quill, Gazette*, and other professional journals. He has been active in the American Society of Journalism School Administrators, a constituent

11.2. Armistead S. Pride, retired director of the journalism department, Lincoln University (Missouri), and historian of black newspapers.

part of the Association for Education in Journalism and Mass Communication (AEJMC), and directly with the AEJMC as well. His bibliography of the black newspaper for the latter's Ad Hoc Coordinating Committee is the most comprehensive thus far issued. He launched the *Lincoln Journalism Newsletter* in 1944, maintaining it as a continuous record of events in black journalism for more than a dozen years.

Marilyn Kern-Foxworth

One of the most professionally active black teachers of communications during the 1970s and 1980s is Dr. Marilyn Kern-Foxworth, an associate professor in the department of journalism at Texas A&M University.

When she joined the faculty there she had been an assistant professor at the University of Tennessee at Knoxville from 1980 to 1987. Before that she worked for a Madison, Wisconsin, black newspaper, the *Midwest Observer*, as a reporter and columnist; she was production manager for radio at WHA radio and TV, and Madison A.M. traffic manager for WWQM radio. Earlier she was coordinator of advertising for the city of Tallahassee, Florida, and a communications specialist at Florida State University in that city. She did her first media work in Jackson, Mississippi, for WJTV as a public relations assistant.

She held some of these jobs while a student. Her education was diversified enough to contribute to her teaching area, public relations. She earned a bachelor's degree at Jackson State University, Mississippi, a master of science degree from Florida State, and her Ph.D. from the University of Wisconsin at Madison in the area of mass communication. Her dissertation title was "A Comparative Analysis of the Portrayal of Blacks and Whites in White-Oriented Mass Circulation Magazine Advertisements During 1959, 1969, and 1979." She believes she was the first, and still may be the only, black person to receive a Ph.D. with a concentration in advertising and public relations.

During these same years she published various professional articles and also wrote for consumer publications. Among these were her biographical entry on Alex Haley for the *Dictionary of Literary Biography*, an article on helping minorities for *Journalism Educator* magazine, and other articles on black minority subjects for the *Black Collegian, Black Journalism Review*, and *Journal of Black Studies*.

Kern-Foxworth has won various awards, grants, and other

honors from the University of Tennessee, Black Women Hall of Fame Foundation, Public Relations Society of America, and Association of Black Communicators. She is the author of several booklets and brochures, all on minority topics and issued by professional organizations, universities, or industries. Her affiliations with professional groups are numerous.

One of her major contributions in the academic field was the founding of Association of Black Communicators (ABC) at the University of Tennessee Knoxville campus. Its members are undergraduate and graduate students in the College of Communications majoring in mass communications.

"The reason a separate group was formed, although SDX/SPJ, WICI, Ad Club and others were there," she explains, "was for the mere fact that those organizations did not network about minority issues."[7]

Through ABC students are able to read publications about minorities in the media, be officers of a group, and come to know one another or, as Kern-Foxworth puts it, "to interact with each other." They went as a group every year, led by her, to attend the Howard University Communications Conference in Washington, D.C.

"They were encouraged, however, to join the other organizations," she pointed out. There was no problem with joining the other groups, but the black students did "get lost" in them. To hold a leadership role in them was extremely difficult.

J. William Snorgrass

Although the literature of black journalism is slender, compared to what is available about mass communications in general, it is an increasingly important body of material. Yet except for the often skimpy bibliographies in the appendices of books — biographies, histories, and reference works — there is little in compact form to aid the researcher.

Some of this lack was corrected in 1985 when a volume entitled *Blacks and Media*, prepared by J. William Snorgrass and Gloria T. Woody, was published by the University Press of Florida A. & M. University in Tallahassee. Snorgrass, who died in 1987, was on the faculty of the university's School of Journalism, Media, and Graphic Arts. Woody is director and librarian of FAMU's library and resources center.

Blacks and Media bears the subtitle *A Selected, Annotated Bibliography, 1962–1982*. It contains more than seven hundred entries "on the relationship between blacks and media" in the United States. The publisher goes on to say that "the compilers have filled a void for persons interested in the media's influence and in how the political, economic, and social conditions of blacks in America are reported." Not only books but also articles in both scholarly journals and general magazines are covered.

The senior author, Snorgrass, had worked on black newspapers and contributed articles on black journalism to important journals dealing with that specialty. He also held high positions in the national organizations of communications, both general bodies and black societies.

A Missourian, he majored in journalism at the University of Nebraska, getting his bachelor's degree in 1970. Three years later he had a master of arts from the University of Minnesota, where he again majored in journalism.

His black press experience included being editor and publisher of the *Black Student Review*, a magazine published in Oakland, California; managing editor of the Post Newspaper Group in Oakland for a year; and a feature writer and newswriter for the Berkeley *Post* in Berkeley, California.

During some of those years and up to 1979 he had decided to make his chief interest teaching and research in journalism and mass communication, with a special emphasis on history. For the five years from 1974 to 1979 he was an instructor in the department of mass communication at California State University in Hayward, teaching courses in news and editorial work, mass communication, and blacks and the media. In 1979 he joined the Florida A. & M. University faculty and became an associate professor in the School of Journalism, Media, and Graphic Arts with the same primary teaching areas as he had had at California State.

His articles appeared in the *Western Journal of Black Studies, Negro History Bulletin, California History*, and *American Journalism*, among other periodicals. He presented historical and biographical papers at meetings of the American Journalism Historians Association, the Research Association of Minority Professors, Association for Education in Journalism and Mass Communication, and the Association for the Study of Afro-American Life and History.

Snorgrass held memberships in various historical and professional bodies, including those named, and the National Newspaper Publishers Association (as an honorary member), College Media Advisors, Southern Conference on Afro-American Studies, and Blacks in Communications. He was president of the American Journalism

Historians Association in 1983–84, vice-president in 1982–83, historian in 1984–87, and served on the board of directors for 1985–87. He directed the FAMU summer high school journalism workshop from 1980 to his death.

A loan fund in his memory was established by the university in 1987.

Lillian Bell

The most successful journalism or communications teachers are those who not only have a sound background of practical experience, academic training, and general education but who also continue to sharpen their skills and knowledge.

Lillian Smith Bell, professor of journalism at Northern Illinois University, DeKalb, Illinois, is an example of such a teacher. From 1977 to 1988 she was a columnist for the *Post-Tribune* of Gary, Indiana, a daily of about 80,000 circulation. Her column, "Person to Person," was a vehicle for local interest features, travel articles, biographical sketches, human interest stories, and other topics. She wrote with knowledge of the community since it was where she and her late husband, Cecil Marvin Bell, made their home for many years until 1987. Beginning in 1988 she became a weekly op-ed page columnist for the South Bend (Indiana), *Tribune*, a daily with more than 92,000 circulation weekdays and more than 123,000 Sundays.

Born in South Bend, Bell is a native Hoosier. She was at Northwestern University for two degrees, the first a bachelor of science in journalism and the second a doctorate from Northwestern's Medill School of Journalism. In between she earned a master's degree in education at Case Western Reserve University, in Cleveland, Ohio. Her doctoral dissertation was on "The Role and Performance of Black and Metro Newspapers in Relation to Political Campaigns in Selected Racially-Mixed Congressional Elections 1960–1970." While working on her doctoral degree she was an instructor of journalism, teaching reporting and editing.

Her first professional journalism experience had come from two years as a reporter and assistant editor on the staff of the Baltimore *Afro-American*. Subsequently she was an editor on the Cleveland (Ohio) *Herald*, where she worked for eight years. In 1956 she went to Hampton Institute (now Hampton University) in Virginia as associate director of public relations.

She returned to Indiana to be a journalism-English teacher at Froebel High School in Gary, handling the school's public relations and advising the student yearbook and newspaper. After six years she entered college journalism teaching as chairperson of the department of journalism at St. Joseph's Calumet College, in East Chicago, Indiana. There she held the ranks of assistant, associate, and full professor and was advisor to the college newspaper staff.

In 1975 she joined the Northern Illinois faculty. In that same summer she was a visiting lecturer in journalism at Northwestern. A decade later she was a visiting professor of journalism at Notre Dame on a summer appointment. In 1988 she became an adjunct professor there.

She worked in black journalism from 1972 to 1982 as a bimonthly columnist for the Gary *Info*, then an 18,000-circulation black weekly. The *Post-Tribune* has at times assigned her writing beyond her column, such as covering a presidential inaugural and the Olympic Games in Los Angeles.

For several years she taught a course on "Ethnic Minorities and the Mass Media" at Northern Illinois. It was part of a Black Studies program. When enrollment dwindled by 1983 it was removed from the curriculum.

"However, I have included the material in my 'Mass Media and Modern Society' course which is much more satisfactory," she said in 1987. "The enlightening of white students is incredible. Primarily seniors and graduate students, they have no knowledge of any minority press and are eager to learn," she added.[8]

Bell has also taught courses on article writing, journalistic writing, teaching journalism, supervision of school publications, principles of public relations, reporting, reporting of public affairs, introduction to mass communication, journalism and mass media, and freshman English.

Bell has been active in various communications organizations. She was executive director of the Chicago Association of Black Journalists, member of the board of directors of the Student Press Law Center, Washington, consultant to the journalism department at Alabama State University, chairperson of the national campus chapter advisory committee of Women in Communications, Inc., and has been a public relations consultant to various organizations and individuals.

She belongs to several of the groups named as well as the Lake County Association of Black Journalists of Indiana and is a lifetime member of the NAACP, to which she has given public relations counsel. She not only works for her own racial group but also is a member of the National Association of Hispanic Journalists. Her interest in the field of nursing has led to her work as consulting editor for the *National Black Nurses Journal* and as a member of the editorial board of the National Black Nurses Association.

Frank W. Render II

Frank W. Render probably is the only head of a journalism school or department to be fired by an American president, and he is certainly the only one of the black race. Now head of the department of mass media arts at Hampton University in Virginia, Render was fired in 1971 after he had been appointed deputy assistant secretary in the U.S. Department of Defense. His special area was equal opportunity. His was the highest rank ever held by a black in the department up to that time. Fourteen months after his appointment he was dismissed by President Richard Nixon, reportedly because he was not a "team player."

Render, a Virginian by birth, has held a large variety of posts in his career, and they have given him preparation for his teaching at Hampton and other colleges and universities offering courses in communications.

A Hampton graduate of the days when it was known as Hampton Institute, he is one of a number of prominent black journalists who earned degrees there. He has a bachelor of science degree in political science and sociology. He earlier had attended Howard University and the New School for Social Research. After Hampton he enrolled at Syracuse University, earning a master's degree in public relations and journalism. Eight years later he was admitted to candidacy for the Ph.D. in mass communication but did not complete the studies.

His professional experience includes numerous appointments, among them executive director of the Human Rights Commission of Syracuse and Onondaga County; consultant and special assistant to the U.S. Department of Education; director of public relations and assistant professor of English at Albany State College, Georgia; a similar position of higher rank at Virginia State University; and lecturer and special assistant at the University of the District of Columbia.

Render also has had wide experience in the private sector: as senior associate with Oram Associates, fund-raising consultants in New York; president of the Economic Growth Systems Information Services Corp., in Washington; vice-president, REM Associates, management consultants; and executive director, National Association of Minority Consultants and Urbanologists. He has received various awards and honors.

Like a number of other communications teachers, he has stressed public relations and human relations rather than participation in production of newspapers, magazines, or broadcasting activities. He was, however, senior editor of *Metro* magazine in Washington.

At Hampton he is an associate professor and department head. The university has a rich curriculum in mass media arts. (See reports on three universities in this chapter.)

Thelma Thurston Gorham

In the first edition of this book Thelma Thurston Gorham, now of Florida A. & M. University, was described as one of the most active practitioners and teachers of journalism.

Early in her career she edited *Step-Up*, a magazine for black businesspeople. She was on the staff of *New Lady*, a creditable magazine for black women. She also went into newspaper work, reaching the executive editorship of the *Black Dispatch*, Oklahoma City, and the managing editorship of the Tulsa (Oklahoma) *Eagle*.

Gorham has had an abiding devotion to black journalism ever since she did this work and wrote her master's thesis at the University of Minnesota. Its title was "Negro Newsmen and Practices of Pressure Groups in the Middle West."

By 1973 she had accomplished still more. She had done public relations work and taught journalism at Hampton University. Before that she had taught in Oklahoma City, Kansas City, and at Southern University in Baton Rouge, Louisiana. While she was on leave from FAMU between 1968 and 1972 she taught at the University of Minnesota.

These are just samples of her extensive career, which also includes being an assistant professor of journalism at Lincoln University, Missouri, news editor of what is now the San Francisco *Sun-Reporter*, pro tem managing editor of the *Crisis*, and news editor and feature writer for the Los Angeles *Sentinel*.

Dozens of other professional activities appear on her vita, an impressive and almost overwhelming report of a person who seems to eat and sleep journalism, especially that of her own race.

Gorham was asked to describe her years at FAMU:

> I came . . . in 1963 as acting director of public relations and associate professor of journalism. Because Dr. George W. Gore, Jr., then presi-

dent of the university, was interested in developing a more structured program in journalism instead of the alternating courses that I taught part-time under the umbrella of the Department of Languages, I moved from P.R. to full-time teaching of journalism in 1967.

In 1968 I took a leave of absence and went back to the University of Minnesota to begin work on a Ph.D. degree. With the inauguration of a new president, Dr. Benjamin L. Perry, my leave in Minnesota was cut short by a request to return and begin working out a full-fledged journalism program.

I returned to FAMU in 1970 as an associate professor. In 1972, a search for a "non-minority male with a Ph.D." was suggested by the Florida State Board of Control. The Board was unable to find a non-minority male with or without a Ph.D. who was interested in the position which was intended to enhance the program in journalism at FAMU for non-minority students. Remember [that] the push was on to get more white students into black schools. I finally received my promotion to full professor [in] July, 1987.

Initially, I organized and advised a Journalism Club, served as advisor of the FAMU chapter of the Society of Professional Journalists, Sigma Delta Chi. When those advisory chores were turned over to other faculty members, I was selected by the student body (non-journalism) to work with the Rattler Yearbook. I had worked with the FAMUAN, the school newspaper, and directed a summer newspaper workshop for minority high school students and teachers.

I teach Introduction to Mass Media, Mass Media Methods (which encompasses our basic newswriting and editing concepts), Feature Writing, Magazine Article Writing, and Editorial Writing; and I began a course in Grammar for Journalists (now called and taught ostensibly as Journalism Skills).

I think Black journalism students from historically Black universities, for whom there have been few newspaper career options, need more role models in the historically important areas of mass communications. The Black press offers such role models and the promotion of this idea may be one way of drawing Black students into the Black media.[9]

Training for Journalism

Education is one road to a place in black journalism. Training is another. They differ: education is a long range plan that may include training but is broader in scope. A black student may, for instance, obtain a bachelor's degree at a particular university or college, which involves study only of standard liberal arts courses (history, psychology, a science, foreign language, and sociology, for instance). No journalism, medical, law, or other professional courses are required in a purely liberal arts degree.

But other students working for an undergraduate degree may decide on a double major and include about 25 percent of their 120 hours for the degree to be in journalism. The bulk of their study, however, is in the liberal arts. Thus there is an element of training in those first four years, but it is subordinated to the broader, cultural courses.

A graduate student also must include, for an advanced degree in journalism, some hours in nonprofessional courses, such as political science, English, or psychology. This student has thereby received further training in communications but shared his or her time with a subject that equips the student to become in time a specialist in a subject matter to which his or her training may be applied.

Training also is obtainable without any connection to an educational institution except that it may be the locale for the work and its facilities. Training programs usually are short term: a summer, twelve weeks, or four to six months are common.

Such nondegree basic training programs have the objective of quickly preparing a candidate for a place in journalism, but it is a beginner's position. Eventually some trainees passing through such a plan go on to degree work. But a training program enables a person to make all or part of a living soon.

Newspapers, magazines, advertisers, and other enterprises in communications look to such basic training plans as a source of personnel, but only for beginning jobs. The time spent in a training program not only will equip a person to hold such a job but also will reveal that some people in the programs are not suited for journalism as a career at that time; i.e., it is a screening process to save the publication or other business from hiring persons unsuited for the profession. It also helps applicants find out their suitability for such jobs.

Advanced training programs run for a year or even two. Typical of these is the Los Angeles *Times*'s 1987–1989 Minority Editorial Training Program (known as METRO for short). It is an intensive plan spread over two years; originally it was started in 1984. Its aim is to increase the number of minority reporters and photographers wishing to work anywhere in the United States.

METRO is funded by the newspaper and its parent company, Times Mirror. Up to 1987, twenty-seven of its graduates were on the staffs of various newspapers.

Plans include training programs and internships. Few trainees can be handled by black publications or stations. A typical example of a white program for minority trainees is provided by Long Island *Newsday* or New York *Newsday*, a large white-owned daily. The program, begun in 1974, has had a dozen trainees since.

One black trainee, Dennis Bell, came into the plan from the paper's pressroom, where he had been a porter. He was hired after his internship. In 1986 he and two other staff members won a Pulitzer Prize for foreign reporting. Soon after, he was named by the National Association of Black Journalists as its Black Journalist of the Year. He was promoted to the Washington bureau.

This newspaper also has a summer intern program, which is more practical for black newspapers and magazines than training programs because the beginner can be of more help during vacation periods. Many such neophytes, however, come with small publication experience (such as high school or college journalism) and some course work in journalism. Training plans mean arranging for classrooms with facilities and at least one full-time director.

Newsday hires thirty-five summer interns each year, and 25 percent of them must be minorities. Marilyn Milloy, formerly a minority intern, became a minority affairs specialist on *Newsday*'s staff.

People interested in these programs—and there are dozens of each type—can obtain the latest information about them from sources such as journalism school offices, units of the Newspaper Guild, career days, high school and college career and job counselors, and local newspaper and broadcasting offices. Booklets, application forms, and other literature can be obtained by writing to these organizations (or others as suggested by local guides): ANPA Foundation, The Newspaper Center, Box 17407, Dulles Airport, Washington, DC 20041; Dow Jones Newspaper Fund, P.O. Box 300, Princeton, NJ 08540; The Society of Professional Journalists, Sigma Delta Chi, 53 W. Jackson Blvd., Suite 731, Chicago, IL 60604-3610; and National Association of Black Journalists, One Herald Plaza, Miami, FL 33102.

Minorities seeking a career in U.S. journalism will find the *Journalism Career Guide for Minorities* an invaluable publication. This fifty-six-page brochure, dated 1986, contains guidance not to be found elsewhere except in portions. It was sponsored by the American Newspaper Publishers Association Foundation, American Society of Newspaper Editors, Associated Press Managing Editors Association, the Society of Professional Journalists, Sigma Delta Chi, and the Dow Jones Newspaper Fund, Inc. (Much of the content appeared in the *1986 Journalism Career and Scholarship Guide* published by the Dow Jones Newspaper Fund, Inc.)

The *Guide* contains specific facts such as a job and salary report, lists of scholarships, programs, and recruiters, as well as grants and programs offered by industry. Internship programs and a list of newspapers that recruit minorities are in it. Academic preparation is explained and illustrated. Various other career questions are answered. The emphasis is heavily on newspaper and news service activity. Individuals may obtain one free copy by writing the Dow Jones Newspaper Fund, P.O. Box 300, Princeton, NJ 08543-0300.

The Career Directory Series provides helpful guidance to persons of any race about various communication careers. By 1987 six volumes had been prepared, several for the second time, with job data and counsel on advertising, public relations, marketing and sales, book publishing, magazines, and newspapers. They are written by various executives from the larger firms, and edited by executives of Career Press. Included in each are chapters on internships and training plans and a list of the available programs.

Grants, Scholarships, Fellowships, Assistantships

Four kinds of financial aid are available to qualified minority applicants. Some assistance is directed solely to members of the black race.

Grants usually are outright and to be used for tuition or other expenses related to education, training programs, or internships. These are obtained as a result of gifts to universities and colleges or are training programs offered by other institutions, such as foundations.

The Knight Foundation, for example, in 1987 gave two grants totaling more than one million dollars to "establish pace-setting programs for recruiting, training, and tracking minority journalists." The University of Florida and the University of Missouri received the grants and sought to guide "promising" high school minority students into journalism education and to track their scholastic and career progress.[10]

Dean Ralph L. Lowenstein of the College of Journalism and Communication at the University of Florida, on receiving the grant, observed that "there are many qualified black students who simply have not been recruited into journalism and advertising. Our study shows that, prevailing myths to the contrary, black students see journalism as a prestigious occupation, see the pay in journalism as attractive, and have confidence in their ability to write and perform as journalists."

Scholarships resemble grants, with at least one major difference. The award of a scholarship to a student may mean that the educational institution pays the student's tuition from money received from a newspaper, a magazine, or some other professional source or from an individual, a family, or a business. Also, the student is expected to meet certain grade requirements and complete a particular educational plan. The scholarship program may be part of a larger plan.

The Alcoa Foundation, for example, donated twenty thousand dollars a year for three years to the University of Missouri. The plan was to have the students study print journalism, broadcasting, advertising, or public relations. A recruiting program was set up and scholarships offered to students who completed their bachelor's degrees so that they could remain for a two-year master's degree. Internships also were to be provided for summer training.

Fellowships differ from scholarships in the requirements upon the winners of such appointments. The university or college expects the student, always a graduate degree candidate, to be an assistant in laboratory courses, to teach elementary classes based on the student's professional experience, or to undertake special research projects.

Assistantships are similar to fellowships except that the student is assigned to a specific member of the faculty to work with him or her in the classroom (according to the graduate student's experience and skills) and to grade papers or projects.

Typical is an assistantship at the School of Journalism at Drake University, for which competent students of any race may apply. This is the Frank Miller Graduate Assistantship, named for a Pulitzer Prize cartoonist for the Des Moines *Register*, in Iowa. It provides a twelve-month stipend of four thousand dollars and twenty-four credit hours of tuition waiver toward the thirty hours required for the master's degree in mass communication. The applicant should have an undergraduate degree or professional experience in the graphic arts, photography, design, or other art and visual communication area of study. "Experience in computer graphics is helpful; interest in computer graphics and desktop publishing is essential," the rules explain.

The graduate assistant, working under the direction of a faculty member specializing in media graphics, is responsible for activities as a laboratory assistant supporting visual communication classes.

Scores of other journalism scholarships or nonjournalism grants may be applied for as short-term study and are not intended necessarily for any particular racial group. Thus considerably more money is available to black students than ever before. But few of the grants are fully adequate to meet the needs of people in the lower economic levels, who sometimes come with insufficient clothing and without the basic supplies.

The Job Situation

Two 1986 studies reached a conclusion that should be heartening to black journalists seeking to join the labor force.

One study was made by the Hudson Institute, which issued a report entitled "Work Force 2000." It noted that "the population and the work force will grow more slowly than at any time since 1980. Minorities will be a larger share of new entrants into the labor force."

The same conclusion was reached, at the same time, by the Department of Labor's Bureau of Labor Statistics in its study, "Project 2000." Both research teams drew on the same sources.

This optimistic outlook may in part be balanced by the fact that staffing may be more difficult than it was in the late 1980s. The present dilemma for the black-owned print and telecommunication companies will simply be heightened: if work conditions in the non-black media become increasingly better for the black journalists, they will not want to work in the black publications and in black stations because they can earn more and have more modern facilities elsewhere.

Shall this boon to the black journalists be cheered, or should there be complaints because the black media cannot improve the lot of the journalists on their staffs sufficiently? This choice faces the black entrepreneurs.

The plaint now often heard is that black communications officers take on promising young people, train them or give them experience, and then lose them to nonblack enterprises. If the black companies cannot meet the salary scales of the nonblack, then they must appeal to motives other than earning more money and having more prestigious professional connections. Thus far black communications firms have not succeeded in finding a formula.

The nonblack companies have been under pressure ever since the

1950s to give all minorities greater opportunities. The response has been slow. The white newspaper companies are under constant criticism for allegedly not hiring and promoting enough black journalists, although the pressures usually are in behalf of all minorities. Most reports on hiring practices do not clearly indicate the percentages of blacks being hired. The 1987 report of the Dow Jones Newspaper Fund, for example, probably seeking not to increase rivalry between minorities, gives figures for all minorities but does not separate them into blacks, Asians, and the other usual categories. Women, not a minority, are included because they, like the minorities, have for some years been excluded.

The extent of the push toward providing new opportunities and training for minorities was summarized in 1987 by Monte I. Trammer, publisher of a white paper in Saratoga, New York, and chairperson of the national minority affairs committee of the Society of Professional Journalists, Sigma Delta Chi. He noted these activities:[11] In 1987 the American Newspaper Publishers Association (ANPA) convention, for the first time, included a panel discussion on minority affairs. It was not well-attended, however. The ANPA also, Trammer observed, sponsors a Task Force on Minorities in the Newspaper Business.

A minorities information booth was available at an Associated Press Managing Editors annual meeting.

Also noted was the statement by Max Frankel, when appointed executive editors of the New York *Times*, that half of all reporters the *Times* hires in future must be black. In 1987 a little more than 8 percent of the professional staff was black, Trammer observed. He admitted that he thinks foot-dragging is going on in the industry as a whole.

Trammer, who was a speaker in 1987 at a rally before a National Association of Black Journalists (NABJ) convention in Miami, said that fifteen persons had appeared for the pre-NABJ meeting three years before but that one hundred were attending in 1987. Other speakers raised questions about lack of minorities in management positions or pointed to increases of minority personnel in that and other areas.

The Gannett Company's hiring of minorities was reported in the *Gannetteer*, the giant firm's internal magazine.[12] The only minorities shown in the five photographs accompanying the article were black. Among other data, the article reports that "only two of 90 Gannett newsrooms had no minorities on the staff last year, 1986, compared with 60 per cent of newsrooms industry wide, according to Mary Kay Blake, Gannett's director/news staff recruiting."

The 4th Estate

By Doug Borgstedt

11.3. One of Doug Borgstedt's weekly cartoons for *Editor & Publisher,* trade journal of the newspaper publishing industry.

Gannett officials, while not satisfied with the results so far, are encouraged by a body founded in 1978 by the Gannett Foundation. Called the Consortium for the Advancement of Minorities in Journalism Education, it was established at the Medill Urban Journalism Center, which is associated with the Medill School of Journalism at Northwestern University.

Another encouraging report came from the American Society of Newspaper Editors (ASNE). It began surveying the nonblack newspapers' hiring of minorities in 1978 and has issued annual reports. The 1986 report noted that for the first time "minority employments in the U.S. newsroom reached 6 percent in 1985."[13]

Another figure, revealing in a different way, was the 57 percent of

U.S. dailies that employ no minorities, reported in *presstime*. Heretofore, however, the figure had been 60 percent or higher, so *presstime*'s writer considered this progress. The ASNE also has been sponsoring job fairs. *MAC News*, newsletter of the Division of Minorities and Communications, reported in 1986 that nearly four hundred students had attended the first two fairs. The one in Boston in October of 1986 attracted three hundred students and one hundred recruiters. The second, in Charlotte, North Carolina, was attended by about one hundred students and twenty-five recruiters.

The NABJ is one of the strongest forces in the effort to ensure that black journalists are employed. The group is the outcome of a meeting of fifty print and electronic media employees in 1975. By 1987 it had nine regions, thirteen hundred members, a quarterly newspaper, and headquarters in Reston, Virginia. It sponsors internships, awards scholarships, and honors outstanding black communicators.

A major event of the past few years on the job scene for black journalists was the winning in 1987 of a discrimination suit against the New York *Daily News* by four black newsroom employees of the paper, one of the largest in circulation in the United States. The charges made by the four plaintiffs (Causwell Vaughn, a copy editor; Steven Duncan, assistant news editor; David Hardy, a reporter; and Joan Shepard, Manhattan cultural affairs editor) were that the paper had discriminated in making assignments, promotions, and salary increases between 1979 and 1982. The complaints had been filed in 1980; the suit was filed in 1982.

It was the first jury case of the sort filed against a major news organization, although cases similar to it had been settled out of court by employees and management of the New York *Times*, Washington *Post*, and Associated Press. As a result of the settlement the plaintiffs accepted $3 million, and the paper agreed not to appeal. The four staffers remained with the paper, although Duncan later took early retirement.

Editor & Publisher reported that Hardy, one of the four, told NABJ members at a 1987 convention that "mainstream news organizations reacted 'hysterically'" to the legal victory. Hardy singled out the *Columbia Journalism Review*, generally criticized by white publishers as being too liberal, because the coverage of the suit was "riddled with inaccuracies." He also criticized NABJ because it had given an award to the *Daily News* city editor at the time: "He was one of the prime architects of a campaign against me and [coplaintiff] Steven Duncan." He also said that only one black organization had given the suing journalists an offer of financial support.

Hardy said that the lessons to be learned from the decision in favor of the plaintiffs were that there should be no negotiation of discrimination complaints against employers and that the employees should organize themselves and confront the management. "I think the time is long past for black journalists to organize and confront for power," Hardy said.

Black journalists have a larger place in print journalism than ever before. But they must make much more progress before there is equality. Yet as some of them make gains in the relatively high-paying general communication field, the reporters, subeditors, and other staffers working for black papers, with some exceptions, will less and less be content that their racial brothers and sisters are doing so much better professionally.

This outcome hangs over the owners, publishers, and top editors of the black media. They believe, with justice in some instances, that their papers should be considered as more than places for neophyte black journalists to get a start in the occupation. Owners in a number of cities believe they have a civic and racial duty to continue printing publications that serve as voices for the black citizens, to fight their battles and keep them informed.

Publishers and Their Problems

Virtually all areas of publishing in the black press offer difficult problems. Advertising, circulation, production, financing, editorial, and promotion are the six principal divisions of a publishing firm. For years each of these has caused extraordinary concern and work in the black press world.

In every major publishing area, the newspaper and magazine, with some exceptions, have had to fight to survive. In many instances the publication has lived because the publishing company has engaged in other money-making enterprises. Especially in the newspaper business this has been true; owners sometimes also are engaged in running insurance businesses, funeral parlors, or automobile salesrooms.

All the normal problems of a publishing venture exist for the heads of papers and magazines, plus certain difficulties stemming from the fact that the publication is a venture by blacks aimed at a black audience and purporting to be improving the status of black citizens.

Advertising

Although more advertising is coming from white-owned firms, mainly on the national level, the rising costs of operation have become so great that more national advertising is needed. The excuse of advertisers is that the black readers do not have the income to spend on more products or services and that to reach those with adequate income it is not necessary to buy space in black media, since so many of what the advertising profession calls "up-scale blacks" read the standard papers and magazines. Most publishers have not found the answer to this problem. Those who have are mostly in the magazine business, where the publications usually are better printed, use color, and have lower copy costs because they are not tied to news events and have longer publishing schedules (monthly rather than weekly).

Circulation

With some exceptions among newspapers and magazines, startling declines have occurred in the circulations of both. The reasons for this are discussed elsewhere. Whatever the causes, the problem is discomfiting for publishers. It has moved more and more of them to give away their publications, calling such distribution "controlled circulation," or dividing the print order between paid and controlled or free. The quantity that is controlled or paid is not always made clear in the raw figures appearing in the directories. There exists within the advertising world a mistrust of circulation statements attributed simply to "Publisher's Reports." Only a handful of black newspapers' circulations are verified by the Audit Bureau of Circulations (ABC). Equally few in the smaller world of black magazines are checked by the ABC.

The average small-circulation newspaper or magazine cannot afford to make demographic studies to discover who readers are, how they respond to various types of content, why they do or do not subscribe, what they desire from their publications, and what competitors to the paper or magazine offer.

A mobile reader group with uncertainties about employment always has been a problem for publishers in this portion of American journalism. High unemployment and rising costs of living exacerbate the problems of selling subscriptions.

Production

Production always has been a major charge on publishers' finances. For many years they chose to buy used equipment—typesetters and presses—sold by white publishing firms. Such purchases were typical of the economical manner in which black newspapers had to run their businesses.

For the paper operating on a margin, purchase of new equipment is more of a problem than ever and not only because of the higher prices of such machinery. While in the long run the new electronic equipment—some of it to be found outside the production department—can be more economical, the first costs can be staggering. The smaller publications find it more satisfactory to contract for the printing. For many years most magazines, black or otherwise, have depended on outside contractors for printing and other services, especially with the advent of extensive use of color printing.

Small publications—newsletters, newspapers, and magazines of modest size—are turning to desktop publishing. That reduces costs in time but does not necessarily result in the most professional-looking publications.

Financing

The publications aimed at the black population in the United States, either on the national or local level, sometimes have not wanted to be dependent on what is called white financing. Members of the black society concerned about content and control falling into white hands used to protest when some publication accepted financial support from white sources. During the past twenty years so many publications have either been discontinued or lost from 30 to 50 percent of their circulations that the purity of financial sources is not so often questioned. Much of the increase in national advertising in black newspapers and magazines is, after all, from white-owned tobacco, liquor, and automobile companies. Most publishers would be glad to accept more such white support. Moving into related and unrelated businesses (job printing and insurance are common) often aids black publishers. One publisher has brought out a weekly newspaper aimed at a multiracial city in the nation; the same publisher has issued a weekly Spanish-language paper for the increasing number of Hispanics within the population. A few publishers have gone into telecommunications.

Promotion

This division of a publishing company's work permits a publisher to take some steps that are generally not costly. In the case of a national magazine the work of promoting it is constant and expensive. In a day when so many Americans pay more attention to radio or television than to the printed word the need for promotion is greater than ever. Astute publishers realize that a publication must have something to promote. Some of the larger papers and magazines have become big because of promotional activities: fashion shows, food fairs, contests, awards of scholarships, and a variety of services to the community.

In an attempt to encourage black enterprise, the Ford Foundation in 1969 granted seventy thousand dollars to a predominantly black publishing firm so it could restart a black women's magazine, *New Lady*. Another seventy thousand dollars was provided to the firm, Mecco Enterprises, Inc., in Hayward, California, by seven Pacific Coast banks. Staffers of *McCall's*, the huge magazine for women in general, agreed to give *New Lady* technical assistance. Later the founders and staff of *Essence*, another magazine for black women, also received financial aid from business sources and technical help from executives of prominent magazines and advertising agencies (see Chapter 7).

The foundation explained the goals, saying that *New Lady* was to be "the first nationally circulated family service publication serving black women." The magazine hoped "to develop a strongly ethnic identity among Negro women as well as serve as a training ground for black editorial and managerial personnel."[1] Commenting on this development before a magazine conference, John H. Johnson, owner of *Ebony* and other magazines directed at black women, including at that time *Tan*, said:

> Your presiding officer was saying something about the fact that
> *Ebony* and our publications were still trying to bridge the gap between
> races and that perhaps the militants wanted to remove that. I also think

that some of the liberal whites are trying to do the same thing. As a case in point [here he restated the *New Lady* plan]. So I want you to know that, in rebuttal, I'm looking for a struggling white publisher who needs money and technical assistance so he can give some competition in the white field.[2]

New Lady, despite the grants, did not live.

Such new competition for black publications came on top of the long-standing editorial and advertising opposition from white newspapers, magazines, and broadcasting companies, emphasized because they were more hospitable to news, articles, pictures, and even fiction about blacks. That the publishers were troubled by it was indicated as long ago as 1956. That year at their annual National Newspaper Publishers Association (NNPA) convention "it was agreed that Negro newspapers . . . would do well to follow the course of national news magazines and attempt to review, analyze and present such news in further detail than the dailies do."[3]

Editorial

Without an adequate staff of writers and editors a publication is hard put to win readers. Yet dozens of black papers have as an editorial staff an editor and two reporters who do virtually all the original journalistic work and depend upon publicity releases, free columns from special pleaders, and other canned material. The papers appear to be largely vehicles for advertising that the publisher has sold, perhaps because the paper is the only one of its kind in the region or because shops intended for black consumers have no other outlet or can afford only a small advertising outlay.

The beckoning finger of opportunity, part of a hand holding far higher salary checks than most of the black press can afford, comes not only from the offices of the relatively few affluent black publishers. A look at the biographies of the black journalists in Chapter 10 shows that a large number either went from small black publications to the larger ones or left black journalism for white entirely. The "come join us" invitations now arrive more often and strongly than ever before from advertising agencies, public relations firms, broadcasting companies, and the public relations, advertising, promotion, and other divisions of white industries and professional groups.

What annoys the publishers and other black executives is that this increased raiding of their staffs may or may not be on merit. It is done, in some instances they suspect, to put some black faces into the office. Robert E. Johnson, executive editor of *Jet*, once observed during a Sigma Delta Chi Headline Club discussion in Chicago that the white publications cannot truthfully allege that they have been unable to get black journalists, because they have been there all the time. Some black students were graduated from schools of journalism in the 1950s and 1960s but few were given opportunities on white publications. The white employers now realize that, and some seek to make up for lost time, a boon to the employee but a headache to the black publisher. This staff raiding undercuts the possibilities of building reasonably permanent staffs on the black publications. Also irritating black owners is the fact that although financial conditions are improving for a few of them, enabling them to do somewhat better with salaries than before, they have not yet become competitive, by any means.

John H. Johnson, now editor and publisher of *Ebony, Jet*, and *Ebony Man* magazines, hearing about an agreement made by the owners of the German magazine *Der Stern* with its editors to give them greater freedom, observed that his company had given its editors more freedom for a long time as an effort to keep them. "Not only have we been working for their independence and freedom," he said, "we've also been working for their happiness, we are forced to give editors what they want in an effort to keep them. As a matter of fact, I have a little sign on my desk . . . 'What should I do today to insure that my editors will be happy and contented and will not leave me?' " He added that "we also have to think about the wives. So we occasionally arrange for an editor to take his wife on a trip overseas, to Africa or to Asia, and when he thinks about leaving, she tells him, 'Oh, remember that nice trip we took, dear,' and this tends to discourage them." He mentioned also that the company reminds single girls just out of journalism school that the Johnson magazines have many single men on their staffs.[4]

But no other company equals the Johnson firm in affluence. The typical black newspaper or periodical publishing house can offer no such inducements, much less hard cash equal to that of white firms of even moderate size. Small community papers, which are the bulk of the black press and could offer opportunities in different regions, employ few people, single or married, and barely can afford to send them to the state capital, much less Asia or Africa.

Journalists traditionally are among society's thoughtful citizens and for years were considered rebels, although today they seem to have been outdistanced by people of all ages and colors who follow programs that mean peaceful or violent revolution against the established order. Although lagging as social critics, black as well as white journalists continue to be skeptical about much that occurs. Increasingly, some are not content with any job, even if it does include Asian or African trips or an opportunity to meet a future mate. These writers and reporters want meaningful work that contributes to the solution of social problems facing the nation or humanity as a whole. The pursuit of personal affluence may be the goal of many journalists or would-be journalists but by no means all. Some uncounted number is standing off, critical of the status quo, seeking ways to have its part in eliminating or correcting what is wrong.

One of the author's black journalism students had opportunities to work on either a large white newsmagazine or on one of the largest black newspapers. The dilemma about which to choose plagued her for months. She realized that her ultimate goal might be a deciding factor. She was torn between her loyalty to her race and a desire to be a success in the white world. This conflict is acknowledged by most of the black students with whom the writer has been in touch during many years of teaching. Those who seized the biggest dollar sign, whatever its source, were few.

This particular student, in her college years as an undergraduate and then a graduate student, had been a girl of comfortable family giving little thought to her race; in fact, she was inclined at first to ignore it. But the drive of many of her black friends—and white ones as well, for some whites can be blacker than blacks—toward pride in her race led her to change her personality. She let her hair grow naturally and gave up trying to make her skin lighter. She had no difficulty being proud of black novelists, poets, painters, athletes, and statesmen. Black, to be sure, was beautiful. Black music was beautiful. "Why wasn't the black press beautiful, in the same way?" she was asked. She persuaded herself that perhaps the black press was, and took editorial work on a major periodical. Her salary was adequate and the working conditions satisfactory. But the idea of meeting single men meant little to her. She had traveled abroad before joining the staff, so that benefit—which was offered to almost no woman, anyway, she reported—was less important to her than it might have been otherwise. What she missed was a direct confrontation of the social issues whose solution she believed so important to the welfare of the black people. After a time she resigned to go to work for a white publication concerned with social problems, not a radical journal but one bringing a scientific approach and as a whole concerned about human beings.

Motivated black journalists such as this young woman want from publishers a more candid attitude. If publishers are to appeal to them to become staff members there must be some compensation for the low comparative salaries, the lack of the usual benefits, such as severance pay, insurance, sharp definition of duties, expanding vacation periods with pay, and retirement plans, often not available in black offices. That compensation might well be a purpose beyond commerce. The freedom fighter dormant in many a black journalistic breast is not unduly upset by inferior working conditions and lack of benefits if the warrior for the right is single and in good health and convinced that by joining the staff of a black publication he can accomplish something for the betterment of the race. If it means only a way to bring money to a few or encouraging black readers to be concerned only about their personal pleasures, black journalism will not command the respect and assistance of these idealists.

"Negro publishers are apt to be primarily businessmen whose interest in race welfare is secondary to their interest in selling newspapers," Thomas Sancton, an astute white observer of the black press, wrote in the World War II years. He went on to describe one that he knew then, as a "patronage politician, a political reactionary, and an anti-Semite. He was exactly like the majority of white publishers."[5] Both black and white publishers are less commercial today and far more socially conscious than they used to be, forced into those positions by events and public opinion. It must be remembered, however, that no business operation that must sell its product and rent its space to advertisers can be expected to put race welfare first even in days of social ferment unless some other source of revenue is available. And the business operations are so complex and hedged with so many problems that little time and energy are left to do much else but keep the publication from sinking into the graveyard of black printed matter. Publishers may have to battle for survival in the marketplace, but their employees usually know what is dearest to their hearts.

The publisher faces a situation not so common before 1960: more and more nonblack general circulation publications have a policy of providing better coverage of the black neighborhoods and the black society as a whole.

Although there are flaws in the way this improved coverage sometimes is provided, it is true, nevertheless, that as blacks have made themselves known in entertainment, sports, and the arts and sciences, they have had a place in the news. In the past such newsworthy persons have found appreciation chiefly in their own media with the exception of certain popular music or other entertainment personalities. Today, however, there are black ballet companies, with worldwide appreciation for their stars, and authors who win awards heretofore restricted to those of other races.

Publishers who have not had the editorial personnel needed to cover such stories can expect to lose readers to the general media. Similarly the coverage of black business is being left largely to one black-owned business magazine, and except for news of local stores and other small businesses, the black press has offered little about finance, industry, and banking news.

The absence during the last quarter of this century so far of a truly well-staffed black news service has deprived the black press of sources for better coverage of national and international news written from a black perspective. Some improvement has been made in the past decade by the inclusion of more news of Africa, in a few instances provided by staff writers but usually from a news agency or the publicity offices of governments and churches and others interested in the problems in black Africa. Although black people live in more than Africa and the United States, such as in the Caribbean, only a few publications report news developments from there, South America, and other areas with black populations of considerable size.

These are only some of the problems facing publishers in the six standard divisions of their publishing companies.

External Problems

Another set of problems is external rather than internal; publishers have a responsibility to their readers to help overcome those problems. Among the most frustrating situations facing not only publishers of black media but also the black population as a whole are the apparently unceasing attacks upon each other by black citizens occurring within the black neighborhoods often accurately described as ghettos. The sociological explanations are common and the correction of the causes complex. When publishers tackle this problem in editorials, they seem to stop at lamenting the situation and appealing to the pride of black citizens.

Related to this problem is the equally wide one of drug use and drug trafficking. It has been an editorial topic for years. But as with black on black crime, the black press is not equipped to do more than lament the situation. It has neither the financial capability nor the personnel to mount an all-out campaign of education and crusading. The drug problem involves personal danger and is best left to official task forces.

Newspapers in particular have been led by some publishers to avoid printing news of crimes committed by blacks. Publishers at times compromise by keeping such stories off the front page instead of ignoring the news completely. Still others print the news of crime freely, believing it is of guaranteed reader interest. Publishers are not agreed on ways of handling such news, and discuss policies on it at their conventions. This news comes close to home when crimes are committed against the newspaper carriers.

A crusade in which many black papers and magazines have joined with zest is the battle against racism. Much attention is given to evidences of discrimination against black people. This crusade against racism can be thought of as the most successful of any special campaigns by the press in the 1970s and 1980s. The publications have pointed out instances of unfairness in basic pay, working conditions, promotion, housing, job opportunities, and other such typical mistreatment of minorities. Violence is not condoned in these campaigns, but encouragement is given to resist substandard conditions through strikes and boycotts.

The Philosophical Battles

From the owner or publisher's point of view, especially if he or she attempts to stand off from the scene either to keep from entanglement with any faction or because he or she respects the long-held view of American journalists that the press is a watchdog, not a partisan, the various philosophies of social change are confusing. And some are a threat to the publishers or owners of the publication.

Like their fellow white publishers, the black entrepreneurs are subject to the many pressures of change; they now are felt sharply. Lerone Bennett, Jr., *Ebony*'s executive editor and a historian of Afro-Americanism, once told a conference on "The Media and The Cities" in Chicago that "the black revolution is a total revolution, every institution in the black community is bending to the winds of change.

Black media are becoming more militant, more black. There is a new tide of black consciousness in the black community. Black readers are more assertive, more demanding, more militant. They are demanding more information about themselves and their struggle. As a result, new media are springing up across the country, and established media are expanding their formats to satisfy new demands."

So publishers raise questions. Is their audience actually more militant? No doubt only a portion, but how large a segment? And what is militancy? Is the reader in a small southern city just as militant as one in a far western community or that of Harlem or Bedford-Stuyvesant, that other restless part of New York? How militant must the editor be to retain the respect of readers and, not so incidentally, the patronage by them of advertisers? And how much militancy will advertisers stand for? One month comes this anonymous letter:

> I am not renewing my subscription because I believe that your magazine has become too militant. I am not renewing because I believe that you now cater to the vocal minority which does not abide by our democratic traditions.
>
> Your magazine began to lose favor with me after an editorial a few months ago in which you advocated that all blacks get together and vote as a bloc, and vote only for the candidate who says he will do most for this segment of our population. . . . I think that your proposal . . . could lead to the worst form of divisiveness and demagoguery that this present generation has yet witnessed. Also, getting back to general attitudes, has the word "Negro" gone out of favor? You don't seem to use it anymore. I don't think that's right, either.[6]

Later comes another signed letter, reading:

> I have just finished reading the letter by the "Former Subscriber" . . . I am going to keep on subscribing to your magazine if nobody does, because I am proud of it. I'm not a militant; I am just concerned about my race. I take every issue of Ebony to school and show my classmates that black is not only beautiful, but very interesting and educational as well. I am proud to be black and you've made me even prouder.[7]

Can publishers judge by the number of letters how their readers react? Probably not. Should they make a reader interest survey? If they can afford it, they do, but it may be necessary to conduct more than one and even if a series is completed there is no certainty that it portrays readers' reactions, for the climate of opinion is changing rapidly.

Favoring the Advertiser

Although it is not by any means exclusively a practice of black publishers, they are particularly vulnerable to the temptation to favor their advertisers and have been since the press was founded, purely because advertising space has been so difficult to sell. All publications are so accustomed to doing something extra for advertisers that the practice is overlooked or condoned. Travel, automobile, and real estate pages in even the largest white papers, with few exceptions, set no example for the black publisher, for they are laden with free advertising. The degree to which such special favors go is great in any journalism. But a publication that runs laudatory articles about its advertisers, sometimes in columns adjoining the paid space, is hardly being subtle. If its editorial policies are generally namby-pamby or nonexistent, it seems reasonable to assume that the owner has no intention of telling the whole truth, as the masthead slogan may declare, because the owner is not expected to bite the hand that signs the checks to pay for space. Or, it may be that it simply is inexpedient to do anything but ignore what it is pleasanter to ignore: the questionable methods of a political boss or the prejudiced hiring policies of an industry or store or bank that advertises. It is difficult to know what a publication omits without living in the community it serves, but there are clues from towns and cities with competing black papers.

Gratifying the Reader

Closely related to that practice of letting, or having to allow, the advertiser call the tune is that of giving the reader solely what he or she wants. Oft-debated by the press as a whole, both newspapers and magazines face the decision. All publications, to some extent, give the public what it wants, but it is a question of how much and which of the public's wants are gratified, and which public is being catered to. The readers of a black religion paper, for example, have a deep interest in the spread of their beliefs and in the righting of wrongs practiced against blacks in general and certain ones in particular. A reader who is against racial intermarriage is pleased to see that the editor has included news or views concerning that policy. If the majority of the publication's readers follow that philosophy the editor is giving his readers what they want. Yet the editor may consider himself an independent editor, beholden only to the organization's officers. That same editorial staff does not, as did some of the white/ black underground papers of the 1960s, condone acceptance of lubricious advertising or print articles laden with obscene words; it is likely that a considerable number of readers would enjoy such material. A line has been drawn, after all. Copy encouraging superstition, news stories furthering rumor, or fiction pandering to the desire of some readers for vicarious sexual thrills, all published for the sake of selling the publication, are giving the public — a portion of the public, in any case — what it wants at the expense, perhaps, of the public's moral fiber or sense of fair play toward others.

Black publishers learned long ago that the practice of giving the public what it wants without much concern for its effect upon the public sells papers or magazines; in the long run the policy is not enough to produce papers that influence public opinion on major social issues, as has been shown by the early history of the Chicago *Defender*, in black journalism, and the Hearst chain, in white journalism. There always will be some audience for the sensational; if the level of education of readers is not yet such as will make them demand a higher quality of content giving them the better quality can be a failure. When Mr. and Mrs. V. P. Bourne-Vanneck, an English couple, took over the black weekly the New York *Age*, in 1949, they found they could not succeed with the paper with their policy of omitting sensational copy. They observed: "A lot of people preach progress, integration, and the need for a new clean newspaper in Harlem. But did you know that some of these same people do everything possible to hinder and crush our 'new' paper with malicious lies and rumors?" The Bourne-Vannecks were reported, along with other investors, to have lost considerable sums by the time the Chicago *Defender* took over the paper in 1952.[8]

As with playing favorites among advertisers by cutting rates or running free plugs for them, the practice of pandering to a certain element among readers still goes on in the black press. It has been much criticized (see Chapter 1). Some weeklies fill their first pages with crime stories, others play as the main story of the week a crime report in which blacks are the major figures. Crime sells papers. The publisher is faced with the questions: Does such treatment overemphasize it? Does it develop an inordinate interest in such happenings? Does it further the concept that the black is naturally criminal? Does it not really become an easy way to obtain a big front-page story rather than do more difficult and controversial reporting of what is happening in the black community in the way of social action or social progress?

Reaching the Educated

A friend of the author who is among the scores who have supplied information for this book one day out of curiosity asked a young black woman, at one time a secretary in a white magazine office, which of the black papers of the city she reads. "Never read them," she told him. Faithfully, however, she reads both the large white dailies. The author asked a black retired official of a racially mixed peace organization her opinion of the black press. She had heard of and glanced at a few papers and magazines. But all her life (she was middle-aged), she insisted, she never had read any of them, always the white press. She had grown up in a fairly well-to-do part of the Midwest and her family had no interest in black news. There was no special interest in blackness for its own sake; on the contrary, they all worked for racial integration. The black press, apparently, simply kept blackness alive and in their opinion to the detriment of all society.

Two decades ago the black publisher therefore welcomed the new interest in Africa and its culture, the attempt to rewrite the U.S. history books to show what part black people had in the story of the country's development, and the efforts to tell their story fully in books devoted to black history. What can be done, however, to reach the well-educated blacks who lack this pride of race, who do not care about the columns of personal news, the accomplishments of individual blacks who are total strangers to them, the goings-on in the black colleges and among black musicians and sportsmen, and much else that fills the pages of black newspapers and magazines? If the publisher's paper is not even a second one to such readers, what hope does the publisher have of gaining them as readers?

The magazine publisher, rather than the newspaper publisher, can hope to reach the black intellectuals, but whether it will pay to do so is another matter. The publisher can offer erudite articles, and literary and art work rather than the straight news, which perforce is largely what appears in newspapers. For while educated blacks may be indifferent to the community life, they often are concerned about the social problems or the cultural progress of blacks and other minorities.

The Tenderest Subject

More sensitive than any of the black social and political programs is the subject of anti-Semitism in the black society. Not a recent development, as is known from the subjection of blacks to attacks by a Jewish editor in New York in the early history of the black press, it is perhaps now more of a problem because of recent events. Aggravating it are the formation of the nation of Israel, with the Arab-Israeli warring, and the fights in black neighborhoods between black and Jewish groups, the blacks asserting their resentment for what they call overcharging by store owners and the Jews resenting what they consider lack of appreciation for their services and their patience. Problems also arose in some cities between Jewish white members of labor unions that will not admit blacks or who work for employers unable or unwilling to hire blacks. The blacks resented the whites' fear of job loss.

Some of this feeling reached the black press world in 1967 when two prominent blacks resigned from the advisory board of *Liberator* magazine in protest against publication of articles they considered anti-Semitic. The protesters were the late James Baldwin, the author, and Ossie Davis, the playwright and actor. Their resignations came about because of a series of articles by Eddie Ellis, a Harlem writer. Called "Semitism in the Black Ghetto," the articles described alleged exploitation by merchants and landlords, charging that Zionists dominated black colleges and organizations and manipulated the civil rights movement.

But such views rarely surface in any large black publication; when they do they are reported guardedly, for the publishers or their editors seem to realize the dangers of sensationalizing or fanning the latent animosity. One important paper, however, took a definite position on the Arab-Israeli War. It was *Muhammad Speaks* (later *Bilalian*), which had a substantial circulation in Chicago, New York, and other large cities with big Jewish and black populations. The paper sided with the Arab nations.

Facing the Middle Class

A problem arose for publishers during the 1970s and 1980s when conditions improved for some black citizens in housing, job opportunities, and wages, with the result that the black middle class became larger. The nature of the audience for black communications changed somewhat because of the choices made in their lifestyle by limited numbers of black physicians, teachers, lawyers, brokers, and other professionals, as well as blue collar workers. So important was this development that books and articles about it began to appear.

The problem created for black media owners was expressed dramatically as long ago as 1973 by the late William O. Walker, while publisher of the Cleveland *Call and Post* Group. He noted that the black middle-class suburbanite "eschews the Negro newspaper." He called this "the cleavage of our best educated, most affluent blacks from the masses." He found this situation to be creating a new dimension in racial problems.

Ebony, since its founding in 1945, has sought to hold up American white middle-class standards as those to which the black society of the United States should look for models. For this aim it won the disfavor of the militant blacks of the 1950s, 1960s, and 1970s. These critics believed that the accumulation of wealth and attempts to obtain the comforts of life were far from the way to solve the problems of the homeless, hungry, poor, and jobless.

Ebony's premise was that black people must help themselves, an application of the philosophy of Booker T. Washington to life in the United States in the second half of the century. It assumed that those blacks who would rise into the middle class would aid those behind them.

To some extent this rise has happened on the general scene, i.e., black organizations are dedicated to improving the lot of black citizens. But this spirit is not so noticeable in the black media, and for understandable reasons.

The successful black publishers and editors, except in the largest establishments, have not been able to provide opportunities to many of their associates. Restrictions on the media industries because of high costs of materials, inability to compete with the general media for advertising and circulation revenue, and failure to offer competitive salary scales are holding them back.

Ebony is not alone in its aims. Some of the newer publications have the same or similar goals, set forth along more specialized lines. These include the magazines *Essence, Excel, Ebony Man, Players, Black Enterprise*, and *Jet*.

  Ebony, however, had made a more forthright attempt than most

12.1. *Ebony* is the circulation leader among black publications in the United States.

others to face the consequences of its campaign. In its 1987 special issue on what it called the new black middle class, it went beyond the 1973 issue on the same topic by raising pertinent questions confronted by certain authorities. A disturbing one was "What can black and white Americans do about the widening gap between the black poor and other segments of the American population?" It also asked if the new black middle class is meeting the responsibility of leadership.[9]

Robert B. Hill, a researcher, wrote in *Ebony* that he had determined that the black middle class is defined by income alone. He used the Tax Reform Act of 1986 as his standard of measurement, thus placing the middle class between those households earning twenty-five thousand dollars annually and those earning fifty thousand. Andrew Brimmer, an economist, in the same issue of the magazine used almost identical figures.

Hill also distinguished between the middle class of earlier in the century, when E. Franklin Frazier wrote his important book, *The Black Bourgeoisie*, and the middle class of the late 1980s. He reported that the middle class in the 1950s was made up mainly of pastors, teachers, doctors, business owners, and artisans; the black middle class of the end of the 1980s comes from the working class and poor blacks who took part in the successful civil rights campaigns and have managed to gain a measure of economic security.

Brimmer, who was the first black to serve on the Federal Reserve Board, found that the gap between the well-to-do and the poor is widening.[10]

Nothing was said in the *Ebony* special issue, however, about what the black middle class reads. That topic may have been avoided as self-serving.

It would be interesting, nevertheless, to visit the large homes in Hamilton Heights, New York City; Baldwin Hills, Los Angeles; MacGregor Park, Houston; Cascade Heights, Atlanta; and Chatham, Chicago, to see what place the black media, including books about blacks, have in the lives of their occupants.

Publishers undoubtedly have encountered persons such as those described in other chapters of this book who have no interest in black literature and communications.

The publishers' problem at this point is diverse. If much of the news and opinion content of the newspapers is of little or no interest to the new black middle class but the best-paying advertising is seeking these readers as consumers, what can a publisher put in the paper not only to hold, but also to increase, readership?

A further question is: If many of the new middle class in the

American black society are trying to meld themselves with the U.S. general middle class, can black journalism ever hope to win their attention unless adversity once more forces them into the old condition of being discriminated against?

A few black newspapers and magazine publishers have confronted these problems, with mixed results. Well-written and well-edited papers such as the Miami *Times* and the Indianapolis *Recorder* have broadened their formulas. *Essence, Black Enterprise, Ebony*, and *Jet* command considerable loyalty still from the black middle class. But others have not succeeded: *Modern Black Men, Freedomways, Amistad* (and numerous other literary or political publications), *Black Politician, Black Theater, Encore, First World, Journal of Negro History, Negro History Bulletin, New Foundations*, and others of highly restricted circulation.

The serious losses in circulation and advertising revenue that have attacked the lives of major newspapers are warnings to be taken seriously.

The United Publishers

Perhaps the problems would be more numerous or even more unsolvable if the nation's black publishers, at least of the larger newspapers and several magazines, were not organized. The black magazines in general are so diversified, being concerned largely with specialties and using a wide variety of formats and formulas, that it would be difficult for them to unite, just as it has been in the white magazine industry, where only the relatively small number of consumer magazines and a minority of the business and religious periodicals have their own organizations.

The newspaper publishers' group grew out of a meeting called in 1943 by Walter White and the NAACP, of which he then was executive secretary. The editors of twenty-four of the largest papers, with an aggregate circulation of three million a week at that time, came together to discuss attacks upon the black press from both black and white critics. The charges were that some papers oversensationalized news, particularly of racial discrimination. The acceptance of doubtful advertising such as that for love potions, dream books, and good luck charms also had been frowned upon. Out of the sessions came the Negro Newspaper Publishers Association, with John H. Sengstacke as the first president. White reported that moderation of the treatment of news followed. The objectionable advertising was dropped, he wrote.[11] Some of it, however, has been resumed since (see Chapter 13).

The group, which later changed its name to National Newspaper Publishers Association (NNPA), is similar in function to the large white organization, American Newspaper Publishers Association, and to numerous state bodies of white published weeklies and dailies. It promotes its particular phase of U.S. journalism, using the annual Negro Press Week to call attention to the black press. This event is its best known effort at developing a favorable public opinion, but it also has rallied aid for publications or individuals it deems unjustly brought before the law. One such was an editor and publisher in the South indicted in connection with stories written about a young black man electrocuted following conviction on a charge of attacking a sixteen-year-old white girl. The editor had not published the girl's name but was indicted under a code statute that prohibits such publication. The paper had printed an interview with the convicted man who alleged that the girl had cooperated.[12]

Other NNPA activities are less dramatic. A high government official may meet with the members; generally he or some other spokesman says something appropriate, such as praising the papers for championing minority rights or being vital sources of information to their readers. At one time NNPA had a national news service to provide news and feature copy for papers published by its members (see Chapter 14). It also has undertaken market studies in recent years. NNPA sends a column called "Coping" to its members which is concerned with problems facing readers.

Just how seriously NNPA's efforts are taken by its public is difficult to say. Certainly intervention in cases of misapplication of the law wins respect for the press and its publishers' organization. The articles lauding the past editors or the present performance of the press probably get little attention. The newspaper business itself, white or not, never has fascinated the customers, who presumably are more interested in the results than in what goes on behind the scene, although they need not be sheltered so thoroughly as they usually are in the press' pages.

NNPA in 1988 had 178 members, almost all newspaper firms. The organization has served to give the publishers and editors a chance to discuss ways to deal with some of the problems faced in common by the nonwhite newspapers.

NNPA sends editorial copy weekly to members, divided between news and commentary. Beginning in 1988 the central office in Washington, D.C., developed a computerized news service staffed by a news editor and two reporters.

"This system," as Steve G. Davis, NNPA executive director describes it, "permits us to cover our interest in national news of concern to our readers — including politics, governmental, economics, social issues and many others. Breaking news in daily media is analyzed for specific impact on black communities." While these items went by mail in the first year, the office has the capability of storing information in its computers for papers to pick up with compatible equipment. Included in the mailings are "Coping" and an article entitled "Business on the March."

For many years the association has sponsored a Merit Award Contest to reward excellence in editorial, circulation, advertising, and other categories. A Russwurm trophy goes to the papers scoring highest. Another activity, originally called Black Press Week, now extends for a month, during which time editors print prepared materials concerning the place and purpose of their press.

The organization also sponsors a Dollars for Black Scholars program, which offers one thousand dollars a year in college for juniors and seniors only. Applicants must be willing to seriously consider working on a black newspaper and have a 2.5 grade point average in their college studies.

The Business Operations

Kinzer and Sagarin, in *The Negro in American Business*, insist that the black press cannot be judged as a business as can other enterprises run by members of that race. "For primarily," they write, "the success of the press is not measured by its financial statements, its ratio of advertising to editorial space, but rather by its influence over its readers, and by its ability to plead their cause and express their hopes."[1]

The black newspaper and magazine should not be downgraded because they have not, throughout their history or to any great extent now, set any records as investments. They should instead be taken seriously as a factor in public opinion about black America and as an influence on that population. Nevertheless they must seek to operate efficiently to survive. In its existence the black press as a whole has had comparatively little opportunity to fall back on resources that would supplement advertising and circulation income. Even returns from running a job printing plant along with the publication of a newspaper or magazine have often not been sufficient. Church, lodge, and college papers have had supporting capital, but never as lushly as have the periodicals of some of the large white denominations or giant universities. Black society's political and social groups have not been in a position to finance in any substantial way publications intended for the general consumer. The press, therefore, has had to depend on its ability to function as a business institution, particularly in the past century. This necessity accounts for the great mortality among the publications since the first was issued in 1827 and the hand-to-mouth existence of many that survived only a few years.

Government, which in recent years has helped other types of business directly through the Minority Small Business Investment Company and other programs, has not been welcome in American journalistic operations during this century, usually for fear of attempts at political control. The black press has been like any other in this respect, but the word *directly* must be emphasized. Distribution of government advertising money has kept many a white newspaper alive, especially in a county seat town, via the official advertising. Black publications have not been so favored until recent years and not widely even so.

And if any publishing ventures could have benefited from financial assistance they are the black newspapers and magazines. Since their beginning, with some exceptions, they have been undercapitalized, underequipped, and understaffed. And many remain so. Kenneth O. Wilson, while a vice-president of the *Afro-American* newspapers, speaking at a panel of six black executives of black publications or members of the staffs of large white firms, said that of the 150-odd black-owned and -operated newspapers . . . there are probably only about sixteen that are doing well.[2]

Yet this picture is different only in degree from a large segment of the white newspaper press. Numerically the bulk of both the black and white presses is made up of weeklies and a few issued twice or three times a week, a few out every other week. Three of the approximately 250–75 black papers (Wilson apparently was using the Ayer figure available at the time) are dailies; about 1,780 of the 12,000 white papers are dailies. For many years the white weeklies had financial troubles similar to those of the black papers, although not so severe or general. The great decrease in their number, from about sixteen thousand in the first part of the century to fewer than ten thousand today, occurred because the financially feeble ones simply lost with the rise in cost of operations.

In recent years the black press, particularly the middle-size and large daily and the consumer magazine, has gained a measure of comparative business stability, but only a measure. What improvement has occurred has taken place largely in the past forty years, reflecting the gradual rise in purchasing power of a segment of the black society and a greater rise of literacy among black workers. It also is evidence of the greater business opportunities of the owners.

The differences between the business operations of the black and white presses are few. Their managers are in the same positions of finding ways to keep publishing. They attend the same workshops or at least the same kind, if they are able to stand the cost of travel and enrollment; they use the same guidebooks; they are quick to appreciate cost savings through new mechanical devices although they can afford few of these inventions. Even the physical quarters are much alike: unpretentious, crowded, and looking a little rundown in many instances. If one wants to understand the inside operations of black publications, one can see them described and explained in the usual books and periodicals devoted to the world of publishing. The equipment is much the same. The black paper's may be somewhat outdated, but it printed, in all likelihood, a white paper once, before it was sold at second hand. Except quantitatively and in some matters qualitatively, the two use the same organizational plans and the same procedures. Black publishers, even if they wished, have no other choice. Presses are made for any user, as are computers, typewriters, file cabinets, and cameras. The equipment is color-blind.

Computers and other modern equipment are used by the more successful and large enterprises in newspaper publishing. Among the magazines this is so because their printing usually is done in plants so equipped. They do not have to own the devices themselves.

The differences are in the race of the owners and most of the staffs, the subject matter of the publications, the number of publications, and some of the particular problems facing those who own and operate this black business. Differences in quantity or number of publications and the quality of their product are serious, but not as much as they used to be. Through the years many black publications have been shoestring operations. Their owners have had no choice but to use ancient equipment or to depend on white printing establishments. They had little access to trained personnel; the more skilled a worker became the more likely he would be enticed by the higher wages and better working conditions of white firms or the few more affluent black ones.

As is traditional with small publications, weekly newspapers especially, publishing a newspaper still is not enough. The press would stand idle six of the seven days. Thus job printing is undertaken — handbills, stationery, posters, leaflets, letters, wedding invitations, business cards, and the like.

Although the basic business operations of a black publication follow in general the lines of any other, several special aspects of advertising, circulation, and production should be scrutinized by persons seeking to understand black journalism. These three areas undergird the business activities of a publishing firm. Other operations, less essential, as well as several services and competitors, are discussed in the next chapter.

Advertising

Functionally, advertising in the black journalism world is no different from that in any other. In both it is intended to provide revenue to the owners, to perform a service to readers by informing them of the availability of products and services, and to aid producers and service institutions to reach their markets. In scope, this advertising is like all other. It is national, regional, or local; when printed it is display or classified. Space and time are sold in the usual ways: agents represent the papers and magazines or the publications' or stations' own salespeople sell it.

Two primary differences exist, however. They are in the slant, appeal, or content of copy and in the volume obtained. Both are changing.

Critics of the black press for years have commented unfavorably on certain types of advertising to be found in it. At one time even the publishers themselves agreed to avoid it, but it continues in some papers. These types were for aphrodisiacs, patent medicines, clairvoyants' services, lucky charms and other appeals to superstition, and skin lighteners. The appeal to superstition and to fakery in religion still can be found in some of the most prestigious papers. Nothing today is as extreme, perhaps, as the patent medicine ad found by Detweiler in the Chicago *Defender* of July 9, 1921, which read:

IF YOU SUFFER FROM

Malaria, Chills and Fever, Loss of Nature, Catarrh, Dropsy, Ulcer, Prickly Heat, Tired Sleepy Feeling, Headache, Pain in Neck, Sides, Shoulders, Back or Hips; Sick Stomach, Kidney and Bladder Trouble, Female Diseases and Women's Troubles, Bad Colds, LaGrippe, Stomach Ulcers, Fever; Mean, Tired Feeling, by all means take a bottle of Aztec Kidney and Liver Medicine. It has made hundreds well and strong again.[3]

More popular today are small ads such as this (the errors are unchanged):

> ### REV. MOTHER
>
> Just back from Haiti with mysterious secrets to help you with your problems. If your loved ones are gone and if you were sick, bring me a coconut or some dust from your floor. I can help yu where others fail. 324-3587.

The New York *Amsterdam News*, a leading weekly of 37,561 circulation, carries as many as three columns of ads from psychics. The one above is typical.

Black people say that aphrodisiac, charm, and fortune-telling advertising, as well as opportunities to play the numbers game through the papers, is important still because of the heritage of the race. Superstitions originating in Africa or the West Indies have not died. They say whites who mount religious images, rabbits' feet, or other symbols of luck on their auto dashboards or consult astrology columns are no different and can point as well to considerable editorial material, such as entire white magazines with similar content, as their support.

Use of such copy, particularly in leading publications not so economically pressed as are most small ones, is out of tune with the ideals expressed by publishers, who must realize that these ads merely trap the gullible. Vishnu V. Oak, a teacher at black colleges who specialized in the study of black press' business operations, pointed out in *The Negro Newspaper* that until the 1920s the papers were dependent for their advertising on black businesses in their own area, a generally feeble source. Their income consequently was both uncertain or low in quality. What advertising outside their own shopping areas they were able to obtain was almost entirely from white companies and only a few of these were large national firms. Among those few were tobacco, soap, bread, and motor car accounts.

The situation improved in the 1930s when a white agency took an interest in selling space for black publications. Within a decade some units of the press were selling to firms producing cosmetics, liquors, and food in addition to the earlier accounts. In two more decades the variety had increased greatly. To all the early advertisers were added more firms producing the same commodities as well as such new accounts as those for men's and women's clothing, musical instruments, travel services, records and tapes, and household equipment.

In recent years an important type of advertising has been display space offering employment opportunities, placed by local, state, and federal government agencies as well as private industry.

Today advertising in the black newspapers, much more so than in the white, is still heavily local. A tabulation made by the author in 1987 shows that advertising occupies, on the average, 25 to 35 percent of a newspaper's total space; of this, from 75 to 100 percent is local in origin.

In contrast, the author found that the advertising in black magazines of all types had an enormous range, from 5 to 60 percent of the total space of the consumer magazines, with an average of 38 percent.

Change in Appeal

Along with the change in kinds of accounts has come altering of the appeal advertisers now make, especially in black magazines. A comparative study of the 1960 advertising in *Ebony* and *Life* made by Dave Berkman brought out the nature of that appeal at the time and continued in the decade that followed. He observed that a basic principle of communication, including advertising, was to address people in their own idiom, but also that "the idiom that a person considers his own may differ with the psychological setting in which the communication is perceived." Thus, if copy appeals to the person's "aspiration to achieve higher status, it will address him not in the idiom of the present and lower situation but in the idiom appropriate to the status to which he aspires," he went on to explain.

Berkman found a great awareness of this condition among advertisers in both magazines. An example in *Ebony* was the presence of copy for lower-priced automobiles and not the higher-priced, although it frequently is thought that possession of a high-priced car confers upon a black owner a status he cannot achieve through home ownership or other symbols. To which might be added the view that when a black citizen is refused a house he wants to buy he enjoys buying what is not denied him: a car, a color television set, or some other commodity.

What has occurred in the decades that followed has not yet, however, confirmed a prediction made by Berkman, a forecast resting upon a statement made also by *Ebony*'s owner, John H. Johnson. "It would seem," Berkman wrote, "that the advertising in Negro publications such as *Ebony* now, and for some time, will continue to reflect the socio-economic dichotomy which exists between the reality of the

Negro's existence, and the status to which he aspires. But as the gulf narrows — as the dominant class status . . . tends to become the same middle-class status which predominates among whites — no longer will *Ebony* advertisements reflect the Negro's 'black reality' as opposed to his 'white aspirations.' " Berkman went on to say that at the time this change occurs, the need for a distinctive Negro magazine will have disappeared and there won't even be an *Ebony*, as its owner himself had predicted.

What Berkman did not and could not anticipate, as did no other scholar or observer of the black press, was the rise of separatism and nationalism and with it a new interest and pride in blackness from which the press has benefited in both advertising and circulation volume (the latter only among magazines). Berkman's "for some time" is sufficiently indefinite, however, to permit the prediction to be correct if the desire for separatism dies out after "some time." But if it persists, advertising in black publications may be greater than ever in both volume and revenue earned and at last may sustain a powerful black journalism.

Separation of the races is less of a goal now than it was before the 1960s. Interracial marriages are greater in number and more acceptable to society in general. The crusade against integration launched by large groups within the black society is less evident, and integration has been furthered by legislative decisions.

Selling the Space

Selling space in black publications is a matter of personal effort by individual publications and the assistance of a few agencies and representatives. The situation was discouraging until the early 1930s, when slight improvement was brought about by the W. B. Ziff Company, then a Chicago firm of advertising representatives but later a book and magazine publishing company, Ziff-Davis. It obtained space sales for a number of papers, supplementing what a few sold by their own efforts. The papers more successful in such individual efforts were several of those nationally known today, such as the New York *Amsterdam News*, Kansas City *Call*, Chicago *Defender*, and Norfolk *Journal and Guide*.

In another decade two Pittsburgh *Courier* executives launched what was to become one of the two major firms of advertising representatives serving the black press, Interstate United Newspapers, Inc., of New York. It made market studies and launched campaigns to obtain accounts for its clients, which, Oak reports, reached 135 newspapers and magazines in 1940, eight years after it was founded.[4] The Ziff accounts multiplied and new ones were added for soft drinks, liquor, sugar, and supermarkets.

The second major firm was founded four years after the first and called Associated Publishers. Interstate ceased in 1961, merging with Associated and the advertising sales activities of the *Defender* publications to become the present Amalgamated Publishers, Inc. At first the combined firm was called Consolidated Publishers; in 1962 the name became Amalgamated. At the time of the merger Interstate had thirty-two member papers, Associated twenty-four, and the *Defender* four. Amalgamated now is known as API, and has offices in new York and Chicago and a special Michigan and Ohio representative. Its offices in 1987 were headed by John H. Sengstacke, president of the newspaper group bearing his name.

Three nationally active advertising agencies were functioning in 1970: Vince Cullers Advertising, Inc., Chicago; Howard Sanders, Ltd., New York; and Zebra Associates, Inc., also of New York. These were dominantly black agencies. Formed in the late 1960s, the latter represented the present-day type of agency operation. It was called Zebra because of its integrated staff (Blacks outnumbered whites by three to two), and it was owned by two blacks, Raymond League, a former account executive for J. Walter Thompson, a worldwide agency and one of the largest, and Joan Murray, a New York television correspondent. Within six months it had annual billings of $1.5 million, including such accounts as Fabergé, Clairol, and Fabricators, Inc. Associated with the agency were Ossie Davis and Godfrey Cambridge, who appeared in a Zebra promotion film.

League told *Newsweek* that the inner city is a large, undeveloped market in which various ethnic groups, while of low income, together spend a total of one hundred billion dollars a year. "But to reach them," he said, "you've got to speak inner city—and fluently." Black dialect was used in the agency's copy. The nonblack staff members enabled the firm to reach other groups, such as Puerto Ricans, Italians, and Jews.

The sales efforts of such firms benefit at least half the black newspapers, but mainly the more substantial ones. Many a small community weekly or monthly magazine must depend on one or two staff members, often not even a full-time person on advertising; whoever does the work often is the owner and editor as well. A large publication, on the other hand, has a sizable staff for such work. *Ebony*, as one would expect on a periodical approaching the two million mark in circulation, has advertising salesmen responsible for selling the magazine's space in a dozen cities where the black population is large. They work with the advertisers' local sales staffs, visit retailers, jobbers, brokers, and wholesalers.

Large or small, these publishing companies try to convince black as well as white advertisers that the black market is an important one and that the black media are needed if they are to reach this market.

Leading Agencies Today

Seventeen agencies are listed in the *Standard Directory of Advertising Agencies* as specializing in advertising directed to blacks.[5] Their total billing, as listed in the 1987–88 edition, comes to nearly $236 million. The highest among the firms was Burrell Advertising, Chicago, with more than $56 million in billings for the year. Next was Mingo-Jones Advertising, New York, with $50 million, and third the Uniworld Group, New York, with $45 million.

Burrell leads also in the number of employees, with 110. Tied for second are Mingo-Jones and Uniworld, with 65 employees each. Third is J. P. Martin Associates, New York, with 30. Five of the remaining firms have billings below one million dollars and all five have fewer than 10 employees each.

Although all seventeen agencies specialize in advertising directed at the black consumer, several have other aims as well. Adelante Advertising, Inc., of New York, as might be guessed from its name, aims at the Hispanic as well as the black markets, as do Fallis Communications of Atlanta and Uniworld. Hamer Advertising & Marketing of New York specifies minorities; J. P. Martin simply says "urban market penetration." Mingo-Jones adds "general" to its black specialization. Several others name no specialization, but other reports show that they sell space in media aimed at the black population.

Frank Mingo, head of the Mingo-Jones agency, in fall 1986 acquired four minority-owned agencies and combined them into a single firm based in Los Angeles. Three of these companies had been headed by Hispanics and the fourth by an Asian. The new agency was named Muse–Cordero–Chen & Baca. His major agency in 1987 joined with Young & Rubicam, one of the largest white-owned agencies, to handle U.S. Army business, according to Crain News Service.

When Lockhart & Pettus, a New York firm, opened in 1977 it planned to go after general as well as black consumer advertising. At the same time some of the white-owned agencies began to see possibilities in the black consumer market.

The total black consumer market expenditures for advertising, therefore, are not represented in the close to $236 million cited above. To this must be added the combined but uncalculated billings of the nonblack agencies.

Profile of an Agency Leader

The fact that Barbara Gardner Proctor became head of her own advertising agency and that it developed into one of the largest black-owned firms of its kind is news in itself.

But one of the company's working policies also is extraordinary: Proctor & Gardner Advertising Inc. of Chicago does not accept liquor or cigarette firms as clients. And the agency, of which Barbara Proctor is chief executive officer, president, and creative director, has not been hurt by this standard, for it has an annual billing of $15 million. Included among its clients are Jewel Food Stores, Kraft, and Sears Roebuck.

Proctor did not allow what has been considered a double handicap (the fact that she is both a woman and black) to discourage her during the twenty-five years since she started her firm. "Racism and sexism were only a challenge to me, not obstacles," she told L. G. Sherrod when she was interviewed by *Modern Black Men* magazine in 1987. "To view every circumstance in one's life in terms of these two small biological characteristics is very self-limiting," she said.[6]

Proctor's career has been described on "60 Minutes" and other television shows and in magazine articles. She went to Talladega College where she earned two bachelor's degrees in four years. Proctor told Mary Daniels, a writer for *Essence* who interviewed her in 1977, that she became a social worker in 1956 in Chicago, but found it too depressing. She sold real estate for six years and at the same time wrote articles for magazines and recording companies about jazz singers and players. For twelve years she was jazz critic for *Downbeat* magazine. She left real estate to become a public relations writer for the Veejay Record Company. In time she joined the international division and traveled often in Europe.

After seven years in small jobs in advertising agency offices, in 1970 Proctor began her own agency with a Small Business Administration loan of eighty thousand dollars. In those early days she did virtually everything in the shop: sold space, made the presentations to potential clients, and attended all meetings with possible buyers.

Her early life had exposed her to bigotry and racism. Now, she thinks, she must oppose them by hard work in her profession.

Research and the Market

Comparatively little research has been done on either black publications or the black consumer market; what results have been recorded are from advertising agencies, university teachers, and graduate students in schools of journalism and business. Most of the research has been conventional or traditional, with history predominating. Market research or product studies, readership or readability surveys, and content analyses on any large scale are few.

That there is a black consumer market is not even agreed upon by all advertisers, advertising agency people, and some analysts of the black press. Louis E. Lomax, black author of several studies of the American black society, discussing the press in one of his books, said that the Negro market as such does not exist. "We respond to a product we already know about when we discover that the makers of that product have invested time and money to make certain that they attract our attention," he observed.[7] One of the leading black publishers calls the expression *Negro market* a misnomer. "It does not mean a market for Negroes," W. Leonard Evans, Jr., while president and editor of Tuesday Publications, said, "but rather it is an abnormal consumption in definable geographic areas of national brands at all economic and educational levels." The Negro market, in his view, was an economic and geographical rather than a racial matter.[8]

Taking another view at about the same time was H. Naylor Fitzhugh, then vice-president for special markets of the Pepsi-Cola Company, and a former professor of marketing at Howard University as well as a black businessman. He said that there is a market and that it has two aspects. The Negro, he said, is both a consumer and a Negro, "and I am not sure the two can be separated. The Negro has to be addressed at both levels with both roles in mind."[9]

Two years later, *Media/scope* magazine examined the matter of advertising to blacks. It learned that "the Negro market means many things to many people." To some agencies and clients the black man is a consumer like anyone else but to others he is among many special markets in the demographic spectrum, it said. "But to an increasing number, he is one of several ethnic groups that deserve consideration, but not quite the same as the others." And Raymond League of Zebra Associates put it succinctly when he said in the same issue that "the black life style is completely different from the white middle-class life style." He also said, for the advertisers: "You can't play the numbers game to reach the Negro market." He went on to note the points made earlier in this book: that the black press serves a function not provided by the white, that is, status and recognition, thus creating a favorable climate for advertisers.[10]

The Attitude of White Advertisers

Perhaps the biggest obstacle to the financial stability of the black press, so far as advertising is concerned, is the attitude of white advertisers. If one riffles through files of back numbers or looks at microfilms of papers it is clear that most of the white advertisers have spent little money on black media, although somewhat more in the 1980s in certain publications. The reasons given usually are that the American blacks can be reached through the white media, circulation is too low, ad budgets are not big enough, or the advertiser does not want to reach this particular market. Other reasons given are that the advertiser is convinced that black citizens buy too little or that they have special choices; that such advertising expenses pay only those who can cater to the black person's needs and that image or trademark advertising is wasted on them; and that the black press is not up to certain physical standards desired by agencies. (See Table 13.1.)

TABLE 13.1. One-insertion advertising page rates (in dollars) of selected consumer magazines

Magazine	1 pg., b/w	½ pg., b/w	1 pg., 1 color	½ pg., 1 color
Ebony	$23,309	$14,568	$26,458	$18,053
Essence	12,820	9,240	15,960	9,585
Jet	10,895	7,315	13,430	8,345
Black Enterprise	9,080	6,500	11,610	9,020

Source: *Standard Rate and Data Service,* 1987.
Note: In the first edition of this book eight magazines were listed in a similar table. Seven of them have ceased publication since.

But some black advertising and marketing people agree that most general advertising agencies have not tried to understand the market.

Several additional reasons for the lack of advertising were uncovered by a study made in 1968–69 by a Syracuse University advertising major. They were noted by advertising agencies.

1. Fear of worsening an already poor image of an advertiser. For example, a company that has been struck can be accused of attempted bribery if it suddenly advertises its product heavily.

2. Reaction to implied threats of a few black media salespeople whose attitude is "Buy our paper—or else."

3. Fear of alienating white customers, especially in the South, with a resulting boycott.

4. Objection to the atmosphere created by the protest aim of some black papers and magazines; firms do not like to associate themselves with it.

5. Belief that the literacy rate of black readers is too low for certain types of advertising or kinds of commodities or services.

The researcher, Sharyn O'Connell, noted answers that she and others give to these objections and others more common reported earlier. A company's poor image can be improved only by fair and honest racial policies and a steady advertising program. Threats by salespeople are rare and do not come from major publication advertising staffers or representatives. Fear of offending white customers is realistic but boycotts have not materialized in any significant way. There are protest publications, to be sure, but most of the larger magazines and papers are not militant. The literacy rate is on the rise as is the general educational level.

On the widely made point that white publications are enough or that radio and television are sufficient, a reply is that the publication issued for whites does not meet the needs of the black consumers, for it does not provide the right atmosphere. The message in the black publication is only for the black citizens, a point about which they are ultraconscious at this time.

On some objections, however, there must be agreement. A large portion of the black press, it is true, is not up to certain physical standards, particularly the newspapers. Even the larger papers, by comparison with white ones of the same importance, are not well printed: cuts reproduce badly; other work, such as page trimming, is inaccurate; printing of the body type often is blurred or smeary. Although it is doubtful that there is much solicitation of firms or organizations whose product or service is of little interest to blacks, where that does occur it is admittedly a misplacement of effort. Like all minority presses, this one has to some extent retained the idea that advertising money should be spent to sustain the press even if there is no direct return. But such reasons as low budgets, lack of purchasing power by blacks, or special choices being paramount in buying decisions appear to be excuses to cover either prejudice or lack of information.

A writer in *Advertising Age* has pointed out, however, that the objection of low quality printing is not taken so seriously anymore. Now that there is a big, desirable market it is discovered, as noted by a Harvard report, "The Management of Racial Integration in Business," that "American advertisers stand to gain image within the Negro community, not only by their identification with the newspapers sincerely directed toward them; they also tend to place more confidence and trust in national advertising when carried in their own press." In other words, more important than physical quality is the rapport between the reader and the paper. If the reader cares not at all if there are errors but is loyal to the paper for its community leadership, the advertising will be taken seriously.

Proud as they are more and more in their blackness, there is reason to think that black citizens will continue to find it easier to use the predominant publications, for they are beginning to see a little more information about their race, more pictures of blacks in both reading matter and advertising, and more direct appeal to them from advertisers in white-owned and -aimed publications. Until black newspapers and magazines are more readily available, the American black is likely to turn to what is at hand. And this matter of availability is the problem of the circulation department.

Circulation

The closed-in-ness of the black society is dramatically demonstrated when one asks white persons about their knowledge of black publications. A well-educated white may know of the high-circulation *Ebony*, but rarely any other. A member of the white intelligentsia may know of one or two scholarly periodicals, such as *Journal of Negro Education*. But other working people— repairmen, drivers of delivery trucks, and factory workers—unless their jobs throw them into close relationship with Afro-Americans, know vaguely that there are such publications and perhaps have seen a copy of *Jet* or one of the newspapers in the hands of a co-worker. Mr. and Mrs. White Citizen appear to be no more aware of the press of the black citizens than they are of the specialized journals for horologists or oculists. Yet these publications are molding opinions, influencing the minds of many members of a different race.

Black citizens' knowledge of their own publications is only a little broader than that of the whites. The surveys made by researchers and the casual questioning by others show that most city blacks are aware of several publications intended for them, usually of one or two newspapers and two or three magazines. But beyond the limits of the consumer publication they rarely can go. White readers are either unaware of them or have little interest in their content. Consequently their circulations in general have been confined to the cities with large black populations. (See Table 13.2.)

TABLE 13.2.   Circulation records of eight general black newspapers in 1966 and 1986

Newspaper	1966	1986	+ or −
Atlanta *Daily World*[a]	30,400	20,000	−
Baltimore *Afro-American*[b]	33,000	40,942	+
Chicago *Defender*	36,541[c]	22,611	−
Detroit *Michigan Chronicle*	49,123	24,447	−
Los Angeles *Sentinel*	34,284	25,225	−
New York *Amsterdam News*	74,213	37,561	−
Norfolk *Journal & Guide*	32,799	7,000	−
Philadelphia *Tribune*	34,816	19,000	−

Source: *Ayer Directory,* 1967, 1968; *Standard Rate and Data Service, 1967; Gale Directory of Publications,* 1987.
[a]Daily.
[b]Semiweekly.
[c]1967 fig., 1966 not stated; daily.

Even black press leaders seem not to have anticipated the fact that some black Americans would lose interest in the black journalism of the country. But as reported previously (see Chapter 12), the increasing numbers of persons who can be considered in the black middle class include uncounted numbers who neither subscribe to nor read black magazines and newspapers and prefer to think of themselves as in a certain financial rather than racial division of the population.

The lack of information among blacks about their own publications is not difficult to explain. In their history, American black citizens have had a low literacy rate. Sparse incomes have kept down their purchases of publications even when they became literate in large numbers. The outlets or sources have been more limited than those for whites. A few newsstands in the black areas are the typical sources; even there only a handful of the existing publications are sold.

The author has walked for many blocks on Chicago's South Side and in Harlem and found few opportunities to buy or see a black paper or magazine. In his own city of Syracuse, which has about

175,000 population, 10 percent of it black, only a few widely separated outlets sell more than two or three black publications. The larger stands on downtown streets or in shopping areas have on sale none of the newspapers and not more than two or three of the popular magazines. Black citizens, unless they happen to live within reach of a black college or university or a well-stocked library such as the Schomburg in Harlem, have little opportunity to see more than a few consumer publications. Such unavailability is built into the circulation system of the black press. It can be compared to the white small literary magazine or some other publication with a limited group of readers. Unless there is a considerable number of readers in each community, the restricted-interest publication will not sell and will be returned or become wastepaper. The black press must base its circulation plans on realistic expectations. If there is insufficient or no demand, one hardly can blame a dealer for not displaying a given publication. The decision may be governed by other factors. In some geographical areas it clearly is prejudice. The dealer may not approve of the publications (it sometimes works in reverse, however). If white, the dealer may not want to encourage black patronage.

Libraries are possibly the most consistent agencies for making black publications available, even when the number of black users of the institution is small. Libraries and library trustees are likely to have a greater sense of obligation to expose different viewpoints, an attitude that few newsstand operators seem to possess or perhaps can afford to hold even if they wished to do so. A small public library — the first free one in the nation — in Peterborough, New Hampshire, population about three thousand, takes *Ebony*, although only a handful of blacks live in the area. The main building of the public library in Syracuse receives scholarly magazines and *Ebony*, but also the New York *Amsterdam News*.

The demand for black publications is so great at the public library in Niagara Falls, New York, that the librarian has to keep *Ebony, Essence*, and *Jet* off the open shelves. They are in a small room with other high-demand periodicals and must be signed out when taken to be read in the library's main room.

Auditing and Other Problems

Vishnu V. Oak, in describing the advertising situation among black publications in his day, quoted a letter he had received from Joseph B. LaCour, then manager of Amalgamated Publishers, Inc. He gave a clue to some of the circulation problems of black publications in the 1940s as well as the 1980s.

"Misrepresentation of circulation and lack of believable and authentic market data have . . . militated against the acceptance of media serving our market and the colored family as a consumer," he wrote. But he saw improvement. And his forecast was correct, for in the next four decades more publications, in proportion to the total number, now are audited, since without such attests some advertisers will not spend their money in a publication.[11]

The auditing picture has been clouded, to some extent, by the practice of some publishers of selling a portion of their circulation and giving away another; the latter, commonly known as controlled circulation, enables them to keep their figures up and to use such copies as promotional samples in the hope of converting their receivers into paid subscribers. Since the reputable auditing firms and organizations, such as the Audit Bureau of Circulations, place limits on the number of free copies, such publishing houses cannot claim convincing audits. The problem is a sticky one especially for new firms seeking to gain a foothold in a community or in some national field for which they are issuing a new specialized magazine that cannot hope to enjoy newsstand distribution.

In an attempt to meet this problem publishers use the verification services of several firms, including Verified Audit of Circulation Corporation (VAC), Certified Audit of Circulation (CAC), and Community Papers Verification Service (CPVS). Publications also cite publisher's statement paid (SWP), publisher's statement paid and free (SWP/F), and controlled circulation (TMC).

Detweiler noted that in 1920 "only four papers in Ayer and Son's Newspaper Directory, out of a total of 217 listed for Negroes, make sworn statements of circulation." The vast improvement is reflected in the fact that most publications now listed in *Gale* (formerly *Ayer*) make such statements and that a number are audited by the Audit Bureau of Circulations. Statements of circulation size coming from publishers alone are not as highly regarded as are verifications from outside agencies.

Pricing has been a troublesome aspect of circulation for some publications. Because of the lack of advertising revenue heretofore, and the small possibilities of profits from substantial job printing contracts, publications have had to price themselves higher than nonwhite papers and magazines, often as much as double (the thoughtless reader, however, did not realize that he was paying 25¢ a week for a weekly and $1.50 or more a week for a daily). This necessary policy limited sales in a day of uniformly low pay for blacks. The differential is not so sharp today, although it persists in per copy sales.

Achieving dependability of circulation has been extremely difficult and damaging to circulation departments. Since the bulk of the distribution of newspapers is in the cities with concentrated black neighborhoods, most of which could be described as substandard areas, the problems were great for distribution of all publications, black or white.

Costs of handling circulation in the central city areas are higher. These charges result from difficulties in "making collections, high turnover of carriers, and lack of parental influence and cooperation." Such difficulties are nothing new to black papers, but as shopping plazas and enlarged stores are set up in or near the black neighborhoods white publications are feeling them sharply for the first time.

Black magazines, except for a small number of community periodicals, are sold largely by subscription and distribution is left to the post office system. But the city or community publications, like the smallest local newspapers, must deliver copies to newsstands and use the mail for distant subscribers.

Production

For years many of the early newspapers and virtually all magazines aimed at black readers were printed on presses owned by white proprietors. The nineteenth-century publishers could not capitalize plants of their own, as did most of their white counterparts in the newspaper business, because if they managed to raise the money for such an investment there was little likelihood that they would get enough general printing business to keep the equipment operating. But a few owners, such as Frederick Douglass, did attempt to do their own printing. When that abolitionist orator opened the offices of his *North Star* in Rochester, New York, he was told by printing experts that he had the best printing equipment obtainable anywhere. Quarles, in his biography of Douglass, describes the plant. It was thought to have been the first possessed by a black citizen. Costing "between nine and ten hundred dollars" in 1848, it was all in one room. A small hand press, a type case, a work table, and a desk were in it. A white apprentice and Douglass's sons were his printing assistants.[12] With this meager equipment, yet luxurious for its time, he and his helpers did all but print the paper, a four-page, seven-column paper much like the other abolitionist publications. It actually was printed on the larger press of the Rochester *Democrat*, a white paper.[13] Douglass kept the *North Star*, and its successor that carried his name, going for sixteen years. In 1850 a new press was bought as well as additional type, and the paper improved in typography and production.

The production setup of the Baltimore *Afro-American*, which was founded before the turn of the century, is in contrast to the small office used by Douglass. The *Afro* considers itself "the largest colored newspaper in the world operating its own plant."[14] In its three-story building at Druid Hill Avenue and Eutaw Street all the usual newspaper publishing departments are housed. Like other large companies, a composing room, an engraving plant, a photographers' studio, and paper storage rooms also are there. The production section has modern equipment.

Development during the 1960s of the cold-type offset printing process using newsprint gave a boost to the small black newspapers that could not afford the big operation, such as that of the *Afro*. It is less expensive than the process of setting type, making up pages, and manufacturing lead plates for a press—the letterpress system long standard in U.S. publishing. It also is speedier, for the staff can paste onto sheets what it wants to reproduce—typed copy, clippings of printed matter of any sort from other publications, cartoons, and photographs, the latter often reproducing better than by the old method of making an engraving on a plate first. The montage or assembled material is photographed; what the camera sees is transferred to a plate from which the final printing is done.

The bigger black newspapers are turning increasingly to use of computerized equipment in one or more of their departments. A sampling by the author of large and small dailies, semiweeklies, and weeklies brought statements that computers are being used in modest numbers in some offices but throughout the plant in others. Since newspapers do not necessarily own printing equipment but sometimes let out their printing, the computerizing may exist in the printer's plant, not the publishing house offices.

The extent to which mechanization exists in the offices of papers interested in investing in such equipment is illustrated by the Miami *Times*. Like the Indianapolis *Recorder* and other papers, the *Times* has been using a Compugraphic computerized typesetting system since it became available in the 1970s. The paper installed in 1988 a system produced by Mycroteck that completely computerized the operation, at a cost of sixty-nine thousand dollars. Certain of the *Times'* business operations are taken care of by a Sperry computer, including general ledger and accounts payable, circulation, advertising billing, and accounts receivable.

The Reporter Publishing Company in San Francisco, which publishes the *Reporter* group of seven area papers and three others in San Francisco, uses three Eagle II computers in its editorial division and two computerized typesetting machines in its production department. The New York *Daily Challenge* reported that all departments are computerized.

Even departments other than editorial at the Cleveland *Call and Post* use some computers or are completely computerized. At the St. Louis *American* all editorial copy is processed on an IBM PC. Preprocessing of type is done on a TAVA, a PC with hard disk. The circulation department keeps the subscription list in a computer. The Los Angeles *Sentinel* uses the Apple Macintosh to a great extent in all phases of the paper's work.

At the Charlotte (North Carolina) *Post* every department was converted to automation in 1987. Seven Apple Macintosh computers were purchased. Both editorial copy and advertising layout are done on a computer. The firm owns a scanner that gives it the capability to read copy sent from outside sources directly into the computer. The prepaid circulation list is handled on a Xerox 744 computer, but plans were being made to convert it to the Apple network. The network also is used for accounting.

Four papers replied that did not use any such equipment.

Whether printed on white-owned or black-owned presses and set by hand or by composing machine in whichever office, the production results, particularly of newspapers of any size and of small magazines, usually have been inferior. Although there has been improvement in recent years because of the bigger incomes of some newspapers and magazines, an examination of a large number of publications shows numerous areas where production improvement still is needed. What Oak wrote in 1948, and others before him, still is true of too many publications: "A study," he wrote, "of 66 representative newspapers revealed that, with the exception of a dozen papers, most of them are typographically inferior. . . . While an assortment of type faces is used for headlines and advertising displays, the quality of printing and typographical arrangement is so poorly done that they often look unattractive. An unbalanced and over-crowded appearance with pictures carelessly scattered everywhere seems to be the rule."[15]

Oak went on to say what he still could of numerous publications: the inking and presswork of many newspapers and magazines are not of high quality. The appearance of some give evidence of worn-out presses. He complained that few better-grade halftones were used by the more affluent papers and that line cuts were too sparingly used. Their appearance led him to conclude that the halftone engraving was poorly done.

Technical perfection is far from realized still, especially with the greater reliance on offset printing, which has led to numbers of small papers with disorderly looking pages produced by little more than a hasty pasteup of material, much of it clipped from other publications. In some papers no thought is given to the clash of type faces, inappropriate typography, tilting columns of type, and unfinished stories cut in midsentence to make them fit space.

Perhaps a larger question should be raised: what standard did Oak and later critics use? What papers were compared? The unit of comparison doubtless was the white press, whose readers by and large were and still are better educated, more discriminating, and more demanding of the press than are black readers as a whole. Furthermore, perhaps the production refinements of white publications are unnecessary, as well as impractical, for most black newspapers but definitely necessary for all black magazines. For, like white magazines, they cater to a more discriminating group of readers and advertisers, and their typographical effects, to be successful, depend on excellent reproduction.

In effecting change in production standards it is necessary to appeal to the publishers, not by pointing to the products of more affluent white firms but to note the arguments on a practical level of gaining more subscribers and advertisers and of more newsstand sales, showing, through research, that lack of better appearance and more careful makeup and better reproduction of halftones puts the black press second to the white, technically. Since it is clear that the trend among blacks is to depend on television more than any other medium and that, in certain communities, as reported elsewhere in this book, black readers either prefer white papers (but not magazines) to black, or read as many white as black, it is necessary for black publishers to give more attention to production quality.

The Policy of Imitating

A characteristic of much black publishing is its imitativeness, a practice not unknown in publications work by whites as well. Pride has observed that "Negro newspapers have usually taken on the fads and fashions of the moment in journalism." He cited the action in the early 1950s when a black paper in Los Angeles had its first page redesigned to be like that of a new daily established in the same city. A Miami weekly then followed suit. Another example was *People's Voice*, an imitation of *PM*, the adless daily of the 1930s.[16]

A classic instance was the long-existing typographical resemblance of the Chicago *Defender*, when it was not a tabloid daily, to the Chicago *Tribune*. When it became a daily it modeled itself on the New York *Daily News*, a highly successful tabloid. Pride could have included, as well, the New York *Amsterdam News*, which for years looked like the now defunct New York *Journal-American*.

Black magazines have followed the same production policy, a notably successful strategy in the hands of the Johnson Publishing Company. The black trade journals and house publications follow the traditional format and typography for such publications in general. A few of the community weeklies are unconventional in format. Here and there a magazine stands out, as does *Essence* or *Excel*.

Unorthodoxy in format and typography is not necessarily a virtue; some experiments in American journalism have not been especially readable. Nor is great originality of design to be expected in a press that has had to struggle to survive and until recently had little reason to trust design to gain support. The imitativeness certainly is understandable and pardonable. Although the black press has contributed little to developments in journalism, as Pride notes, it had neither time nor money for attempts at originality for originality's or art's sake. Furthermore, if a certain format is a factor in one publication's success, it is only sensible and practical to learn from its experience. There were newsmagazines before *Time* and *Newsweek* and picture magazines before *Life* and *Look*; and white newspapers have looked much alike across the nation for many years.

But if the black newspaper in particular is to climb out of the position of being the second paper in the reader's fare, it will more easily do so if it attains a personality of its own. And such personality is based heavily on a publication's physical appearance and quality.

Auxiliaries and Competitors

The three major auxiliaries of the black press examined in the preceding chapter—the departments or hired services devoted to advertising, circulation, and production—are only some of the aids. Less formally tied to publishing because they are external are news services, feature syndicates, and the output of those who do public relations, promotion, publicity work, and broadcasting.

Radio broadcasting is the one direct competitor to be examined in this chapter. White publications and broadcasts are the chief competitors for advertising and readers, but they need no explication in this book.

The News Services

The most important auxiliary outside those originating in the newspaper or magazine company's own precincts is the news service, since it provides copy that publication staffs cannot obtain for themselves without enormous expense.

In practice, however, few black publications use such services. Those that do are a few of the large city weeklies, semiweeklies, and dailies, and the one black newsmagazine, *Jet*. Some larger papers subscribe to United Press International (UPI), a white agency and one of the two largest in the world. The other is the Associated Press (AP), also white-owned but a cooperative. Both agencies also have Wirephoto service.

Black news agencies, with the major exception of the Associated Negro Press (ANP), have had an uncertain history, just as have many of the papers and magazines that have subscribed to their services. Detweiler reports that in 1921 a half-dozen services were available: the reciprocal service of the National Negro Press Association (NNPA), Capital News Service, and the Negro Press Syndicate, all of Washington, D.C.: The NAACP and Exchange News Service of Boston and New York; and the ANP of Chicago. To them he adds the Tuskegee Institute and Hampton Institute Press Services; probably the last two and the NAACP service were free and perhaps closer to publicity offices than objective news agencies.[1] Brooks has noted that in 1945 there were fourteen, attributing this information to the Bureau of the Census. He did not name them and added that he rarely saw any material in the black publications credited to them and surmised that most were highly specialized, dealing with sports, theatrical activities, and comics.[2] Perhaps either he or the Census Bureau confused news services with feature syndicates. Briefly there was a United Negro Press, mailing its service from Durham, North Carolina, beginning in the late 1940s; it specialized in news of blacks living in the southeastern section of the United States and later moved to New York City.

The NNPA service was an outgrowth, begun in 1947, of the desire and need of association members for less costly and better news coverage outside their own communities. Mutually owned and operated, it began with a bureau in Washington. Among the larger papers behind its operation were the Baltimore *Afro-American*, Kansas City *Call*, Norfolk *Journal and Guide*, and Atlanta *World*. Heading it was Louis Lautier, with correspondents in New York and Washington, two out-of-town columnists, and a sports editor in Philadelphia. The NNPA members, Brooks reports, did not respond heartily to the service, however. Some of the larger papers' owners believed that the service duplicated coverage they already were receiving from their own correspondents in Washington. Nevertheless, by 1948 it had thirty-three members. In a year this figure dropped to twenty. The service was ended in 1960. John H. Sengstacke, NNPA president in 1970, explained its cessation a decade later as the result of more local community coverage.

The original ANP was founded in 1919 by Claude A. Barnett. News was supplied by mail, since most black papers are published weekly. As with the white AP, this black agency was a cooperative, i.e., each member agreed to supply ANP with news of its own area and shared in its expenses. Barnett was joined by Nahum D. Brascher, the first editor in chief. He had worked for the Indianapolis *Recorder* and the Chicago *Defender*. P. L. Prattis, onetime editor of the Pittsburgh *Courier* and an early associate of Barnett, credits the founder with building and stabilizing the black press in his day through the service. His career was one of unusual devotion to black journalism and the black race. Widely known as he was to black journalists, he was little known to the world of journalism in general.

By training, Barnett was an engineer. Born in Sanford, Florida, in 1889, he went to public school in Oak Park, Illinois, and then to Tuskegee Institute, from which he received his engineering degree. But he entered journalism instead when, after nine years of working for the Chicago Post Office, he became an advertising salesman for the Chicago *Defender*.

Traveling around the United States for his paper, he realized that the black publications needed news of the black people, so he decided to form the ANP.[3] He remained as its head until its cessation in 1964. During his career he was a special assistant to the secretary of agriculture during the third Roosevelt and Truman administrations, a director of the Supreme Life Insurance Company, and devoted to studying the African nations, in which he spent much time. He was particularly aroused by the demoralizing effects of segregation in the armed forces and is credited with having brought about some of the decrease in its practice.

After World War II Barnett traveled to Africa and added one hundred publications to the list of ANP subscribers. He made fifteen trips to that continent for this purpose as well as to obtain information for his writing about the black society. He died in Chicago in 1967.

Lomax quotes him as having said: "It's a shame that we have a separate Negro society in this country and a separate wire service for Negro newspapers. We are working toward the end that some day there will be no more need for my news service and no need for anything else—including society—which at present the white community does not allow us to share."[4]

The highest number of domestic subscribers in any one year, according to Beard and Zoerner, was 112, in 1945. The African service in number of subscribers, in 1964, was large. More than 200 papers on that continent received it, some translating it into French, Portuguese, or other non-African languages. Of Africa's 158 daily papers, 108 received ANP material. During its last years under the original management, the American services of ANP were used somewhat less. The drop occurred because the black press was losing advertising and circulation to television and the competition of white newspapers that began giving improved coverage to black news events in the realm of civil rights. In 1964 it was going to 101 papers, 3 magazines, 2 radio stations, and 21 private individuals. It was appearing in 90 percent of the total circulation of black papers.[5]

During the completion of the agency's sale in 1964, some staff members established another service, a feature agency called Negro Press International. In 1969 its name was changed to Black Press International, the news service owned by the now defunct *Muhammad Speaks* and issued from its Chicago offices. At this time the black press has no major news agency of its own comparable to what was once provided by ANP or NNPA.

News credits, when they appear in the black press, are to the publication's own staff writers, to stringers, or to a black college free news service mainly devoted to covering the college.

Liberation News Service (LNS) was used by only a few black publications, largely such advocacy organs as the *Black Panther* or some of the more militant small community papers, the latter tending merely to clip material from the larger papers that pay for it. Founded in 1967, the LNS stories (or some distributed by the similar Underground Press Service) were chiefly in the white underground periodicals and papers, college papers, and magazines of the critics of society that considered themselves in the Third World or "The Movement," as they put it. A typical report, datelined Saigon, detailed a crackdown on black-market operators, concluding: "No wonder so many South Vietnamese people are siding with the revolutionaries. In liberated zones there's no black market — but also no inflation, no unemployment."

Community News Service (CNS) came into being after the Kerner report indicated the lack of coverage of minority group events in New York City. "You've made your point. It's true. We are not doing a proper job of covering the communities and the neighborhoods. But, you see, we are not geared to do this well. We don't have the time or talent." This is what media people in the city said to people seeking a solution to the communication problem.[6] CNS was begun in 1968 with a Ford Foundation grant of $275,000. It covered the black and Puerto Rican neighborhoods of the New York metropolitan area five days a week. The service was sold on a subscription basis not only to newspapers and broadcasting stations but also to organizations and businesses wanting information about trends, events, and issues in the ethnic living areas of New York. Administered by the Center for New York Affairs of the New School for Social Research, CNS was staffed by journalists experienced in either the black or white press.

The use by the black media of news services intended especially for print is at a low point, most specialized agencies having succumbed to the high cost of operating and the decline in circulation of many publications.

The Need for Service

The need for a large-scale black news-gathering service persists. Although the white media cover more news of the black society than before, it generally is only major events, particularly those that will have direct impact upon the white society, that get much attention: demonstrations, disturbances, honors for prominent blacks, political action, crime. The black press could use a large agency intended not as a political tool but as an attempt at reporting with a measure of objectivity those events and trends not observed and passed on to their subscribers by the other agencies. Such a service is needed because:

1. White news agency charges are too high for most black owners' budgets.

2. Black subscribers to white services receive much news not useful to them; furthermore, black papers are second papers to many readers, so they must concentrate on what the rest of the press does not contain; the black press also has no room for much of what is sent.

3. Only the major black news stories are received via the white-owned agencies. For example, most of the Richmond and Washington news in the Baltimore *Afro-American* would not come from such services. The matter of emphasis also enters.

4. A black service is written by writers with an understanding of the readers and their interests that white writers for a black service do not possess. Even black wire service correspondents working for a white agency find that their copy has been filtered through white editorial minds.

Syndicates

Closely related to these news-gathering services are the feature syndicates, in principle the same sort of operation, for they send material uniformly to their subscribers. These are firms that sell comic strips, panel cartoons, personal columns, and other content for release everywhere on the same date. In the white world they bear such names as King Features Syndicate and United Features Syndicate. UPI and AP also send out nonnews materials, as do various individual newspaper and magazine publishing companies, such as the Washington *Post*, the *Christian Science Monitor*, and some units of the Newhouse newspapers and magazines. A few black writers appear in white papers via white syndicates: Carl T. Rowan, Les Payne, William Raspberry, and Chuck Stone, each with a column bearing the writer's name.

Syndicated Writers & Artists, Inc., a black news and feature syndicate, was founded in 1984. Its output is sold to various black papers, including the Miami *Times*, Indianapolis *Recorder*, Charlotte *Post*, Atlanta *Voice*, and Sacramento *Observer*. Sent to subscribers are a black family comic strip called "Hobson's House," features on parenting, a senior citizens column and two dozen others, which are sold as a package, in several packages, or separately.

The hope of the syndicate, which was begun by Eunice Trotter, editor of the Indianapolis *Recorder*, is that it will appeal to white editors and readers as well as to those in minorities. Various writers and artists are drawn from any race or nationality. The syndicate, of which Trotter was president and executive editor in 1987, has its headquarters in Indianapolis.

Black Conscience Syndication, established in 1987 in Wyandanch, New York, lists more than two hundred publications and other communications offices as its clients. Two-thirds are black-owned. It distributes "Ralph," a humorous panel cartoon by James A. Malone, and editorial page cartoons and caricatures by William D'Arcy. Clyde Davis, editor and publisher of the syndicate, also issues the *Wyandanch Intellect*, a monthly magazine consisting largely of reprints from other publications and articles or advertisements for books on black topics.

Changing the Black Image

Public relations has been called the science of attitude control. Its practitioners are trained to use whatever psychological and communications tools are available to develop in various publics a favorable attitude toward the institution or person concerned. Some institutions in the black society have been aware of the power of such an activity, but not many have had the money to use it in any nationally dramatic way. Publicity and promotion are simply tools of public relations, methods by which to influence a public to a view or an attitude; publicity using news releases to the press and broadcasters, for example; promotion turning out printed matter, films, and setting up special events that it publicizes. The distinction is largely a theoretical one today, for publicity promotes and promotion publicizes.

At its best, public relations wins understanding. Publicity helps by spreading information. So does promotion, by calling attention to special efforts. The black press is at one and the same time the target, and the projector, of publicity and promotion; it is used to affect public opinion, and it itself wishes to influence the public's opinion about itself and about the race it serves.

For years the black press was not much of a target nor much of a user of public relations techniques. Publicity offices of industry, government, and organizations, white or black, that prepare news releases, feature stories, take photographs, and supply other free materials boosting their products, services, or aims either were not much interested in cooperation from the black press or saw little point outside the sports and entertainment worlds. Travel publicity is an example. Why should a steamship company operating luxury liners spend money on publicizing its service (including the purchase of paid advertising space) to a small group of readers most of whom could only dream of making such a journey? Until the Caribbean, former family home for many an American black family or at least its forebears, became a popular playground for Americans and within economic reach of an increasing number of black travelers, there was no point in having travel editors and travel columns or in making space for travel releases, especially if they were not tied into space that had been bought. The growing middle class in American black society is changing that, however, and travel agencies and airlines have another segment of the public to seek to influence. Black publication offices are finding more free copy coming to their desks and, while they throw much of it away, they use more than ever before, as an observant reading of almost any large black publication and many a small one reveals.

The Black Counselor

A black public relations firm seeking to go well beyond the commercial function of public relations (i.e., do more than soften up a public so that families will buy many packages of frozen food or women will invest in wigs) makes a social contribution. It comes on the scene at a time when the image of black America is changing and made up of sharply contrasting concepts. These images exist in the minds of all occupants of U.S. territory (beyond whose borders this study of black journalism does not venture). The black citizens have their images of the black people and the whites theirs; the Orientals, too, have their impressions of their fellow minority group. There no more is one black image than there is one white or yellow. And the blacks' concept of their fellows can be as erroneous as whites' views of their black neighbors. To many, a white or black person has certain characteristics. W. Leonard Evans, while publishing *Tuesday*, said that one common stereotype is false ("lower mentality, a higher crime rate, think he's lazy, laughs a lot, steals chicken, and eats watermelon"). To others the black image is that of a gun- or knife-carrier bent on robbing banks or breaking into private houses.

The professional black publicist or public relations counsel is interested, outside the commercial area, in projecting what he or she deems a correct image of the American black society, whatever that may be, for it varies in different minds. He or she seeks to do so through black social organization channels, through white-sponsored enterprises working among blacks, and through church and educational institutions. The practice of public relations counseling under such circumstances is likely to resemble missionary work. In the commercial world, however, it is colored by the aims and purposes of all business. There it has been more scientifically and systematically carried out, for capital is available. Consequently, more and more public relations counsels are being called into service to advise dominantly white organizations, particularly government bodies, business corporations, and political groups and individuals, as well as others that may not have full rapport with black people or simply want to spread their gospel to the black society. It is assumed by those who employ them that a black public relations firm has more entrée to the ghetto or black neighborhoods and organizations than a white firm doing such propaganda or opinion-molding work.

Stanley Penn, a former *Wall Street Journal* reporter, in 1965 surveyed the development of black-run public relations firms. It is likely that what he discovered more than ever is so today. He traced the rise in business for black companies working for the business world to the civil rights movement, which resulted in what he called "the new awareness . . . of the importance of the Negro as a customer and an employee." Listing what firms are asked to do, he noted that they advise corporations on racial hiring practices, create contacts between black leaders and corporate executives, advise companies on participating in local civic movements, interpret the mood of the black community, arrange for company participation in conventions, and help determine the best advertising and merchandising methods for cultivating the black market.[7]

These activities, it should be noted, illustrate the basic difference between public relations and publicity or promotion. Every assignment is a matter of giving advice, counsel, or guidance in some way, with a few adding research techniques to discover the facts that serve as a basis for later judgments, as in interpreting the mood of the community.

Black personalities, particularly entertainers, more than ever are turning to counsels to manage their public problems as racial conflict becomes more acute. With the greater acceptance of nonwhites as television entertainers, actors, newscasters, interviewers, and behind-the-scenes managers, the black "public relations person" as well as the white has more clients. The black press cannot escape the impact of these communicators.

Public Information Directors

When they practice outside of business circles, public relations counsels sometimes are called directors of public information. The aim is the same, whatever the title: to obtain greater empathy for the institutions they represent, be they churches, colleges, or hospitals. Black journalists at times start their communications careers in the public relations field, particularly for black colleges and universities. Such institutions have had to pay such low salaries for all staff that it has been difficult to fill the position, which frequently (as in many a white college as well), includes disseminating news, advising the student paper, teaching a journalism class or two, and running the alumni office. Thus bright students have been appointed, or new graduates, or young people just out of undergraduate journalism school, or newsmen with little or no practical experience or training in public relations work, which they reduce to writing news releases.

Usually these neophytes move on to jobs in the professional journalism field, but some remain as public relations or information directors, never having time to obtain the necessary media experience or any more special training than attending a workshop sponsored by the American College Public Relations Society. In the late 1930s, for example, a prominent black college had as its public relations director an eighteen-year-old who was not to be handed his first college degree (nor was it in journalism) for another decade. Several other black colleges later hired men without media experience of any sort. One began doing such work in 1946, and went successively from that college to two others, and was at the third until the 1970s. He had published some magazine and newspaper articles but had no other practical media experience in his quarter of a century in public relations and publicity; in addition he taught journalism classes at two of the colleges, relying wholly on uncompleted master's degree work in journalism. Some of these men and others like them have taught themselves much about media operations by spending time in newspaper, magazine, and broadcasting company offices and observing what is done and how. Others have sunk into the routines and exert little influence for their institutions except in a small local circle and are minor auxiliaries of the black press. Few such self-taught information executives are aware of the more sophisticated public information methods or the social contribution that public relations directors can make when at their best.

The diversity of what comes under the heading of public relations is demonstrated by the activities of Terrie Williams, vice-president and director of corporate communications at Essence Communications.

An umbrella organization of which *Essence* magazine is one of the units, Essence Communications includes also a television program, two clothing labels, and a direct mail marketing firm. Williams joined *Essence* in 1982 as director of public relations with responsibility only for the magazine's image, since it was the only Essence enterprise at the time.

Describing her work to Shelley Moore, a writer for *Modern Black Men* magazine, Williams listed a variety of duties: she arranges speaking engagements for the top executives; provides representation for *Essence* at major meetings, luncheons, conferences, and other gatherings, especially if of national importance; and sees to it that the company and its products are the subjects of newspaper and magazine articles and noted on radio and television broadcasts; she also serves with black organizations and assists in fund-raising for them by organizing parties.

Little of this activity differs from public relations as practiced in any area of the business world. What is most important is that more and more black enterprises are aware of the value of such work in the life of any black business, including the press.

Another area in which black communicators practice the art of opinion management and direction is in the government and social information office. Several black journalists have gained national attention for their work as government information specialists. Perhaps best known is Carl T. Rowan, who was head of the U.S. Information Agency (USIA—see Chapter 10); others are William Gordon, who had American government information duties in Africa, Sweden, and the United States, and Henry Burrell Woods. Before he became associate director, program development, of the USIA, Woods had a successful background of black newspaper and radio experience. He was with the St. Louis *Call* from 1935 to 1940, chief of the bureau there for the Chicago *Defender* from 1942 to 1949, a newscaster for WMTV between 1951 and 1954, and executive editor of the St. Louis *Argus* for the next eleven years. During his news career he won various awards for news and editorial writing. Still other men and women, both with and without journalism training, have been sent by the State Department to Africa, Asia, and the West Indies as information officers. And all, as part of their duties, have worked with the press, either that of the country where they were or the black press, or along with the white, on the American continent, gaining understanding of the government body they represented.

For all such work is bound to affect the black press. It means visits from public relations representatives to editors seeking cooperation or vice versa. It means much more free copy—text as well as illustrations—coming into offices for use by editors. It means activities stimulated by public relations counsel, which will lead to creation of news that must be reported by the media. It produces problems as well: where to draw the line between news and publicity or promotion, the risk of undue influence by publicists, and the demands of advertisers that they receive a given amount of space as "free readers" in addition to what they pay for, an attitude they often believe to be part of obtaining good public relations.

Promoters of the Press

Black publications have made little use of public relations skills in the larger sense. Usually they rely on proved promotion ideas only. These are not involved with applications of psychology's principles and often are mixed, instead, with human concerns, a natural consequence of seeking to serve a group of people facing multitudes of everyday problems. These plans and ideas may have a by-product of generating goodwill toward the publication. Like many other black activities, the publication must rely on its own community for support, although white interest sometimes is manifested via financial aid and personal participation.

Examples of one idea are Negro Press Week and Black History Month. Although not entered into with much zest in recent years, the press as a whole every February or March since 1941 has conducted, via the National Newspaper Publishers Association (NNPA), a Negro Press Week. Then, or just before or after, the papers print articles on heroes of black journalism—usually Cornish, Russwurm, or Douglass—drawings, photographs, and special articles supplied by the NNPA committee that supervises the observance. Sometimes a radio program has been included with outlets in cities served by black papers. Schools and colleges are asked to cooperate by drawing attention to the black press. Exhibits are staged also in schools and other public places. Like white publishers, the black owners and managers appear to be convinced that the reader is indifferent to the publication per se and therefore bored by historical or laudatory articles about black journalism. Thus recognition of the black press at times is allowed to go by with one brief article noting it or an editorial saying little beyond the customary.

The promotions staged or sponsored by individual publications at other times of the year are neither extremely costly nor inordinately fancy, mainly because the more elaborate, such as fashion shows and contests, usually are tied in with advertisers, who supply materials or awards. Newspaper and magazine staff people engaged in this aspect of publishing are busy with charity drives, scholarship programs, amateur photography and other contests, honor rolls, youth clubs, beauty queen competitions, and sports events. These goings-on often are responses to the needs of readers as much as to the desire of publishers to ingratiate themselves with those who buy the paper or magazine, as a brief review of some typical promotion enterprises indicates.

Perhaps the best-known activity launched by a black magazine is *Ebony*'s "Fashion Fair" held in many parts of the nation. Sponsored by the National Council of Negro Women in conjunction with the magazine, it is staged in a local theater or auditorium of a city with a substantial black population. Often it is an important annual women's social event in a community, especially since a scholarship fund benefits. *Ebony* representatives accompany the fair, which seeks to tie into the fashion trends of the day. Displayed is everything from beachwear to wedding gowns; when traditional African clothing was popular, it was shown.

A far different sort of promotion, and perhaps more individually useful, is the column run in a newspaper to which readers may send requests for assistance. For instance, a reader of the Philadelphia *Tribune* sent its "Mr. Help" column a complaint about a backing sewer. The paper arranged for the water commissioner's office to correct the situation. The Baltimore *Afro-American* for years offered a similar service, "Afro Line," in its local edition, describing it as "a community service to help you solve problems, whatever they may be." Readers sent a postcard asking their question and identifying themselves. A typical question and answer:

> Q: My wife and I are separated. I have custody of our six children. I want to know, is there any place a broken man can get a divorce or legal separation. I can't afford a lawyer.
>
> A: At the Legal Aid Bureau, in People's Court Building, Fayette and Gay Sts., you can get help.

The Detroit *Michigan Chronicle* service is called Chronicle Information Center. Much older than the "Life Line" type of service is that of the San Francisco *Sun-Reporter*, which has maintained a Public Affairs Bureau to call attention to "special aspects of new problems," as the newspaper explains. International as well as local matters are given attention. The late Tom Mboya, Sir Adetokunbo Adesnola, and other African leaders or American visitors to Africa have been lecturers or guests. This paper also sponsors an annual Merit Award Program that rewards local people for outstanding community service. That particular old reliable among promotions has been used also every year since 1939 by the Baltimore *Afro-American*. Pictures of the winners are printed in the paper. A related feature is Good Neighbor of the Week, an article about someone in an area of the city. Charity campaigns are among the oldest of the traditional plans.

Black Press Hall of Fame

In 1987 the *Afro-American* newspapers founded a Black Press Hall of Fame (BPHF), "honoring those who have made significant contributions to the black press." Leaders in formulating the plan were Frances H. Draper, president of the firm, and John J. Oliver, Jr., publisher of the papers.

The first celebration of the BPHF was held in Baltimore, the home of the *Afro-American* papers, October 23–25. Financing of the plan was through Afro-Charities, Inc., in Baltimore, which carried out the plans and is related to the papers.

The purposes of the BPHF are "to preserve and perpetuate Black Newspapers as a vigorous American institution; to honor past and present contributors and supporters of Black Newspapers; and to encourage pursuit of careers in journalism." To be qualified for selection, a nominee must have three years of black newspaper experience out of a total of ten years' newspaper experience as a founder/ publisher, journalist, photographer, graphic artist, cartoonist, salesperson, circulation person, marketer, distributor, technical pioneer, spokesperson, promoter, production person, or some other person related to that press. The nominees must meet criteria of professionalism, influence, commitment, morality, and experience. The latter is divided into two categories: newspaper people, who must have ten years media experience, three on black newspapers; and newspaper advocates, who must have a five-year record of consistent support of the black newspaper industry. The advocates are to be chosen from financiers, spokespersons, educators, volunteers, advertisers, promoters, journalists, and others.

The nine black journalists, in alphabetical order, and the one black organization first named to the Hall of Fame were Samuel E. Cornish; Frederick Douglass; Carlton B. Goodlett; John H. Johnson; John Henry Murphy, Sr.; Christopher J. Perry, Sr.; John B. Russwurm; John H. Sengstacke; Ida Baker Wells-Barnett; and the National Newspaper Publishers Association. The judges were Moses J. Newson, former editor of the *Afro-American* papers; Harry Amana, former reporter for the Philadelphia *Tribune*; and Brenda Andrews, publisher of the Norfolk *Journal and Guide*. The next year six more were inducted: Sam Lacy, the sportswriter; Carl Murphy, the late head of the *Afro-American* chain; Lutrelle F. Palmer, Jr., a Chicago newsman; E. Washington Rhodes, the late editor and publisher of the Philadelphia *Tribune;* and Ernest Withers, Sr., a news photographer.

Special crusades, part of the black press since its founding, have a by-product of promotional value, even when not successful. As a crusading press, this one has a fine record that can be illustrated from the history of most newspapers and a few magazines. In recent years they have centered on eradicating slum housing, righting injustices to individuals, opposing rent-gouging tactics by landlords, and working for the hiring of blacks by firms doing business with them. Nor are these all only recent campaigns. P. Bernard Young, while editor of the Norfolk *Journal and Guide*, was looking out the window of his office one day in 1933, when he saw the collapse of a decaying house used by black people. He took a picture of the ruins and wrote a story and an editorial demanding action on housing in that Virginia city. Later Young was appointed head of the Negro Housing Advisory Commission of the city; by 1949 Norfolk had four modern housing developments for black residents. The paper was successful with other campaigns. *Time* reported in 1949 that it was responsible for the county floating a $750,000 bond issue to improve black schools and for changes in pay scales so black and white teachers were treated equally.

The Bud Billiken Club

One of the most effective promotions by a black publication was the early Bud Billiken Club of the Chicago *Defender*. Begun in 1924, its major event was an annual parade and picnic in Chicago. As many as 150,000 youngsters came with their parents and friends to the mammoth picnic. Chicago society women helped stage the affair.[8] Each member received a wallet card and an identification button; at one time membership totaled nearly one million. The club was intended to attract and interest black children and perhaps eventually make them readers and possible advertisers. The plan centered on a club called The Defender Junior, with a regular page or two for children's writings and drawings and reports of their activities. The staff member in charge called himself "Bud Billiken."

The first Bud Billiken was Willard Motley, later known as the black novelist who wrote *Knock on Any Door*. Motley was only a ten-year-old at the time Robert S. Abbott, the publisher, selected him for the job. The plan built incalculable goodwill for the paper and continues to do so with an annual Billiken Club king and queen contest.

Another *Defender* promotion device that was different, one which spread to other cities and became part of the language, was election of a mayor of what the paper called Bronzeville. Such mayors held unofficial conventions; the mayor became the official host to celebrities who visited the black neighborhoods.

Tons of literature are among the promotional materials issued by the black press over the years. The simplest are rate cards and leaflets describing the paper and its coverage, promotion letters, and booklets.

Competitors of the Black Press

Every other medium, whatever the race or color of its owners, is a competitor for black publications: other newspapers and magazines, billboards, car cards in subways and buses, books (especially paperbacks), television, radio, what the advertising business calls point of purchase displays, direct mail, and cassette and videocassette tapes. Such competition is at the usual two levels: for readers and for advertising accounts. Any revenue-producing form is competition. Any activity that consumes a potential reader's time is competition, even spectator sports and adless books. In this book, however, the concern is with the black-owned and -operated radio and television. They directly affect the publications. Little information has been set down about them as journalistic phenomena in the world of the minorities.

About 150 radio stations and 15 television stations are owned and operated by black citizens. By all logic, if the black press, to be so considered, must be owned, operated, and staffed by, and aimed at the black race, with content about it, then black broadcasting is genuinely black only when it also has a similar description. The reasons are much the same, and just as they are articulated for the press by black journalists so are they expressed by black broadcasters.

Dr. Haley Bell, when co-owner of several black radio stations, told an interviewer that black ownership establishes an atmosphere of trust with the black listener and that creates a better selling atmosphere. And Gregory Moses, while vice-president of James Brown Enterprises, said to the same writer that "there is a great pride factor" involved and that is why stations tell the listener that the operation is black. It "gives our people the feeling of voices, of someone looking out for their interests."[9] Bernard Howard, then president of a station advertising representative company bearing his name, called black radio "the only medium through which the Negro himself believes he can receive the happenings of the day as they happen, and he feels they should be reported. It gives him more of his side of the story, more of the internal facets non-Negro stations overlook; it gives him more of the editorials he likes to hear, delivered by announcers he knows are on his team, and it does this more consistently and more often than any other medium."

As journalism, black broadcasting is not yet socially significant in its everyday operations. Taking into consideration both its manifestations (as wholly or only partly black), it can be important in times of crisis, and has been in cities where disturbances have occurred (as for example after the assassination of Martin Luther King, Jr., in 1968). Day in and day out it is competition for the community newspaper owner, for he or she knows that a radio station in the area is being listened to and can command thousands of dollars in advertising accounts. Such publishers are perhaps not primarily concerned with the racial nature of the station's ownership, unless they share in the advertising budgets of local merchants, banks, and other businesses. They have no illusions about a competitor's effectiveness.

Black radio has grown to the point where it needs unity of its owners. In 1976 what is commonly called NABOB was formed, the National Association of Black Owned Broadcasters, Inc. It was organized, its leaders said, "as a response to the abysmal under-representation of minorities in the communications industry." Its members are not only the 150 black-owned radio stations and 15 black-owned television stations in the United States but also, as associate members, law firms, station brokers, national firms of representatives, and other businesses related to broadcasting, including cable television. One of NABOB's functions is to influence national government and industry policies to benefit owners of black and other minority operations.

Advertising in Black Broadcasts

The vital competitive point of black broadcasting is its ability to sell advertising time. Most studies have dwelt on its success in reaching a market, affirming that it is an effective community medium from that standpoint. Especially is that true in towns and cities where there is no black publication. The existence of as many as two to six stations in one city (for example, six in Washington, D.C., three each in Augusta and Albany, Georgia, and two in Atlanta) indicates eagerness to gain a lucrative market. The desirability of the market reached a height in the 1950s when a black radio network was formed.

Before W. Leonard Evans was publisher of *Tuesday* magazine, he was president of the National Negro Network, Inc. (NNN), launched in 1954. It included fifty radio stations and reported that it reached 12 million black listeners. It operated from January 1954 to fall 1956, on a five-times-a-week frequency. The stations were in areas with large black populations. Offered were programs on a network basis to what were called Negro-appeal stations. The first output, a transcribed soap opera that Evans himself wrote (perhaps the first black story of this sort) was called "Ruby Valentine," starring Juanita Hall, who had won great popularity in *South Pacific*. Advertising time was bought by Pet Milk and Philip Morris, among others. The NNN employed annually between 125 and 155 black actors and actresses, 10 to 15 musicians on a regular basis, 6 major writers, and a staff of about 18 in management and production. Because television's advent affected all radio, the network did not survive. Evans explained that it was discontinued also "primarily because of inability to resolve economic differences with a group of three radio chains that represented 11 of the 50 stations involved in network operations."[10]

Another black-owned radio network operated briefly in 1969, American Freedom Network. Stimulated by the demand for news after the assassination of Dr. King, coverage of that tragedy's aftermath was provided 240 stations in the United States and Canada. From thirty to thirty-five reporters provided news from throughout the nation for the new pool.[11]

Now black radio stations broadcast the usual kinds of commercials, with heavy accent on local accounts. Success in obtaining national advertising usually depends on the rating of each station in relation to others in the community. They carry out promotion schemes somewhat like those of the black newspapers, hoping similarly to endear themselves to listeners and thus boost their ratings. Public service announcements are broadcast about lost articles and animals, and the station acts as a job clearinghouse.

Competition in New Form

Black communications media now are experiencing a new turn in the competitive business world. Already noted is the situation wherein magazine publishers of long standing now see white foundations, banks, and periodical publishers combining to strengthen or launch black magazines that will seek to share in the budgets of their advertisers and appeal to their readers for subscriptions (see Chapters 7 and 12).

Newspapers will be affected by such support, if it should increase, more than magazines not only because listeners or viewers do not usually read at the same time but also because money spent on advertising over broadcasts perhaps is that amount not devoted to the print media. The black press has enough problems without unexpected strength being given to its major competitor from within the racial ranks. Editors and publishers can take the view, however, that whatever improves the lot of black citizens is helpful to their papers and periodicals, for it can mean more purchasing power and better educated citizens, and therefore more readers.

Pro and Con
on the Black Press

Is black journalism "good" journalism? Before any answer can be given, other questions must be raised: What standards have been used? Who set up the criteria?

Black people, in defending certain attitudes and actions of their race, make the point at times that whites use white measuring sticks when assessing black performance and say that the requirements and ways of black people are not those of whites and need not be. Consequently they believe different standards should be used.

The criteria for judging the technical performance of the black press, however, have been color blind. Judgment of it should not be confused with past or present estimates of its efficacy as an advertising medium, its assertion of its right to exist, or the validity of the points of view expressed. Racial prejudice has been a factor in denying the press its share of advertising revenue, and it also has operated against establishment or continuation of black publications in prejudiced communities.

This chapter is concerned with evaluation of the black newspaper and magazine as a piece of journalism. The criteria generally applied admittedly have been set up by white people, but they are for the most part internationally accepted and respected in Africa and Asia as well as Europe and America. They are not necessarily American in origin, for the designers, typographers, editors, and writers of many countries (particularly Britain) contributed, over the years, to their formation. The criteria range from technological details such as legibility of type to more debatable aspects such as fairness in news coverage.

What may be lacking in white criticism of the black press, in applying abstract standards, is understanding of why that press may not measure up at all times in all departments. Certainly in U.S. journalism, and that of many other countries, the major standards—at least theoretically—are:

1. Integrity: being detached from political or commercial influence that might deny readers the truthful information they are led to expect.
2. Fairness, which in journalism means giving all sides (not just two) of a news event, restricting the paper's or magazine's opinions to the editorial columns, and avoiding printing opinions as news.
3. Technical excellence, including legibility of printed matter, correctness of grammar and spelling, readability by the audience selected, originality in illustrations, suitability of subject matter for readers, professionalism in preparation of headings, layouts, and makeup.

To these could be added standards set up for noneditorial operations: advertising, circulation, promotion, and management. These standards were established for the business world and apply to the business operations of the black press. They imply, for example, honesty in circulation statements, impartial treatment of advertisers in the rate structure, making only legitimate claims for a publication in its promotion material, and providing adequate working conditions, salaries, and fringe benefits for employees.

The first two standards for operation—integrity and fairness— are within the reach of publishers of all types of media. They are matters of policy rather than of technical expertise. Not that they are easy to attain or inexpensive. Covering all angles even of a fire story breaking out in a black neighborhood, for example, takes time and staff; similar coverage of a larger and more complicated event, such as a demonstration or strike, can be costly.

The third standard—technical excellence—often is much less attainable because it requires substantial capital investment, trained personnel, and high regular expense. Furthermore, in many communities, a black newspaper (and here the newspaper is more in question than the magazine) is quixotic if it spends large sums on achieving technical perfection that its audience is not interested in or perhaps even prepared to appreciate fully, a situation common in all shades and types of journalism.

Under what conditions, then, is it important that a black paper have the most highly recommended type dress, a horizontal rather than a vertical makeup, optically attractive page designs or tabloid instead of standard size, or some other technical characteristic? The answers are several. If: (1) it is economically no more costly than any other way; (2) competing papers are succeeding because of such practices, and one's own is suffering as a result of not keeping pace; (3) readers demand but also respond; (4) advertisers respond more readily as a result; (5) the owner can afford it.

In this third area of technical excellence compromises are possible and sometimes necessary for survival. Failure to live up to this standard is understandable and to be preferred to the stilling of a printed voice in a community. The danger in compromise is that it can and does result in contentedness with slovenly reporting, careless writing, confusing makeup, and a generally mediocre publication, technically speaking, especially in a one-paper community where a white press is indifferent to the ethnic group.

In applying all such standards, ethical as well as technical, which have nothing to do with race per se, the black newspaper press of today as a whole comes off with a moderate grade only. As second newspapers and quasi-protest journalism, they, like their predecessors in the nineteenth century, can be considered possibly more successful as propaganda organs than as journalistic media devoted to offering their readers as much news as possible in the most objective way available. The early protest papers were influential and important not for their total content but for their value as outlets for opinion. As sermonizers, as exhorters, they were effective, but their readers still had to become informed of facts and strategies after the sermons were over. For those simpler times the protest papers performed a function, but it was not, and still is not, the sole function of a press that wants protection of its freedom. And, since then, papers have had to do more than supply such leadership and give their readers more nearly objective content.

Implicit in this assessment is the idea that the ideal black paper or magazine is one that informs its readers fully and also provides analysis, interpretation, and opinion material to help them comprehend the meaning and significance of events occurring in their own society and in the surrounding white society. On that basis, few black publications of today or the past score high. In proportion to number, neither do many white publications for that matter, a criticism made for many years by individuals and organizations. Insofar as the white press has to some extent overcome the faults of bias and exaggeration, it has made more progress toward meeting the standards than has the black press. But it must be remembered that it has been in a far better position to do so; in fact, it can be criticized for not having made more progress by now.

That portion of the literature on black journalism in the United States that has attempted to evaluate the press has been predominantly adverse. One finds few defenders outside the writers of high-sounding, idealistic perorations published during black press celebrations, the official time for praise. The whole American press, for that matter, has been a favorite whipping boy of politicians, reformers, and presidents throughout history. The serious students of the black publications—Frazier the sociologist, Sancton the journalist, Brown the public affairs scholar, and numbers of other black and white journalists discussing the profession—have had many faults to find. Those few who came to praise—Villard, Baldwin, and Waters stand out—are outnumbered. The writers who sent down a balanced verdict—Myrdal is the best known of these few—generally are overlooked, as center-of-the-roaders usually are, because partisans cannot use them. Furthermore, the evaluations have come at different times and on different aspects of the black press performance. For present purposes they sometimes are valueless because conditions have changed.

The Classic Adverse Criticisms

Perhaps the most quoted critic of the black publications during any time in their history is the late E. Franklin Frazier, still regarded as one of the leading black sociologists, albeit somewhat outmoded. In *Black Bourgeoisie*, a book that the civil rights movement and later racial developments have made a landmark volume, he devoted a chapter to "The Negro Press and Wish-Fulfillment." It was an application of the volume's thesis: that the black, up to the early 1960s, was living in a make-believe world of his own creation; out of the black business and society world has arisen what he described as a Negro bourgeoisie.

Frazier called the press "not only one of the most successful business enterprises owned and controlled by Negroes" but also the "chief medium of communication which creates and perpetuates the world of make-believe."[1] He accused the press of representing only the bourgeoisie, not the black society as a whole, adding that it "promulgates the bourgeois values." He selected certain types of content to support his point, noting the stories of accomplishments of widely known Negroes or prominent persons thought to have black blood (such as Pushkin and Dumas) but also the accomplishments of unknowns. These latter are exaggerated, he insists. A student who has a good college record is reported to be a genius; a black police magistrate is dubbed "judge." Such treatment of the news generates myths, he wrote.

But the darts thereafter in his chapter hit mainly at *Ebony*, as it was in the 1950s. Then it was emphasizing accounts of black men who became millionaires, with emphasis on their luxurious homes and cars; a few wealthy widows also were glorified. He reported that each month financially successful black businessmen were played up. The bourgeoisie and its press, Frazier insisted, ignore "the broader issues facing the modern world" because the black intelligentsia has developed an opportunistic philosophy.

His charges, which rested on now-outdated issues of publications, hold true today only on some points. The creation of a black world of society people continues in the large publications, especially the bigger newspapers. The reporting of relatively trivial accomplishments as significant goes on, particularly in the small weeklies (it is not only their reporting but the way they report that is also debatable). But the important issues facing and affecting all citizens, not blacks alone, are being dealt with somewhat more than before editorially. They may not strike hard, but at least there is a group of papers with something to say. The problems of the rank-and-file black citizens, not the interests of the bourgeoisie mainly, are being reported in a substantial number of publications.

Few black publications, then or now, really qualified for his rating of being "one of the most successful Negro business enterprises," as the mortality rate and its owners' dependence upon outside enterprises (funeral parlors, banks, and insurance companies) shows. And too much of his writing about the black press is purely subjective. Sweeping generalizations are based on a few major publications. What is true applies to a handful, but at the time, as today, there were responsible publications not given to exaggerations of which all are accused.

After World War II was underway, attacks upon the black press began to mount, written by blacks and whites alike. Warren H. Brown, a black who at that time directed Negro relations for the Council for Democracy, late in 1942 published an article that drew fire. Some of the people who objected to it did so particularly because it appeared in a then relatively small public affairs magazine and simultaneously in the *Reader's Digest*, with its multimillion circulation even in those days. Most newspapers are Negro first and American second, he charged, increasing segregation because they are race-conscious before being America-conscious. "They feed and prosper by sensationally playing up the Negro at his worst," he wrote. "When they publish news of the white community, it is generally an account of the white man at his worst . . . breeding ill-will between the races."[2]

In short, Brown's view was that the black press presented a dishonest picture of the United States and of the opportunities for blacks. He then went after Adam Clayton Powell, Jr., who was editing *People's Voice* at the time, and quoted some of the melodramatic editorial writing of that excitable minister-politician. There then followed numerous citations showing the headlines in various black papers that attacked the military establishment for its treatment of black troops, headlines that Brown considered "blatantly sensational and hate-making." He asked not for censorship but that the press not be "encouraged to run at a venemous, hate-making pace."

An article in reply appeared in *Saturday Review* but not in *Reader's Digest*. It was written by Vishnu V. Oak, a Wilberforce University professor of sociology and journalism, who some years later was to publish one of the few books on black journalism in this country. Oak, a strong critic of the press, in his reply to Brown made the point that the American Negro would be unintelligent indeed if he did not, through his press, demand greater freedom for himself, "especially when he is fighting abroad for the preservation of democracy. . . ."

Several white writers joined in the criticism nevertheless. Two prominent southern journalists, John Temple Graves and Virginius Dabney, published articles. Graves's, in the *Virginia Quarterly Review*, received much less attention than that of Dabney, then editor of the white Richmond (Virginia) *Times-Dispatch*, for Dabney's appeared in several publications, including the *Atlantic Monthly*. He accused the press of stirring dissension between blacks and whites, publishing this view also in *Negro Digest* and the professional magazine for journalists, the *Quill*. He exhibited no such restraint as did Brown, but proposed that "the disturbing elements on both sides of the color line . . . be muzzled for the duration."[3]

Walter White, by then secretary of the NAACP, placed some of the blame for whatever truth such criticisms contained upon certain press weaknesses. These were the lack of staff or carelessness that led to publication of unverified copy and use of sensational headlines that gave the news a distorted emphasis. But, White declared in an autobiography, the fault was not all to be assigned to the black papers. They were doing only what white ones had begun to do long before, and to greater excess. Also, news of discrimination against blacks had long gone unpublished in the white press, and black readers wanted to know of it. White reported that he learned of pressure being brought upon President Franklin D. Roosevelt and the Department of Justice to indict some of the black newspaper editors. But the president discouraged that move. Then there were plans, White added, to deny newsprint to papers thought to be seditious. These, too, were discouraged. The NAACP early in 1943 called a meeting of editors of two dozen prominent black papers. The association's Washington office was made available for checking stories and the papers agreed to help each other in news verification. From this session came the National Newspaper Publishers Association.[4]

These actions were in response to wartime criticism of the press. But there were other charges. Brooks summarizes the major adverse criticisms generally leveled at midcentury. The newspapers were accused of sensationalism, questionable advertising policies, and overemphasis on the racial angles of the news. One coming from fewer sources was that certain unnamed leading journals were leftist or Communist inspired. It was this latter charge that Brooks studied, providing a quantitative report on the leading black papers of 1948. His findings were that these papers "reflect those values consistent with the American tradition rather than the espousal of doctrine alien to it," that they were fundamentally concerned with promoting civil liberties and other citizenship rights for the whole population, and that there was "uncompromising rejection of segregation and discrimination" as well as many other social practices "affecting adversely the status and role of colored minorities in American society." He also observed that these papers were not primarily organs of protest but were more journals of reform.[5]

About this same time Roi Ottley, later to be the biographer of Robert S. Abbott and himself an experienced black newsman, attacked the commercialism of the papers. "Once the stuff of idealism is cut away," he wrote, "they are operated primarily for profit and in this sense are like their white contemporaries. What is good business in the judgment of the owners rarely is hampered by the nonsense about race."[6] Earl Conrad, the white man who left the white press to work in a black newsroom and wrote sympathetic and understanding articles about the black papers, in a 1946 article said that some publishers in the postwar period accepted money from the highest bidder for their political support. He thought the owners and other heads of these publishing companies hardly needed the dollars. Such selling out, he wrote, was a violation of trust. Conrad considered such blacks as traitors among their people. Nor did he exempt white leaders of the two major parties for making such deals. He pointed to the political stances taken in 1944 when Thomas E. Dewey and Franklin D. Roosevelt contended for the presidency. Some big, black papers supported Dewey but the black citizens in their communities voted overwhelmingly for FDR.[7] Whites similarly repudiated their press. In contrast to this was the 1968 election, when Hubert H. Humphrey was heavily supported by the black press as well as the black citizenry.

Now and again, in the next quarter of a century, came other adverse criticisms, these largely from within the fold. The late James Baldwin, the novelist, although in reality more of a defender than an adverse critic, did write in 1948 that the black press "supports any man, provided he is sufficiently dark and well known. . . . The Negro press has been accused of not helping much—as indeed, it has not, nor do I see how it could have. And it has been accused of being sensational, which it is."[8]

Enoch R. Waters, who was Associated Negro Press editor in the early 1960s, was unhappy about what he called the sameness of the black papers and the "narrow rut in which they operate." He called for more creativity and imagination. The reporting was "too prosaic and conventional." A crusading spirit was lacking; editors needed more of a sense of mission.[9]

Relative quiet prevailed until 1967, when Elaine Kendall, a magazine writer and author, writing in the unlikely snob-appeal *Holiday*, cast "The Critical Eye" department of the sophisticated magazine on the black press. Angry letters followed. She had analyzed mainly several of the larger magazines (those from Johnson and the now gone *Elegant*) and the usual national papers, generalizing about all from these. She saw these publications as not being realistic enough about the true condition of the black people of the country. "Moreover, the papers are disdained and unread by the young and impatient Negro leaders and intellectuals," she wrote. "When they do see them, they are dismayed and irritated by the galloping materialism they find there."[10]

Her opponents chastised her for accepting *Elegant*'s alleged circulation of 200,000, for omitting the New York *Amsterdam News* and

Tuesday magazine, for comparing the black weeklies to the white dailies, and for holding views she actually did not express. Hoyt W. Fuller, managing editor of *Black World* (then *Negro Digest*), offended perhaps because Kendall brushed off his magazine merely by saying it had the smallest circulation of the Johnson group, which was correct, called the article names but gave no evidence and scolded *Holiday* for printing it.

Two years later appeared, during national Negro Press Week, ample substantiation of Kendall's view about the disenchantment of the young black intellectuals with the press. It probably was as untypical a press week or month piece as can be found.

Dan Aldridge, in his "Serious Business" column for the *Michigan Chronicle*, the large Sengstacke paper in Detroit, commented on an editorial in his own paper, which had praised the press. With that as a springboard he made these assertions:

"There are very few newspapers in the country that can rightly be called the 'black press.' The only two that come to mind are the papers put out by the Black Panther Party and the Nation of Islam." He admitted that there might be "a few others around the country." "Negro press," he said, was a better label for "our so-called printed media." He then called to his support the familiar views, referring to the press of two decades earlier, of Frazier the sociologist, already introduced in this chapter. Next he presented his own opinions, noting that "too much of most Negro newspapers is concerned more with the social life of the few than with the political life of the many. Valuable space which could be used to educate, mobilize and guide our people is used to talk about cocktail parties, ski parties, and dating games. This misuse of valuable news space is more than naive. It is criminal."

He then observed that the Detroit *News*, a large white daily, although criticized for carrying so much crime news, "is no match for most Negro newspapers." Their front pages, he wrote, "are filled with the words rape, murder, kill, loot, rob, stab, shot, stomp, cut and blood." He labeled them "crime shooting journals."

Further objects of the attack were what the press omits (knowledge of Africa and leading Africans, what really is going on in China and Cuba, and other events), the press' practice of service as "agents for cheating real estate dealers," even defending them, and its failure to take a position, on public issues, with specific examples.[11]

A leading black journalist, C. Sumner Stone, Jr., formerly editor of three major black newspapers and more recently columnist for the white Philadelphia *Daily News*, one of the large Atlantic Seaboard dailies, as long ago as 1977 expressed doubts about the willingness of the black press publishers to take steps to improve their papers.

When the white-owned press began in the 1970s to offer jobs to black reporters the black press executives resented it, as some still do. "Many black publishers bitterly criticized the white press for this journalistic black 'brain drain.' But more accurately stated, a mediocre black press had drained itself," Stone wrote in *Editor & Publisher*. "Even though race relations had changed dramatically and men had walked on the moon, the black press continued to reflect all the editorial and typographical authority of a horse-and-buggy blueprint for orbital flight."[12]

A scholar of black journalism, Dr. Henry G. La Brie III, has observed that the black press is being weakened by lack of advertising, that its management practices are poor, that readers are leaving it, and that white-owned publications are attracting black journalists away from the black papers. La Brie said that this assessment was not meant as criticism but is chiefly a list of trends. Certainly most of these trends are clear with the exception of one that is purely subjective (that management practices are poor) and difficult to substantiate except in certain instances. No broad and deep study has been made of this aspect.

In the mid-1980s criticism began to come from the advertising agency and representative worlds. Executives of agencies specializing in the black consumer market acknowledged that more mainline advertisers are using black publications. "For improvement and continuation of this kind of advertising support," said Karl Jackson, then general manager of Amalgamated Publishers, Inc., to an *Advertising Age* writer, means that "the editorial content of black newspapers must be geared to captivating more of their targeted readership."

Eugene Morris, in 1985 senior vice-president at Burrell Advertising, Chicago, the largest black-owned advertising agency, said: "I think black newspapers could do a better job editorially." He noted that for a long time the tendency was to sensationalize the news instead of covering substantive community issues. He also noted that the black press has traditionally been most effective in that area.

On the Positive Side

When it is not praised for its courage in fighting for the black American's rights, the positive criticism of the black press is more a matter of justifying or explaining its policies and viewpoints than compliments on its performance.

Praise for the press came in 1944 from Oswald Garrison Villard, grandson of William Lloyd Garrison and himself at one time editor of the New York *Evening Post* and owner and publisher of the *Nation*. He also was a founder of the NAACP. The Negro press, as he called it, was the only one that had developed swiftly. Many of the editors, he believed, had shown and were then demonstrating great ability and power. Its growth in numbers and in the extent of its support by members of the race was astounding, he said, to many persons who had been unaware of the tensions from discontent and anger among the black people.

"Born of these bitter passions, the new Negro press speaks with vigor, and far too often with a violence, that have startled the whites who have suddenly been brought into contact with it." Viewing the same headlines as did Warren Brown, Villard saw them in a different light. "It is not cowed because this is war-time, it does not tremble before authority," he wrote. "It uses little or no restraint in discussing the refusal of this government to grant to our Negroes not only their constitutional privileges, but full equality in the army and the navy, the right to fight for their country on equal terms with white citizens. These militant newspapers are both creators of the suddenly developed Negro sense of solidarity and themselves an index of a developing race consciousness and unwillingness to remain in a subordinate position, a helotry in a democracy."[13]

He recognized weakness, as well, adding that it was then unfortunately true that many Negro dailies and weeklies had to go to censurable excesses and injure their case by their unbridled attacks in what he considered an explosive period in the nation's history. He placed responsibility for these excesses mainly on those whites who believed that the United States, as a democracy, could live part servile and part free. Villard thought that the white press might "similarly catch fire" after the war. He did not live to see this happen, nor has it happened since his death in 1949.

The late James Baldwin, in one of his autobiographical essays, wrote in 1948: "Negroes live violent lives, unavoidably; a Negro press without violence is therefore not possible; and, further, in every act of violence, particularly violence against white men, Negroes feel a certain thrill of self-identification, a wish to have done it themselves, a feeling that old scores are being settled at last.[14]

After describing Harlem as it existed in the late 1940s and noting that some steps were being taken to "make it less of a social liability," such as opening a boys' club, a playground, and a housing project, he said that most of the projects were stimulated by Negro leaders and the Negro press [using *Negro*]."[15] Baldwin added that it can be forgiven for its preoccupation considering the indifference and hostility of the white press. "The Negro press has been accused of not helping much—as indeed it has not, nor do I see how it could have," he wrote. He also did not hold it against the press of that time for being sensational. He added that the terrible dilemma of the press is that it had to imitate the white, not having any other.

Baldwin seems to forget that the situation may have existed in the nineteenth century, but in this century, when the press was somewhat more oriented, there was less necessity for using white models. Even today, as noted in the discussion of production of black publications in the preceding chapters, little experimentation is taking place; like other American publishers, black ones evidently have found little or nothing to attract them in the press of other nations. Later Baldwin says that the critics of the press are irrational when they demand that "the nation's most oppressed minority" conduct itself with a skill and foresight not asked of Joseph Medill Patterson (founder of the New York *Daily News*) or of William Randolph Hearst, Sr.

What Baldwin calls the press' "innate desperation" is betrayed in its tone, he writes. He would be cheered to note today that with improvement in the condition of some blacks, at least, the press tone has changed somewhat. Its militancy is not so much born of desperation as of occasional victories and possibilities of more to come—blacks in high political office, such as mayors of large cities; in important educational posts (presidencies of black and white colleges); in government positions (senators, representatives, ambassadors); and in the sciences, arts, and letters.

A positive view of the black press can be obtained by noting certain of its actions in comparison to those of the white. Chuck Stone went into battle with Ben H. Bagdikian, one of the leading critics of the white press. In a *New Republic* article Bagdikian discussed the political views of American newspapers, saying at one point that President John F. Kennedy had no editorial support in certain cities, including Chicago. Stone accused him of racial myopia that, he said, characterizes the press of America, noting then that the Chicago *Daily Defender* (of which Stone once was chief editor) had supported Kennedy, as had many black weeklies.

"Negro newspapers simply are not recognized as co-equals or even respected for their editorial integrity and power," Stone wrote in his answering letter, "even if they are larger, far more wealthy, influential and professional than the smallest, most impoverished racist and editorially unkempt white rag."[16] Bagdikian in rebuttal wrote that

"Negro newspapers are not the co-equals of papers like the Chicago *Tribune, Sun-Times, Daily News* or *American*, not because they are Negro, but because they are specialized papers, edited for the particular interest of one ethnic group."

His answer, in this author's view, was not adequate. To be sure the black papers are second papers, but not in the same sense as is the *Financial World* of New York for financiers, or *Women's Wear Daily* for buyers and merchandisers. For those papers do not deal to any appreciable extent with social issues, nor are they expected to take political positions. Racial problems today enter many areas: religion, employment, health, education, and government are only a few. But any of the large black major weeklies, and many of the moderate-size papers and the few dailies have their following, even though almost everyone in that following may read a white newspaper and some a white newsmagazine at the same time, for the followers do not see in their primary papers the social issues that concern them treated from the black viewpoint. Thus it is important for any politician gauging public opinion to be aware of what the black press is urging upon its readers or even exposing them to by way of news coverage. With black Americans more and more voting as a group, their press is to be reckoned with.

Still another defense of the press came in 1969 from W. Leonard Evans, then editor and president of *Tuesday*. Speaking in a panel on marketing, he chided white advertisers and agencies when he said that "the black newspapers, after being 100 years old, have never gotten their just dollars. Therefore, they are being criticized, they don't cover this news, or have this type of reproduction. How can they, when they have to live off circulation?"

The Myrdal study of the black people of America noted the charge that the black papers were sensational. It quoted the defense of their editors and publishers, i.e., they wanted to reach as many readers as possible so as to widen their chance of influencing them to improve and advance the race. Myrdal said that "the main factor" was that "the Negro community, compared with the white world, is so predominantly lower class." He also noted that the black paper was sensational because it was an "additional" paper.

The black paper still is a second paper and no longer relies so heavily on sensationalism, an indication of the belief among publishers that the economic condition of readers is improved, that the taste for sensationalism has lessened, that other media are gratifying it, or that to attract the best advertisers such sensationalism must be decreased.

The Unmentioned Weaknesses

Defenses and explanations have been entered for the faults usually mentioned by adverse critics: questionable advertising, inadequate facilities and low salaries for employees, technically low-grade publications, accepting political bribery. These weaknesses are not attributed to all publications, although those resulting from inadequate and insufficient capitalization are general.

Several other weaknesses are not pointed out in the usual discussions of this press, possibly because they are to be found in portions of the American press of any color. They are inadequate news coverage, blatant use of publicity copy to please advertisers or extend policy, lack of attribution of much material, plagiarism, outcroppings of racial bigotry, indifference to skilled workmanship, and self-promotion by owners and editors.

Few black papers, or few white ones, are free of many dozens of inches of promotional copy for new movies, packaged products, television programs, night club entertainers, recordings, and other advertised products and services. A respected black journalist, L. F. Palmer, Jr., has put it thus: "Black newspapers . . . are greedy for handouts." This attitude is explained by lack of qualified editorial personnel and the impossibility of covering the black communities in competition with the metropolitan dailies.

The entire special sections of the general dailies that deal with the new automobile models, real estate developments, and general business progress in a community contain largely articles praising or in some way publicizing local business enterprises. This copy helps fill a few spaces on each page between the advertisements solicited especially to sustain these sections. In the black press such supplements are less common than in the white and are confined largely to the major papers and to areas in which advertising can be solicited: black educational institutions, local industry, and the national automobile companies. Such special sections, and the thousands of alleged news stories printed in the run of the paper, are handled with little subtlety. Hardly any attempt is made to print only such free publicity as contains genuine news value. Publicity copy is not useless per se; the best of it contains genuine news elements. But the black press often shows little discrimination in its use of such handouts.

On the women's page are the free publicity stories and pictures one has become accustomed to finding in these pages of gratis space for advertisers. On a typical day the page carries a fourteen-inch double-column story about the loveliness of Haiti — a land not known for its freedom from the conditions and restraints of which many blacks long have complained in the United States — accompanied by a twenty-inch photograph of a female tourist on a Haitian beach. Adjoining is a two-column photo of a girl cooking jellies, a picture provided by the firm that makes some of the ingredients mentioned in the recipes, obviously trade names. And at the bottom of the page is a five-column spread of four pictures, all of whites, supplied by a firm that makes clothing materials; its name is mentioned five times in the underlines.

The cutline below, including the misspelling, came from one of the major papers.

> JEWELLED — Model displays an assortment of modern costume jewelry by designer Robert Lee Morris. The bold "Disc" earrings and sculptural "beta cuffs" that are Morris' perennial bestsellers are often imitated and are an accessorey retailers like to recommend with sophisticated business clothes.

Publicity material of this type is blatant. One day alongside an advertisement for a car repair shop is a picture of the proprietor and a story praising his enterprise. On the front page is a three-column picture of the proprietors of a local supper club, its name in capitals, having "an impromptu chat" with a "popular" representative of a brewing company, the latter's personality reported to be one of the chief reasons that his products are highly favored by many tavern patrons. Such material is to be seen in the nonblack press as well, but that is no suitable model for the black papers.

Insufficient News Content

Aside from the large weeklies and certain middle-size city papers, the black newspaper publishers are engaged in producing many newspapers offering readers little news. This statement is not intended as a generalization about the black press. But in the author's possession are more than a score of current papers, the majority of them commercial ventures and not propaganda organs for groups defending causes, which present themselves to their readers as purveyors of news but actually contain little and make virtually no attempt at a systematic canvas of the black news sources, local, national, or international. He has seen as many more in libraries and in black publications offices, where they are received as exchanges. These publishers paste up material lifted from the large white papers or from magazines, print publicity releases without editing, and in other ways evade the responsibility for genuine local coverage and origination of news on their own. Usually there is some local news, perhaps four or five stories, most of them routine, but what actually is going on in the black community is only skimmed over. In one community there were serious racial disturbances in several parts of the city. The local black paper not only left the coverage to the white press (which published biased stories) but failed to provide any interpretation of the events in an effort to clarify causes.

As long ago as 1955 Simeon Booker pointed out that the surest way for white dailies to gain black readers is to print news of all kinds of black life. He noted that the Chicago *Tribune* outsold the more liberal Chicago *Sun-Times* and the Chicago *Daily News* in the black neighborhoods. "The *Trib*," a black told him, "was the first to pay attention to Negro news. They not only attend our meetings and affairs but they do feature stories on our leaders and outstanding citizens."[17]

The same principle holds for black publications, as the failures of some of the newsless cause papers should show as clearly as do the failures of the more-or-less newsless commercial papers intent on selling advertising space and pushing the news out of the columns to make room for it.

The contention is that it takes too much staff, and hence too much money, to cover the black community. But to go to press with a pasteup consisting of an editorial, many columns of free publicity stories containing few news elements, and nonlocal news filched from other papers shows little serious interest in being a newspaper. It shows only an interest in making money or an attempt to survive until money is made.

Failure to attribute the source of material occurs constantly in both small and large publications, newspapers and magazines alike. In many areas of the country are papers produced by the photocomposition process, which requires that the staff mount on sheets corresponding to pages the copy they wish reproduced, including illustrations and advertising. Thus it is a temptation to lift whatever is desirable from anywhere. One practice is to clip wire service stories from white dailies or other black papers that have paid for such copy, and trim out the initials or name of the agency. This deliberate plagiarism is known to the agencies and papers thus being robbed. But they are helpless to correct it, for the publications that resort to such practices have no money and a legal case would be fruitless. A further complication is that news is perishable and in the public domain the second day after it has been published. Damages would be difficult to prove if a weekly or biweekly lifted copy originally published ten days earlier. Readers have no knowledge of this background and credit such papers with being newsy. But alert readers remember having seen the identical material in the source publications and can draw their own conclusions about the initiative and integrity of the papers that clip and print so freely.

Even in some of the largest black weeklies many columns of news appear without indication of or even a clue to source. Some clearly is from the news bureaus of black institutions — colleges, National Urban League, and the NAACP. Many stories are matter-of-fact and are a service to an understaffed publication. But others are supposedly from the paper's own bureaus and stringers and are by no means impartial accounts of the news they allegedly report. When such stories come from small towns and large cities alike, the implications are that the paper has its own sources there.

The view that skilled workmanship is of little importance on many publications is easily enough supported. Although it is lessening as a fault because of the training more easily available to potential and practicing black journalists, it still is true that too little concern is shown for correctness of grammar, rhetoric, and spelling, journalistic form, conciseness, and clarity in writing. Ted Poston, one of the most capable black journalists, a prizewinning and courageous writer long identified with the New York *Post*, said in an article on the black press that "the average news story is badly written, poorly edited, and often based on rumors which could be easily checked."[18] There has been improvement in the decades since, but it is largely in some of the larger or exceptional middle-size papers. One can forgive such unprofessionalism in some small community paper conducted as a workshop experiment whose staff has no guidance or coaching and works as a group of volunteers.

The defenses are familiar. The alternative, the owners say, is to have no newspaper at all, for there is no time, between attempting to sell advertising space, obtain subscribers, write the copy, deal with the public, and do dozens of other jobs, to write headlines carefully, edit copy precisely, and plan artistic makeup. Especially if these are not crusading publications, the reply to that might be that perhaps some of these badly written and poorly edited papers are not needed, that they do more damage than good in their communities, and that they mar the influence and image of the black press as a whole.

Individual Attitudes

Articulate members of the black race are more specific than scholarly studies. Scientifically they may have no validity, but individual reactions of blacks to their own press are worth noting. Conversations with them bring results that are interesting, if nothing more.

There was the woman to whom the black press had meant nothing in a life spanning more than sixty years. Always employed in desk work by white organizations, this woman never used the black press or had it in evidence in her offices.

"Have you no interest, then, in the problems of the black race?" she was asked.

"On the contrary, indeed I have," she answered. "But the black papers never were needed in my work or my thinking about racial problems." The basic ones she depended on, it turned out, were those produced by the Society of Friends (Quakers), never lacking in understanding and assistance to the black people.

Another conversation was with a college-trained man about to get a law degree. It essentially was like those with an engineer, a social worker, housewife, teacher, and businessman on other occasions.

"Now and then I look at *Ebony*," the about-to-be lawyer said.

"Anything else?"

"Johnson has other publications I am aware of." He seemed to be groping for the titles. He assented when they were named.

"Yes, that's right. But I don't read them. I've just heard of and seen them. I also used to read the Pittsburgh *Courier*. But I don't read black papers any more. Too much in them is of no interest to me now. Too much family stuff and I'm still single. *Ebony* has a lot of everything but doesn't stand for anything editorially. No editorials."

His error about no editorials went unchallenged. Usually there is some such error about the black press in these conversations (one young man insisted *Esquire* is a black magazine), showing little close acquaintance with certain periodicals or papers. From others, mainly militant students and organization workers, comes the view that most black publications are Uncle Toms. In the late 1960s and early 1970s a well-edited press seemed less stimulating than that of the militant organizations. The frame of mind of those holding the latter view is represented by a letter in a newsmagazine that had carried an article about the black-owned Zebra advertising agency.

"What America's black community does not need," the letter

writer said, "is advertising that, like all advertising, will sell them $32 billion worth of generally useless and superfluous goods. I'm all in favor of black entrepreneurs in the black community, but not when they only turn out to be as destructive as the self-serving leeches in the drugs and numbers racket—they may be more legal but they are no more moral."[19]

With the major militant press now mute, its readers in some instances have abandoned the regular black publications entirely.

Constructive Efforts

Although there seems to have been no follow-up, early in 1969 there was formed a Black Student Press Association (BSPA) whose purpose was to improve the quality of the news media and to establish job opportunities for fellow college editors, as it was described.[20] Meeting in Washington, the college editors announced: "We don't necessarily want jobs in the mainstream of white journalism; we would like to devote our energies to making the black press a much more effective and relevant medium." The executive director of the group then was Jay Harris, of Lincoln University (Pennsylvania), who stressed the fact that the group intended to form a network of news communications involving students from both black and white schools. Although this plan appears to have petered out, others on foot to strengthen black journalism education may bring improvements such as were envisioned by BSPA.

Another scheme, to encourage publishers and owners of black publications to conduct community service programs, was that of the Coca-Cola Company, long a big advertiser. Annually since 1968 the firm has given an award to some paper during the NNPA convention. Named for the late Carl Murphy, of the *Afro-American* papers, it consisted of a plaque and one thousand dollars. Insofar as such a plan makes the black papers more useful to their communities, black citizens may feel a little closer to the press and support it.

From time to time the black publications have been told, usually by whites, that the black press needs to present a clearer image of itself to the country's advertisers if it is to have a favorable response from them. The owners need to develop sound reasons why their papers and magazines should be used as advertising tools.

The events of the past two decades have provided them with their opportunity, as some elements in business, industry, and government have made special efforts to employ blacks and have used both the display and classified advertising columns of the press to recruit. The moderate papers and magazines, which are the bulk of the journalism, have had such support and hence a way to keep an editorial message before their constituencies. And the backing has given them a new opportunity, in some instances, to offset the adverse criticisms that have surrounded the black press for many years, by correcting the faults so often attributed to that press. Some of the older publications have made such efforts. But the publishers of the new papers and magazines, often little more than neophytes, have failed to keep to the high standards. They cannot express all the reasons that genuinely explained why the early protest press was journalistically unprofessional.

If the economic pressure to survive can be relaxed still further, the black press already possesses an agency through which editors and publishers can work if they seek to raise standards or bring about more interest in reaching existing standards: the National Newspaper Publishers Association (NNPA). As with other press groups, it is the national organizations of those engaged in the work that can affect standards.

The NNPA might be preparing to launch activities other than its annual convention and its promotional plans in an effective effort to meet the kinds of unfavorable criticism being made now. It could do so through regional workshops, contests for greater technical excellence, community service and editorial courage, and the stimulation of research into the causes for the weaknesses and ways to eradicate them. But above all, it might help black journalists and publishers decide on their ever-important ideological positions in the light of developments toward the end of the twentieth century.

The NNPA cannot do all this without greater support from its members. Although its membership has grown in numbers, for financial reasons and consequent lack of staff it has lessened its activities. Plans exist to carry out programs likely to benefit the NNPA. Such programs would portray the black press favorably and gain more understanding of its purposes and potentialities.

The Future

Where is the black press heading? That question has been raised for years in newspaper and magazine articles and in parts of several books on this special journalism. The predictions are almost always confined to the press literally and do not include electronic journalism. They fall into three groups: the press will disappear, it will diminish but survive, or it will be a strong element in communication in this country.

Whatever the forecast, it is accompanied by suggestions for change, either to hold off death or to strengthen the press in the future.

As with all predictions, many uncertainties surround them: inventions, economic rises and falls, international wars or peace, worldwide health disasters or triumphs. All could sweep away hopes or elevate the press victoriously for the good of all. Assuming that the world and this nation remain on a more-or-less even keel and that plans can be made one should examine the points of view.

In the first edition of this book (1971), the author made no outright prediction. What was said, however, was interpreted by some readers and critics as a forecast of disaster. The situation was broken into parts, and the future was considered as it related to newspapers as distinguished from magazines and as each depended on social developments. In an article in *Commonweal* in 1950,[1] also published in *Negro Digest*, the author offered the view that full integration of the races could make the black press unnecessary. Both these publications and the book provoked rebuttal and helpful discussion.

The excitement over such ideas was reviewed in 1972. Henry G. La Brie III, who became a Ph.D. that year at the University of Iowa, wrote his dissertation on black journalists. He based his study on the results of interviews with scores of reporters, editors, and other black newspeople in various parts of the country. Subsequently he did considerable other writing on the black press and published his findings in various newspapers and magazines of both the black and white races. He produced substantial reports and edited and coauthored *Perspectives of the Black Press 1974*. In one chapter he reported that the black papers of the future are likely to be largely community publications.

Five years later, writing in *Editor & Publisher*, La Brie, under the title "The Disappearing Black Press," supplied figures showing that in number of papers, size of circulations, and number of employees, "the black press, as we have known it since 1827, is dying." He concluded the article thus: "The Black newspapers which will pass from the scene are those still relying on racism to guarantee their future. The publisher doesn't need to continue to remind advertisers of the buying power of the Black community. These facts are abundantly clear now. Instead, the Black publisher needs to impress corporations with his business acumen, his marketing research reports, his audited circulation and the journalistic skills of his newspaper."

The next year he had a strong ally. That ally was one of the most pessimistic prophets and at the same time an outstanding leader of the black newspaper business: John H. Sengstacke, head of the four-unit chain of papers bearing his name, and more than forty years ago founder of the National Newspaper Publishers Association (NNPA).

"The black press," Sengstacke wrote in 1980 for the NNPA convention journal, "is at a crossroad." In his opinion the press does not quite measure up to the demands of the time. "It is a question," he wrote, "whether we shall preserve our identity and continue the emphasis on black news or shift our focus."

He advised fellow publishers to consider integrating "in the social and economic spheres."

Chester Higgins, Sr., a prominent editor and publicist in the black communications realm, said, "We must do something, for our survival is at stake."[2]

These observations and predictions brought strong reaction. La Brie was told in an *Editor & Publisher* letter that he was right but had failed to give the reasons for the decline. The writer, W. Earl Douglas, a black columnist, was not pessimistic because he saw leadership that would solve the problems.

Thomas A. Johnson, a black reporter for the New York *Times*, covered the NNPA meeting and quoted one publisher with whom the delegates agreed generally when he said, "As long as there is racism in America, there will be a black press. I guess that assures us of life eternal."[3]

Dennis Schatzman, then city editor of the *New Pittsburgh Courier*, in 1979 published a lengthy article in *Editor & Publisher* defending the press and confronting the predictions of its demise. He said that the state of the black press came about because it was in a time of regression, "a resurgence of black press leadership and white power brokers" who want to downplay the future importance of the press, and the 152d anniversary of the press gave an opportunity to "access ["assess" was intended] its overall condition."

Schatzman reviewed the criticisms of La Brie, Gunnar Myrdal (discussed later in this chapter), and Carl Morris. The latter was a former general manager of the *Courier* who became a general assignment reporter for the large white-owned daily, the Pittsburgh *Gazette*. Morris had written in 1978 that there was danger the black press would become extinct.

Schatzman then cited the reasons he saw for circulation drops: establishment of more papers, false good feelings of blacks about white attitudes toward them, a decrease in reading as television became popular, the problem of nepotism, the NNPA being (in his opinion) a closed corporation. He also mentioned low salaries and mistakes in spelling, grammar, and typography. All then were excused by him on the basis that the same conditions exist in the white press world.

He concluded that the black press will survive because racism will keep it alive and the white press will not "truly cover the Black community as well as we do." To achieve this Schatzman said the papers must take the leadership role again in the black community, and publishers must become broad-based information providers and "gain support in home territory."[4]

In the late 1940s difficulties clearly were ahead for the American black press. Racial integration in education was on the move. This meant to some observers that in a few decades black newspapers and magazines would have little or no place. Newspaper circulations began dropping dramatically. Advertising space was as difficult to sell as at any time in the century, except for a few publications. Black consumer magazines were only just taking hold. Television was soon to become popular and to compete sharply with the print media.

Then, as the civil rights movement gained legal support, as there appeared a measure of popular backing for it from whites, and as the black Americans made known their desire for change in different ways, the future started to look less gloomy. A few consumer magazines became amazingly successful. Advertising dollars began to flow a little more easily. The purchasing power of some black citizens increased, as did their literacy. Racial pride stirred; there was an eagerness for knowledge of the black past in Africa as well as in America. The outlook improved for the black press.

A quarter of a century ago a leading black journalist, Chuck Stone, addressing the NNPA, urged the editors and publishers to take six steps.

He suggested that they "go daily." There are three dailies. Two appeared in 1964.

He urged publishers to "help inculcate in Negroes a reaffirmed pride in being Negro." There is considerable activity in showing pride in heritage, but it has not extended toward supporting a black institution like the press, except in a small number of communities.

Stone asked for unity in the black press by calling for it to pursue "power and speak as one voice on the great issues of the day."

He asked also for support of voter registration. More has been accomplished with this suggestion than any of the others.

He encouraged papers to improve their image, modernize typography, and the like. To some extent this has occurred, but scores of publications still have writers who use clumsy and incorrect English and editors who mar the papers with spelling errors in headlines and titles. And what may be worse, they call themselves newspapers but print little news while carrying numerous long articles based on wholly subjective views. The pages of papers both large and small carry many blatant, newsless publicity releases from advertisers or special pleaders. Some of the advertising space is bought, especially in magazines, by tobacco companies and wine and liquor firms. In this author's view, neither is needed by people in the black communities. Many of these living areas still do not have adequate housing, employment, and food.

His last proposal was that "the Negro press must find the soul of the Negro community and reflect it in its news pages."[5] Few black publications approach this challenge and most of those that have attempted to do so have failed because of rising costs and the indifference of black readers who did not give sufficient support to keep these periodicals afloat.

With the twentieth century only a handful of years from its end, the question of survival of the black press is being raised again. Some of the same reasons for doubts or hope exist, but new conditions must be taken into account. There are the rebels, for in some areas the revolutionary spirit of the 1960s and 1970s survives among black people. Government policies on both international and domestic affairs have polarized the American people regardless of race or color. Employment and income have improved for the black society at the same time that a minority of its members have opted for separatism and self-sufficiency. Television competition for the time of the audience has reached a new height. Integration of the races in education has been impeded in some quarters.

A Mortal Press

Always in danger of failure, the black press has survived despite great losses. No publication begun a century and a half ago has survived. Most of even fifty years ago are gone. Yet as an institution the press has continued, urged on by leaders who needed propaganda organs, by politicians who wanted voices, by white enemies who forced blacks to realize that their church and their press were their only outlets of expression.

At almost any point in its history it would have been reasonable to forecast the end of the press, either for economic or social reasons. In the late 1940s and early 1950s the speculators on the future of this press were in exactly opposite camps. One group, including Thomas W. Young, former president of the NNPA and business manager of the Norfolk *Journal and Guide*, thought that the black paper should see to its own disappearance by fighting against the injustices practiced against the black citizen, helping bring about democratic conditions that would make the papers unnecessary. Close to this school of thought were those who believed that racial integration would remove the need for a separate press. The author of this book, writing in 1949, observed that the press might be destined to remain a segregated one, and eventually would vanish as its readers lost their racial identity.[6]

The wrath produced by this prediction and similar ones was based more on fear of the implications to those connected with the press than on realization of the trends. Various side issues were introduced—whether the black people wanted segregation or were to blame for it, for example.

Subsequent events that no one had foreseen made the predictions of disappearance invalid in part. No one predicted that new social legislation would give blacks hope for just treatment. No one predicted a new rise to political power. Nor did anyone see that illegal wars would sharpen the contrast between an announced battle to the death for the rights of Asians to democratic freedoms and the treatment of minorities at home.

But the central idea persists: if there is racial amalgamation, a separate press may not be needed.

Simeon Booker, veteran black newsman and magazine writer, predicted in 1964 that "One of these days, the Negro press will be out of business. But it won't be for a generation or so. . . . It will continue to try to be the voice of the people inhabiting the ghettos in the cities with the poorest housing and the menial jobs. As long as the voice is strident, clear and militant, its function will be valued."[7] And in 1970 James D. Williams, a former editor of black newspapers and at the time director of the office of information and publication of the U.S. Commission on Civil Rights, wrote that "in a fully integrated society, the black press would shrink and eventually vanish, much in the manner of the foreign language press." He added, however: "Pending that . . . it is alive and well."[8] It should be noted, however, that the foreign language press has not vanished; because of the influx of Puerto Ricans and Cubans the Spanish segment has become one of the strongest, for example.

Chain Ownership: A Danger?

From the viewpoint of the readers, listeners, and viewers of the black media, there is a certain danger lurking in its future.

Consumers of all types of communications are in line to be victims of a trend gradually developing not only among black-owned media but also white-owned, including the book industry. That is the trend toward forming chains, or groups of publications or stations, into conglomerates. As small as the black press is by comparison with the huge nonblack enterprises, the process is still occurring. Some of the chains have a half-dozen units.

Such an assembly is minuscule when compared with those of the general field. The Gannett Company, for instance, owns about one hundred newspapers as well as radio and television stations, magazines, and other units. Also large are the white chains of Knight-

Ridder, Thomson, Hearst, Ingersoll, Murdoch, Donrey, Park, and Newhouse. The latter owns large book and magazine publishing companies and a syndicate in addition to a dozen major newspapers and as many broadcasting stations.

Chain ownership has been debated for many years. Its pros and cons are now well understood. Such ownership makes for more economical operations. Supplies can be bought in quantity, and some firms are so large they can own and operate their own supply sources. Editorial and advertising copy can be shared by two or more units. Staff can gain a variety of experience by working on different units within the firm. Profits can be higher, with advantages to stockholders or individual owners.

But what also can occur under ownership of multiple units is elimination of competition with the likelihood of an unopposed editorial policy. Reducing direct competition not only stifles discussion but also decreases the number of publications or stations and consequently the number of jobs. It also gives publishers an advertising monopoly. In the United States only fifty-five cities have competing dailies, and of these twenty-one are issued from printing plants owned jointly with another paper and sometimes with common advertising or business departments.

Among black weeklies, since the three dailies are in only that many cities, there is proportionately more competition. Thirty-three U.S. cities have two or more black papers, almost all weeklies. Seven have three papers each, three have four each, one has five papers, and one has six. These figures are from a base of ninety-seven papers. Some of the chains have units in multiple weekly cities but at the same time own the single paper in other places.

The success of chain ownership inevitably will move publishers who find the going financially rough either to turn to chain publishing or to cease publishing. In either case, the cause of democracy will not be served, since there will be fewer voices or more dissemination of a single point of view.

The Myrdal View

Gunnar Myrdal, the Swedish economist, in his landmark study of the American black society interpreted the situation in the 1940s differently than did the prophets of doom. "The

Negro press is bound to become even stronger as Negroes are increasingly educated and culturally assimilated but not given entrance to the white world," he wrote.[9] He was even more encouraging than that. He also said that better coverage of black activities by the white press would not substitute for the black publications. The news of blacks would continue, he believed, to have a relatively low news value to whites. An editor of a white paper, no matter how sympathetic to blacks, would reach a point where he could not satisfy the demand for black news without alienating whites. He would not have room for the news wanted by the white majority. The newspapers—and Myrdal concerned himself largely with them and not magazines—would grow as the level of education rose, the cultural differences between blacks and other Americans decreased, race consciousness and race solidarity were intensified, and the protests were stronger. Because circulations would be larger, more advertising would be obtained. The resulting income would produce material improvements—better equipment and enlarged and more capable staff. Weekly frequency would dominate, but a few dailies might succeed.

Earl Conrad was one of the few to contest Myrdal's views. He pointed out that the forecast was concerned with the press only as a business institution and that in effect Myrdal said that the press had to base its future on the continuance of segregation.[10]

Forty years later parts of Myrdal's predictions had been fulfilled. The optimism still exists, but for other reasons than those he gave. Some newspaper circulations grew for a time but then fell off badly. Advertising revenue increased, not because of larger circulations but because the white advertisers wanted a share of the black consumer market, needed black personnel, or wished to support the moderate black press as a force against revolutionary elements. Some improvements in equipment resulted, but staff was not, on the whole, much enlarged or even professionally so much better trained, especially on the many new publications launched in the 1960s and 1970s. The papers did persist as weekly publications, a few became semiweeklies, and two were coming out four or five times a week.

What Myrdal and the contributors to his remarkable study did not foresee was the rise of the black consumer magazines. Only *Opportunity* and the *Crisis* were mentioned; the first disappeared and the second remained an organization spokesman until the early 1980s. Nor did they anticipate the impact of general television on newspaper advertising sales and reading and its domination of viewers' time.

Other Hopeful Prophets

Myrdal was not the only optimist. Armistead S. Pride, while chairman of the journalism department at Lincoln University; Louis E. Lomax, black author and journalist; and D. Parke Gibson, publicist, in subsequent years were among those who were hopeful of growth and strength. Pride, writing in 1951, wondered what the size and character of the black press would be fifty years later or at that great division year, A.D. 2000. He decided that "it seems reasonable to expect that Negro newspapers will be published for a long time to come," an opinion to be taken seriously, since it came from a scholar of black newspaper history. He relied for this view on "the momentum which the larger Negro papers have gained, their growing prestige and know-how, their knack of appealing to a special class as well as to an enlarging clientele of different races, and their role as special pleaders for the rights of minority groups. . . . "[11]

But Pride also said that this future depended on their honesty in "throwing the spotlight on injustice, graft, lawlessness, discrimination, inferior educational facilities, hunger, lack of sanitary and healthful conditions." The rise of new protest papers, apparently at the expense of the standard weeklies, temporarily indicated that enough of the black people did not believe the press was fighting their cause hard enough to support his prophecy, but that protest diminished.

Lomax, writing ten years later, said that at the time it was true that there was a separate group of readers with "special interests that can be appealed to and exploited." But he predicted that there would come a time when the Negro revolution will make it less true and "it is against this day that the Negro individual who is a publisher must begin now to make his plans."[12] He did not reckon, however, with the rise of separatism and the growth of pride in being black that led the black society, by the end of that decade, to be more loyal to what is its own, at least in the form of magazines and radio programs and books. But not newspapers.

He faced the idea, in a short-range forecast, of the black press becoming a general news medium. He feared that if it did it would be moving in "a market where new entries die like flies. The immediate future of the Negro press seems to be that of a community newspaper and its future to be tied to that of the Negro church and Negro social clubs."[13] The rise of small community papers, the great reliance of the large weeklies on such church and club news to hold circulation, are evidence of the shrewdness of his forecast. In the long run, however, he was pessimistic. He noted that the other American ethnic groups at that time had their own newspapers, churches, and clubs. But the support of the institutions of these other groups was beginning to shrink, and he believed that that would happen to the black press and church, in time. "For, as housing and job barriers fall, Negroes will drift from the ghetto into general American life, where they will rise to positions of prominence and leadership in the general American community, as Americans rather than as Negroes."[14]

Gibson, with the optimism so typical of the public relations man who moves among advertising executives and marketing experts, in another decade wrote that he believed that the Negro market "will continue to exist for years to come" because of the factors that formed it, for they continue to exist. A market is available, therefore, to advertisers via either the black or white press; it is implied that a black press will be needed to service the advertisers. He saw population concentration going on, the birth rate continuing to exceed that of the whites, income on the increase. He also saw a new mood in the black community. That mood is "an increasing pride in blackness that for so long was denied. The Negro is becoming more self-conscious of being a Negro, and he is accepting this with pride," Gibson wrote.[15]

Two young black journalists, both experienced in white as well as black news work, in 1970 gave still other reasons for their view that the press will continue. L. F. Palmer, Jr., then a columnist and reporter for the white Chicago *Daily News*, wrote that the established black press will survive because, as Louis E. Martin, onetime vicepresident of the Sengstacke Newspapers has said, so long as there is white racism there will be black papers. But Martin admitted that the black papers will have to become more relevant in point of view as well as in news presentation.[16] George M. Daniels, a former Associated Negro Press staffer and reporter for the Chicago *Defender* and later a church publicist, was optimistic about the future of the press. Speaking about it at Syracuse University, he said he believed it would remain a protest organ but politically moderate. It will continue to grow because, when measured by the number of new publications that continue rather than by the size of circulations, there was growth already evident in the early 1970s. This stability, he explained, is limited to the rise in advertising expenditures by black business, giving black publications less dependence on white advertisers; especially, Daniels believes, is this true of the small community papers.

Other stabilizing trends he saw were the policy of diversifying being practiced by increasing numbers of publishing firms, the purchase of small papers by bigger ones to increase chain or group holdings, the raising of capital by companies going public, and the lower costs of production possible through technological developments such as offset printing.

"A black press always will be needed," Daniels said, "because the white cannot cover the black news in detail, such as marriages, births, and the activities of blacks in government." He predicted also resumption of a national black wire service and expansion of Washington coverage and foresaw more journalism education at black colleges.[17]

Internal Handicaps

The future of the black press is greatly dependent on external developments such as acceptance or rejection by its natural audience or its success in selling advertising space to both black and white buyers. Population growth, internal conditions, and attitudes are important also.

The press of the United States, black and white alike, never has been known for its progressiveness, either in its social ideas or its technology. Except for a minority of newspapers and magazines, it generally has opposed social changes and defended the status quo.[18] For many years the nation's conservatives have been able to count on the consumer or general circulation newspapers and magazines for support. Democratic party presidential candidates, from Franklin D. Roosevelt on, with the exception of Lyndon B. Johnson, have not gained the editorial backing of the bulk of the white newspaper owners, and most magazines, being highly specialized, have not raised their voices. Minority party candidates, such as Norman Thomas, Henry Wallace, and George Wallace, although at opposite poles ideologically, have had little support from the consumer press, including the black.

Such caution extends even to the physical aspects and management of the press itself, particularly the newspaper segment, for it has been slow to effect internal changes that would enable it to keep pace with the times. For that reason, and also for some lesser ones, some of the nation's most famous white dailies and periodicals disappeared between 1950 and 1985, including the New York *Herald Tribune*, the New York *World-Telegram*, the original *Saturday Evening Post*, the *American*, and *Collier's*.

The black press is no exception although it never has been, nor could it have been, in a financial position to keep up with the times in techniques and methods. Thus it cannot be blamed for failing, since it could not be expected to try. But ideologically, by and large, it has played safe, earning for itself the condemnation of the black race's noted sociologists and of some of the few other scholars who have sought to evaluate it.

As the last decade of the twentieth century nears, the standard American black press finds itself confronting a public split as never before in its history. Its potential black audience is, on the one hand, a large middle-class group of economically and educationally develop-ing citizens still getting their entertainment from the mass media, black or white; and on the other, a small, potent group—the militant blacks who want change and want it at once and have among them a few leaders determined to get it by any means that will work. A third group, not part of its potential audience, is the lower economic and education population from whence statistics about black poverty and illiteracy still are drawn.

For awhile, the established black press also saw the development of an underground or advocacy press serving the militants and scorn-ing the traditional publications or those who direct and edit them. The regular press sought to adjust, taking over some of the less dis-turbing causes on which there would not be much weakening of the rapport with advertisers. It also began seeking ways, therefore, to keep its circulation from slipping away to the outright protest publica-tions.

The slowness to improve their plants, forced upon them by low income and lack of capital, was challenged by plans for new publish-ing projects. These came, for example, from the Black Economic Development Conference, a group that demanded a half-billion dol-lars from white churches in 1969. Although the program received little of the money wanted, some grants were made. Neither this effort nor the experiment with facsimile transmission succeeded and thus had no effect on the black press. Cable television, however, has added strength to the competition from broadcasting.

Despite these and other technological changes the papers still were being thrown onto the porches or the apartment doorsteps, and the magazines continued to arrive by mail or to crowd each other out of sight on newsstands, the technological miracles confined to using computers in typesetting and other behind-the-scenes operations, such as circulation-list updating and selection of subscribers' names for special promotion schemes. Since little of this technology has as yet touched the black press, it may be some time before present-day publishers will gain the advantages or be faced with the necessity to scrap their present equipment.

Continuing as Protestors

Some observers of the black press, mainly of the newspaper, have said that to survive it must continue to fulfill its original mission as a protest press. Even so moderate a businessman at Kenneth O. Wilson, when vice-president of the *Afro-American* papers, has been quoted as saying that the papers have the role of creating a climate in which business and industry can participate and that those black papers are strong that take up the great issues that affect the black consumer most, giving as examples the war on poverty, open housing, equal public accommodation, and representation at the very highest state, county, and municipal levels. The editors will keep their ears to the ground for the big story that affects Negroes one way or the other, he said.[19]

Similar advice came from Simeon Booker. He said that the press must be simultaneously a service and an entertainment institution. It must engage in what he calls "uplift projects, self-improvement and educational campaigns and inspirational stories to revive our discouraged populace." It also will need to continue giving attention to the lives of stars, personalities, society queens, and cultists.[20]

The likelihood of the black press becoming uniformly more outspoken in its protest function may be hampered by several circumstances. One is the climate of opinion existing at any one time in the nation. A black publication could hope to do little protesting in one of the notoriously repressive communities of the country, where even white protest journalism has hard going. Another danger, one that may seem remote at this time, is that as black people more and more break out of second-class citizenship and gain access to middle-class comforts and conveniences, they will be captured by the hedonism so typical of the white society. The white press and broadcasting media have played a large part in firming up the philosophy of the worth of pleasure and ease for their own sakes.

Signs can be found that this tone is rising in the black press, particularly in certain of the magazines, which through their editorial and advertising matter treat as of paramount importance the achievement of status by possessions. It is made to seem significant that the black woman use the right shade of lipstick or see the merit of false eyelashes, and that she think it desirable to dress as does the reigning black queen of the television screen or Las Vegas nightclubs—or that the primary goals of young black men should be to become nationally famous sports stars paid millions and owning posh homes. Such is not the atmosphere in which a fight for civil rights or social justice thrives.

Black publishers doubtless do not believe that the emphasis on luxury items such as perfumes, furs, extra television sets, record players, videos, and home computers is a contradiction in any program of crusades for social reform; when such items mean more advertising income it is difficult to denigrate them. But even if they do object, it is unlikely that they can do more than drift, as the white press has been drifting for years. All are dependent on the economic order. Only correctives for that order, joined with a new moral concept that defies the hedonists and gives whites as well as blacks long-lasting goals, can arrest the trend.

The altruism and goodwill that have guided black Americans in the fight for justice may dissipate in the pursuit of pleasure, which seems to be the main occupation of many middle-class citizens of any race or color. And the black press, for the sake of its own survival, has an opportunity now to play an important part by providing leadership to its readers by its editorial emphasis.

The Place of Racial Harmony

Racial harmony is another factor in the black press' future. Some blacks have come to believe that they have a greater awareness of blackness by being among nonblacks than by being among persons of their own race. This view causes them sometimes to take positions in white institutions rather than in black. But others would reverse that—and they are the black segregationists. Two groups—those with a loyalty to the idea of blacks overriding their desire to be among whites and those who feel uncomfortable and in need of more self-confidence when not among black people—also will keep a black press alive. The press depends on such racial harmony, limited as it may be.

But a larger harmony is possible: the harmony of the American people. And such harmony may, in the long run, benefit the black press more than the harmony of like minds about racial segregation to preserve the black heritage. If John W. Gardner, the former Health, Education and Welfare secretary, was right, the black press may someday play a larger part after an unhappy schism in American society. For in the 1960s he predicted that if no way was found to reverse the trend of that time — increasing conflict between the races — the United States would end up as two nations, "with an embittered and angry nation within a nation, with two peoples who don't know each other, don't mingle, and meet only to vent their hostility."[21]

It takes but little imagination to see the entire black press function as did the militant press of the 1960s and 1970s, leading a nationalist movement and fighting for separatism. But it will come about only if there is one or the other kind of harmony: complete separatism or complete cooperation with other races. What is demanded of the black press is that it have the same zeal and devotion for harmony as the separatists have for their philosophy.

To sum up, it appears that in the future the black press may:

1. Survive and thrive because black Americans are proud of their race and are working for the survival of their culture. The press should benefit from that trend. But its owners must be alert, if they are to keep pace. They cannot fall behind the educational growth and cultural development of their readers, nor do they dare move too much in advance of them. At the same time, they must solve the difficult problem of crusading for causes important to black people while not alienating the business interests on which they depend. The publishers have the possibility of seeing the press grow slowly but firmly in economic security, either because of the unity of separatism or the unity of cooperation between the races.

2. Fail because of the separatism desired by numbers of black people — intellectual leaders, such as teachers, authors, clergy, and students — and the possibility that it will be weak, with the result that integration of the races may resume in full strength and the press may be faced with the threat of the 1940s and 1950s once more. Unless it makes itself essential to the black people, it might disappear as an unnecessary journalism.

3. Succeed because, at least for many generations, there will be a black race, for the eventual amalgamation of the races will not occur as rapidly as integrationists desire. It will be a small press still. The success, it now appears, lies more with the magazines than the news-

papers, which are weaker in number and circulation and, for many, still are not well established as advertising carriers. These conditions limit their outreach and influence. The new magazines often are professional and commercial ventures and dependent less on an organization than on general public support — readers and advertisers. The magazine's economic plan is a sounder and more independent one in a participatory democracy. As the white newspapers cover the black society more and more, the black magazine will supply readers with in-depth writing, fiction, and other materials for the ethnic group that will not, in sufficient quantity, be available through white periodicals and that cannot reasonably be expected to appear there.

Since the early 1960s the author has contended in various books and articles that the future of the magazine industry in the United States as a whole is with the specialized periodicals, not the giant consumer-aimed ones.[22] Events have borne out the prediction, for the *Saturday Evening Post* failed a few years after *Collier's* and a few other leaders, and in the early 1970s both *Life* and *Look* were having their economic troubles as were some other large periodicals. The *Post* and *Life* were reborn, but they are not comparable to their earlier versions.

That the future of the black magazine is in the hands of the specialized periodical rather than the consumer is even more certain. The black population, even if it someday reaches the point when economically it could support many large consumer magazines, would be no more likely to do so than the general public. What is even more important, or at least less speculative, is that the costs of production and distribution, which are enormous portions of the large magazine's cost schedules, not only will continue to increase but also will be even more difficult for the black magazine publisher to handle. With the exception of *Ebony, Jet*, and *Essence*, none ever has been able to command a volume of advertising at all comparable to that of the large white publications. The small, less costly operation of the specialized magazine aimed at a definable reader group can hope for survival. *Black Enterprise* is a prime example.

If the large black magazine survives it must win white as well as black readers to be of influence in the white world as well as the black. This effort can be motivated by both the desire for commercial success as well as the hope of bringing about greater understanding between the people of each race. It is dubious, however, that it can offset the economic hazards of mass circulation.

It is likely, therefore, that a black press of some sort always will be available in the United States, unless *fully integrated* means the complete eradication of the black experience, culture, temperament, and personality. Whether it will be an important and influential press depends on the social changes occurring without respect to race.

NOTES

Preface to the Second Edition

1. S. E. Anderson, review of *Neo-African Literature*, by Janheinz Jahn, *Black Scholar* 1, nos. 3, 4 (Jan.–Feb. 1970): 76, 79.

1 / The Black Press Defined

1. Kent de Felice, "The Black Press Defined" (Syracuse, N.Y.: School of Journalism, Syracuse University, Jan. 1969).
2. "Negro Paper Gives Backing to Wallace," *Press* State Service account in Cleveland *Press*, 17 Nov. 1968; "Whites Own Negro Paper for Wallace," Associated Press dispatch in Cleveland *Plain Dealer*, 22 Nov. 1968.
3. "Neutral Term," *Editor & Publisher* 101, no. 11 (Mar. 1968): 7.
4. "Black Militants Flay D.C. Press Policies," *Guild Reporter* (20 June 1969): 2.
5. Clyde Reid, "Why There's a Need for a Black Press Today," *Editor & Publisher* 12, no. 10 (7 Mar. 1967): 60.
6. Henry Lee Moon, "Beyond Objectivity: The 'Fighting Press,'" in *Race and the News Media*, eds. Paul L. Fisher and Ralph R. Lowenstein (New York: Praeger, 1967), 139.
7. Susan Rittenhouse, Syracuse University.
8. O. Rudolph Aggrey, former U.S. Ambassador to The Gambia and Romania, letter to the author, 14 May 1987.
9. George E. Daniels, executive editor, *New World Outlook* magazine, letter to the author, 13 May 1987.
10. Charles V. Willie, professor of education and urban studies, Harvard University, letter to the author, 15 July 1987.

2 / The Beginnings

1. Earl Conrad, *Jim Crow America* (New York: Duell, Sloan & Pearce, 1947), 6.
2. Rosalynde Ainslie, *The Press in Africa* (London: Gollancz, 1966), 21–22.
3. I. Garland Penn, *The Afro-American Press and Its Editors* (Springfield, Mass.: Willey, 1891; New York: Arno Press, New York *Times*, 1969), 28.

405

4. Bella Gross, "Freedom's Journal and the Rights of All," *Journal of Negro History* 17, no. 3 (July 1932): 241–86.
5. Penn, *Afro-American Press,* 30.
6. Armistead S. Pride, "A Register and History of Negro Newspapers in the United States: 1827–1950" (Ph.D. diss., Northwestern University, 1950), 4.
7. Carter Bryan, "Negro Journalism in America before the Emancipation," *Journalism Monographs* 12 (Sept. 1969): 30.
8. Ibid., 1.
9. Ronald K. Burke, "The Anti-Slavery Activities of Samuel Ringgold Ward in New York State," *Afro-Americans in New York Life and History* 2, no. 1 (Jan. 1978): 17. See also Penn, *Afro-American Press,* 62.
10. Penn, *Afro-American Press,* 67.
11. Theodore Draper, "The Father of American Black Nationalism," *New York Review of Books* 14, no. 5 (12 Mar. 1970): 33.
12. Frederick Douglass, *Narrative of the Life of Frederick Douglass* (New York: New American Library, 1968), 21–22.
13. For discussion of the differences see Benjamin Quarles, *Frederick Douglass* (Washington, D.C.: Associated Publishers, 1948), 70–79.
14. Philip S. Foner, *Frederick Douglass* (New York: Citadel Press, 1963), 278–79, 311–12.
15. Frederick Douglass, *My Bondage and My Freedom* (New York: Miller, Orton & Mulligan, 1885), 389–90.
16. Charles S. Johnson, "The Rise of the Negro Magazine," *Journal of Negro History* 13, no. 1 (Jan. 1928): 10.
17. Frederick G. Detweiler, *The Negro Press in the United States* (Chicago: University of Chicago Press, 1922; College Park, Md.: McGrath, 1968), 42–43.
18. Penn, *Afro-American Press,* 78–79.
19. Detweiler, *Negro Press,* 44.
20. Pride, "Register and History," 97.
21. See Chapter 5 for discussion of black daily papers.
22. Pride, "Register and History," 71.
23. Penn, *Afro-American Press,* 114.
24. Armistead S. Pride, "Negro Newspapers: Yesterday, Today, and Tomorrow," *Journalism Quarterly* 28, no. 2 (Spring 1951): 180–81.
25. Earl Conrad, "The Negro Press," *Tomorrow* 6, no. 3 (Nov. 1946): 6.
26. Penn, *Afro-American Press,* 367.
27. Arna Bontemps and Jack Conroy, *They Seek a City* (Garden City, N.Y.: Doubleday, Doran, 1945), 77–79.

3 / Black Journalism Enters the Twentieth Century

1. The original Baltimore edition was founded in 1892. Other editions: Washington, 1933; Philadelphia, 1934; Richmond, 1939; New Jersey, 1940.
2. *Good News for You! The Afro-American Newspapers* (Baltimore: The Afro-American Co., 1969), 5–7.
3. Charles Flint Kellogg, *NAACP*, vol. 1 (Baltimore: Johns Hopkins Press, 1967), 70.
4. Frederick G. Detweiler, *The Negro Press in the United States* (Chicago: University of Chicago Press, 1922; College Park, Md.: McGrath, 1968), 55–56; I. Garland Penn, *The Afro-American Press and Its Editors* (Springfield, Mass.: Willey, 1891; New York: Arno Press, New York *Times*, 1969), 133–38.

5. Detweiler, *Negro Press*, 56.

6. Jack Lyle, *The News in Megalopolis* (San Francisco: Chandler, 1967), 167.

7. Penn, *Afro-American Press*, 133–38; "Negroes on Dailies," *Lincoln Journalism Newsletter* 2, no. 6 (15 June 1946): 7.

8. Detweiler, *Negro Press*, 55; the passage appeared originally in the Autumn 1920 issue of *Favorite* magazine.

9. W. E. B. Du Bois, *The Autobiography of W. E. B. Du Bois* (New York: International Publishers, 1968), 238.

10. Lerone Bennett, Jr., *Pioneers in Protest* (Baltimore: Penguin Books, 1969), 221.

11. Bennett has brought together the basic facts; Du Bois gives various personal glimpses; a useful supplement is Carl Senna, "The Man Who Published 'The Guardian,'" Boston *Sunday Globe*, 1 Dec. 1968.

12. Roi Ottley, *The Lonely Warrior: The Life and Times of Robert S. Abbott* (Chicago: Regnery, 1955), 2. The major events in Abbott's life are summarized here; all other sources are brief passages in books or short articles.

13. E. Franklin Frazier, *Black Bourgeoisie* (Glencoe, Ill.: The Free Press, 1957), 149.

14. Enoch R. Waters, *American Diary: A Personal History of the Black Press* (Chicago: Path Press, 1987), Chapter 10.

15. Du Bois, *Autobiography*. Material for this section was drawn not only from this autobiography but also from Francis L. Broderick, *W. E. B. Du Bois: Negro Leader in Time of Crisis*; Elliott M. Rudwick, *W. E. B. Du Bois: Propagandist of the Negro Protest*; and the chapter on Du Bois in Bennett, *Pioneers in Protest*. See Bibliography for complete information.

16. Bennett, *Pioneers in Protest*, 249.

17. Detweiler, *Negro Press*, 165–66.

18. Ibid., 171.

19. Ibid., 170.

20. Ottley, *Life and Times*, 291.

21. Frank W. Miles, "Negro Magazines Come of Age," *Magazine World* 2, no. 8 (1 June 1946): 12–13.

22. Ottley, *Life and Times*, 125.

23. Du Bois, *Autobiography*, 241.

24. Bennett, *Pioneers in Protest*, 237.

25. "Rangel Seeks Exoneration of Marcus Garvey," States News Service, New York *Times*, 5 Apr. 1987.

26. Edmund David Cronon, *Black Moses: The Story of Marcus Garvey and the Universal Negro Improvement Association* (Madison: University of Wisconsin Press, 1955), 46.

27. Allon Schoner, ed., *Harlem on My Mind: Cultural Capital of Black America, 1900–1968* (New York: Random House, 1968), 54.

28. "Publisher of Nation's First Negro Daily Is Dead," Buffalo *Evening News*, 22 June 1961.

29. James Booker, *History of the New York* Amsterdam News (New York: *Amsterdam News*, 1967), 1–4.

30. Armistead S. Pride, "A Register and History of Negro Newspapers in the United States: 1827–1950" (Ph.D. diss., Northwestern University, 1950), 161.

31. Ibid., 138–39.

32. Detweiler, *Negro Press*, 68.

33. Ibid., 154.

34. Ibid., 155.

35. Ibid., 156.
36. William O. Walker, "Anniversary of the Negro Press," Atlanta *Daily World*, 12 Mar. 1970.
37. Earl Conrad, "The Negro Press," *Tomorrow* 6, no. 3 (Nov. 1946): 8.

4 / World War II and After

1. As quoted from a 1942 syndicated column in Maxwell R. Brooks, *The Negro Press Re-examined* (Boston: Christopher, 1959), 24.
2. "Publishers: Owners of Negro Newspapers Are Hard-Headed, Farsighted, Race Conscious Businessmen," *Ebony*, Nov. 1949, 47–51.
3. Roi Ottley, *The Lonely Warrior: The Life and Times of Robert S. Abbott* (Chicago: Regnery, 1955), 363.
4. "Powell on Press," *Lincoln Journalism Newsletter* 1, no. 5 (Feb. 1945): 11.
5. Chuck Stone, *Black Political Power in America* (Indianapolis, Ind.: Bobbs-Merrill, 1968), 189.
6. "Matthews on Powell," *Lincoln Journalism Newsletter* 1, no. 5 (Feb. 1945): 11.
7. "Harlem Paper Held Aiding Negroes' Foes Plays 'Uncle Tom' Role, Red Critic Says," New York *Times*, 19 Dec. 1947.
8. James Baldwin, *Notes of a Native Son* (New York: Bantam Books, 1968), 50.
9. Gordon Parks, *A Choice of Weapons* (New York: Harper & Row, 1966), 192.
10. As related to the author by Johnson in 1969.
11. A. James Reichley, "How Johnson Made It," *Fortune* 77, no. 1 (Jan. 1968): 152.
12. Ibid., 178.
13. Ibid.
14. Walter Goodman, "*Ebony*: Biggest Negro Magazine," *Dissent* 15, no. 5 (Sept.–Oct. 1968): 404.
15. Institutional advertisement printed in various white newspapers and magazines at different times in the early 1960s.

5 / Today's Major Newspapers

1. A group consists of directly linked papers, each responsible to the same headquarters office; a chain is a series of more or less independent papers under a common ownership.
2. Robert D. Bontrager, "An Investigation of Black Press and White Press Use Patterns in the Black Inner City of Syracuse, New York" (Ph.D. diss., Syracuse University, 1969), 93.
3. Andrew Radolf, "More at Stake than Profits for National Black Weekly," *Editor & Publisher* 116, no. 23 (4 June 1983): 13, 20–22.
4. Officially a six-day daily, in 1969 and 1970, because of a strike by employees, its frequency varied from three to four issues a week; it went on a four-day schedule thereafter.
5. L. F. Palmer, Jr., "The Black Press in Transition," *Columbia Journalism Review* 9, no. 1 (Spring 1970): 36.
6. Armistead S. Pride, "The Negro Newspaper in the United States," *Gazette* 2, no. 3 (1956): 143.
7. Robert U. Brown, "Shop Talk at Thirty: The Negro Press," *Editor & Publisher* 97, no. 29 (18 July 1964): 54.

6 / Local Newspaper Voices

1. John Reid, "Black America in the 1980s," *Population Bulletin* 27, no. 4 (Dec. 1982): 23–24.
2. "Editors Die Poor," *Lincoln Journalism Newsletter* 10, no. 9 (Sept. 1955): 1–2.
3. "Fresno State Hears Black Publisher," *Quill* 58, no. 5 (May 1970): 35.
4. D. Parke Gibson, *The $30 Billion Negro* (New York: Macmillan, 1969), 31–46.
5. Cited by Sharyn Smith in a study of this and other black community papers made in 1968–69 at Syracuse University.
6. Jack Lyle, *The News in Megalopolis* (San Francisco: Chandler, 1967), 163–82.
7. Ibid., 164.
8. Frederic C. Coonradt, *The Negro News Media and the Los Angeles Riots* (Los Angeles: School of Journalism, University of Southern California, 1965), 47.
9. Brian White, "Black Newspapers Add to Media Mix," *Business Journal, Focus: Printing and Graphics*, magazine section, 14 Sept. 1987, 5.
10. "College Aroused by Negro Paper/Revolutionaries Gain Control of Wayne State Daily," New York *Times*, 21 Feb. 1969.
11. "CSU Blacks Publish Own Paper," Cleveland *Plain Dealer*, 20 Jan. 1970.

7 / The Black Magazines—the Front-runners

1. Raymond Franzen, *Magazine Audiences in the Urban Negro Market* (New York: Our World Publishing Co., 1951), 9.
2. *"Our World* Goes Bankrupt Owing 20 Ad Agencies," *Advertising Age* 16, no. 49 (Dec. 1955): 109.
3. Walter Goodman, *"Ebony:* Biggest Negro Magazine," *Dissent* 15, no. 5 (Sept.– Oct. 1968): 407.
4. Letter to the editor, *Ebony* 23, no. 8 (June 1968): 21.
5. *Ebony* 24, no. 3 (Jan. 1969): 14.
6. *"Jet,"* *Lincoln Journalism Newsletter* 8, no. 2 (15 Feb. 1952): 3.
7. Alfred Balk, "Mr. Johnson Finds His Market," *Reporter* 21, no. 8 (12 Nov. 1959): 35.
8. Robert E. Johnson, "President Johnson Gives Views on Riot Report/Says Report Is 'Most Important,' " *Jet* 33, no. 26 (Apr. 1968): 14.
9. Letter to the editor, *New Lady* 2, no. 3 (Nov. 1969): 2.
10. Thomas H. Allen, "Mass Media Use Patterns in a Negro Ghetto," *Journalism Quarterly* 45, no. 3 (Aug. 1968): 525.
11. Jack Lyle, *The News in Megalopolis* (San Francisco: Chandler, 1967), 178.
12. William David Stephenson II, "Magazines and Black Americans: An Evolving Relationship" (Master's thesis, Syracuse University, 1969), 149–63; Robert D. Bontrager, "An Investigation of Black Press and White Press Use Patterns in the Black Inner City of Syracuse, New York," (Ph.D. diss., Syracuse University, 1969), 197–203.
13. Paul M. Hirsch, "An Analysis of *Ebony:* The Magazine and Its Readers," *Journalism Quarterly* 45, no. 2 (Summer 1968): 261–70, 292.
14. Gary A. Puckrein, letter to the author, 6 May 1987.
15. "The New Achievers," *Black Enterprise* 16, no. 1 (Aug. 1986): 29.
16. *"Black Enterprise* Plans Research on Black Consumer," *Advertising Age* 43, no. 29 (17 July 1972): 20.
17. Communication businesses included in the 1987 report were Johnson Publishing

Co., which was No. 1 in the entire list; Inner City Broadcasting, N.Y., No. 26; Essence Communications, Inc., No. 42; Queen City Broadcasting, N.Y., No. 54; and Earl G. Graves Ltd., No. 87. "The Top 100 Black Businesses," *Black Enterprise* 17, no. 11 (June 1987): 131–37.
18. Frank C. Kent, "Publisher's Message. Frankly Speaking," *Black Family*, Spring 1986, 4.
19. Thomas L. Atkins and Michael H. Sussman, "Reaganisms, Reaganauts and the NAACP," *Crisis* 89, no. 1 (Jan. 1982): 5–8.
20. Earl G. Graves, "What the Constitution Means to Black America," *Black Enterprise* 17, no. 12 (July 1987): 11.

8 / The Black Magazines—the Specialists

1. Carolyn Gerald, "The Measure and Meaning of the Sixties," *Negro Digest* 19, no. 1 (Nov. 1969): 27.
2. Ibid., 28.
3. Ernest Kaiser, "Five Years of *Freedomways*," *Freedomways* 6, no. 2 (Spring 1966): 103.
4. Letter to the author, 19 Feb. 1970.
5. Henry Raymont, "Black Writers Win Literature Awards," New York *Times*, 27 Mar. 1970.
6. Ibid.
7. For background on *Black World* see the preceding chapter where it is discussed under its former name, *Negro Digest*.
8. B. J. Nolen, letter to the author, 15 June 1970.
9. Frank Luther Mott, *A History of American Magazines*, vol. 2 (Cambridge: Harvard University Press, 1957, 1958), 68.
10. Nolen letter.
11. Mott, *A History of American Magazines*, vol. 3, 71.
12. Ibid.
13. Carolyne S. Blount, "Advocate for Economic Development," *about . . . time* 15, no. 4 (Apr. 1987): 14–16.
14. Ibid.

9 / What Is in the Black Press?

1. Frederick G. Detweiler, *The Negro Press in the United States* (Chicago: University of Chicago Press, 1922; College Park, Md.: McGrath, 1968), 110–11.
2. Ibid., 126.
3. Ibid., 79.
4. Ibid., 106.
5. Armistead S. Pride, "The Negro Newspaper in the United States," *Gazette* 2, no. 3 (1956): 141–49.
6. Elizabeth Murphy Moss, "Black Newspapers Cover News Other Media Ignore," *Journalism Educator* 24, no. 3 (1969): 6–11.
7. "Barbershop Burned After Threats," Atlanta *Daily World*, 12 Mar. 1970.
8. "Man Beaten for Speeding," Milwaukee *Courier*, 3 Jan. 1970.
9. "Pastor Hits Racist Headlines," *Greater Milwaukee Star*, 7 June 1969.
10. Moss, "Black Newspapers," 6–11.
11. "Cartoonist and College Journalism Dean Will Speak at Press Institute," Cleveland *Press*, 9 Oct. 1969.

12. Ollie Harrington, "How Bootsie Was Born," in *Harlem, U.S.A.*, ed. John Henrik Clarke (Berlin: Seven Seas, 1967), 90.

13. Trevor Wyatt Moore, "Cool Cat with a Warm Message," *Ave Maria* 109, no. 11 (15 Mar. 1969): 18–19.

10 / The Modern Black Journalist

1. "We Quote *Time*," *Lincoln Journalism Newsletter* 7, no. 7 (15 July 1951): 6–7.

2. "Press," *Time* 95, no. 14 (6 Apr. 1970): 89.

3. David L. Lewis and Judy Miao, "America's Greatest Negroes: A Survey," *Crisis* 77, no. 1 (Jan. 1970): 17.

4. *This Is Our War: Selected Stories of Six Afro-American War Correspondents* (Baltimore: Afro-American Publishing Co., 1945), 63–66, 79–80, 154–56.

5. Armistead S. Pride, "Opening Doors for Minorities," *Quill* 56, no. 11 (Nov. 1968): 24.

6. Woody Klein, "News Media and Race Relations: A Self-Portrait," *Columbia Journalism Review* 7, no. 3 (Fall 1968): 43–45.

7. Walter White, *A Man Called White* (New York: Arno Press; New York: New York Times, 1969), 209.

8. See Paneth's *The Encyclopedia of American Journalism*, Taft's *Encyclopedia of Twentieth Century Journalists*, Stein's *Blacks in Communications*, Buni's biography of Robert L. Vann, Bynum's and Zehnpfennig's books on Carl Rowan, Hill's *Who's Who in the American Negro Press*, Hogan's *A Black National News Service: The Associated Negro Press and Claude Barnett, 1919–1945*, Stevens's *From the Back of the Foxhole: Black Correspondents in World War II*, and Waters's *American Diary: A Personal History of the Black Press*. See Bibliography for complete information.

9. Enoch R. Waters, *American Diary: A Personal History of the Black Press* (Chicago: Path Press, 1987), 429.

10. Kim Hessberg, "William Worthy: He Broke Through the Bamboo Curtain," *Baltimore* 72, no. 4 (Apr. 1979): 13–14.

11. Ibid.

12. Ibid.

13. See "Petition for a Writ of Certiorari to the District of Columbia Court of Appeals," Supreme Court of the United States, October term 1977, no. 77.

14. Samuel F. Yette, letter to the author, 6 Jan. 1988.

15. Alex Haley, "A Black American's Search for His Ancestral African Roots," *Ebony* 31, no. 10 (Aug. 1976): 100, 102, 104, 106–7.

16. "Haley Denies Copying *Jubilee*," Minneapolis *Tribune*, 24 Apr. 1977 (New York *Times* Service).

17. Walter Goodman, "Fact, Faction or Symbol?" New York *Times*, 15 Apr. 1977.

18. Thomas Sancton, "The Negro Press," *New Republic* 108, no. 17 (26 Apr. 1943): 559.

19. Edmund David Cronon, *Black Moses: The Story of Marcus Garvey and the Universal Negro Improvement Association* (Madison: University of Wisconsin Press, 1955), 181.

20. Henry Scarupa, "Black Sportswriting Legend Still Going Strong at 84," Baltimore (Maryland) *Sun*, 23 Oct. 1987.

21. "Chuck Stone Quits TV Spot After 'Hate' Mail," Norfolk *Journal and Guide*, 6 June 1970.

22. "*Jet* Editor Refuses to Censor Speech, Leaves Group," *Jet* 36, no. 4 (May 1969): 8.

23. The author is indebted to Mary Male for some of the information on Robert Johnson.
24. Letter requested by the author from Dr. Aggrey written 14 May 1987.
25. Tricia Drevets, "He Moved from the Trib to TV and Back," *Editor & Publisher* 120, no. 44 (31 Oct. 1987): 38.
26. Thomas A. Johnson, "A Graduate of the Black Press Looks Back," in *Perspectives of the Black Press 1974*, ed. Henry G. La Brie III (Kennebunkport, Maine: Mercer House Press, 1974), Chapter 16.
27. Pamela Noel, "Robert Maynard: Oakland's Top Newsman," *Ebony* 40, no. 8 (June 1985): 105.
28. M. J. Stein, "Financially Troubled Oakland, Calif., Paper Announces Layoffs," *Editor & Publisher* 120, no. 46 (14 Nov. 1987): 12.
29. B. Denise Hawkins, "The Essence of Success. Editor Advises Students the Future of Black America Depends upon Youth," Syracuse (New York) *Post-Standard*, 7 Feb. 1987.
30. Marilyn A. Batchelor, letter to the author, 6 June 1987.
31. Jane Rhodes, "A Page One Story," Syracuse (New York) *New Times*, 20 Jan. 1982.
32. "New Black Journalists Group Backs Reporter," New York *Times*, 29 June 1970.
33. Advertisement in the New York *Amsterdam News*, 21 Feb. 1970.
34. Mark Fitzgerald, "Black Journalists Urged to 'Confront' Newsroom Discrimination," *Editor & Publisher* 120, no. 35 (29 Aug. 1987): 14.
35. Jules Witcover, "Washington's White Press Corps," *Columbia Journalism Review* 8, no. 4 (Winter 1969–70): 42–48.

11 / Journalism Education and Training

1. The author distinguishes between training and education thus: training emphasizes learning of skills and procedures, often using workshops, practice sessions, and internships; education may include training but also adds mental development and imparting knowledge (or guiding toward it) beyond the technical field, using standard classroom procedures, such as lectures and seminars.
2. "Report of Ad Hoc Coordinating Committee on Minority Education," Association for Education in Journalism, Aug. 1969, Foreword.
3. Ibid.
4. Simeon Booker, *Black Man's America* (Englewood Cliffs, N.J.: Prentice-Hall, 1964), 143.
5. Professor Hattie S. Knight, letter to the author, 16 Nov. 1987.
6. Kevin C. Douglass, "Howard University: A Glorious Reality in Higher Education," *MBM* (*Modern Black Men*) 3, no. 3 (Mar. 1987): 74–75. Also letters and other communications from Raymond H. Boone, lecturer, Howard's School of Communications faculty.
7. Dr. Marilyn Kern-Foxworth, letter to the author, 16 Sept. 1987.
8. Dr. Lillian Bell, letter to the author, 30 May 1987.
9. Professor Thelma Thurston Gorham, letter to the author, 4 Jan. 1988.
10. "Knight Foundation Awards $1 Million in Grants to Two Universities," *Minorities in the Newspaper Business* 3, no. 3 (May–June 1987): 7.
11. Monte I. Trammer, "Gaining Ground Slowly," *Quill* 76, no. 8 (Sept. 1987): 45.
12. Cynthia Friedheim, "Gannett Minority Hiring, Coverage: There Is Work Yet to Be Done," *Gannetteer*, Sept. 1987, 20.
13. "Minority Newsroom Employment Up, Annual ASNE Survey Shows," *presstime* 8, no. 5 (May 1986): 88.

12 / Publishers and Their Problems

1. "News from the Ford Foundation," 20 May 1969, 4.
2. John H. Johnson, "Understanding: The Key to Effective Communication" (Address, International Magazine Conference, Williamsburg, Virginia, 25–28 May 1969), 1.
3. "Negro Press Advised to Analyze More," *Editor & Publisher* 89, no. 29 (July 1956): 60.
4. Johnson, "Understanding," 4.
5. Thomas Sancton, "The Negro Press," *New Republic* 108, no. 17 (26 Apr. 1943): 560.
6. Letter to the editor, *Ebony* 25, no. 4 (Feb. 1970): 16–17.
7. Letter to the editor, *Ebony* 25, no. 6 (Apr. 1970): 25.
8. "Who Owns the *Age?*" *Lincoln Journalism Newsletter* 5, no. 4 (15 Apr. 1949): 6.
9. *Ebony* 42, no. 10 (Aug. 1987), special issue on the black middle class: 22–162 (except departments). Drawn upon were the articles "The Black Middle Class Defined," by Robert Hill; "Income and Wealth," by Andrew F. Brimmer; "Speaking Out: Is the Black Middle Class Blowing It? Yes!" by Nathan Harc.
10. Andrew F. Brimmer, "Income and Wealth," *Ebony* 42, no. 10 (Aug. 1987): 42, 46, 48.
11. Walter White, *A Man Called White* (New York: Arno Press; New York: New York Times, 1969), 208–9.
12. "NNPA Winter Meeting," *Lincoln Journalism Newsletter* 6, no. 2 (15 Feb. 1950): 2–3.
13. Enoch R. Waters, *American Diary: A Personal History of the Black Press* (Chicago: Path Press, 1987), 423–24.

13 / The Business Operations

1. Robert H. Kinzer and Edward Sagarin, *The Negro in American Business* (New York: Greenberg, 1950), 115.
2. "Black Is Beautiful But Maybe Not Profitable," *Media/scope* 13, no. 8 (Aug. 1969): 100.
3. Frederick G. Detweiler, *The Negro Press in the United States* (Chicago: University of Chicago Press, 1922; College Park, Md.: McGrath, 1968), 116.
4. Vishnu V. Oak, *The Negro Newspaper* (Yellow Springs, Ohio: Author, 1948), 114–16.
5. See *Standard Directory of Advertising Agencies*.
6. L. G. Sherrod, "Barbara Gardner Proctor," *MBM* (*Modern Black Men*) 3, no. 5 (May 1987): 61.
7. Louis E. Lomax, *The Negro Revolt* (New York: Harper & Row, 1962), 204.
8. "Courting the Black Billionaire," *Media/scope* 11, no. 11 (Nov. 1967): 70.
9. Ibid.
10. "Black Is Beautiful But Maybe Not Profitable," 41–42.
11. Oak, *The Negro Newspaper*, 118–19.
12. Benjamin Quarles, *Frederick Douglass* (Washington, D.C.: Associated Publishers, 1948), 83; Foner, in his more detailed biography by the same name, relates that there were two white apprentices who helped with typesetting, wrapping, and other chores.
13. Philip S. Foner, *Frederick Douglass* (New York: Citadel Press, 1963), 84.
14. *"Good News for You! The Afro-American Newspapers"* (Baltimore: The Afro-American Co., 1969), 14.

15. Oak, *The Negro Newspaper*, 72–73.
16. Armistead S. Pride, "Negro Newspapers: Yesterday, Today, and Tomorrow," *Journalism Quarterly* 28, no. 2 (Spring 1951): 186.

14 / Auxiliaries and Competitors

1. Frederick G. Detweiler, *The Negro Press in the United States* (Chicago: University of Chicago Press, 1922; College Park, Md.: McGrath, 1968), 28.
2. Maxwell R. Brooks, *The Negro Press Re-examined* (Boston: Christopher, 1959), 82.
3. Luther A. Townsley, "ANP Provides International Coverage for 78 Member Papers in America," *Lincoln Journalism Clipsheet*, Feb. 1945, 1.
4. Louis E. Lomax, *The Negro Revolt* (New York: Harper & Row, 1962), 72.
5. Richard L. Beard and Cyril E. Zoerner II, "Associated Negro Press: Its Founding, Ascendancy, and Demise," *Journalism Quarterly* 46, no. 1 (Spring 1969): 51; this account contains the commonly known facts about the ANP and Claude Barnett. See also Lawrence D. Hogan, *A Black National News Service: The Associated Negro Press and Claude Barnett, 1919–1945* (Rutherford, N.J.: Fairleigh Dickinson University Press, and Cranbury, N.J.: Associated University Presses, 1984).
6. "Helping to Close the Communications Gap," Empire Features release, 18 Apr. 1970, 5.
7. Stanley Penn, "Major Concerns Seek Help from Negro-run Public Relations Firms," *Wall Street Journal*, 12 Nov. 1965.
8. "Chicago *Defender* Observes 50th Year of Service," *Editor & Publisher* 88, no. 34 (Aug. 1955): 58.
9. "Empathy: The Vital Plus of Negro Radio," *Sponsor*, 26 Aug. 1963, 61.
10. W. Leonard Evans, letter to the author, 2 Feb. 1970.
11. Bernard E. Garnett, *How Soulful is "Soul" Radio?* (Nashville, Tenn.: Race Relations Information Center, 1970), 12.

15 / Pro and Con on the Black Press

1. E. Franklin Frazier, *Black Bourgeoisie* (Glencoe, Ill.: The Free Press, 1957), 146.
2. Warren H. Brown, "A Negro Looks at the Negro Press," *Saturday Review of Literature*, 12 Nov. 1942, 5–6.
3. Virginius Dabney, "Nearer and Nearer the Precipice," *Atlantic Monthly* 171, no. 1 (Jan. 1943): 100.
4. Walter White, *A Man Called White* (New York: Arno Press; New York: New York Times, 1969), 208.
5. Maxwell R. Brooks, *The Negro Press Re-examined* (Boston: Christopher, 1959), 15, 98–101.
6. Roi S. Ottley, *New World A'Coming* (New York: Literary Classics, 1943), 280.
7. Earl Conrad, "The Negro Press," *Tomorrow* 6, no. 3 (Nov. 1946): 5–8.
8. James Baldwin, *Notes of a Native Son* (New York: Bantam Books, 1968), 49.
9. Enoch R. Waters, "The Negro Press: A Call for Change," *Editor & Publisher* 95, no. 19 (May 1962): 67–68.
10. Elaine Kendall, "The Negro Press," *Holiday* 41, no. 5 (May 1967): 84.
11. Dan Aldridge, "Black Press—Where Are You?" *Michigan Chronicle*, 29 Mar. 1969.
12. Chuck Stone, "Black Press: Democracy's Stepchild or a Successful Exercise in Ethnic Pride?" *Editor & Publisher* 110, no. 11 (12 Mar. 1977): 18.

13. Oswald Garrison Villard, *The Disappearing Daily* (New York: Knopf, 1944), 24–25.
14. Baldwin, *Notes of a Native Son*, 53.
15. Ibid., 54.
16. Letter from C. Sumner Stone, *New Republic* 151, no. 18 (Oct. 1964): 29–30.
17. Simeon Booker, "The New Frontier for Daily Newspapers," *Nieman Reports* 9, no. 1 (Jan. 1955): 12.
18. Ted Poston, "The Negro Press," *Reporter* 1, no. 7 (6 Dec. 1949): 16.
19. Letters, "Zebra Associates," *Newsweek* 75, no. 5 (2 Feb. 1970): 9.
20. "Form Group to Make Black Press 'More Relevant,'" *Jet* 35, no. 24 (Mar. 1969): 53.

16 / The Future

1. Roland E. Wolseley, "The Vanishing Negro Press," *Negro Digest* 9, no. 2 (Dec. 1950), 64–68.
2. Chester Higgins, Sr., "Is the Black Press Dying?" *Crisis* 87, no. 7 (Aug.–Sept. 1980): 240.
3. Thomas A. Johnson, "Despite Decline in Number of Black Papers, Publishers Predict Era of Strong Growth," New York *Times*, 31 Jan. 1979.
4. Dennis Schatzman, "The Black Press and Its Role in Modern Society," *Editor & Publisher* 120, no. 10 (21 Apr. 1979): 16–18, 30.
5. The text of these proposals can be found on pp. 72–75 in *Tell It Like It Is*, a collection of Stone's columns published by Trident Press, although this is the key-note address he made to the NNPA while editor in chief of the Chicago *Defender*; it also appeared, in shorter form, in an article by Stone in *Editor & Publisher* magazine for 22 Mar. 1977, pp. 18–19.
6. Wolseley, "The Vanishing Negro Press," 64–68.
7. Simeon Booker, *Black Man's America* (Englewood Cliffs, N.J.: Prentice-Hall, 1964), 152–53.
8. James D. Williams, "Is the Black Press Needed?" *Civil Rights Digest* 3, no. 1 (Winter 1970): 15.
9. Gunnar Myrdal, *An American Dilemma* (New York: Harper & Bros., 1944), 912.
10. Earl Conrad, "The Negro Press," *Tomorrow* 6, no. 3 (Nov. 1946): 8.
11. Armistead S. Pride, "Negro Newspapers: Yesterday, Today, and Tomorrow," *Journalism Quarterly* 28, no. 2 (Spring 1951): 188.
12. Louis E. Lomax, *The Negro Revolt* (New York: Harper & Row, 1962), 204.
13. Ibid., 206.
14. Ibid.
15. D. Parke Gibson, *The $30 Billion Negro* (New York: Macmillan, 1969), 262.
16. L. F. Palmer, Jr., "The Black Press in Transition," *Columbia Journalism Review* 9, no. 1 (Spring 1970): 36.
17. Address to journalism students at Syracuse University, 4 May 1970.
18. See such discussions as George L. Bird and Fredrick E. Merwin, eds., *The Newspaper and Society* (New York: Prentice-Hall, 1942), *The Press and Society* (New York: Prentice-Hall, 1951); A. J. Liebling, *The Wayward Pressman* (New York: Doubleday, 1947); Curtis D. MacDougall, *Newsroom Problems and Policies* (New York: Macmillan, 1941), *The Press and Its Problems* (Dubuque, Iowa: Brown, 1964); Oswald Garrison Villard, *The Disappearing Daily* (New York: Knopf, 1944); Carl E. Lindstrom, *The Fading American Newspaper* (New York: Doubleday,

1960); J. Edward Gerald, *The Social Responsibility of the Press* (Minneapolis: University of Minnesota Press, 1963); Fredrick S. Siebert, Wilbur Schramm, and Theodore Peterson, *Four Theories of the Press* (Champaign: University of Illinois Press, 1956); Ben H. Bagdikian, *The Effete Conspiracy and Other Crimes of the Press* (New York: Harper & Row, 1972), *The Information Machines* (New York: Harper & Row, 1971), *The Media Monopoly* (Boston: Beacon Press, 1983); Edwin Diamond, *Good News, Bad News* (Cambridge: MIT Press, 1978); David Halberstam, *The Powers That Be* (New York: Knopf, 1979).
19. Gibson, *The $30 Billion Negro*, 160.
20. Booker, *Black Man's America*, 156.
21. John W. Gardner, *No Easy Victories* (New York: Harper & Row, 1969), 17.
22. Roland E. Wolseley, *Understanding Magazines*, 2d ed. (Ames: Iowa State University Press, 1969), 432.

BIBLIOGRAPHY

No extensive, readily obtainable, and annotated, selected bibliographical guide exists as yet to aid the searcher for information about the books on the black press of the United States. In fact, only one up-to-date general bibliography covering the entire U.S. press scene is in print, and it is flawed by omissions.

Scholars, therefore, have had to rely on long-outdated general bibliographies, almost all of which have been on special areas and are likely to be found in histories or biographies of black journalism and journalists.

One exception stands out: *Blacks and Media*, by the late J. William Snorgrass and Gloria T. Woody, of Florida A. & M. University. It is a substantial and readily available reference volume, but it covers books, articles, and other items published only between 1962 and 1982. Happily it is selected and annotated.

Biography is the strongest area of the literature of black journalism. And it quickly became richer after 1970, encouraged by the greater interest in black history, culture, and social problems. Much of the recent biographical work goes beyond the long popular figures for such books as Douglass, Du Bois, and Garvey. The work of Quarles, Foner, Cronon, Ottley, Broderick, Bennett, Fox, Buni, Thornbrough, and Rudwick in producing full-length biographies or analytical biographical studies so far has been the extent of superior biographical writing. Penn's history is more a mélange of brief biographies than a sustained study of the publications and persons of a century or more ago.

Press history is next in strength, although it is a spotty area, lacking a first-class overview that should begin with the first paper in 1827. It would take a team of historians to produce it, for so many of the approximately thirty-five hundred newspapers issued since then are lost, as are facts about their editors and writers.

Consequently, scholars have a little help from the few books on segments of the history. Penn's book, though adjective-laden, nevertheless supplies some information about many nineteenth-century publications and editors. A better-written history is Detweiler's, but it is too brief, old, and narrow in scope.

Why Does This Situation Exist?

One explanation for the lack of available information is that for most of the existence of black American educators in the history of the nation, they were not accepted on the faculties of many nonblack colleges and universities. In some geographical areas neither were the students.

The black scholars were forced to work in black institutions which themselves were victims of discrimination and segregation, were underfinanced, and therefore unable to provide the facilities, salaries, and opportunities for publication.

Another reason is that books about small areas of American journalism such as the black press had little likelihood of profitable sales to their publishers, much less their authors. The literacy rates and income levels of black citizens until recent years were far below the whites' records.

But literacy is now vastly higher and income has improved, at least for the new black middle class. The interest may increase, at least in the academic realm where there are general media programs and courses dealing with the black publications.

There is little encouragement for this optimism, however, among the consumers of journalism. Circulations of many papers are down, and failures have become more common among specialized magazines and general papers. It is misleading to think that *Black Enterprise, Essence, Jet, Ebony*, and a few other periodicals are typical in circulation, advertising volume, and readership. If readers are lacking in the others the advertising will fall as well, and the publishers must either go kaput or find a subsidy.

Where to Find Reviews

Clues to what is being published are still available, in spite of the great mortality in recent years among magazines and newspapers. Among important sources for review and criticism of books are the *Black Scholar, Ebony, Black American Literature Forum*, the *Negro Educational Review*, and the *Western Journal of Black Studies*.

If merely lists of newspapers and magazines, with or without addresses and other data, are needed, three publications are of help: the periodically issued *Standard Rate and Data Service* reports, *Gale Directory of Publications*, and *Editor & Publisher International Year Book* (newspapers only).

The bibliographical facts that follow are not only a record of the materials used by the author but also a miniguide to the sparse literature on the black press. All the books and articles have been read by the author of this volume.

(Note: The printed sources consulted in preparation of this book are in categories for easy use by readers. In some instances brief annotations are provided. To help keep the listings up-to-date consult the periodicals noted above.)

Books and Monographs Concerned Mainly with the Black Press and Black Journalists

Biography (See also History)
Robert S. Abbott

Ottley, Roi. *The Lonely Warrior: The Life and Times of Robert S. Abbott.* Chicago: Regnery, 1955. 381 pp. Abbott was the founder of the Chicago *Defender*, a major newspaper in the history of black journalism.

Pride, Armistead S. "Robert S. Abbott." In *Dictionary of American Biography*, Supplement 2, edited by Edward T. James, 2–4. New York: Scribner's, 1958.

James Baldwin

Baldwin, James. *Notes of a Native Son*, 49–53. New York: Bantam Books, 1968. 149 pp. The late novelist had his turn in journalism.

Claude Barnett

Hogan, Lawrence D. *A Black National News Service: The Associated Negro Press and Claude Barnett, 1919–1945.* Rutherford, N.J.: Fairleigh Dickinson University Press; Cranbury, N.J.: Associated University Presses, 1984. 260 pp. Founder of the Associated Negro Press, Barnett also gave black journalism its best news agency.

Martin R. Delany (also spelled Delaney)

Rollin, Frank A. *Life and Public Services of Martin R. Delaney*. Boston: Lee & Shepard, 1868. 367 pp. Reprint. New York: Kraus Reprint Co., 1969. A talented early leader in politics, social problem solving, and journalism.

Sterling, Dorothy. *The Making of an Afro-American: Martin Robeson Delany, 1812–1885*. New York: Doubleday, 1971. 352 pp.

Ullman, Victor. *Martin R. Delany: The Beginnings of Black Nationalism*. Boston: Beacon Press, 1971. 534 pp.

Frederick Douglass

Bontemps, Arna. *Free at Last: The Life of Frederick Douglass*. New York: Dodd, Mead, 1971. 310 pp. An appreciative biography by a leading black scholar and poet reviewing the already widely known facts about Douglass, but recording them in an attractive style.

Douglass, Frederick. *Life and Times of Frederick Douglass*. New York: Collier Books, 1962. 640 pp. Reprint of 1895 revised edition. Rayford W. Logan, who wrote the introduction to this version of Douglass's autobiography, explains its background thus: *"The Life and Times . . .* is the final form of an autobiography first published as a small Narrative in 1845, expanded in *My Bondage and My Freedom* in 1855, further extended in the first edition of *Life and Times* in 1881, and completed and revised in 1892." This edition is a reprint of the 1892 book that appeared in 1895, itself a revision.

————. *My Bondage and My Freedom*. New York: Miller, Orton & Mulligan, 1885. 464 pp. Reprint of 1855 edition.

————. *Narrative of the Life of Frederick Douglass*. New York: New American Library, 1968. 126 pp. Reprint of 1845 edition.

Foner, Philip S. *Frederick Douglass*. New York: Citadel Press, 1963. 444 pp. Foner's two books and those by Douglass himself are considered the best sources on the famous editor.

————. *The Life and Writings of Frederick Douglass*. 4 vols. New York: International Publishers, 1950, 1952.

Graham, Shirley. *There Was Once a Slave . . .: The Heroic Story of Frederick Douglass*. New York: Messner, 1947. 310 pp.

Holland, Frederick May. *Frederick Douglass: The Colored Orator*. Rev. ed. New York: Funk & Wagnalls, 1895. 430 pp.

Huggins, Nathan Irvin. *Slave and Citizen: The Life of Frederick Douglass*. Boston: Little, Brown, 1980. 194 pp.

Miller, Douglas T. *Frederick Douglass and the Fight for Freedom*. New York: Facts on File Publications, 1988, 152 pp.

Quarles, Benjamin. *Frederick Douglass*. Washington, D.C.: Associated Publishers, 1948. 378 pp.

————, ed. *Frederick Douglass*. Englewood Cliffs, N.J.: Prentice-Hall, 1968. 184 pp.

W. E. B. Du Bois

Broderick, Francis L. *W. E. B. Du Bois: Negro Leader in Time of Crisis*. Palo Alto, Calif.: Stanford, 1959. 259 pp.

Clarke, John Henrik, Esther Jackson, Ernest Kaiser, and J. H. O'Dell, eds. *Black Titan: W. E. B. Du Bois*. Boston: Beacon Press, 1970. 333 pp. A collection of articles on different aspects of Du Bois's work, many of which appeared in *Freedomways* in a 1965 issue dedicated to him. These are by various scholars and writers—two pertaining to journalism are one on the *Brownie's Book*, a children's magazine he founded and edited, and another an excerpt in which Du Bois describes his work at the *Crisis*.

Du Bois, Shirley Graham. *His Day Is Marching On: A Memoir of W. E. B. Du Bois*. Philadelphia: Lippincott, 1971. 384 pp. Shirley Graham, an author in her own right, was Dr. Du Bois's second wife, forty years his junior. He was far younger than his years, so they had a busy life together—here she tells of their travels around the world, their increasing disenchantment with American life, and their appreciation of the social changes made in China, Russia, and other totalitarian lands. Both idealists, they saw mainly bad in China and good in the Soviet Union. The book provides insights into the extraordinary Du Bois and also into the tastes and views of his widow.

Du Bois, W. E. B. *The Autobiography of W. E. B. Du Bois*. New York: International Publishers, 1968. 448 pp.

Hamilton, Virginia. *W. E. B. Du Bois*. New York: Crowell, 1972. 218 pp.

Lacy, Leslie Alexander. *Cheer the Lonesome Traveler: The Life of W. E. B. Du Bois*. New York: Dial, 1970. 183 pp.

Logan, Rayford W., ed. *W. E. B. Du Bois: A Profile*. New York: Hill & Wang, 1971. 325 pp. Ten reproductions of chapters from early books, articles, or speeches about Du Bois.

Moore, Jack B. *W. E. B. Du Bois*. Boston: Twayne, 1981. 185 pp.

Partington, Paul G. *W. E. B. Du Bois. A Bibliography of His Published Writings*. Whittier, Calif.: Author, 1977. 202 pp.

Rudwick, Elliott M. *W. E. B. Du Bois: Propagandist of the Negro Protest*. New York: Atheneum, 1968. 390 pp.

T. Thomas Fortune

Thornbrough, Emma Lou. *T. Thomas Fortune: Militant Journalist*. Chicago: University of Chicago Press, 1972. 388 pp. A noted editor of powerful newspapers.

Marcus Garvey

Clarke, John Henrik, ed. *Marcus Garvey and the Vision of Africa*. New York: Vintage Books, 1974. 498 pp. A major work by a prominent black historian and educator, useful in view of changing minds about Garvey in the mid-1980s. See also Cronon.

Cronon, Edmund David. *Black Moses: The Story of Marcus Garvey and the Universal Negro Improvement Association*. Madison: University of Wisconsin Press, 1955. 278 pp.

Garvey, A. Jacques. *Garvey and Garveyism*. Kingston, Jamaica: Author, 1963. 287 pp.

Hill, Robert A., ed. *The Marcus Garvey and Universal Negro Improvement*

Association Papers. 5 vols. Berkeley: University of California Press, 1981–86.

Jean-Charles Houzeau

Houzeau, Jean-Charles. *My Passage at the New Orleans* Tribune. Baton Rouge: Louisiana State University Press, 1984. 168 pp. Houzeau was a Belgian white man who passed himself off as black; he was with the New Orleans *Tribune*, the first black daily. A Civil War figure, Houzeau was an astronomer and bibliographer.

James Weldon Johnson

Johnson, James Weldon. *Along This Way.* New York: Viking, 1933. 418 pp. An editor, poet, and lyricist, Johnson also was a leader in black organizations; his own book and Levy's are sound.

Levy, Eugene. *James Weldon Johnson: Black Leader, Black Voice.* Chicago: University of Chicago Press, 1973, 1976. 380 pp.

Tarry, Ellen. *Young Jim.* New York: Dodd, Mead, 1967. 230 pp. Young Jim was James Weldon Johnson; the book is intended for young people.

Joseph E. Mitchell

Mitchell, Edwina W. *Crusading Black Journalist: Joseph Everett Mitchell.* Philadelphia: Farmer Press, 1972. 77 pp. Biography by the widow of Mitchell, founder, editor, and publisher of the St. Louis *Argus* until 1951. An admiring account, but poorly organized.

Raymond Mungo

Mungo, Raymond. *Famous Long Ago: My Life and Hard Times with Liberation News Service.* Boston: Beacon Press, 1970. 202 pp. Since a number of black publications have used Liberation News Service copy the references to the organization, although few, are worth noting.

Roi S. Ottley

Ottley, Roi S. *New World A'Coming.* New York: Literary Classics, 1943. 364 pp. The autobiography of a foreign correspondent, writer, and editor in the United States; his biography of Robert Abbot was a major contribution to black journalism.

Gordon Parks

Parks, Gordon. *A Choice of Weapons.* New York: Harper & Row, 1966. 274 pp. One of the three autobiographical books the photographer, filmmaker, and novelist has written. *The Learning Tree* has little concerning writing; *To Smile in Autumn* deals with his work on *Life* and in other media.

———. *To Smile in Autumn: A Memoir.* New York: Norton, 1979. 249 pp.

A. Philip Randolph

Anderson, Jervis. *A. Philip Randolph: A Biographical Portrait*, Chapters 5–13. New York: Harcourt Brace Jovanovich, 1973. 398 pp. Long a leader for working black men's rights, he was in early days editor of *Messenger*, an influential magazine.

Kornweibel, Theodore, Jr. *No Crystal Stair: Black Life and the* Messenger, *1917–1928.* Westport, Conn.: Greenwood Press, 1975. 306 pp.

Carl T. Rowan

Bynum, Lynn. *Carl T. Rowan: Journalist Extraordinary*. Bloomington, Ind.: Afro-American Institute, 1975. 35 pp.

Zehnpfennig, Gladys T. *Carl T. Rowan: Spokesman for Sanity*. Minneapolis, Minn.: Denison, 1971. 314 pp. Zehnpfennig's full-length biography should be used except for ordinary identification of the columnist in the other.

John Brown Russwurm

Sagarin, Mary. *John Brown Russwurm: The Story of* Freedom's Journal, *Freedom's Journey*. New York: Lothrop, Lee & Shepard, 1970. 160 pp. Russwurm was the cofounder of the first black newspaper in the United States.

George S. Schuyler

Peplow, Michael W. *George S. Schuyler*. New York: Twayne, 1980. 144 pp. Controversial, changeable politician, and able writer and editor, these books on and by him are valuable.

Schuyler, George S. *Black and Conservative*. New Rochelle, N.Y.: Arlington House, 1966. 362 pp.

Ellen Tarry

Tarry, Ellen. *The Third Door*. New York: McKay, 1955. 304 pp. Autobiography of a Southern teacher, journalist, and social activist.

William Monroe Trotter

Fox, Stephen R. *The Guardian of Boston: William Monroe Trotter*. New York: Atheneum Press, 1970. 307 pp. Trotter was a fiery, courageous, and feared Boston editor who got new appreciation after 1960.

Robert L. Vann

Buni, Andrew. *Robert L. Vann of the Pittsburgh* Courier: *Politics and Black Journalism*. Pittsburgh: University of Pittsburgh Press, 1974. 410 pp.

Samuel Ringgold Ward

Ward, Samuel Ringgold. *Autobiography of a Fugitive Negro*. Reprint. Chicago: Johnson Publishing Co., 1970. 277 pp. A little-known figure, but strongly active as a religious leader against injustice to blacks, and founder of several newspapers for them in the United States and Canada. Originally published in 1855.

Booker T. Washington

Harlan, Louis R. *Booker T. Washington: The Making of a Black Leader, 1856–1901*. New York: Oxford University Press, 1973. 379 pp. This and other books deal with his behind-the-scenes ownership or control of numerous black publications.

Mathews, Basil. *Booker T. Washington: Educator and Interracial Interpreter*. Cambridge: Harvard University Press, 1948. 350 pp.

Enoch R. Waters

Waters, Enoch R. *American Diary: A Personal History of the Black Press*. Chicago: Path Press, 1987. 520 pp. Hardly an adequate history but a readable account of Waters's work as foreign correspondent and editor for the Chicago *Defender*. His social views are stimulating.

Ida B. Wells-Barnett

Duster, Alfreda M., ed. *Crusade for Justice: The Autobiography of Ida B. Wells*. Chicago: University of Chicago Press, 1970. 434 pp. Much honored in the 1980s, Wells-Barnett early in the century was a reformer, journalist, and public speaker of great power.

Walter White

White, Walter. *A Man Called White*. New York: Arno Press; New York: New York *Times*, 1969. 382 pp. White was black by race but so white physically he was usually mistaken for white. He was head of the NAACP and somewhat controversial.

Roger A. Wilkins

Wilkins, Roger A. *A Man's Life*. New York: Simon & Schuster, 1982. 384 pp. Related to the more noted Roy Wilkins, Roger Wilkins has been a writer for the New York *Times* and other publications and organizations.

Roy Wilkins

Wilkins, Roy, and Tom Mathews. *Standing Fast: The Autobiography of Roy Wilkins*. New York: Viking Press, 1982. 361 pp. Remembered now for his leadership of the NAACP, his journalism undergirded him for it. He edited his university student publications, worked on black papers, was a columnist, and edited the *Crisis*.

Malcolm X

Malcolm X. *The Autobiography of Malcolm X*, Chapter 14. New York: Grove Press, 1968. 460 pp.

Groups of Black Journalists

Adams, Russell L. *Great Negroes Past and Present*. 2d ed. Chicago: Afro-Am Publishing Co., Inc., 1964. 182 pp.

Bennett, Lerone, Jr. *Pioneers in Protest*, Chapters 5, 14–17. Baltimore: Penguin Books, 1969. 263 pp. Early editors are included.

Franklin, John Hope, and August Meier, eds. *Black Leaders of the Twentieth Century*. Urbana: University of Illinois Press, 1982. 372 pp. Chapters on seven with close journalism connections.

Marzolf, Marion. *Up from the Footnote: A History of Women Journalists*. New York: Hastings House, 1977. 310 pp. See pp. 25–26, 90–92 for recognition of black journalists.

Mills, Kay. *A Place in the News*. New York: Dodd, Mead, 1988. 378 pp. Includes the biographies of several modern female journalists, including Marvel Cooke, Dorothy Gilliam, Nancy Hicks Maynard, Sheila Rule, and others.

Paneth, Donald. *The Encyclopedia of American Journalism*, 35–38. New York: Facts on File Publications, 1983. 548 pp. Considerable information is here about the black press: biographies, press history, press directories, and lists of newspapers.

Stein, M. L. *Blacks in Communications.* New York: Messner, 1972. 191 pp. For young black people: brief historical background but mostly short biographical sketches of black journalists on black or white media.

Sterling, Dorothy, and Benjamin Quarles. *Lift Every Voice.* New York: Doubleday, 1965. 116 pp.

Stevens, John D. "From the Back of the Foxhole: Black Correspondents in World War II." *Journalism Monographs* 27 (Feb. 1973). 61 pp.

Taft, William H. *Encyclopedia of Twentieth Century Journalists.* New York: Garden, 1986. 408 pp. Eighteen entries are of black journalists; some not usually found are Betty Anne Williams, Robert Maynard, Earl G. Graves, and Lerone Bennett.

This Is Our War: Selected Stories of Six Afro-American War Correspondents. Baltimore: Afro-American Publishing Co., 1945. 216 pp.

Business

Gibson, D. Parke. *$70 Billion in the Black.* New York: Macmillan, 1978. 230 pp. Gibson's books describe the black consumer market and suggest advertising and public relations strategies to reach it.

_____. *The $30 Billion Negro.* New York: Macmillan, 1969. 311 pp.

Kinzer, Robert H., and Edward Sagarin. *The Negro in American Business.* New York: Greenberg, 1950. 220 pp. This book and the next two are useful for comparisons only.

Lancaster, Emmer Martin. *A Guide to Negro Marketing Information.* Washington, D.C.: U.S. Department of Commerce, 1966. 50 pp.

The Negro Market. New York: Department of Media Relations and Planning, Young & Rubicam, Inc., 1969. 164 pp.

Education and Training

Becker, Lee B., Jeffrey W. Fruit, and Susan L. Caudill. *The Training and Hiring of Journalists in the U.S.A.* Norwood, N.J.: Ablex Publishing Corp., 1987. 196 pp. Data about minorities, some specifically on black students of journalism and practicing black writers and editors, are here and there in the chapters.

Careers for Negroes on Newspapers. Rev. ed. Washington, D.C.: American Newspaper Guild, 1966. 28 pp. Useful for comparative purposes only.

Journalism Career Guide for Minorities. American Newspaper Publishers Association Foundation and other groups, 1986. 56 pp.

Recruiting and Retaining Newspaper Minority Employees: How to Do It. Washington, D.C.: American Newspaper Publishers Association Foundation, 1986. 28 pp.

Telfer, Judie. *Training Minority Journalists: A Case Study of the San Francisco* Examiner *Intern Program.* Berkeley: Institute of Governmental Studies, University of California, 1973. 124 pp.

Evaluation of the Black Press

Brooks, Maxwell, R. *The Negro Press Re-examined*. Boston: Christopher, 1959. 125 pp.

Coonradt, Frederic C. *The Negro News Media and the Los Angeles Riots*. Los Angeles: School of Journalism, University of Southern California, 1965. 49 pp.

Finkle, Lee. *Forum for Protest: The Black Press During World War II*. Rutherford, N.J.: Fairleigh Dickinson University Press; London: Associated University Presses, 1975. 249 pp.

Frazier, E. Franklin. *Black Bourgeoisie*. Glencoe, Ill.: The Free Press, 1957. 264 pp. A trenchant attack.

Johnson, Abby Arthur, and Ronald Maberry Johnson. *Propaganda and Aesthetics: The Literary Politics of Afro-American Magazines in the Twentieth Century*. Amherst: University of Massachusetts Press, 1979. 248 pp.

Myrdal, Gunnar. *An American Dilemma*. New York: Harper & Bros., 1944. 1,483 pp. One of the most referred to and useful studies.

Oak, Vishnu V. *The Negro Newspaper*. Yellow Springs, Ohio: Author, 1948. 170 pp. Adversely critical but not well documented.

Stevens, John D. "Black Journalism: Neglected No Longer." In *Mass Media and the National Experience*, edited by Ronald T. Farrar and John D. Stevens. New York: Harper & Row, 1971. 196 pp. See pp. 97–111.

————, and William E. Porter. *The Rest of the Elephant: Perspectives of the Mass Media*. Englewood Cliffs, N.J.: Prentice-Hall, 1973. 186 pp. See pp. 26–30, 33–37, and 165–71.

Washburn, Patrick S. *A Question of Sedition: The Federal Government's Investigation of the Black Press During World War II*. New York: Oxford University Press, 1986. 296 pp.

Williams, James D. *The Black Press and the First Amendment*. New York: National Urban League, 1976. 23 pp.

General

"The Black Image in the Mass Media." *Freedomways* 14, no. 3 (1974). 108 pp.

Bullock, Penelope L. *The Afro-American Periodical Press 1838–1909*. Baton Rouge: Louisiana State University Press, 1981. 330 pp.

Dodson, Don, and William A. Hachten. "Communication and Development: African and Afro-American Parallels." *Journalism Monographs* 28 (May 1973). 37 pp.

Garnett, Bernard E. *How Soulful is "Soul" Radio?* Nashville, Tenn.: Race Relations Information Center, 1970. 61 pp.

La Brie, Henry III, ed. *Perspectives of the Black Press 1974*. Kennebunkport, Maine: Mercer House Press, 1974. 231 pp. Chapters by various black or white journalists, teachers, and researchers on different aspects.

Meier, August. *Negro Thought in America, 1880–1915*. Ann Arbor: University of Michigan Press, 1963. 336 pp.

Murphy, Sharon. *Other Voices: Black, Chicano, and American Indian Press.* Dayton, Ohio: Pflaum/Standard, 1974. 133 pp.

Reilly, Tom, ed. "The Black Press Roots 150 Years Deep." *Journalism History* 4, no. 4 (Winter 1977–78). 47 pp. The entire issue is devoted to articles by Pride, La Brie, and other authorities; Pride's bibliography to 1968 is included; other clues are in the individual articles.

Sandman, Peter M., David M. Rubin, and David B. Sachsman. *Media: An Introductory Analysis of American Mass Communications.* 3d ed., 472–75. Englewood Cliffs, N.J.: Prentice-Hall, 1982.

Tinney, James S., and Justine J. Rector, eds., *Issues and Trends in Afro-American Journalism.* Lanham, Md.: University Press of America, 1980. 363 pp.

Welsch, Erwin K. *The Negro in the United States.* Bloomington: Indiana University Press, 1968. 142 pp.

Wolseley, Roland E. *The Black Press, U.S.A.* Ames: Iowa State University Press, 1971. 362 pp. The first edition of the present book; it was re printed and some changes made. Many of the 1968–78 events in the field not included in this revision make the book still useful.

History (See also Biography)

Ainslie, Rosalynde. *The Press in Africa.* London: Gollancz, 1966, 21–22.

Booker, James. *History of the New York* Amsterdam News. New York: *Amsterdam News*, 1967. 4 pp.

Bryan, Carter R. "Negro Journalism in America before Emancipation." *Journalism Monographs* 12 (Sept. 1969). 33 pp.

Dann, Martin E., ed. *The Black Press, 1827–1890.* New York: Putnam, 1971. 384 pp. An anthology of materials from the black publications.

Detweiler, Frederick G. *The Negro Press in the United States.* Chicago: University of Chicago Press, 1922. 274 pp. Reprint. College Park, Md.: McGrath, 1968.

Emery, Edwin, and Michael Emery. *The Press and America.* 6th ed. Englewood Cliffs, N.J.: Prentice-Hall, 1988. 786 pp. See pp. 150–54, 265–70, 490–94, 655.

Emery, Michael, and Ted Curtis Smythe, eds. *Readings in Mass Communications.* 6th ed. Dubuque, Iowa: Brown, 1987. 549 pp. See pp. 140–50.

Garnett, Bernard E. *Invaders from the Black Nation: The "Black Muslims" in 1970.* Nashville, Tenn.: Race Relations Information Center, 1970. 32 pp.

Good News for You! The Afro-American Newspapers. Baltimore: The Afro-American Co., 1969. 64 pp.

Hughes, Langston. *Fight for Freedom: The Story of the NAACP,* 40, 43, 46–48, 77, 95, 154, 203. New York: Norton, 1962. 244 pp.

———, and Milton Meltzer. *A Pictorial History of the Negro in America.* Rev. ed. New York: Crown, 1963. 347 pp. Originally published in 1956; contains brief reports on Douglass, Du Bois, and a few other leaders, and references to several historical papers, especially Douglass's.

Kellogg, Charles Flint. *NAACP*, vol. 1, Chapters 3, 5, 7. Baltimore: Johns Hopkins Press, 1967. 332 pp.

Lincoln, C. Eric. *The Black Muslims in America*. Boston: Beacon Press, 1961. 276 pp.

Meier, August. *Negro Thought in America, 1880–1915*. Ann Arbor: University of Michigan Press, 1963. 336 pp. See pp. 114–15, 127, 166, 171, 178–80, 198, 207–8, 224–36, 246–47.

Mott, Frank Luther. *American Journalism*. 3d ed. New York: Macmillan, 1962. 901 pp. An early general history of the U.S. press. While this was one of the best, it gave little attention to the black press. See pp. 794–95, 821.

_____. *A History of American Magazines*. 5 vols. Cambridge: Harvard University Press, 1957, 1958. A Pulitzer prize for history was won by these volumes; like all other early scholars, the author gave little space to black magazines. See Vol. 2, p. 68; Vol. 3, pp. 63, 71, 75, 283; Vol. 4, p. 214.

Muse, Benjamin. *The American Negro Revolution: From Nonviolence to Black Power, 1963–1967*. Bloomington: Indiana University Press, 1968. 345 pp.

Penn, I. Garland. *The Afro-American Press and Its Editors*. Springfield, Mass.: Willey, 1891. 569 pp. Reprint. New York: Arno Press; New York *Times*, 1969. Reprint carries two-page biography of Penn and is a facsimile.

Roucek, Joseph S., and Thomas Kiernan, eds. *The Negro Impact on Western Civilization*. New York: Philosophical Library, 1970. 506 pp. The chapter "Contributions of the Negro Press to American Culture" (pp. 173–94) is by William C. Spragens, then a professor of political science at Bowling Green.

Sinnette, Elinor Desverney. "*The Brownies' Book*, A Pioneer Publication for Children." In *Black Titan*, edited by John Henrik Clarke, et al. Boston: Beacon Press, 1970. 333 pp. About one of the five magazines founded by Du Bois. See pp. 164–75.

Suggs, Henry Lewis, ed. *The Black Press in the South, 1865–1979*. Westport, Conn.: Greenwood Press, 1983. 468 pp.

Taft, William H. *American Journalism History*. Columbia, Mo.: Lucas Brothers, 1968. 94 pp.

_____. *American Magazines for the 1980s*. New York: Hastings House, 1982. 382 pp. See Chapter 17, "Minority Publications Led by *Ebony*," pp. 241–50.

Vincent, Theodore G., ed. *Voices of a Black Nation: Political Journalism in the Harlem Renaissance*. San Francisco: Ramparts Press, 1973. 391 pp.

Reference Books

Ashley, Perry J., ed. *Dictionary of Literary Biography*. Vol. 43, *American Newspaper Journalists, 1690–1872*. Detroit, Mich.: Gale Research Co., 1985. 527 pp. Frederick Douglass is covered on pp. 160–68.

_____. *Dictionary of Literary Biography*. Vol. 29, *1926–1950*. Detroit, Mich.: Gale Research Co., 1984. 410 pp. The black journalists covered are Robert S. Abbott, George S. Schuyler, and Robert L. Vann. See pp. 12–18, 313–22, 350–60.

_____. *Dictionary of Literary Biography*. Vol. 23, *1873–1900*. Detroit, Mich: Gale Research Co., 1983. 392 pp. T. Thomas Fortune and Ida B. Wells-Barnett are included. See pp. 120, 340–46.

Black List: The Guide to Publications and Broadcasting of Black America, Africa, Caribbean. New York: Panther House, 1971. 289 pp.

The Black Resource Guide. Washington, D.C.: R. Benjamin Johnson, 1985. 217 pp.

Bray, Leonard, ed. *Directory of Newspapers and Periodicals*. Philadelphia: N. W. Ayer & Son, Inc. Covering volumes for the period 1965–70. For comparative use only.

Briscoe, Sherman, ed. *Black Press Handbook*. Rev. ed. of *Black Press Information Handbook 1974–75*. Washington, D.C.: National Newspaper Publishers Association, 1977. 120 pp.

_____. *Black Press Information Handbook 1974–75*. Washington, D.C.: National Newspaper Publishers Association, 1974. 74 pp.

Daniels, Walter C. *Black Journals of the United States*. Westport, Conn.: Greenwood Press, 1982. 433 pp. One of the more valuable bibliographies, with sketches of magazines.

Directory of Minority Media. Washington, D.C.: Office of Minority Business Enterprises, U.S. Dept. of Commerce, 1973. 89 pp.

Domenech, Margie, and Matthew Manning, eds. *The Standard Periodical Directory*. 10th ed. New York: Oxbridge, 1987. 1,474 pp.

Editors of *Ebony*. *The Negro Handbook*, 377–86. Chicago: Johnson Publishing Co., 1966. 535 pp.

Franzen, Raymond. *Magazine Audiences in the Urban Negro Market*. New York: Our World Publishing Co., 1951. 63 pp.

Gale Directory of Publications, 1988. 120th ed. 2 vols. Detroit, Mich.: Gale Research Co., 1988. 2,345 pp. Includes a partial list of black newspapers and magazines; for many years known as the *Ayer Directory*.

A Guide to Negro Media: Newspapers, Magazines, Radio and College. New York: Deutsch & Shea, Inc., 1968. 38 pp. For comparison use only.

Hill, Roy L. *Who's Who in the American Negro Press*. Dallas: Royal Publishing Co., c. 1960. 80 pp.

Johnson, Ben, and Mary Ballard-Johnson. *Who's What and Where*. Detroit, Mich.: Who's What and Where, 1985. 478 pp.

Kimbrough, Marvin. *Black Magazines: An Exploratory Study*. Austin: Center for Communication Research, University of Texas, 1973. 78 pp. The first substantial checklist of U.S. magazines for the black race in the U.S., based upon a survey made by Kimbrough as a university project.

La Brie, Henry G. III. *The Black Press in America: A Guide*. Iowa City: Institute for Communication Studies, University of Iowa, 1970. 64 pp. Reprint. Coralville, Iowa: Mercer House Press, 1972. 80 pp.

————. *A Survey of Black Newspapers in America.* Kennebunkport, Maine: Mercer House Press, 1979. 72 pp.

Paine, Fred K., and Nancy E. Paine. *Magazines: A Bibliography for Their Analysis.* Metuchen, N.J.: Scarecrow Press, 1987. 690 pp. Thirty-nine entries deal with black magazines or related topics; most are post-1978.

Ploski, Harry A., and James Williams, comps. and eds. *The Negro Almanac.* 4th ed. New York: John Wiley & Sons, 1983. 1,550 pp. A 38 pp. segment is highly valuable.

Porter, Dorothy B., comp. *The Negro in the United States: A Working Bibliography.* Ann Arbor, Mich.: University Microfilms, 1969.

Pride, Armistead S. *The Black Press: A Bibliography.* Madison, Wis.: Association for Education in Journalism, 1968. 37 pp. A fundamental list greatly in need of updating.

Sawyer, Frank B., ed. *Amalgamated Publishers Rate & Data List of 70 Black Newspapers in 28 States; Malcolm X Reference Section.* New York: *U.S. Negro World*, 1969. 87 pp. Useful source for comparative statistics, but found in few libraries.

————, ed. *1967 Directory of U.S. Negro Newspapers, Magazines & Periodicals in 42 States: The Negro Press—Past, Present and Future.* New York: *U.S. Negro World*, 1968. 40 pp.

————, ed. *1966 Directory of U.S. Negro Newspapers, Magazines & Periodicals.* New York: *U.S. Negro World*, 1967. unpaged.

————, ed. *U.S. Negro World.* Vol. 9. New York: *U.S. Negro World*, 1970. 137 pp.

Snorgrass, J. William, and Gloria T. Woody. *Blacks and Media. A Selected and Annotated Bibliography 1962–1982.* Tallahassee: Florida A. & M. University Press, 1985. 150 pp. See comments on p. 1.

Spradling, Mary Mace, ed. *In Black and White.* Detroit, Mich.: Gale Research Co., 3rd ed., vol. 1, 1980. 643 pp. Vol. 2, 1980, 639 pp. Subtitled "A Guide to Magazine Articles, Newspaper Articles, and Books Concerning More than 15,000 Black Individuals and Groups."

Staff of Hallie Q. Brown Memorial Library, Central State University. *Index to Periodical Articles about Blacks: 1981.* Boston, Mass.: G. K. Hall & Co., 1984. 240 pp. First published in 1941, this index has appeared irregularly and often late, but is an invaluable guide to the content of numerous black magazines as well as to their contributors.

Standard Directory of Advertising Agencies, no. 21 (October-January 1987–88). Wilmette, Ill.: National Register Publishing Co. 1,012 pp.

Velez, Orlando, ed. *Editor & Publisher International Year Book, 1988.* 7 sections. New York: *Editor & Publisher Magazine*, 1988. It includes a list of black weeklies; Henry G. La Brie III, its compiler, identified 175 papers.

Weiner, Thomas, ed. *Analytical Guide and Indexes to the* Voice of the Negro *1904–1907 .* Westport, Conn.: Greenwood Press, 1974. 451 pp. A bibliography of the magazine the *Voice of the Negro*, published from 1904–7; at first published in Atlanta and continued there under three owners.

West, Earle H., comp. *A Bibliography of Doctoral Research on the Negro 1933–1966*. Ann Arbor, Mich.: University Microfilms, 1969.

Wolseley, Roland E., and Isabel C. Wolseley. *The Journalist's Bookshelf: An Annotated and Selected Bibliography of United States Print Journalism*. 8th ed. Indianapolis, Ind.: R.J. Berg & Co., 1986. 400 pp. Five-page minorities section and entries on fourteen black journalists on whom biographies have been written.

Yuster, Leigh Carol, ed. *Ulrich's International Periodicals Directory*, 1987–88. 26th ed. 2 vols. New York: Bowker, 1987. 2,361 pp.

Miscellaneous

Bontemps, Arna, and Jack Conroy. *They Seek a City*. Garden City, N.Y.: Doubleday, Doran, 1945. 266 pp.

Booker, Simeon. *Black Man's America*, Chapter 10. Englewood Cliffs, N.J: Prentice-Hall, 1964. 230 pp.

Chambers, Bradford, comp. and ed. *Chronicles of Negro Protest*. New York: Parents' Magazine Press, 1968. 320 pp.

Clarke, John Henrik, ed. *Harlem, U.S.A.* Berlin: Seven Seas, 1967. 361 pp.

Conrad, Earl. *Jim Crow America*, Chapter 7. New York: Duell, Sloan & Pearce, 1947. 237 pp.

Daly, Charles U., ed. *The Media and the Cities*. Chicago: University of Chicago Center for Policy Study, 1968. 90 pp.

Drake, St. Clair, and Horace R. Cayton. *Black Metropolis*, Chapter 15. New York: Harcourt, Brace, 1945. 809 pp.

Drotning, Phillip T., and Wesley W. Smith. *Up from the Ghetto*. New York: Cowles, 1970. 207 pp.

Fisher, Paul L., and Ralph L. Lowenstein, eds. *Race and the News Media*, 123–40. New York: Praeger, 1967. 158 pp.

Ford, Hugh, ed. *Negro: An Anthology Edited by Nancy Cunard*. New York: Frederick Ungar, 1970. 464 pp.

Greenberg, Bradley S., and Brenda Dervin. *Communications Among the Urban Poor*. Michigan State Reports, no. 1. Lansing: Michigan State University, 1967. 86 pp.

Lomax, Louis E. *The Negro Revolt*. New York: Harper & Row, 1962. 271 pp.

Lyle, Jack. *The News in Megalopolis*. San Francisco: Chandler, 1967. 208 pp.

MacDonald, J. Fred. *Blacks and White TV*. Chicago: Nelson-Hall, 1983. 288 pp.

Pantell, Dora, and Edwin Greenidge. *If Not Now, When?* New York: Delacorte Press, 1969. 216 pp. Subtitled *The Many Meanings of Black Power*.

Report of the National Advisory Commission on Civil Disorders. New York: Bantam Books, 1968. 659 pp.

Romm, Ethel Grodzins. *The Open Conspiracy*. Harrisburg, Pa.: Stackpole, 1970. 256 pp. About the alternative and underground publications of the time.

Schoener, Allon, ed. *Harlem on My Mind: Cultural Capital of Black America, 1900–1968.* New York: Random House, 1968. 255 pp.

Stone, Chuck. *Black Political Power in America.* Indianapolis, Ind.: Bobbs-Merrill, 1968. 261 pp.

Villard, Oswald Garrison. *The Disappearing Daily.* New York: Knopf, 1944. 295 pp.

Welsch, Erwin K. *The Negro in the United States.* Bloomington: Indiana University Press, 1968. 142 pp.

Williams, John A. *Flashbacks: A Twenty-Year Diary of Article Writing.* New York: Doubleday, 1971. 440 pp. A collection of articles by Williams, a novelist and journalist, including brief introductory essays for each giving the origins and backgrounds of the pieces.

Winks, Robin W. *The Blacks in Canada.* New Haven, Conn.: Yale University Press, 1971. 546 pp.

Articles and Pamphlets

Aldridge, Dan. "Black Press — Where are You?" *Michigan Chronicle,* 29 Mar. 1969.

"Alex Haley Settles Suit Out of Court: $500,000." *Jet* 55, no. 16 (4 Jan. 1979): 47.

Alexander, Charles T. "Is *Anything* Being Done to Interest Blacks in Journalism?" *Bulletin,* no. 535, American Society of Newspaper Editors (Nov. 1969): 16–18.

Allen, John E. "More Media Planning at Client Level Is Needed for Negro Radio." *Media/scope* 10, no. 12 (Dec. 1966): 162.

Alsbrook, James E. "Historic Color Bias in Print: Career Aid to Three 'Black' Officials." *Journalism Quarterly* 48, no. 3 (Autumn 1971): 480–85.

Anderson, Monroe. "Black Advertising Agencies Woo the Black Dollar." *National Observer* 10, no. 46 (13 Nov. 1971): 11.

Anderson, S. E. Review of *Neo-African Literature,* by Janheinz Jahn. *Black Scholar* 1, nos. 3, 4 (Jan.–Feb. 1970): 76, 79.

Andrews, Brenda H. "That Remarkable Black Press." *Virginia Humanities Newsletter* 13 (Winter 1987): 1–4.

Aronson, James. "The Inspiration of the Freedom Movement." *National Guardian,* 5 Sept. 1963. About W. E. B. Du Bois.

———. "Mediations." *Antioch Review* 31, no. 3 (3 Nov. 1971): 423–36.

Ashyk, Loretta. "*Independent* Set to Try Again." *Crain's Cleveland Business* 8, no. 49 (7 Dec. 1987): 15

Astor, David. "Columnist Is a 'Voice of the Opposition.'" *Editor & Publisher* 119, no. 49 (6 Dec. 1986): 52.

Atkins, Thomas L., and Michael H. Sussman. "Reaganisms, Reaganauts, and the NAACP." *Crisis* 89, no. 1 (Jan. 1982) 5–8.

"Backstage." *Ebony* 33, no. 1 (Nov. 1977): 22.

"Baldwin Leaves Negro Monthly." New York *Times*, 28 Feb. 1967.

Balk, Alfred. "Mr. Johnson Finds His Market." *Reporter* 21, no. 8 (12 Nov. 1959): 34–35.

Barger, Harold M. "Images of Political Authority in Four Types of Black Newspapers." *Journalism Quarterly* 50, no. 4 (Winter 1973): 645–51, 672.

Bayton, James A., and Ernestine Bell. "An Exploratory Study of the Role of the Negro Press." *Journal of Negro Education* 20 (Winter 1951): 8–15.

Beard, Richard L., and Cyril E. Zoerner II. "Associated Negro Press: Its Founding, Ascendancy, and Demise." *Journalism Quarterly* 46, no. 1 (Spring 1969): 47–52.

Bennett, Lerone, Jr. "Founders of the Black Press." *Ebony* 42, no. 4 (Feb. 1987): 96, 98, 100.

———. "Founders of the Negro Press." *Ebony* 19, no. 9 (July 1964): 96–98, 100, 102.

———. "Frederick Douglass: Father of the Protest Movement." *Ebony* 18, no. 9 (Sept. 1963): 50–51, 56.

Berkman, Dave. "Advertising in *Ebony* and *Life*: Negro Aspirations vs. Reality." *Journalism Quarterly* 40, no. 1 (Winter 1963): 53–64.

"The Big, Rich Sound at the End of the Dial." *Black Enterprise* 1, no. 4 (Nov. 1970): 30–34.

"The Birth, Death, and Resurrection of TLV." *Liberated Voice*, 11 Dec. 1968.

"*Black Enterprise* Plans Research on Black Consumer." *Advertising Age* 43, no. 29 (17 July 1972): 20.

"Black is Beautiful But Maybe Not Profitable." *Media/scope* 13, no. 8 (Aug. 1969): 31–37, 39, 65, 91, 95–96, 100.

"Black Journalists Win Discrimination Suit Against *Daily News*." Associated Press dispatch in the Syracuse (New York) *Post-Standard*, 16 Apr. 1987.

"The Black Market." *Chain Store Age* 46, no. 5 (May 1970): 100–138.

"Black Press Does Its Own Thing, Spurs Readers' Heavy Buying." *Advertising Age* 41, no. 16 (20 Apr. 1970): 192–93.

"Black Reporters Organize Trade Association." *Editor & Publisher* 109, no. 3 (17 Jan. 1976): 22.

Blank, Dennis M. "Integrated Comic Strives for Success." *Editor & Publisher* 100, no. 46 (18 Nov. 1967): 13.

Blount, Carolyne S. "Advocate for Economic Development." *about . . . time* 15, no. 4 (Apr. 1987): 14–16.

Blount, James M. "Charlayne Hunter-Gault: Outstanding Print and Broadcast Journalist." *about . . . time* 9, no. 3 (Mar. 1981): 9–11, 25–28.

Booker, Simeon. "E. Fannie Granton, 66, Dies of Natural Causes." *Jet* 58, no. 16 (3 Sept. 1980): 14–15.

———. "A Negro Reporter at the Till Trial." *Nieman Reports* 10, no. 1 (Jan. 1956): 13–15.

_____. "The New Frontier for Daily Newspapers." *Nieman Reports* 9, no. 1 (Jan. 1955): 12–13.

Boyd, Dale E. "Black Radio: A Direct and Personal Invitation." *Media/scope* 13, no. 8 (Aug. 1969): 14–15.

Braithwaite, William Stanley. "Negro America's First Magazine." *Negro Digest* 17, no. 2 (Dec. 1947): 21–26.

Brown, Robert U. "Shop Talk at Thirty: The Negro Press." *Editor & Publisher* 97, no. 29 (18 July 1964): 54.

Brown, Warren H. "A Negro Looks at the Negro Press." *Saturday Review of Literature*, 12 Nov. 1942, 5–6.

Burke, Ronald K. "The Anti-Slavery Activities of Samuel Ringgold Ward in New York State." *Afro-Americans in New York Life and History* 2, no. 1 (Jan. 1978): 17–28.

"Cartoonist and College Journalism Dean Will Speak at Press Institute." *Cleveland Press*, 9 Oct. 1969.

Cartwright, Marguerite. "Big Wheel of the National Negro Network." Pittsburgh *Courier*, 16 Aug. 1954.

_____. "Magazines in Sepia." *Negro History Bulletin* 17, no. 4 (Jan. 1954): 74, 94.

Christmas, Faith. "A Fond Farewell to a Great Newsman." Editorial, Chicago *Defender*, 13 June 1987. About Enoch R. Waters.

Citations of Merit for Outstanding Performance in Journalism. Jefferson City, Mo.: Department of Journalism, Lincoln University, 1969. Unpaged.

Click, J. W. "Comparison of Editorial Content of *Ebony* Magazine, 1967 and 1974." *Journalism Quarterly* 52, no. 4 (Winter 1975): 716–20.

Cohen, Shari. "A Comparison of Crime Coverage in Detroit and Atlanta Newspapers." *Journalism Quarterly* 52, no. 4 (Winter 1975): 726–30.

"Color Success Black." *Time* 92, no. 5 (2 Aug. 1968): 32.

Conrad, Earl. "The Negro Press." *Tomorrow* 6, no. 3 (Nov. 1946): 5–8.

Cooper, Ann. "Positively Upbeat." *Advertising Age* 57, no. 29 (5 May 1986): 40–41. About Joel P. Martin.

Cornish, Lori. "Samuel Cornish: Co-Founder of the Nation's First Black Newspaper." *Media History* 7, no. 1 (Spring–Summer 1987): 25–28.

"Court Holds Guild Unfair; Not Publisher." *Editor & Publisher* 97, no. 18 (2 May 1964): 49.

"Courting the Black Billionaire." *Media/scope* 11, no. 11 (Nov. 1967): 41–42, 66, 69–70, 82.

Cox, Clinton. "Abandoning the Brother on the Street." *(more)* 5, no. 8 (Aug. 1975): 8–9, 12–23. About the New York *Amsterdam News*.

Crain News Service. "Mingo Aims to Build First-class Agency." *Advertising Age* 54, no. 5 (23 Feb. 1987): 89.

Dabney, Virginius. "Nearer and Nearer the Precipice." *Atlantic Monthly* 171, no. 1 (Jan. 1943): 94–100.

Dallos, Robert E. "Black Radio Stations Send Soul and Service to Millions." New York *Times*, 11 Nov. 1968.

Daniels, Mary. "Woman with a Destiny: Barbara Proctor." *Essence* 3, no. 3 (July 1977): 44–45, 56.

Davis, Lee. "Black Press—The Sleeping Giant." *California Publisher* nos. 2–3 (Nov.–Dec. 1971): 19–20.

Dingle, Derek T. "Doing Business John Johnson's Way. *Black Enterprise*'s Entrepreneur of the Decade." *Black Enterprise* 17, no. 16 (June 1987): 150–52, 154, 156, 158, 160, 162, 164.

"The Doctor Who Built Harlem's *Amsterdam News.*" *Quill* 66, no. 10 (Nov. 1978): 37.

Dodson, Angela. "Black Journalists Urged to Take Stand on Issues." *Editor & Publisher* 114, no. 36 (5 Sept. 1981): 14–15.

Donath, Bob. "After Five-year Struggle, *Essence* Turns a Profit." *Advertising Age* 46, no. 30 (28 July 1975): 22–23.

_____. "*Essence* Moves to Courts." *Advertising Age* 48, no. 19 (9 May 1977): 4.

Draper, Theodore. "The Father of American Black Nationalism." *New York Review of Books* 14, no. 5 (12 Mar. 1970): 33–41. About Martin R. Delany.

Drevets, Tricia. "He Moved from the Trib to TV and Back." *Editor & Publisher* 120, no. 44 (31 Oct. 1987): 38–39.

Dullea, Georgia. "*Essence* Marks 15 Years of Serving Black Women." New York *Times*, 5 Apr. 1985.

Dunnigan, Alice E. "Early History of Negro Women in Journalism." *Negro History Bulletin* 28, no. 5 (May 1965): 178–79, 193, 197.

Eaton, Iris. "An Empire Built on a 'Magic Month.'" *News Workshop*, New York University, May 1954, 5–6.

"*Ebony*'s Johnson: 'Long Term, We'll Win.'" *Folio* 15, no. 7 (July 1986): 41–42.

Edwards, Audrey. "Charlayne Hunter-Gault." *MBM* (*Modern Black Men*) 3, no. 5 (May 1987): 48–49.

_____. "Susan L. Taylor." *MBM* (*Modern Black Men*) 3, no. 5 (May 1987): 21, 64.

Enrico, Dottie. "The Black-owned Agency Club." *Advest*, 16 March 1987, 47.

Evans, W. Leonard, Jr. "After 3 Years from Hope to Solution." *Tuesday* 4, no. 1 (Sept. 1968): 5.

Farrell, Charles S. "Students Read *Black Collegian* to Find How to Win Jobs in Booming Fields." *Chronicle of Higher Education,* 8 Aug. 1984.

"Few Negroes Are Enrolled in J-Schools." *Editor & Publisher* 102, no. 18 (3 Apr. 1969): 35.

Finkle, Lee. "Quotas or Integration: The NAACP Versus the Pittsburgh *Courier* and the Committee on Participation of Negroes." *Journalism Quarterly* 52, no. 1 (Spring 1975): 76–84.

First Black Press Hall of Fame Induction Ceremonies. Baltimore: Afro-Charities, Inc., 1987. 24 pp.

Fitzgerald, Mark. "Black Journalists Urged to 'Confront' Newsroom Discrimination." *Editor & Publisher* 120, no. 35 (29 Aug. 1987): 15.

Forkan, James P. "Black Ownership of Radio Grows—Slowly." *Advertising Age* 41, no. 6 (9 Feb. 1970): 10, 62–63.

"4.7% of Newspaper Workers Are Negro." *Guild Reporter* 36, no. 1 (27 Dec. 1968).

Fraser, Gerald C. "Haley Is Hoping to Debate Reporter." New York *Times*, 10 Apr. 1977.

———. "Ted Poston, Veteran Reporter, Dies." New York *Times*, 12 Jan. 1974.

Friedheim, Cynthia. "Gannett Minority Hiring, Coverage: There's Work Yet to Be Done." *Gannetteer*, Sept. 1987, 20–21.

"Friends, Admirers Honor *Jet* Columnist at Lavish Reception." *Jet*, 14 June 1979, 14–15.

Garland, Phyl. "The Black Press: Down But Not Out." *Columbia Journalism Review* 21, no. 3 (Sept.–Oct. 1982): 43–49.

Gatewood, Willard B., Jr. "A Negro Editor on Imperialism: John Mitchell, 1898–1901." *Journalism Quarterly* 49, no. 1 (Spring 1972): 43–50, 60.

Gerald, Carolyn. "The Measure and Meaning of the Sixties." *Negro Digest* 19, no. 1 (Nov. 1969): 24–29.

Gilliam, Dorothy. "What Do Black Journalists Want?" *Columbia Journalism Review* 11, no. 1 (May–June 1972): 47–52.

Gitter, A. George, Stephen M. O'Connell, and David Mostofsky. "Trends in Appearance of Models in *Ebony* Ads over 17 Years." *Journalism Quarterly* 49, no. 3 (Autumn 1972): 547–50.

"Good-bye Hambone." *Newsweek* 72, no. 4 (22 July 1968): 36.

Goodman, George, Jr. "George S. Schuyler, Black Author." Obituary in the New York *Times*, 7 Sept. 1977.

Goodman, Walter. "*Ebony*: Biggest Negro Magazine." *Dissent* 15, no. 5 (Sept.–Oct. 1968): 403–9.

———. "Fact, Faction or Symbol?" New York *Times*, 15 April 1977.

Greenlee, Ruth, and Robert L. Allen. "The Black Press—An Interview with Hoyt Fuller." *Ball and Chain Review* 1, no. 2 (Nov. 1969): 3.

Gross, Bella. "*Freedom's Journal* and the Rights of All." *Journal of Negro History* 17, no. 3 (July 1932): 241–86.

Grosvenor, Verta Mae. "Susan L. Taylor: Working for Us All." *Excel* 2, no. 2 (Fall 1987): 10–15.

Haley, Alex. "A Black American's Search for His Ancestral African Roots." *Ebony* 31, no. 10 (Aug. 1976): 100–102, 104, 106–7.

"Haley Denies Copying *Jubilee*." Minneapolis *Tribune*, 24 Apr. 1977. New York *Times* service story.

Hamilton, Stephanie. "*Black World*: Evolution and Extinction." *Black Voice* 9, no. 14 (3 May 1976): 6, 9.

"Harlem Mourns Dr. Powell." New York *Amsterdam News*, 1 Oct. 1977.

Harsch, Jonathan. "America's Leading Black-owned Newspaper Enters Its 75th Year." *Christian Science Monitor*, 14 May 1980.

Hawkins, B. Denise. "The Essence of Success." Syracuse (New York) *Post-Standard*, 7 Feb. 1987.

Help Wanted: More Black Newsmen. Associated Press Managing Editor's Black News Committee, undated (c. 1969). 35 pp.

Hessberg, Kim. "William Worthy: He Broke Through the Bamboo Curtain." *Baltimore* 72, no. 4 (Apr. 1979): 13–14.

Hicks, James L. "The Life of Our Dr. C. B. Powell." New York *Amsterdam News*, 1 Oct. 1977.

Higgins, Chester, Sr. "Is the Black Press Dying?" *Crisis* 87, no. 7 (Aug.–Sept. 1980): 240–41. Also *about . . . time* 8, no. 5 (May 1980): 20, 21.

Hogan, Lawrence D. "A Case of Mistaken Identity." *Editor & Publisher* 117, no. 46 (17 Nov. 1984): 44–30 [sic]. On Claude Barnett and ANP.

_____. "Claude Barnett, Founder: The Associated Negro Press (1919–1964)." *about . . . time* 12, no. 5 (May 1984): 26–29.

Hooker, Robert. "The News Appears in Black and White." *Floridian*, 7 Jan. 1973. Newspaper published by Florida Agricultural and Mechanical University, Tallahassee. Reprinted from St. Petersburg (Florida) *Times*.

Howard, Bernard. "Empathy: The Vital Plus of Negro Radio." *Sponsor*, 26 Aug. 1963, 61.

Hunter, Charlayne. "A Homecoming for the First Black Girl at the University of Georgia." *New York Times Magazine*, 25 Jan. 1970.

_____. "*Roots* Getting a Grip on People Everywhere." New York *Times*, 28 Jan. 1977.

Hurley, Kay. "Gordon Parks: Shaper of Dreams." *This Week*, 19 Oct. 1969.

Hutton, Frankie P. "Historians Still Ignore the Black Press." *Journalism Educator* 28, no. 1 (Apr. 1973): 48.

"Interview with Hoyt Fuller." *Black Collegian* 1, no. 3 (Apr.–May 1971): 24–26, 38.

"Is the Black Press Still Needed Today?" Richmond *Afro-American*, 5 Sept. 1987.

"J. L. Sylvahn Dies; Owned Newspaper." Syracuse (New York) *Post-Standard*, 20 May 1977.

Johnson, Charles S. "The Rise of the Negro Magazine." *Journal of Negro History* 13, no. 1 (Jan. 1928): 7–21.

Johnson, Hershel. "Dr. C. B. Powell's $6 Million Legacy." *Ebony* 33, no. 11 (Sept. 1978): 130–31, 134, 136, 137–39.

"Johnson Publishing Co. Announces New Magazine; To Discontinue *Black World*." *Jet* 49, no. 26 (25 Mar. 1976): 54, 56.

Johnson, Thomas A. "Despite Decline in Number of Black Papers, Publishers Predict Era of Strong Growth." New York *Times*, 31 Jan. 1979.

_____. "68 Million Saw 'Roots' Sunday, Setting Record." New York *Times*, 2 Feb. 1977.

Jones, Alex S. "Black Papers: Businesses with a Mission." New York *Times*, 17 Aug. 1987.

Jones, Marsha. "Moneta Sleet, Jr.: Pulitzer Prize Photojournalist." *about . . . time* 14, no. 10 (Oct. 1986): 12–13.

Joseph, W. Franklyn. "Identity Crisis Hurts Minority Press." *Advertising Age* 56, no. 54 (15 July 1985): 51–52.

Kaiser, Ernest. "Five Years of *Freedomways.*" *Freedomways* 6, no. 2 (Spring 1966): 103–17.

Kendall, Elaine. "The Negro Press." *Holiday* 41, no. 5 (May 1967): 82–84.

Kent, Frank C. "Publisher's Message. Frankly Speaking." *Black Family*, Spring 1986, 4–5.

Kern, Marilyn L. "Helping Minorities: Author Finds a Lack of Activity in J-department Minority Programs, Suggests That Minority Student Organizations Can Fill Gaps." *Journalism Educator* 27, no. 2 (Summer 1982): 6–10.

Kilgore, Margaret A. "Magazine Tells Black Woman How to Turn Over a New Leaf." Cleveland *Plain Dealer* (Los Angeles *Times*/Washington *Post* News Service), 13 June 1975.

Klein, Woody. "News Media and Race Relations: A Self-Portrait." *Columbia Journalism Review* 7, no. 3 (Fall 1968): 42–49.

Koontz, E. C. "Pittsburgh *Courier* Leads Fight for American Negro Equality." *Quill* 54, no. 10 (Oct. 1966): 44.

La Brie, Henry III. "The Arrival of the Black Newspaper." Part 1. *National Scene* 1, no. 11 (Aug. 1972): 7–8. As reproduced in the Hartford (Connecticut) *Star.*

――――. "Concealed Champions: The Black Pulitzers and Hearsts." *National Scene* 1, no. 12 (Sept.–Oct. 1972): 4, 5–8.

――――. "A Difficult History." *Black Enterprise* 1, no. 10 (May 1971): 42.

――――, and William J. Zima. "Directional Quandaries of the Black Press in the United States." *Journalism Quarterly* 48, no. 4 (Winter 1971): 640–44, 651.

Lacy, Sam. "Black Sportswriters Play Major Role in National Turnabout in Pro Sports." *Dawn*, 30 Mar. 1974.

"Lawsuit Filed in Fight for Control of *Essence* Magazine." *Jet*, 5 May 1977, 8–9.

League, Raymond A. "Be Subjective in Evaluating Negro Media." *Media/scope* 13, no. 8 (Aug. 1969): 18–19.

Lee, Don. "The Black Writer and the Black Community." *Black World* 21, no. 7 (May 1972): 85–87.

Levy, Raymond L. "Journalism's Place in Black Studies." *Journalism Educator* 25, no. 3 (Fall 1970): 26–28.

Levy, Renee Gearhart. "Bylines in Black Ink." *Syracuse University* 4, no. 1 (Nov. 1987): 24–25.

Lewis, David L., and Judy Miao. "America's Greatest Negroes: A Survey." *Crisis* 77, no. 1 (Jan. 1970): 17–21.

Lincoln Journalism Newsletter. Lincoln University, Jefferson City, Mo.: "NNPA Winter Meeting." 6, no. 2 (15 Feb. 1940): 2–3. "Matthews on Powell." 1, no. 5 (5 Feb. 1945): 11. "Powell on Press." 1, no. 6 (5 Feb. 1945): 10. "Negroes on Dailies." 2, no. 6 (15 June 1946): 7. "Who Owns the *Age*?" 5, no. 4 (15 April 1949): 6. "We Quote *Time*." 7, no. 7 (15 July 1951): 6–7. "*Jet*." 8, no. 3 (15 Feb. 1952): 3. "Editors Die Poor." 10, no. 9 (Sept. 1955): 1–2.

Lubasch, Arnold H. "*Roots* Plagiarism Suit is Settled." New York *Times*, 15 Dec. 1978.

———. "Suit Says *Roots* Copied from Novel." New York *Times*, 9 Nov. 1978.

McFadden, Robert D. "Some Points of *Roots* Questioned; Haley Stands By Book as a Symbol." New York *Times*, 10 Apr. 1977.

McGeehan, Pat. "The Burrell Style: Building a Solid Base on Michigan Avenue." *Advertising Age* 56, no. 98 (19 Dec. 1985): 4–5, 7.

McLellan, Diana. "Color *Essence* Editor Bittersweet." Cleveland *Plain Dealer*, reprinted from Washington *Star*, 27 July 1975.

McManus, Marjorie. "The *Essence* Magazine Success Story." *Folio* 5, no. 11 (Dec. 1976): 27–29.

Massaquoi, Hans J. "Alex Haley: The Man Behind *Roots*." *Ebony* 32, no. 6 (Apr. 1977): 33–36, 38–40.

Mencher, Melvin. "Recruiting and Training Black Newsmen." *Quill* 57, no. 9 (Sept. 1969): 22–25.

"Methodist Agencies Help Blacks Get Radio Stations." Baltimore *Afro-American*, 28 Mar. 1970.

Miles, Frank W. "Negro Magazines Come of Age." Parts 1, 2. *Magazine World* 2, no. 8 (1 June 1946): 12–13. 2, no. 10 (1 July 1946): 12–13, 18–20.

Milloy, Courtland. "The Black Press: A Victim of Its Own Crusade?" *Washington Journalism Review* 6, no. 5 (June 1984): 50–53.

"Minority Newsroom Employment Up, Annual ASNE Shows." *presstime* 3, no. 5 (May 1986): 80.

Moore, Gregory L. "Trouble in the Black Press." Cleveland *Plain Dealer Magazine* (22 May 1982): cover, 10–13, 17.

Moore, Shelley. "Terrie Williams." *MBM* (*Modern Black Men*) 3, no. 5 (May 1987): 72.

Moore, Trevor Wyatt. "Cool Cat with a Warm Message." *Ave Maria* 109, no. 11 (15 Mar. 1969): 17–20.

Morrison, Allan. "The Crusading Press." *Ebony* 18, no. 9 (Sept. 1963): 204, 206–8, 210.

Moss, Elizabeth Murphy. "Black Newspapers Cover News Other Media Ignore." *Journalism Educator* 24, no. 3 (1969): 6–11.

"The Negro Market—Two Viewpoints." *Media/scope* 11, no. 11 (Nov. 1967): 70–72, 74, 76, 78.

"Negroes Insist on Recognition by Advertisers and Newspapers." *Publishers' Auxiliary* 98, no. 34 (28 Sept. 1963): 2.

"The New Achievers." *Black Enterprise* 16, no. 1 (Aug. 1986): 29.

"New Prosperity for the Black Press as Readership, Revenue Move Up." *Black Enterprise* 1, no. 10 (May 1971): 38–40.

"Newspapers—Playing It Cool." *Time* 90, no. 4 (28 July 1967): 66.

Noel, Pamela. "Robert Maynard: Oakland's Top Newsman." *Ebony* 40, no. 8 (June 1985): 105, 108, 110.

Ottley, Roi. "The Negro Press Today." *Common Ground*, Spring 1943, 11–18.

"Our Black Guardians." *Afro-American* magazine section, 21 Feb. 1970, 1.

Palmer, L. F., Jr. "The Black Press in Transition." *Columbia Journalism Review* 9, no. 1 (Spring 1970): 31–36.

Patterson, Pat. "Editing an Ethnic Business Magazine." *Better Editing* 7, no. 3 (Fall 1971): 21–23.

_____. "The Editor Speaks." *Black Enterprise* 1, no. 10 (May 1971): 12.

"Percival L. Prattis, 85, Editor and Columnist at Pittsburgh *Courier*." New York *Times*, 3 Mar. 1980.

Peterson, Franklynn. "Color Comes to the Color Comics." *Sepia* 20, no. 11 (Nov. 1971): 68–78.

Pietila, Antero. "White SUN Reporter Writes About the *Afro*." Baltimore *Afro-American*, 23 Sept. 1971.

"The Pittsburgh *Courier*." *Tide*, 25 Aug. 1950, 68.

Poston, Ted. "The Negro Press." *Reporter* 1, no. 7 (6 Dec. 1949): 14–16.

Powell, Adam Clayton. "Need for Militant Voice Led Powell into Journalism." *Lincoln Journalism Clipsheet*, Feb. 1945.

Prattis, P. L. "Racial Segregation and Negro Journalism." *Phylon* 8, no. 4 (1947): 305–14.

"The Press." *Frontier*, June 1955, 14–15.

Pride, Armistead S. "America's Negro Newspapers." *Grassroots Editor* 2, no. 3 (July 1961): 9–10.

_____. "The Negro Newspaper in the United States." *Gazette* 2, no. 3 (1956): 141–49.

_____. "Negro Newspapers: Yesterday, Today and Tomorrow." *Journalism Quarterly* 28, no. 2 (Spring 1951): 179–88.

_____. "Opening Doors for Minorities." *Quill* 56, no. 11 (Nov. 1968): 24–27.

Pristin, Terry. "Is Anybody Downtown Listening?" (*more*) 1, no. 3 (Oct. 1971): 6–8.

Raymont, Henry. "Black Writers Win Literature Awards." New York *Times*, 27 Mar. 1970.

Read, Beverley. "Amy Jacques Garvey: Black, Beautiful & Free." *Ebony* 26, no. 8 (June 1971): 45–46, 48, 50, 52, 54.

Reasons and Patrick. "They Had a Dream: Martin R. Delany." The Troy (New York) *Record*, 17 Feb. 1972. The authors contributed a biographical sketch to the Troy general paper, omitting their first names; it evidently is one of a series.

Reichley, A. James. "How John Johnson Made It." *Fortune* 77, no. 1 (Jan. 1968) 152–53, 178, 180.

Reid, Clyde. "Why There's a Need for a Black Press Today." *Editor & Publisher* 120, no. 10 (7 Mar. 1987): 60, 50 [sic].

Reimel, Mimi. "Black Book." *Philadelphia* 62, no. 5 (May 1971): 62, 64, 65, 66, 68, 70, 72, 75.

Rhodes, Jane. "A Page One Story: Publisher Pam Johnson Brings Minorities to the Top of the Masthead." Syracuse (New York) *New Times*, 20 Jan. 1982.

Robinson, Louie. "Cartoonist with a Conscience." *Ebony* 28, no. 4 (Feb. 1973): 31–34, 38, 40, 42.

"*Roots* Breaks All Records." Associated Press report in the New York *Times*, 24 Jan. 1977.

Ross, Irwin. "Roy Wilkins—'Mr. Civil Rights.'" *Reader's Digest* 92, no. 549 (Jan. 1968): 86–91.

"Rousing." *New Yorker* 63, no. 26 (21 Aug. 1987): 22–24.

Rozen, Leah. "*Essence* Celebrates Its 10th with a New Project." *Advertising Age* 51, no. 34 (11 Aug. 1980): 34, 36.

Sale, J. Kirk. "The *Amsterdam News*." *New York Times Magazine*, 9 Feb. 1969: 30–31, 37, 39–40, 42, 44, 46, 49, 52.

Sampson, Larry. "Chris Powell—'Drummer' for Revolution Edits Newspaper for Blacks." Syracuse University *Daily Orange*, 14 Nov. 1968.

Sancton, Thomas. "The Negro Press." *New Republic* 108, no. 17 (26 Apr. 1943): 557–60.

Scarupa, Henry. "Black Sportswriting Legend Still Going Strong at 84." Baltimore *Sun*, 23 Oct. 1987. About Sam Lacy.

Schatzman, Dennis. "The Black Press and Its Role in Modern Society." *Editor & Publisher* 112, no. 16 (21 Apr. 1979): 16–18, 30.

_____. "Meet the NABJ." *Quill* 76, no. 3 (Mar. 1987): 37.

Schemmel, William. "Press—Black Voices Filling a Void." *Atlanta Magazine* 10, no. 1 (May 1970): 48, 50, 52, 54.

"Scholars Protest Closing of *Black World* Magazine." Hartford (Connecticut) *Inquirer*, 21 Apr. 1976.

Schwadel, Francine. "In Philadelphia, Many a Person Turns Himself in to Stone." *Wall Street Journal*, 5 Feb. 1987.

Seeman, Howard L. "The Editor-Publisher of a Black Daily: A Case Study." *Journalism Quarterly* 49, no. 1 (Spring 1972): 140–42.

_____. "Keeping the Gates at the Chicago *Defender*." *Journalism Quarterly* 48, no. 2 (Summer 1971): 275–78.

Senna, Carl. "The Man Who Published *The Guardian*." Boston *Sunday Globe*, 1 Dec. 1968.

Shenker, Israel. "Some Historians Dismiss Report of Factual Mistakes in *Roots*." New York *Times*, 10 Apr. 1977.

Sherrod, L. G. "Barbara Gardner Proctor." *MBM* (*Modern Black Men*) 3, no. 5 (May 1987): 60–61.

Stevens, John D. "The Black Press Looks at 1920's Journalism." *Journalism History* 7, nos. 3,4 (Autumn–Winter 1980): 109–13.

_____. "'Bungleton Green': Black Comic Strip Ran 43 Years." *Journalism Quarterly* 51, no. 1 (Spring 1974): 122–24.

_____. "Conflict—Cooperation Content in 14 Black Newspapers." *Journal-*

ism Quarterly 47, no. 3 (Autumn 1970): 56–68.

Stone, Chuck. "Black Press: Democracy's Stepchild or a Successful Exercise in Ethnic Pride?" *Editor & Publisher* 110, no. 11 (12 Mar. 1977): 18–19.

———. "Teaching Minority Journalists." Los Angeles *Sentinel*, 20 Aug. 1978.

Suggs, Henry Lewis. "P. B. Young of the Norfolk *Journal and Guide*: A Booker T. Washington Militant. 1904–1928." *Journal of Negro History* 64 (Fall 1979): 365–76.

A Survey of the Mass Communications Areas in 66 Predominantly Black Four Year Accredited Colleges and Universities. New York: United Negro College Fund, Inc., 1969. 16 pp.

"Text of the Moynihan Memorandum on the Status of Negroes." New York *Times*, 1 Mar. 1970.

Thornbrough, Emma Lou. "American Negro Newspapers, 1880–1914." *Business History Review* 40 (Winter 1966): 467–90.

Tomkinson, Craig. "The Weekly Editor—New Orleans Weekly." *Editor & Publisher* 103, no. 23 (6 June 1970): 68.

"The Top 100 Black Businesses." *Black Enterprise* 17, no. 11 (June 1987): 131–37.

Townsley, Luther A. "ANP Provides International Coverage for 78 Member Papers in America." *Lincoln Journalism Clipsheet*, Feb. 1945, 1.

"Training of Blacks a Step Beyond Tokenism." *Media/scope* 13, no. 8 (Aug. 1969): 77–79.

Trammer, Monte I. "Gaining Ground Slowly." *Quill* 76, no. 8 (Sept. 1987): 45.

Trayes, Edward J. "Black Newsmen." *Quill* 59, no. 9 (Sept. 1970): 16–18.

———. "Blacks Triple Enrollment as J-majors in 3 Years." *Journalism Educator* 26, no. 3 (Fall 1971): 14–18.

———. "Still Few Blacks on Dailies but 50% More in J-schools, Recent Surveys Indicate." *Journalism Quarterly* 47, no. 2 (Summer 1970): 356–60.

Twitty, John C. "150 Negro Papers and Their Fight for Civil Rights." *News Workshop*, New York University, 20 Nov. 1950, 7–8.

"The Value of Grassroots Journalism." *College Management*, June 1969, 40–42.

Van Breems, Arlene. "New Magazine Tries to Fill Void for the Black Woman." Part 4. Los Angeles *Times*, 18 Aug. 1969.

"A Victim of Negro Progress." *Newsweek* 62, no. 9 (26 Aug. 1963): 50–51.

Walker, William O. "Anniversary of the Negro Press." Atlanta *Daily World*, 12 Mar. 1970.

Ward, Carl. "The Need for Black Journalists." *Tuesday* 4, no. 1 (Sept. 1968): 10, 22.

Waters, Enoch R. "The Negro Press: A Call for Change." *Editor & Publisher* 95, no. 19 (May 1962): 67–68.

Watson, Walter Ray. "Adam Clayton Powell III Named Head of NPR News." *New Pittsburgh Courier*, 12 Sept. 1987.

Weaver, Bill L. "The Black Press and the Assault on Professional Baseballs' 'Color Line.'" *Phylon* 40 (Dec. 1979): 303–17.

Weaver, Robert C. "Ted Poston: July 4, 1906–January 11, 1974." *Crisis* 81, no. 3 (Mar. 1974): 97–98.

Weyr, Thomas. "Minorities in Publishing." *Publishers Weekly* 218, no. 16 (17 Oct. 1980): 31–35.

"Whatever Happened to Charlayne Hunter?" *Ebony* 27, no. 9 (July 1972): 138.

White, Brian. "Black Newspapers Add to Media Mix." *Business Journal, Focus: Printing and Graphics*, magazine section, 14 Sept. 1987, 5–6.

White, Jack E. "Color and the Comics." *Columbia Journalism Review* 8, no. 4 (Winter 1969–70): 58–60.

Williams, James D. "Is the Black Press Needed?" *Civil Rights Digest* 3, no. 1 (Winter 1970): 8–16.

Williams, Roger M. "Journalism Expands on Black Campuses." *Columbia Journalism Review* 10, no. 2 (July–Aug. 1971): 21–26.

Williams, Rudy. "Second-Guessing the Black Press." *Columbia Journalism Review* 11, no. 4 (Nov.–Dec. 1972): 34.

Williamson, Lenora. "Specialists Cover Minority Communities for News Media." *Editor & Publisher* 106, no. 10 (16 May 1970): 13.

Wilson, Quintus C. "J-schools Adopt Black Studies Slowly." *Journalism Educator* 26, no. 3 (Fall 1971): 12–14.

Winfrey, Carey. "Volume I, Number 1 – Birth of a New Black Magazine." *New York* 3, no. 17 (27 Apr. 1970): 58–60.

Winski, Joseph M., and Kathy Lanpher. "He Said 'No Thanks!' to Handouts." *Advertising Age* 53, no. 9 (1 Mar. 1982): M2, M3.

Witcover, Jules. "Washington's White Press Corps." *Columbia Journalism Review* 8, no. 4 (Winter 1969–70): 42–48.

Wolseley, Roland E. "The Black Magazines." *Quill* 57, no. 5 (May 1969): 8–11.

_____. "The Developing World of the New Black Press." *Black Business Digest* 2, no. 5 (Feb. 1972): 41–43.

_____. "Jobs and Black Journalism." *Equal Opportunity* 6, no. 1 (Jan. 1973): 15, 18, 20.

_____. "The Vanishing Negro Press." *Negro Digest* 9, no. 2. (Dec. 1950): 64–68.

Young, A. S. "Doc." "The Black Sportswriter." *Ebony* 25, no. 12 (Oct. 1970): 56–58, 60–62, 64.

Dissertations, Theses, and Addresses

Bontrager, Robert Devon. "An Investigation of Black Press and White Press Use Patterns in the Black Inner City of Syracuse, New York." Ph.D. diss., Syracuse University, 1969. 317 pp.

Burd, Gene. "Magazines and the Minority Messages of Poets and Blacks." Address, Magazine Division Meeting, Association for Education in Journalism, 27 Aug. 1969. 26 pp.

Burke, Ronald K. "Samuel Ringgold Ward and *The Impartial Citizen*." Unpublished paper, Syracuse University, 17 Mar. 1977. 13 pp.

Del Gatto, Michele. "Histories and Policies of the New York *Amsterdam News*." Term paper, Syracuse University, 1969. 9 pp.

Fleming, G. James. "The Negro Press." Manuscript prepared for Myrdal study, *An American Dilemma*, New York, 1942, New York Public Library. Microfilm.

Goodlett, Carlton B. Address, Association of Afro-American Television Producers, Racine, Wisconsin, 27 Feb. 1970. 13 pp.

Grayson, William P. "Some of Your Best Customers Are Negro." Address, Second District Convention, American Advertising Federation, Pocono Manor, Pennsylvania, 8–10 Nov. 1968.

Johnson, John H. "Understanding: The Key to Effective Communication." Address, International Magazine Conference, Williamsburg, Virginia, 25–28 May 1969.

O'Connell, Sharyn. "Why Not the Black Press?" Research report, School of Journalism, Syracuse University, Jan. 1969. 13 pp.

Pride, Armistead S. "A Register and History of Negro Newspapers in the United States: 1827–1950." Ph.D. diss., Northwestern University, 1950. 426 pp. Microfilm. Pride found twenty-seven hundred in his search; an additional five hundred for the four decades since 1950 is a conservative estimate.

Report of the Ad Hoc Coordinating Committee on Minority Group Education. Lionel C. Barrow, Jr., chairman, and William R. Stroud, secretary, Association for Education in Journalism, Feb. 1969. 12 pp.

Report of the Ad Hoc Coordinating Committee on Minority Education. Lionel C. Barrow, Jr., chairman, and William R. Stroud, secretary, Association for Education in Journalism, Aug. 1969. 13 pp.

Stephenson, William David II. "Magazines and Black Americans: An Evolving Relationship." Master's thesis, Syracuse University, 1969. 209 pp.

INDEX

445